Destination London

Film Europa: German Cinema in an International Context
Series Editors: **Hans-Michael Bock** (CineGraph Hamburg);
Tim Bergfelder (University of Southampton); **Sabine Hake**
(University of Texas, Austin)

German cinema is normally seen as a distinct form, but this new series
emphasizes connections, influences, and exchanges of German cinema
across national borders, as well as its links with other media and art forms.
Individual titles present traditional historical research (archival work,
industry studies) as well as new critical approaches in film and media
studies (theories of the transnational), with a special emphasis on the
continuities associated with popular traditions and local perspectives.

The Concise Cinegraph: An Encyclopedia of German Cinema
General Editor: Hans-Michael Bock
Associate Editor: Tim Bergfelder

**International Adventures: German Popular Cinema and European
Co-Productions in the 1960s**
Tim Bergfelder

**Between Two Worlds: The Jewish Presence in German and Austrian
Film, 1910–1933**
S. S. Prawer

Framing the Fifties: Cinema in a Divided Germany
Edited by John Davidson and Sabine Hake

A Foreign Affair: Billy Wilder's American Films
Gerd Gemünden

**Destination London: German-speaking Emigrés and British Cinema,
1925–1950**
Edited by Tim Bergfelder and Christian Cargnelli

Michael Haneke's Cinema: The Ethic of the Image
Catherine Wheatley

Willing Seduction: *The Blue Angel*, **Marlene Dietrich and Mass Culture**
Barbara Kosta

DESTINATION LONDON

German-speaking Emigrés
and British Cinema, 1925–1950

Edited by

Tim Bergfelder and Christian Cargnelli

Berghahn Books
New York • Oxford

First published in 2008 by

Berghahn Books

www.berghahnbooks.com

Library of Congress Cataloging-in-Publication Data

Destination London : German-speaking emigrés and British cinema, 1925-
1950 / edited by Tim Bergfelder and Christian Cargnelli.
   p. cm. -- (Film Europa : German cinema in an international context ; v. 6)
Includes bibliographical references and index.
ISBN 978-1-84545-532-3
1. Motion pictures--Great Britain--History. 2. Germans--Great Britain. I.
Bergfelder, Tim. II. Cargnelli, Christian, 1962-

PN1993.5.G7D47 2008
791.430941--dc22
                                        2008026234

British Library Cataloguing in Publication Data
A catalogue record for this book is available from
the British Library.

Printed in the United States on acid-free paper

ISBN 978-1-84545-532-3 hardback

CONTENTS

ACKNOWLEDGEMENTS

We would like to thank the Arts and Humanities Research Council (AHRC) for financing a three-year project on the subject of German-speaking émigrés in British cinema. This book is one of the outcomes of this project, following an international conference in 2005, and two smaller symposia in 2006 and 2007. The AHRC also funded a period of research leave for Tim Bergfelder, to complete the research and writing on his two main contributions to this collection. Our gratitude goes to the School of Humanities at the University of Southampton for hosting this project, and for providing the appropriate environment and essential infrastructure. In Germany and Austria, the research centres CineGraph and SYNEMA offered encouragement and contributed to the 2005 conference.

A number of individuals helped to instigate the project, especially Dr Kevin Gough-Yates, whose advice and expertise was indispensable on many occasions, and whose pioneering research on exiles in British cinema no scholar working in the field can ignore. We thank Kelly Robinson, whose PhD on German cinematographers in the British film industry was funded as part of the project, for her generous sharing of archival research, which contributed not only to her own work but to the project as a whole. Hans-Michael Bock and Sabine Hake supported the publication with Berghahn and made invaluable suggestions. We thank the two external anonymous reviewers whose positive assessment of the manuscript made the publication possible, and the team at Berghahn, in particular Marion Berghahn and Mark Stanton.

At the 2005 conference, we had the pleasure of welcoming one of the last surviving émigrés of the period at the core of this anthology. The career of the Viennese-born cinematographer and photographer Wolfgang (Wolf) Suschitzky, encompassing documentaries made during the war and the acclaimed thriller *Get Carter* (1971), exemplifies the diverse and important creative contributions of German-speaking exiles who first came to the UK from the 1920s to the 1940s, which we wish to recall in this present collection. Moreover, in founding a veritable cinematographer's dynasty, Suschitzky – who retired from active filmmaking in the late 1980s – leaves a continuing legacy to a vibrant and internationally oriented film culture, through the work of his son Peter (e.g. David Cronenberg's *Spider*,

2002, and *Eastern Promises*, 2007) and his grandson Adam whose television credits include the successful BBC series 'Hustle' (2004), 'Life on Mars' (2006), and 'Jekyll' (2007). We owe a lot to Suschitzky and his generation, and thus dedicate this book to him.

Tim Bergfelder
Christian Cargnelli
Southampton and Vienna, September 2007

Chapter 1

INTRODUCTION: GERMAN-SPEAKING EMIGRÉS AND BRITISH CINEMA, 1925–50: CULTURAL EXCHANGE, EXILE AND THE BOUNDARIES OF NATIONAL CINEMA

Tim Bergfelder

Britain can be considered, with the possible exception of the Netherlands, the European country benefiting most from the diaspora of continental film personnel that resulted from the Nazis' rise to power.[1] Kevin Gough-Yates, who pioneered the study of exiles in British cinema, argues that 'when we consider the films of the 1930s, in which the Europeans played a lesser role, the list of important films is small.'[2] Yet the legacy of these Europeans, including their contribution to aesthetic trends, production methods, to professional training and to technological development in the film industry of their host country has been largely forgotten. With the exception of very few individuals, including the screenwriter Emeric Pressburger[3] and the producer/director Alexander Korda,[4] the history of émigrés in the British film industry from the 1920s through to the end of the Second World War and beyond remains unwritten. This introductory chapter aims to map some of the reasons for this neglect, while also pointing towards the new interventions on the subject that are collected in this anthology.

There are complex reasons why the various waves of migrations of German-speaking artists to Britain, from the mid-1920s through to the postwar period, have not received much attention. The first has to do with the dominance of Hollywood in film historical accounts, which has given prominence to the exodus of European film artists to the United States. Numerous studies since the 1970s have charted the trajectories of German-speaking (and other European) film personnel to Los Angeles, especially after 1933, and their eventual integration or failure within the studio system.[5] A succession of scholars has traced the legacy of 'mittel-European' émigrés either through high-profile biographical trajectories (e.g., Ernst Lubitsch, Marlene Dietrich, Fritz Lang, Billy Wilder, and Peter Lorre),[6] or in terms of specific genres such as film noir.[7] Other studies have documented how Hollywood became a dead end for formerly successful or promising filmmakers, including directors Joe May, Reinhold Schünzel, E.A. Dupont, Richard Oswald, and Gustav Machaty.[8]

Thus, emigration in film historical terms has been mostly associated with the lure of Hollywood as the focal point or as the crucible of the global film business. This perception gains even more strength given the fact that indeed many relocations within Europe during the 1930s often only marked an intermediate stopover for émigrés who would continue and usually end their journey (by the outbreak of the Second World War at the latest) in the USA. In terms of the sheer volume of individuals, the dominance of this particular stream of migration is thus undoubtedly justified. However, as a result of the overwhelming focus on Hollywood, a whole range of other, and culturally significant, migratory processes and cultural exchanges, some permanent and some more temporary, have been ignored.[9]

Exiles or Emigrés?

The assessment of the legacy of émigrés is complicated by the very definition of the word 'émigré'. This umbrella term has been used in film historical accounts, sometimes too indiscriminately, for a range of quite different existential experiences, encompassing purely economically motivated, brief and voluntary production trips between countries, extended and often permanent periods of enforced exile and personal reinvention, and a number of ambiguous cases in between. For an accurate assessment of émigré activities it is essential to differentiate their place within wider paradigms, such as sociopolitical events and developments (e.g., the migrations from and within Central and Eastern Europe prior, during and after the First World War; and the rise of fascism and ethnic and political persecution that follow in the 1930s), but also within the parameters of national and transnational economic strategies and policies.

For the film historian, it is important not to conflate these contexts too readily, as the aims and requirements associated with politics and economics may indeed sometimes coincide, but may on occasion also pull in different directions. As I have argued in a previous essay, the history of European cinema has frequently been 'characterised by two simultaneous yet diverging processes, namely the film industries' economic imperative of international expansion, competition and cooperation (often accompanied by a migration of labour), and the ideological project of re-centring the definition of national cinema through critical and public discourse, and film policy'.[10]

The case of British cinema from the 1920s through to the 1940s, and its shifting relations with other film industries in Europe as well as with Hollywood, is particularly instructive in this respect. As several scholars have suggested, the deliberate adoption of internationalist principles, looking across the English Channel for artistic inspiration and technological innovation and training, and across the Atlantic for economic success and potential distribution markets, was key to the resurgence of the British film industry in the second half of the 1920s and the mid-1930s, and resulted in a busy transnational traffic of production strategies, generic formulae and personnel.[11]

The same period, however, saw the emergence of protectionist measures, such as the introduction of national quotas in the 1927 Cinematograph Act (designed primarily to stem the growing influence of Hollywood), and from the early 1930s the attempts by the film technicians' union, the Association of Cine-Technicians (ACT), to block and prevent the employment of foreigners in British studios (a policy that was primarily aimed at continental technicians).[12] It is against this context of contradictory forces impacting on the film industry that émigré activity in Britain during this period needs to be seen, while it is also important to acknowledge that the exchange and migration of film personnel was well established before the Nazis' rise to power initiated a far more urgent and existentially motivated wave of emigration.

Extending the time frame of émigré activity back into the 1920s allows one to recognise filmmakers and artists who, within the parameters of reciprocal arrangements between national film industries, travelled between, and made films in, different countries. Such an understanding would encompass on the British side temporary 'émigrés' such as Alfred Hitchcock who made his first films in Germany in 1925, but also Graham Cutts, Ivor Novello, Henry Edwards, Mabel Poulton, Warwick Ward, Robert Stevenson and a host of other names, all of whom were filming at one time or another in German studios. Michael Powell, meanwhile, began his career at about the same time working for American director Rex Ingram in the South of France. To these names one could add the British-born actors Lilian Harvey or Jack Trevor, who predominantly worked in German cinema. Arriving from the continent were figures such as the directors E.A. Dupont, Arthur Robison and Paul Czinner; actresses including Anny Ondra, Pola Negri, Olga Chekhova and Lya de Putti; cinematographers Werner Brandes and Theodor Sparkuhl; and set designer Alfred Junge, who made films in Britain in the late 1920s, joining other professionals who were arriving from the United States.

In a previous article I referred to this category of film personnel as 'commercial travellers'.[13] Such purely industry-determined migrations extended to some extent from the late 1920s until the late 1930s, reaching its peak during the years of multilingual sound film production early to mid-decade, which is mapped in this volume by Chris Wahl's essay on

Ufa's English-language projects.[14] However, from 1933 onwards, the term émigré became more prominently associated with the experience of exile, as numerous film artists were forced to leave Nazi Germany, and subsequently other European countries, to escape persecution on racial and/or political grounds. The commercial two-way traffic of the late 1920s thus gradually turned into a forceful one-way exodus, with the number of émigrés in the British film industry in the late 1930s and 1940s rising to around 400, a significant amount considering the size of the British film industry.

Again, it is necessary to distinguish between individual cases, as the emerging differences often challenge a straightforward historical narrative of a clear-cut caesura, or normative experiences of exile. As a part of the close relationship between the German and British film industries in the 1920s and 1930s, a number of German-speaking filmmakers working on Anglo-German co-productions or multilingual versions of the early sound period later became established in the film industry of the Third Reich, including cinematographer Robert Baberske (*A Knight in London*, 1929) and Hans Steinhoff (*Nachtgestalten/The Alley Cat*, 1929), the latter one of the most prominent directors of Nazi propaganda films and prestige productions from 1933 onwards. Although far less common than before 1933, German film personnel continued coming to Britain on purely professional temporary visits for the remainder of the decade (often under contract with Korda), including cinematographers Franz Weihmayr, Sepp Allgeier, and Hans Schneeberger.

Other film artists, however, such as the set designers Alfred Junge or Oscar Werndorff, may originally have moved to Britain for economic reasons, but they effectively changed into political exiles after 1933 when a return to Germany became a definitive impossibility. They thus shared the same fate, though not the same professional status, as those filmmakers who entered Britain as refugees. Indeed, while many of the émigrés of the late 1920s could attain a relatively stable position within the British studios, for later émigrés the situation looked far bleaker. Influential studio positions such as the one Alfred Junge enjoyed at Gaumont-British and later at M-G-M British, or the public profile of émigré actors such as Conrad Veidt, Elisabeth Bergner, Richard Tauber, Anton Walbrook or Lilli Palmer remained relatively isolated occurrences in the British film industry of the 1930s and 1940s.

In some cases, exile could spell the end of one's career altogether. Brigitte Mayr's moving account in this volume of the screenwriter Carl Mayer's years in British exile documents one of the more tragic examples in this respect. Penniless and unemployed, the celebrated creator of Robert Wiene's *Das Cabinet des Dr. Caligari* (1920) and F.W. Murnau's *Sunrise* (1927) could in his final years at least rely on the kindness and pity of his British friends. Kevin Gough-Yates has previously pointed to similar destinies of formerly celebrated artists of Weimar stage and screen, including the directors Leo Lasko and Max Mack.[15] Meanwhile, not even established industry figures such as Junge were immune from being interned as 'enemy aliens' following the outbreak of the Second World War, let alone artists who were less settled at this moment in time, such as another Powell and Pressburger stalwart, Hein Heckroth, who was temporarily deported to Australia.

In between those 'who had to flee' and those 'who stayed' were, especially during the 1930s, a number of more ambiguous career trajectories. Actress Lilian Harvey and the Czech-born cinematographer Franz Planer, for example, continued prolific pan-European careers until the late 1930s, which significantly included working for the Nazi film industry. Planer's credits in Britain included Vistor Saville's *The Dictator* (1935) and Curtis Bernhardt's *The Beloved Vagabond* (1936), while in Germany he worked until 1937 with directors such as Gustaf Gründgens and Carl Froelich. As Michael Omasta in his essay in this book notes, the cinematographer Günther Krampf returned in 1935 from Britain to Nazi Germany to shoot Gustav Ucicky's *Das Mädchen Johanna* (Joan of Arc). Harvey made her last film in Germany in 1939 (see Chris Wahl's chapter in this volume). That same year, she fled to Hollywood via France while Planer and his Jewish wife also sought safety in the USA. They were part of a final wave of émigrés that included directors Douglas Sirk and Frank Wysbar. There were some last-minute émigrés to Britain too, including the Czech actor Karel (Karl) Stepanek, who had appeared in German productions up to the outbreak of the Second World War, and who from 1942 became one of the most reliable foreign villains in British films.

It is worth remembering in this context that although the German film industry introduced racial exclusion policies almost immediately after the Nazis took control and summarily dismissed the overwhelming majority of Jewish film personnel (including such prominent figures as the producer Erich Pommer), until the late 1930s policies of exclusion on ethnic or political grounds were applied expediently. In the early years of the regime, Jewish or half-Jewish directors such as Kurt (Curtis) Bernhardt or Reinhold Schünzel (who both eventually emigrated to Hollywood) were given special permission not only to direct films in Germany, but also to provide with their work an illusion of continuity from Weimar cinema in terms of visual style and urbanely modern narratives.[16] Prior to his emigration to London (via Hollywood, an unusual trajectory), Anton Walbrook was (as Adolf Wohlbrück) an established matinee idol of German-speaking productions until 1936.

A particularly ambiguous case is the career of producer Günter Stapenhorst during the 1930s and 1940s. A lifetime personal friend of Emeric Pressburger, he did not face any personal threats from the Nazis on either political or racial grounds; indeed he had endeared himself to the regime by producing two of the most nationalistic films at Ufa in the early 1930s, *Morgenrot* (Dawn, 1933) and *Flüchtlinge* (Refugees, 1933). As a former 'old school' naval officer, however, Stapenhorst (reputedly a model for Anton Walbrook's Theo Kretschmar-Schuldorff in Pressburger's 1943 *The Life and Death of Colonel Blimp*) refused to join the Nazi Party and emigrated to Britain in 1935.

Working for Korda, he produced Milton Rosmer and Geoffrey Barkas' *The Great Barrier* (1937), with an uncredited contribution to the screenplay by Pressburger. The film was an adventure spectacle about the building of the Canadian Pacific Railway that featured the exile actress Lilli Palmer, but was photographed by Sepp Allgeier, previously one of the principal cameramen on Leni Riefenstahl's *Triumph des Willens* (Triumph of the Will, 1935). Stapenhorst's other contribution to British cinema was *The Challenge* (1938), a remake of Luis Trenker's mountaineering drama *Der Berg ruft* (The Mountain Calls, 1937), a film that in its German version displayed explicit nationalist tendencies. After a failed attempt to return to Germany in the late 1930s, Stapenhorst spent the war years in neutral Switzerland, supporting and employing genuine exiles, but also surreptitiously receiving financial support from the Nazi film industry, which brought him under suspicion of espionage.[17]

Stapenhorst's biography illustrates the murky distinctions between a more traditional form of German nationalism and National Socialism, and the rather dubious importation of at best ambivalent ideological messages into British cinema; and it helps to disperse the assumption that all exiles and émigré technicians working in Britain prior to the Second World War were politically on the left (although some, such as the cinematographer Wolfgang Suschitzky, or the set designer Ernö Metzner, indisputably were).

There were, of course, numerous émigrés who actively campaigned during the 1930s against fascism, German nationalism, and anti-Semitism, and who subsequently made significant contributions to Britain's war effort, both on-screen and off. It is no coincidence that some of the most prominent attacks on Hitler's Germany in British cinema during the 1930s (as far as this was possible given the stringent restrictions by the British censorship board, BBFC), including Lothar Mendes' *Jew Süss* (1934) and Karl Grune's *Abdul the Damned* (1935),[18] were made by film teams comprising a high proportion of émigrés, including the non-Jewish Conrad Veidt who through his role in *Jew Süss* effectively and very publicly declared his rejection of the Nazi regime. As Gerd Gemünden in his essay on Veidt in this book demonstrates, this not only earned the star the status of a *persona non grata* in the eyes of the Nazis, but also placed him in genuine danger during his final visit to Germany in 1934. During the Second World War, émigrés supported the war effort by playing Nazi villains in, or contributing in other technical capacities to, British propaganda productions (feature films as well as documentaries), or making German-language broadcasts for the BBC's German service. Tobias Hochscherf's essay in this volume provides a number of examples of such activities.

Finally, there is the generation of émigrés in British cinema that emerges after 1945, comprising genuine exiles who fled as very young children or young adults and who either began to make their mark in the British film industry after the war (the James Bond set designer Ken Adam is a prominent example), or returned to Germany (such as the later stage and film director Peter Zadek), alongside a new succession of professional travellers who have moved across the Channel from the 1950s to the present for a variety of reasons.[19]

All these very diverse examples raise fundamental questions for an assessment of émigrés within British cinema. For example, a simplistic celebration of the creative transnational imagination of émigré production across different decades could be accused of ignoring the crucial differences in actual lived experience that I mapped above; and it might well end up underestimating or glossing over the sometimes traumatic dimension of diasporic biographies. Conversely, approaches that are exclusively concerned with the tragic aspects of the exile's condition and that lament a loss of culture are in danger of perpetuating narratives of victimisation and of unproblematically stable categories of belonging. Such narratives can be seen to disallow the possibility of individual resilience, personal as well as creative reinvention, and they deny the (at least for some individuals) positive potential of cultural adaptation and change. As Gerd Gemünden argues in his chapter in this volume:

> [R]esearch on exiled artists has long emphasised the significance of the disabling, paralysing, and traumatic dimension of exile, but has mostly neglected to consider the more productive dimension that forced displacement and disorientation can create.[20]

Exile studies is often more interested in the nature and consequences of exile as an existential condition than in questions of aesthetic influence. From this perspective the émigré's work is of interest where it engages with or reflects the exilic experience. In studies on film exile there consequently has been a tendency to prioritise the biographical/personal dimension over the aesthetic, professional and economic. This has to be understood both as an act of ongoing resistance against the political forces that aimed to displace the respective biographies in the first place, and as a commitment towards acknowledgement and remembrance. Thus, the process of discovering forgotten careers, and of giving a voice and afterlife to destroyed, interrupted or redirected careers is part and parcel of creating a wider picture of exilic experience that extends beyond the narrow concerns of film history.

For the film historian, on the other hand, the social and existential dimension of exile is important primarily where it impacts on wider patterns of a national film culture. The fact that the number of émigrés in the British film industry increased dramatically after 1933, for example, does not necessarily entail that the actual influence of émigrés increased accordingly. Determining 'influence' is notoriously complex. In the sense of meaning popularity, it can be assessed by economic data, in other words, what films, stars and directors attained the greatest number of audiences. At the level of production it can encompass an effect on specific studio practices (e.g., technological innovations, management and organisation), a training function for younger personnel (i.e., British technicians learning from European cinematographers or set designers), but it can also mean determining a film's visual style and its narrative content.

As far as the 'influence' on narrative content and style is concerned, one needs to ask how far 'authorial' control among émigrés actually extended. In the case of relatively independently working filmmakers such as Emeric Pressburger, an exilic perspective is perhaps most easily identified.[21] In other cases, such an approach may be more difficult. Thus, while it is legitimate to point to émigrés' personal investment in contributing to wartime propaganda (e.g., as a way of demonstrating loyalty to their host country), assumptions about their ability to exert influence on the content and narrative of their respective films often overestimate the position of émigrés within studio hierarchies. This is not to say that tracing an émigré 'sensibility' is impossible. In this volume, the contributions by Gerd Gemünden and Michael Williams on Conrad Veidt and Anton Walbrook exemplify analytical approaches that identify a particularly exilic 'inflection' in the respective stars' performance style.

To reiterate, then, individual, economic, political and cultural contexts constitute a complex and sometime contradictory force field that determines the assessment of exiles in British cinema; and it is crucial to realise that none of the different markers by which one could measure their influence (economic success, technological know-how, stylistic legacies, audience popularity, or narrative/political content) necessarily need to overlap or coincide at any given time.

Emigrés and National Film Histories

As we have seen, by the very nature of their cultural background and career trajectory, émigrés destabilise fixed notions of national identity. As a result their disjointed biographies and creative efforts (dispersed across two, or more, cultural contexts) have often fallen through the net of standard narratives of national cinemas, presented at best as a parallel history that can never be totally integrated into the mainstream of the national canon.

In an influential essay, Jan-Christopher Horak has pointed to the difficulties histories of cinema have had in situating émigré activity within national boundaries.[22] In Germany, particularly in the West, it took a long time after the end of the Second World War for the contributions and experience of exile filmmakers to be acknowledged. References to émigré artists during the 1950s and 1960s frequently glossed over their fate under the Nazis, skipped the years 1933 to 1945 altogether, or euphemistically presented their departure from Germany in retrospect as a voluntary career choice.[23] Moreover, émigrés to the United States frequently faced criticism for having succumbed during their time in Hollywood to brash American populism, and were thus seen as part and parcel of an unwanted postwar American colonisation of Germany.[24] Some émigrés, the most prominent example being Marlene Dietrich, encountered open hostility on their return to Germany for having 'betrayed' their country during the Second World War.

Emigrés to Britain received little attention within discourses on German cinema, while most of the wider studies of artistic exile to Britain have originated with British or British-based scholars.[25] The émigré background of the few exiles to Britain who managed to reestablish a career in postwar Germany (mainly the West) or who maintained a dual career between the United Kingdom and the Continent (e.g., actors such as Lilli Palmer, Albert Lieven, Lucie Mannheim and Walter Rilla, or the set designer Hein Heckroth) was frequently overlooked. Since the 1970s, Germany has witnessed a veritable academic industry of exile studies, yet the problem of how to reconcile narratives of German cinema and exile trajectories persists. Horak's above-mentioned essay represents one particular approach to the historical integration of exile. For Horak exile constitutes an integral part of a comprehensive history of German cinema, and is chronologically placed between a chapter on Weimar cinema and one on National Socialism. He argues that

> the history of exile film must not be considered as a peripheral aspect of the national canon of individual countries of exile; it needs to be seen as part of German film history, running parallel to the film of the 'Third Reich', as a piece of film culture associated with a non-fascist, 'other Germany'.[26]

Horak distinguishes between 'exile films' as a temporary generic category, valid for the duration of the Third Reich, as long as there was no possibility of a 'free German film production', and 'film exile', which in the case of many individual émigrés became a more permanent, and often life-long condition. It is precisely the latter term that marks the gradual transition towards the adoption by the émigré of a new national identity, which however never fully loses all traces of its former cultural formation. Between the poles of Horak's proposal to integrate émigré activity into the national canon, and postwar Germany's attempts to keep émigrés out of it, more recent studies have attempted to use the narrative of exile and émigrés as a means of challenging the concept of national cinema itself. Nationally discrete film histories are opened up in terms of their relation to other film cultures, transnational migration, and to the wider context of a global film industry.[27]

As with discourses on German cinema, British film historiography has in the past often avoided addressing the complex processes of cultural exchange and exile in favour of simpler and culturally 'purist' historical narratives. This striving for exclusivity has to be partly understood, as scholars such as Charles Barr and Alan Lovell have argued, as a reaction against a longstanding and unjustified international perception of British cinema as artistically insignificant.[28] On the other hand, Kevin Gough-Yates has pointed to an equally long tradition within Britain of underestimating or denigrating foreign contributions to the national canon.[29] One can find the origins of this tradition in the sometimes virulently xenophobic attacks on émigré filmmakers and producers (particularly Alexander Korda and Max Schach) in Graham Greene's film reviews of the 1930s,[30] which mark the beginning of an all too familiar rhetoric that equates a serious, and nationally pure (and overwhelmingly masculine) British cinema with 'realism', whereas commercial, popular genres (particularly those of the 1930s and 1940s) were seen to be tainted by their association with both feminine tastes and with the foreign, the latter of which was not infrequently portrayed as an 'invasion'.[31]

An apparent division between a nationally rooted realism and a foreign-influenced populism in British films continues to inform the public perception of the national cinema to the present day. Even scholars who have questioned the supposed superiority of the realist canon and who champion non-realist traditions on the whole accept this division. Among the most notable examples of such interventions is the feminist reassessment since the 1980s of Gainsborough's melodramas, and of historical costume drama more generally.[32] Yet a distinction between realist and non-realist strands in British cinema, at least as far as émigré involvement is concerned, is rarely clear-cut. Foreign filmmakers and personnel prior, during and after the war could be found contributing to the documentary tradition (e.g., the cinematographer Wolf Suschitzky, or the composer Ernst Meyer) as much as to melodrama (e.g., the composer Hans May). (See Geoff Brown's chapter in this volume). Alan Lovell has convincingly argued against a discourse that separates realist and non-realist traditions in British film history, suggesting that 'contemporary scholarship has fallen into a trap by posing excess and restraint against each other. British cinema is often most exciting when restraint and excess interact'.[33]

As I have argued elsewhere, the coding of 'foreign' influence in British cinema as 'non-realist', 'excessive' or 'Expressionist' not only homogenises the range of aesthetic approaches among exile filmmakers, but also resorts to reductive assumptions about the nature of foreign versus indigenous film styles.[34] After all, realist traditions were and are hardly exclusive to British cinema; indeed, many of Britain's avowed documentarists had themselves been influenced in the late 1920s by realist filmmakers from Russia, Germany and France. The preferences of the socialist critic, historian and filmmaker Paul Rotha provide an interesting test case in this respect. An admirer of German cinema (and, as Brigitte Mayr's chapter in this book outlines, a supportive personal friend of Carl Mayer, he was also one of the founding figures of the documentary movement in British cinema.

Rotha had no difficulties in reconciling non-realist and realist traditions as well as foreign and indigenous styles. The real schism for him was between commercial mass culture on one hand and 'quality' art cinema on the other; and the ultimate aim was to strategically promote the production and distribution in Britain of films with an educational, artistic, and socially engaged remit.[35] In his major historical survey, *The Film Till Now*, Rotha did take continental filmmakers working in the UK in the 1920s and 1930s to task for 'failing to understand British temperament and trying to mix German psychology with British bourgeois unintelligence'.[36] Yet it is clear from this waspish comment that his real target was less the émigré, but the – in his view – mediocre state of a class-driven and middlebrow British culture at the time.

Historical narratives persist that pit émigré activity (seen as either refreshingly non-realist or alternatively as weird and alien, depending on one's critical agenda) against an unproblematised indigenous canon; and such narratives can be found in academic discussions as much as in more populist representations. An example of the latter is Matthew Sweet's television documentary *Silent Britain* (2006), co-produced by the BBC and the British Film Institute. Sweet's approach marks a refreshing departure from the highbrow assessment of British realist cinema as the pinnacle of national achievement. To that extent, he can be congratulated for promoting a 'forgotten' and 'underrated' history.[37] At the same time he maintains suspicious of foreign influence, demonstrating that in discourses on British cinema foreigners can conveniently function both as pedlars of populist Eurotrash (as Greene perceived it) and as role models for an un-British, elitist art cinema.

In Sweet's version, British cinema drew primarily on native cultural references, and provided a staunch defence of British values and traditions in the face of an economic threat from Hollywood and the more insidious cultural infiltration from the continent. There is no mention here that already in the earliest years of cinema, British film pioneers were actively pursuing international contacts;[38] no mention either of early incursions of foreign companies into Britain, including two that would later transform into genuine British enterprises, Gaumont and Pathé.

Whereas for the earliest periods the omission of cross-national exchanges between Britain and continental Europe may be explained as a way of keeping the story simple, in Sweet's discussion of developments in the 1920s his bias towards national exclusivity comes to the fore. Thus, a German influence on Alfred Hitchcock (difficult to ignore altogether)[39] is summarily dismissed, discounting the fact that the director himself acknowledged this influence throughout his career. Similarly, viewers of *Silent Britain* are not told that many of the major directors and stars feted by Sweet as local heroes, including Graham Cutts, Henry Edwards, Guy Newall, Joan Morgan, Ivor Novello, Betty Balfour, and Miles Mander, worked on films that were either made in continental studios or produced in collaboration with European partners. Not much mention either that the Film Society, led by the committed internationalists Ivor Montagu and Adrian Brunel, provided an additional forum for foreign films and their specific stylistic innovations to be disseminated and discussed in Britain.[40]

Far from being an insular cultural backwater, Britain during the 1920s was keen to engage with European and wider international trends in culture and intellectual thought, as well as with more specific cinematic innovations and developments from abroad. Yet instead of celebrating this cosmopolitanism, Sweet champions the ideal of a Little Englander film culture. It comes as no surprise that although E.A. Dupont's *Piccadilly* (1929) and Arthur Robison's *The Informer* (1929) are justifiably hailed as masterpieces of late British silent film, unlike any of Sweet's other film examples, the non-British directors alongside other continental collaborators on these productions remain nameless.

The real villains of Sweet's narrative, however, are British 'cinema intellectuals'. He specifically singles out the critics associated with the magazine *Close Up*, who, in Sweet's words, 'wrote gushing fan letters to foreign directors, while dismissing the work of British film directors as third-rate and uninspired'. This argument creates simplistic dichotomies between filmmakers and critics, and between the terms 'British' and 'foreign'. Thus, some of the unnamed *Close Up* critics, including Rotha and John Grierson, in fact were or became significant British filmmakers themselves. Grierson, in particular, was hardly writing fan letters to foreign directors, certainly not gushing ones. In 1927, he considered the imitation of German styles by British directors 'a fallacy and a very dangerous one'.[41]

It is true that *Close Up* celebrated the work of Pabst and Eisenstein, but it was far less enamoured of popular imports from the continent.[42] It was also highly critical of the collaboration between continental and British filmmakers, as its harsh review of Dupont's *Piccadilly* attests to, which specifically criticised the film's multinational film crew.[43] Thus, while there is scope to criticise the elitist scope and limitations of *Close Up*'s aesthetic criteria, there is a a more complex attitude at work towards the place of the 'foreign' in British cinema than Sweet gives the magazine and its writers credit for.

It might seem churlish and ungracious to berate an all too rare attempt to promote the history of (especially silent) British film in the popular media, whatever its flaws and generalisations may be. Nevertheless, *Silent Britain*'s parochialism is symptomatic of a latent hostility in Britain towards cultural cosmopolitanism that was already much in evidence in the 1920s and 1930s, as Amy Sargeant's chapter in this book documents. Sweet's TV programme demonstrates how foreign, and particularly European, contributions to British cinema continue to be almost instinctually negated.

Emigrés and British Cinema: Whose Cultural Imaginary?

Over the past two decades, academic research has witnessed British film historiography focusing on questions of national identity, or, to be more precise, specifically on 'Englishness'.[44] On the whole, this emphasis is quite different from the perspective that *Silent Britain* exemplifies. Taking note of the devolution of Britain and acknowledging the ongoing regionalisation of Europe within the framework of wider globalisation processes, studies associated with this approach have overall avoided the homogenising tendencies of previous national film histories, and replaced them with nuanced arguments concerning the relationship between the national, the regional and the foreign. In this respect, studies on English cinema have been complemented by studies on the 'Scottishness' of Scottish films, by histories of Welsh cinema, and by the relations between Ireland, Britain and Europe.[45]

One of the most sophisticated recent studies representing this focus on English cinema is Christine Gledhill's *Reframing British Cinema 1918–1928. Between Restraint and Passion*.[46] Arguing for a 'locatedness of art practices' within discourses and traditions of nationhood, Gledhill provides a particularly useful suggestion for reconciling transnational traffic and local impact:

> If notions such as 'cultural poetics', 'horizon of expectation' or 'cultural imaginary' hold any force, then ideas and practices crossing national and cultural boundaries are subject to locally conditioned uses and interpretations even as they contribute to shifting, expanding, or contracting the frames within which local cultural practices operate.[47]

Gledhill's notion of Englishness in British cinema, then, functions less as an inherent characteristic or stable identity, but rather as a local negotiation of cultural practices that embraces cultural exchange, and thus also appears to be able to encompass the contribution of the émigré. It is interesting that one of Gledhill's main theoretical references is the work of a Jewish-German exile, the Leipzig-born art historian Nikolaus Pevsner's *The Englishness of English Art* (originally delivered as a BBC Reith lecture in 1955).[48] One can speculate whether Pevsner's investment in stable national roots of artistic expression was motivated by his own biographical experience, but his lecture – and his encyclopaedic assessment of English art and architecture in their regional variations – certainly demonstrate that some of the most articulate definitions of national identity, culture and history are formulated by the immigrant or the exile (see also Amy Sargeant's discussion of Pevsner in her chapter in this volume).

Given the inclusivity of Gledhill's theoretical framework, however, it is disappointing that when it comes to cinematic examples, her book once again omits the contributions by émigré filmmakers. This may in part be due to her schematic differentiation between 'American filmmaking' (continuity cinema) and 'continental modernism', with 'English pictorialism' as a distinctive aesthetic running parallel to both. But while Gledhill acknowledges the exportability of some features of British cinema (especially acting conventions), there is much less discussion on whether the indigenous aesthetic itself is hybrid and the result of cultural mixing. Amy Sargeant has pointed out that Gledhill's book has 'scant regard for international cooperation as a conscious policy to secure screenings for British films abroad and to enhance their popular and critical standing at home'.[49]

Justifying her choice of case studies, Gledhill argues that she wanted 'to avoid cherrypicking the few titles already feted in the British historical canon: the silent Hitchcocks, the Duponts and Asquiths'.[50] Yet while it is true that Hitchcock and Asquith's films of the late 1920s have indeed been discussed previously, where is the extensive literature on Dupont or, for that matter, Robison or Bolvary; and where are the émigrés (once again, later exceptions such as Pressburger and Korda excluded) 'feted in the historical canon'?[51] If one takes the major academic surveys from the late 1990s as a measure of what constitutes the canon in British cinema, one finds that in 1997 Dupont's *Piccadilly* was still too obscure to feature in Sarah Street's first edition of *British National Cinema*, making a brief, but hardly extensive appearance in an article on BIP by Tom Ryall in Robert Murphy's *British Cinema Book*, and only latterly gaining in prominence in Amy Sargeant's *British Cinema. A Critical History*, following the film's restoration, high-profile recommendation from Martin Scorsese, and re-release by the British Film Institute on DVD.[52] As noted above, by the time of *Silent Britain*, *Piccadilly* had become an apparently unauthored masterpiece of 1920s British film. In the sleeve notes of the BFI's DVD edition of *Piccadilly*, Ian Christie comes closer to the mark when he suggests:

> Arguably, internationalism has been the true strength of British cinema; and this sumptuous revival allows us to discover an almost forgotten moment when London seemed to be the capital of European cinema.[53]

Towards a Transnational History of British Cinema

One influential approach of assessing the intersections between the national and the international is the concept of an 'accented' cinema.[54] The work of Iranian-American film theorist Hamid Naficy has become a major reference point for many recent studies of exiles, émigrés, and cultural exchanges in cinema. In this volume both Gerd Gemünden and Tobias

Hochscherf cite his ideas.[55] His study posits that the emergence of a new exilic or diasporic cinema is primarily a post-1945 phenomenon. Naficy sees exile cinema as a consequence of 'Third World decolonization, wars of national liberation, the Soviet Union's invasion of Poland and Czechoslovakia, Westernization, and a kind of "internal decolonization" in the West itself'.[56]

Couched in an *auteurist* discourse, informed by postcolonial theory, and resolutely committed to alternative or art cinema practices, Naficy's book provides many useful insights on how an exile filmmaker's work can be stylistically informed by their own biographical background, and how it can intersect with diasporic communities and networks. At the same time, one has to be cautious about how far his model can be extended retrospectively to production practices and career trajectories in the first half of the twentieth century. Naficy's insistence on relative authorial autonomy, for example, does not easily fit the working conditions in British, European or Hollywood studios of the 1930s and 1940s, because the majority of émigrés prior to 1945 did not work on art cinema productions, but more often on popular genre films. These, however, rarely fit Naficy's suggestion that an accented cinema can be understood as a countercurrent to the mainstream. Identifying 'embedded criticism' as a cornerstone of an accented style, Naficy argues:

> By its artisanal and collective mode of production, its subversion of the conventions of storytelling and spectator positioning, its crucial juxtaposition of different worlds, languages, and cultures, and its aesthetics of imperfection and smallness, it critiques dominant cinema.[57]

Although Naficy qualifies this statement by saying that accented films are not necessarily politically progressive, it is problematic to simply import his definitions to production practices of the 1930s and 1940s. To give an example, the films of exile Alexander Korda in the 1930s did not adopt an 'artisanal' aesthetic of 'smallness and imperfection' – in fact, they specifically attempted to compete with Hollywood in the field of big-budget spectacles in order to gain a foothold in the US market.[58] Also, Korda's glorification of British imperialism hardly constitutes a politically marginal position. His productions are thus not immediately conducive to the kind of postcolonial subversion that Naficy's own case studies suggest; indeed many of them, for example *Sanders of the River* (1935), represent the pinnacle of colonial discourse itself. Nevertheless, despite or even because of their adherence to the ideological and the artistic mainstream, there is scope to explore films by the Kordas and indeed by other émigrés of the period according to some of Naficy's 'accented' motifs that mark them as the work of exiles: for example in terms of storytelling and spectator positioning, their insistent articulation of themes of nationhood, and their juxtaposition of public and private histories.

Elsewhere I have proposed understanding transnationalism in cinema not as a recent phenomenon, nor as a practice that is necessarily marginal or alternative, either in political, aesthetic or commercial terms, but rather as a succession of persistent exchanges that have characterised film history from its very beginning.[59] More crucially, and in this respect I echo Gledhill's earlier quotation, I argue that transnationalism always needs to encompass a dialogue between transitoriness and location, and between émigrés and hosts, and involve a process that blurs and ultimately dissolves the boundaries between these oppositions.

Destination London:
German-speaking Emigrés and British Cinema, 1925–50

The subsequent chapters will engage in varying degrees with the issues and debates outlined in the previous pages, although not all of the contributors necessarily share my theoretical premises or conclusions. The essays in this volume, the majority of which were originally presented as papers at an international conference at the University of Southampton in July 2005, deliberately comprise a diversity of approaches that can be applied to the subject, ranging from biographical studies to cultural and industrial contextualisations, as well as close textual readings. They encompass – and allow comparisons between – perspectives and prevailing perceptions from different national contexts (Germany, Austria, the United States and Britain) and different disciplines (musicology, exile history and film studies). The émigrés discussed in this volume include directors and cinematographers, set designers and composers, actors and writers, as well as specific German and British production companies. Of these various professional groups, it is primarily the cinematographers and set designers whose influence on British cinema has previously been acknowledged.[60]

The present anthology does not claim, nor could it realistically achieve, comprehensiveness. Although some of the names covered in this anthology are well known (e.g., Conrad Veidt or Alfred Junge), the contributions of others discussed here have barely been recognised in previous accounts, despite the fact that some of these individuals worked on major British productions. This collection explicitly does not want to create the impression that all émigrés managed to have a marked influence on the direction of British filmmaking. Laurie Ede's essay on Ernö Metzner and Brigitte Mayr's study of Carl Mayer in particular demonstrate the inability of some émigrés to integrate or to find employment, and as a not infrequent experience this fact needs to be documented. Conversely, we felt that the two most prominent and influential émigrés in the British cinema canon, Emeric Pressburger and Alexander Korda, had been amply as well as ably discussed in previous accounts. Thus, although their names come up repeatedly (for example in the essays by Tobias Hochscherf and

K.J. Donnelly), there are no specific chapters devoted to them. In any case, given the extent and volume of film émigrés working or living in Britain during the 1930s and 1940s in particular (numbering in the hundreds across these two decades), any anthology on this topic can inevitably only provide a snapshot of a few individuals.

The contributions in this volume are structured chronologically and in thematic clusters. The essays by Tim Bergfelder, Lawrence Napper, Chris Wahl and Kelly Robinson are all concerned with the early period of exchange between Britain and the German film industry. While Bergfelder and Robinson analyse respectively the work of director E.A. Dupont and cinematographer Werner Brandes in the context of the British studio system in the late 1920s, Napper and Wahl discuss 'British' productions made in German studios. Napper's study of Geza von Bolvary's *The Ghost Train* (1927) demonstrates how British reviews camouflaged the film's hybrid production context in order to make it more appealing to British audiences. Wahl's essay, meanwhile, is concerned with Ufa's short-lived strategy in the early sound period of making English-language versions of their box office hits, and analyses the input from British production personnel (in particular the script-doctor and later director Robert Stevenson) in the process. Evaluating the ultimate cultural as well as economic failure of multilingual productions, Wahl points to the technically efficient, but also inflexible organisation of German studios in the early 1930s, the seemingly inevitable national differences in temperament and attitude; and it documents the fascinating and often highly creative attempts by British script-doctors to adapt German narratives for a British market. Despite their eventual discontinuation as a production practice, multilingual versions nevertheless paved the way for subsequent exchanges and film personnel coming to Britain. For while German-made films may not have appealed to large sections of the British audience, British-made films based on continental sources and benefiting from continental technical know-how certainly did.

The contributions by Michael Omasta, Amy Sargeant, Sarah Street, Laurie Ede, Christian Cargnelli, Gerd Gemünden and Michael Williams (and partly Barbara Ziereis) concentrate on developments and individual careers during the 1930s. Omasta's essay on Günther Krampf complements Robinson's piece on Brandes, and demonstrates a distinctive visual imagination at work in Krampf's films in Britain. Sargeant situates émigré activity in the film industry of the 1930s within wider contexts of artistic exchanges and developments in modern design. Drawing in particular on the case of former Bauhaus guru Laszlo Moholy-Nagy, she argues that artistic activity during the 1930s should be seen as an itinerant practice that cannot be contained by singular national developments.

Street and Ede offer contrasting assessments of émigré production designers in 1930s British film. Street makes a persuasive case for the set designer Alfred Junge to be recognised as an important contributor to the visual style of many British films of the period, significantly enhancing the look and atmosphere of musicals and thrillers, while also transporting ideas about modernity and design trends. Ede's essay on Ernö Metzner, on the other hand, while acknowledging the quality and imagination of some of his British films, comes to the conclusion that his specific working style did not match the practices of the British studio system, which resulted in Metzner leaving Britain for Hollywood.

Christian Cargnelli discusses the work of director Paul L. Stein who, though prolific and successful at the time, has been entirely forgotten by film history. Cargnelli explores the images of Vienna Stein created in his British films, memorably starring fellow exile Richard Tauber. Alongside Tauber and Elisabeth Bergner, Conrad Veidt and Anton Walbrook were the most popular émigré actors working in Britain during the 1930s. They are discussed here respectively by Gemünden and Williams. Both authors detect an émigré inflection in the on- and off-screen personae of the two actors, and suggest how their image underwent significant changes as a result of their move from one country to another.

Lilli Palmer also emerged as a popular actress in the latter half of the 1930s, but unlike Veidt and Walbrook, she had no experience in the continental film industry prior to her arrival in Britain. Ziereis's essay documents the difficulties involved in an unknown émigré actress establishing herself in British cinema, and looks at the range of roles and types she was assigned according to her perceived national background, in particular in films made during the Second World War. In this emphasis, her essay overlaps with the next contribution, focusing on the 1940s: Hochscherf concerns himself with a number of wartime feature films, looking in particular at the contributions by émigré writers and actors, including Emeric Pressburger and Anton Walbrook.

As the chapters by Williams, Gemünden, Ziereis and Hochscherf make clear, linguistic factors, such as a foreign accent and linguistic ability more generally, played an important part in how successful émigré actors became, and what kind of roles they were given. The loss of one's own language was even more acutely felt among writers. Thus, while British cinema throughout the 1930s relied heavily on stories and remakes of films from the continent (comedies, operettas and costume dramas in particular often had continental origins), the number of exiled screenwriters who managed to establish a career for themselves in England is negligible. Emeric Pressburger's success is a notable exception in this respect. Far more representative trajectories are the erratic careers of authors such as Anna Gmeyner (aka Anna Reiner) and Wolfgang Wilhelm, or indeed the dead end mapped for Carl Mayer in Brigitte Mayr's chapter.

The volume concludes with three essays on film composers, bridging the war years and the late 1940s. Geoff Brown's comparison between the divergent and yet complementary careers of Ernst Meyer and Hans May illustrates émigré activity in a range of different genres and production environments, and in the context of the conflicting demands of serious, politically motivated art versus mass entertainment. K.J. Donnelly sees Allan Gray's score for Powell and Pressburger's Scottish-set *I Know Where I'm Going* (1945) as a crucial element in the film's narrational strategies, and as an example of the importation not only of Scottish idioms, but also of 'Germanic' musical conventions into the repertoire of British cinema. Florian Scheding, meanwhile, makes an interesting case for an émigré inflection in Mátyás Seiber's score for the animated experimental film *The Magic Canvas* (1948).

As suggested previously, to some extent the temporal demarcation of émigré activity and cultural exchange between Britain and Germany between 1925 and 1950 is an artificial one. One could find earlier examples, while some significant émigré careers really only begin in the 1950s. The latter would include the eminently influential émigré producer, writer and director Rudolph Cartier, and his contributions to the development of both quality and popular British television drama, and the set designer Ken Adam, in particular in his work for the James Bond series and for Stanley Kubrick. Meanwhile, as Sarah Street's chapter demonstrates, some prewar careers such as Alfred Junge's very successfully continued into the postwar period. All of these examples (to which one could easily add more) underline the point made earlier in this introduction that émigré activity in British film does not just encompass the 1930s and 1940s, but constitutes an ongoing and productive element in the continual regeneration of British cinema. It is our hope that this collection may not only provide the incentive to consider British cinema in more international (or cosmopolitan) terms, but that it may also trigger the rediscovery of a host of forgotten names, who – in similar ways to the case studies presented here – left their mark on the history of British and global film culture.

Notes

1. See, for instance, 'Deutsche Künstler im englischen Film. Eine vorläufige Bilanz', *Pariser Tageblatt*, 12 December 1934, p. 4; Kevin Gough-Yates, 'The British Feature Film as a European Concern. Britain and the Emigré Film-Maker, 1933–1945', in Günter Berghaus (ed.), *Theatre and Film in Exile. German Artists in Britain, 1933–1945* (Oxford, New York, Munich: Berg, 1989), pp. 135–66; Gough-Yates, 'Exiles and British Cinema', in Robert Murphy (ed.), *The British Cinema Book* (London: BFI, 1997), pp. 104–13.
2. Gough-Yates, 'The British Feature Film as a European Concern', p. 140.
3. Since the rediscovery of The Archers in the late 1960s, an extensive literature on the partnership between Michael Powell and Emeric Pressburger has emerged. Among the best-known publications on the subject are Kevin Gough-Yates, *Michael Powell in Collaboration with Emeric Pressburger* (London: BFI, 1971); Ian Christie, *Arrows of Desire. The Films of Michael Powell and Emeric Pressburger* (London: Waterstone, 1985); Kevin Macdonald, *Emeric Pressburger: The Life and Death of a Screenwriter* (London: Faber and Faber, 1994); and Andrew Moor, *Powell and Pressburger. A Cinema of Magic Spaces* (London: I.B. Tauris, 2005).

4. See Karol Kulik, *Alexander Korda, the Man Who Could Work Miracles* (London: Allen & Unwin, 1975); Charles Drazin, *Korda: The Definitive Biography* (London: Sidgwick & Jackson, 2002).

5. Among the most notable studies are: John Baxter, *The Hollywood Exiles* (New York: Taplinger, 1976); Otto Friedrich, *City of Nets: A Portrait of Hollywood in the 1940s* (Berkeley: University of California Press, 1977); Maria Hilchenbach, *Kino im Exil. Die Emigration deutscher Filmkünstler* (Munich: K.G. Saur, 1982); John Russell Taylor, *Strangers in Paradise: The Hollywood Émigrés 1933–1950* (London: Faber and Faber, 1983); *Exil. Sechs Schauspieler aus Deutschland* (Berlin: Stiftung Deutsche Kinemathek, 1983); Jan-Christopher Horak, *Fluchtpunkt Hollywood. Eine Dokumentation zur Filmemigration nach 1933* (Münster: MakS, 1986); Ronny Loewy (ed.), *Von Babelsberg nach Hollywood: Filmemigranten aus Nazideutschland* (Frankfurt am Main: Deutsches Filmmuseum, 1987); Christian Cargnelli and Michael Omasta (eds.), *Aufbruch ins Ungewisse. Österreichische Filmschaffende in der Emigration vor 1945* (Vienna: Wespennest, 1993); Helmut G. Asper, '*Etwas Besseres als den Tod …' Filmexil in Hollywood. Porträts, Filme, Dokumente* (Marburg: Schüren, 2002); Helmut G. Asper, *Filmexilanten im Universal Studio, 1933–1960* (Berlin: Bertz und Fischer, 2005); and Alastair Phillips and Ginette Vincendeau (eds.), *Journeys of Desire. European Actors in Hollywood* (London: BFI, 2006). See also a special edition on 'Film and Exile', edited by Gerd Gemünden and Anton Kaes, in the journal *New German Critique*, no. 89 (Summer 2003).

6. The following titles constitute a small selection of an extensive literature on the subject: Werner Sudendorf (ed.), *Marlene Dietrich* (Frankfurt am Main, Berlin and Vienna: Carl Hanser, 1977); Scott Eyman, *Ernst Lubitsch: Laughter in Paradise* (New York: Simon and Schuster, 1993); Cameron Crowe, *Conversations with Wilder* (New York: Alfred Knopf, 1999); Tom Gunning, *The Films of Fritz Lang: Allegories of Vision and Modernity* (London: BFI, 2000); Michael Omasta, Brigitte Mayr and Elisabeth Streit (eds.), *Peter Lorre: Ein Fremder im Paradies* (Vienna: Zsolnay, 2004); Erica Carter, *Dietrich's Ghosts* (London: BFI, 2004); Stephen D. Youngkin, *The Lost One. A Life of Peter Lorre* (Lexington: University of Kentucky Press, 2005); and Gerd Gemünden, *Filmemacher mit Akzent: Billy Wilder in Hollywood* (Vienna: Synema, 2006).

7. See Thomas Elsaesser, 'A German Ancestry to Film Noir?', *Iris*, no. 21 (1996), pp. 129–44; Christian Cargnelli and Michael Omasta (eds.), *Schatten. Exil. Europäische Emigranten im Film Noir* (Vienna: PVS, 1997); Lutz Koepnick, *The Dark Mirror. German Cinema Between Hitler and Hollywood* (Berkeley: University of California Press, 2002); Tim Bergfelder, 'German Cinema and Film Noir', in Andrew Spicer (ed.), *European Film Noir* (Manchester University Press, 2007), pp. 138–63.

8. Jörg Schöning (ed.), *Reinhold Schünzel. Schauspieler und Regisseur* (Munich: edition text+kritik, 1989); Helga Belach and Wolfgang Jacobsen (eds.), *Richard Oswald. Regisseur und Produzent* (Munich: edition text+kritik, 1990); Hans-Michael Bock and Claudia Lenssen (eds.), *Joe May. Regisseur und Produzent* (Munich: edition text+kritik, 1991); Jürgen Bretschneider (ed.), *Ewald André Dupont. Autor und Regisseur* (Munich: edition text+kritik, 1992); Jürgen Kasten and Armin Loacker (eds.), *Richard Oswald: Kino zwischen Spektakel, Aufklärung und Unterhaltung* (Vienna: Filmarchiv Austria, 2005); and Christian Cargnelli (ed.), *Gustav Machaty. Ein Filmregisseur zwischen Prag und Hollywood* (Vienna: Synema, 2005).

9. An example of particular cultural influence constitutes émigré activity in the French film industry of the 1930s. Cf. Sibylle M. Sturm and Arthur Wohlgemuth (eds.), *Hallo? Berlin? Ici Paris! Deutsch-französische Filmbeziehungen 1918–1939* (Munich: edition text+kritik, 1996); and Alastair Phillips, *City of Darkness, City of Light. Émigré Filmmakers in Paris 1929–1939* (Amsterdam: Amsterdam University Press, 2004). For migrations between Russia, Germany and France, see Jörg Schöning (ed.), *Fantaisies Russes. Russische Filmmacher in Berlin und Paris 1920–1930* (Munich: edition text+kritik, 1995). German-speaking emigration to the Netherlands is explored in Kathinka Dittrich van Weringh, *Der niederländische Spielfilm der dreißiger Jahre und die deutsche Filmemigration* (Amsterdam: Rodopi, 1987), while the work of exiles in 1930s Austria has been analysed in Armin

Loacker (ed.), *Unerwünschtes Kino: Der deutschsprachige Emigrantenfilm 1934–1937* (Vienna: Filmarchiv Austria, 2000). A range of other migratory trajectories, including to Mexico and China, were covered in articles in the unfortunately now defunct journal *FilmExil* (1992–2004). See also a number of essays in Erwin Rotermund and Lutz Winckler (eds.), *Exilforschung. Ein internationales Jahrbuch, Band 21: Film und Fotografie* (Munich: edition text+kritik, 2003).

10. Tim Bergfelder, 'The Nation Vanishes', in Mette Hjort and Scott Mackenzie (eds), *Cinema and Nation* (London and New York: Routledge, 2000), p. 139.

11 See Jeffrey Richards (ed.), *The Unknown 1930s. An Alternative History of the British Cinema, 1929–1939* (London and New York: I.B. Tauris, 1998); Andrew Higson and Richard Maltby (eds.), *'Film Europe' and 'Film America': Cinema, Commerce and Cultural Exchange 1920–1939* (Exeter: Exeter University Press, 1999); Mark Glancy, *When Hollywood Loved Britain: The Hollywood 'British' Film, 1939–1945* (Manchester: Manchester University Press, 1999); and Sarah Street, *Transatlantic Crossings. British Feature Films in the USA* (New York: Continuum, 2002).

12. For a discussion of the ACT's actions with regard to émigré personnel, see Kevin Gough-Yates, 'The British Feature Film as a European Concern', and Tim Bergfelder, 'The Production Designer and the *Gesamtkunstwerk*: German Film Technicians in the British Film Industry of the 1930s', in Andrew Higson (ed.), *Dissolving Views. Key Writings on British Cinema* (London: Cassell, 1996), pp. 20–37.

13. Bergfelder, 'The Production Designer and the *Gesamtkunstwerk*', p. 22.

14. See the three special thematic editions of the journal *Cinema & Cie* on multiple-language versions in early 1930s European cinema: no. 4, Spring 2004; no. 6, Spring 2005; and no. 7, Fall 2005.

15. Kevin Gough-Yates, 'Jews and Exiles in British Cinema', in *Leo Baeck Yearbook*, vol. 37 (1992), pp. 520–21.

16. See Thomas Elsaesser, *Weimar Cinema and After. Germany's Historical Imaginary* (London and New York: Routledge, 2000), pp. 383–91.

17. For more detailed information on Stapenhorst, see the biographical entry in *CineGraph* (Hamburg 1984–) which can also be viewed online: www.filmportal.de

18. See Richard Falcon, 'No Politics! "German Affairs" im Spionage- und Kostümfilm', in Jörg Schöning (ed.), *London Calling. Deutsche im britischen Film der dreißiger Jahre* (Munich: edition text+kritik, 1993), pp. 77–88; and Christian Cargnelli, '*Abdul the Damned* (1935) und *These Are the Men* (1943): Anmerkungen zu Robert Neumanns Filmarbeit im englischen Exil', in Anne Maximiliane Jäger (ed.), *Einmal Emigrant – immer Emigrant? Der Schriftsteller und Publizist Robert Neumann (1897–1975)* (Munich: edition text+kritik, 2006), pp. 102–8.

19. Examples of German-speaking actors to cross over the Channel to work on British productions in the 1950s and 1960s include Hardy Kruger, Curd Jürgens, Peter van Eyck, and Horst Buchholz. See Melanie Williams, '"The most explosive object to hit Britain since the V2!": The British films of Hardy Kruger and Anglo-German relations in the 1950s', *Cinema Journal* 46 (1): 2006, pp. 85–107; Tim Bergfelder, 'The Passenger – Ambivalences of National Identity and Masculinity in the Star Persona of Peter van Eyck', in Sabine Hake and John Davidson (eds.), *Take Two: German Film in the 1950s* (Oxford and New York: Berghahn, 2007).

20. p. 143.

21. For recent evaluations of the respective contributions of Michael Powell and Emeric Pressburger to The Archers, see Charles Barr, 'The First Four Minutes' (pp. 20–35), and Ian Christie, 'Another Life in Movies: Pressburger and Powell' (pp. 171–86), in Ian Christie and Andrew Moor (eds.), *Michael Powell. International Perspectives on an English Film-Maker* (London: BFI, 2005).

22. Jan-Christopher Horak, 'Exilfilm, 1933–1945', in Wolfgang Jacobsen, Anton Kaes and Hans-Helmut Prinzler (eds), *Geschichte des deutschen Films* (Stuttgart and Weimar: Metzler, 1993), p. 102.

23. See my study of the reception in postwar West Germany of former émigré actor Peter van Eyck in 'The Passenger – Ambivalences of National Identity and Masculinity in the Star Persona of Peter van Eyck'.

24. See Lutz Koepnick's discussion of Robert Siodmak's postwar German reception in *The Dark Mirror*, pp. 192–200. See also my chapter 'Artur Brauner's CCC: Remigration, Popular Genres, and International Aspirations', in *International Adventures. German Popular Cinema and European Co-Productions in the 1960s* (Oxford and New York: Berghahn, 2005), pp. 108–25.

25. See Berghaus (ed.), *Theatre and Film in Exile*. The notable German exception is Schöning (ed.), *London Calling*.

26. Horak, 'Exilfilm, 1933–1945', p. 103. My translation.

27. See the representation of exile and cultural exchange in Sabine Hake, *German National Cinema* (London and New York: Routledge, 2002); and in Tim Bergfelder, Erica Carter and Deniz Göktürk (eds.), *The German Cinema Book* (London: BFI, 2002).

28. Cf. Charles Barr, 'Amnesia and Schizophrenia', in Barr (ed.), *All Our Yesterdays. 90 Years of British Cinema* (London: BFI, 1986), pp. 1–26; Alan Lovell, 'The British Cinema: The Known Cinema', in Robert Murphy (ed.), *The British Cinema Book*, 2nd edition (London: BFI, 2001), pp. 200–6.

29. Gough-Yates, 'Jews and Exiles in British Cinema', p. 517.

30. See Bergfelder, 'The Production Designer and the *Gesamtkunstwerk*', p. 32.

31. See the chapter on 'The German Invasion' (meaning the work of émigré filmmakers, not the attacks by Hitler's Luftwaffe) in C.A. Oakley's jingoistic historical survey of British cinema, *Where We Came In* (London: Allen & Unwin, 1964).

32. See Sue Aspinall and Robert Murphy (eds.), *BFI Dossier, no. 18: Gainsborough Melodrama* (London: BFI, 1983); Sue Harper, *Picturing the Past. The Rise and Fall of the British Costume Film* (London: BFI, 1994); Pam Cook, *Fashioning the Nation. Costume and Identity in British Cinema* (London: BFI, 1996); Pam Cook (ed.), *Gainsborough Pictures* (London: Cassell, 1997); Claire Monk and Amy Sargeant (eds.), *British Historical Cinema* (London: Routledge, 2002); and Andrew Higson, *English Heritage, English Cinema. Costume Drama since 1980* (Oxford: Oxford University Press, 2003).

33. Lovell, 'The British Cinema: The Known Cinema', p. 202.

34. Bergfelder, 'The Production Designer and the *Gesamtkunstwerk*', pp. 33–37.

35. See John Ellis, 'The Quality Film Adventure: British Critics and the Cinema, 1942–1948', in Higson (ed.), *Dissolving Views*, pp. 66–93. See also Leo Enticknap, 'This Modern Age and the British Non-Fiction Film', in Andrew Higson and Justine Ashby (eds.), *British Cinema, Past and Present* (London and New York: Routledge, 2000), pp. 207–220.

36. Paul Rotha, *The Film Till Now: A Survey of World Cinema*, rev. edn. (London: Vision Press, 1951), p. 254.

37. Of course, there had been a significant amount of prior academic groundwork in rediscovering these forgotten histories, most notably the efforts of the scholars associated with Nottingham's annual silent British cinema events. See Alan Burton and Laraine Porter (eds.), *Pimple, Pranks and Pratfalls. British Film Comedy Before 1930* (Trowbridge: Flicks Books, 2000); Andrew Higson (ed.), *Young and Innocent? Cinema and Britain 1896–1930* (Exeter: Exeter University Press, 2002); Jon Burrows, *Legitimate Cinema. Theatre Stars in Silent British Films, 1908–1918* (Exeter: Exeter University Press, 2003); Michael Williams, *Ivor Novello. Screen Idol* (London: BFI, 2003); and Michael Hammond, *The Big Show: British Cinema Culture in the Great War (1914–1918)* (Exeter: Exeter University Press, 2006).

38. See Martin Loiperdinger, *Film und Schokolade. Stollwercks Geschäfte mit lebenden Bildern* (Frankfurt am Main and Basle: Stroemfeld/Roter Stern, 1999).

39. For a discussion of Hitchcock's first two German films, see Charles Barr, *English Hitchcock* (Moffat: Cameron & Hollis, 1999), pp. 215–17; and Joseph Garncarz, 'German Hitchcock', in Sidney Gottlieb (ed.), *Framing Hitchcock: Selected Essays from the 'Hitchcock Annual'* (Detroit: Wayne State University Press, 2002).

40. See Jamie Sexton, 'The Film Society and the Creation of an Alternative British Film Culture in the 1920s' (pp. 291–305), and Gerry Turvey, 'Towards a Critical Practice: Ivor Montagu and British Film Culture in the 1920s' (pp. 306–20), both in Higson (ed.), *Young and Innocent?*

41. Ian Jarvie, 'John Grierson on Hollywood's Success', in *Historical Journal of Film, Radio and Television* 9.3 (1989), p. 323.

42. See James Donald, Anne Friedberg and Laura Marcus (eds.), *Close Up 1927–1933. Cinema and Modernism* (London: Cassell, 1998).

43. *Close Up*, July 1929.

44. Other prominent examples include Andrew Higson, *Waving The Flag. Constructing a National Cinema in Britain* (Oxford: Oxford University Press, 1995); Jeffrey Richards, *Films and British National Identity. From Dickens to Dad's Army* (Manchester: Manchester University Press, 1997); Barr, *English Hitchcock*; and Higson, *English Heritage, English Cinema*.

45. See John Hill, Martin McLoone and Paul Hainsworth (eds.), *Border Crossing: Film in Ireland, Britain and Europe* (Belfast, Dublin and London: Institute of Irish Studies/BFI/University of Ulster, 1994); Dave Berry, *Wales and Cinema – The First Hundred Years* (University of Wales Press, 1996); and Duncan Petrie, *Screening Scotland* (London: BFI, 2000).

46. Christine Gledhill, *Reframing British Cinema 1918–1928. Between Restraint and Passion* (London: BFI, 2003).

47. Ibid., p. 5.

48. Nikolaus Pevsner, *The Englishness of English Art* (London: The Architectural Press, 1956).

49. Amy Sargeant, 'Review of *Reframing British Cinema 1918–1928*', in *Modernism/Modernity* 12.4 (2005), p. 732.

50. Gledhill, *Reframing British Cinema*, p. 1.

51. Among the very few essays in English on Dupont is Andrew Higson, 'Polyglot Films for an International Market: E.A. Dupont, the British Film Industry, and the Idea of a European Cinema, 1926–1930', in Higson and Maltby (eds), *'Film Europe' and 'Film America*, pp. 274–301.

52. Sarah Street, *British National Cinema* (London and New York: Routledge, 1997); Murphy (ed.), *The British Cinema Book*; Amy Sargeant, *British Cinema. A Critical History* (London: BFI, 2005).

53. *Piccadilly* (London: BFI video, 2004). It is encouraging to see that similarly affirmative acknowledgments of the productive and positive contribution of internationalism to British film are becoming more common. See, e.g., Sarah Street, 'British Cinema: Introduction', in Pam Cook (ed.), *The Cinema Book*, 3rd edn. (London: BFI, 2007), pp. 175–76.

54. For introductions to this debate, with a particular emphasis on the British case, see Andrew Higson, 'The Instability of the National', in Higson and Ashby (eds), *British Cinema, Past and Present*, pp. 35–47; and Tim Bergfelder, 'National, Transnational, or Supranational Cinema? Rethinking European Film Studies', *Media, Culture and Society*, vol. 27, no.3 (Spring 2005), pp. 315–31.

55. Hamid Naficy, *An Accented Cinema: Exilic and Diasporic Filmmaking* (Princeton: Princeton University Press, 2001).

56. Naficy, *An Accented Cinema*, p. 10.

57. Ibid., p. 26.

58. See Street, *Transatlantic Crossings*, pp. 43–69.

59. Bergfelder, 'National, Transnational, or Supranational Cinema?'

60. See Catherine A. Surowiec, *Accent on Design. Four European Art Directors* (London: BFI, 1992); Duncan J. Petrie, *The British Cinematographer* (London: BFI, 1996); Tim Bergfelder, Sue Harris and Sarah Street, *Film Architecture and the Transnational Imagination. European Set Design in the 1930s* (Amsterdam: Amsterdam University Press, 2007).

Chapter 2

LIFE IS A VARIETY THEATRE – E.A. DUPONT'S CAREER IN GERMAN AND BRITISH CINEMA

Tim Bergfelder

Studies of émigré filmmakers often mirror the disjointed lives of their subjects, focusing on a selective body of work that either precedes or postdates their emigration, and thus fixing this fragmented work within the stable parameters of a single national cinema. Only in a few cases do surveys manage to convey either a sense of artistic continuity, or else document a significant departure in the émigré's work from their previous career. As I have outlined in the introduction to this volume, assessments of émigré artists are frequently couched in not always accurate assumptions concerning the cultural context these filmmakers emerged from, and, especially, the perceived difference of this context to that of the host country. I have argued that in the case of émigré directors and technicians coming to Britain from Germany in the 1920s and early 1930s, the standard historical narrative has been to subsume their original formation, stylistic preferences and artistic directions under the rubric of 'Expressionism', which in turn is seen as antagonistic to a British preponderance for realism. Meanwhile, a focus on the émigré's career prior to their emigration often fails to acknowledge the crucial influence a change in industrial context has on a filmmaker's output.

In this chapter, I shall argue that it is no coincidence which German-speaking artists came to Britain, especially in the late 1920s, when there were fewer political motivations for emigration. I shall suggest that the films the émigrés made in their home context can give an indication of what they could offer the British studios, and will examine in what ways their work was adaptable to British generic strategies and working conditions. The chapter will look at the trajectory of the arguably most prominent émigré director working in Britain in the late 1920s and early 1930s, E.A. Dupont. Although my approach will draw largely on his biography, the primary aim of this chapter is not to reify him as a misunderstood *auteur* (even if this does emerge as one of the outcomes of this discussion), but instead to identify his career and production strategies as symptomatic of wider patterns within European cinema of the time. The recourse to biographical chronology suggests, especially in the case of Dupont, that the reasons for success or failure in another national industrial context may not always be caused by irreconcilable cultural differences or incompatible production methods, but might be the result of issues of personality, and sometimes pure chance.

In order to situate Dupont's stylistic and narrative contributions to British cinema, one first has to qualify a common misunderstanding of 1920s German film as a homogeneous and essentially non-realist art cinema, exemplified by iconic productions such as Robert Wiene's *Das Cabinet des Dr. Caligari* (The Cabinet of Dr Caligari, 1920), Paul Wegener's *Der Golem, wie er in die Welt kam* (The Golem, 1920), F.W. Murnau's *Nosferatu* (1922) and *Faust* (1926), and Fritz Lang's *Die Nibelungen* (1924) and *Metropolis* (1927). Lang and Murnau in particular have been portrayed as the star *auteurs* of a national cinema canon that drew on indigenous visual and literary traditions, and whose films reflected as well as articulated national concerns, desires, and anxieties.[1]

Within Germany itself, this kind of prestige cinema represented a minority mode of production, albeit internationally a highly visible one. Producers, most notably Erich Pommer at Ufa, promoted a specifically national German cinema in the early to mid-1920s as an international brand, while a culturally more promiscuous and less highbrow indigenous cinema appealed to domestic audiences. Dupont, alongside other directors including Richard Eichberg, Reinhold Schünzel, Richard Oswald, Joe May, Paul Ludwig Stein (see Christian Cargnelli's contribution in this volume), Geza von Bolvary and Friedrich Zelnik are prime examples of this 'other Weimar cinema', a cinema dedicated to popular generic conventions, stars, and couched within the demands of an industrial mode of production. As with the more prestigious productions at Ufa (equally only representing a partial output within the company), Weimar's popular cinema comprised a close-knit group of frequent artistic collaborators; indeed, many of the above-mentioned filmmakers repeatedly worked on each other's films and relied on recurrent technical teams. These teams would eventually support the directors in their émigré productions, and in some cases technicians and craftsmen managed to establish a more settled position in the British film industry than the directors themselves.

Although Weimar's popular cinema shared certain characteristics with the period's prestige productions in terms of narrative themes, visual style and techniques, its primary aim was commercial appeal. Another characteristic was the directors' indebtedness and intertextual references to other popular entertainment media of the time: in the case of Dupont and Eichberg circus, cabaret and variety theatres; in the case of Bolvary and Zelnik the operetta and the pulp novel. Meanwhile, in their reliance on specific generic formulae (especially serial narratives, thrillers and melodrama), directors tapped into internationally circulating, in some cases universal paradigms, providing a localised version of the kind of popular cinema that became from the late 1910s increasingly identified with Hollywood.

During the 1920s, Dupont, Eichberg and Bolvary (all of whom would later work in Britain) were celebrated by critics and producers alike for their ability to make films that could compete, both in terms of professional quality and box office potential, with productions imported from Hollywood. Indeed, all three of them were at one point approvingly seen as German cinema's most 'American' directors. I argue that it was this quality that facilitated their movements across different national film cultures. In the remainder of this essay, I shall look at Dupont's specific trajectory, primarily prior to his final emigration to the United States after 1933, and situate his films not simply within the specifics of respective production systems, but also within a framework of transnational exchanges of generic formulae.

Since the restoration and acclaimed re-release of *Piccadilly* (1929) in 2003, the film has been celebrated as a central example of late 1920s British cinema. Visually dazzling and highly modern in its narrative of the erotic attraction between an English nightclub owner and a Chinese scullery maid (Anna May Wong), her rise to become the club's star performer, and her eventual murder by a jealous boyfriend, the film seems to have struck a chord with audiences in the new millennium, but its success seems to have come out of nowhere. Although not exactly unknown in previous decades, *Piccadilly* was nonetheless overlooked. More recently it has been analysed in relation to its function within British production strategies of the late 1920s, and as a vehicle for its Chinese-American star.[2] However, relatively little has been written in the context of *Piccadilly* about its German director.

Indeed, prior to the critical renaissance of *Piccadilly*, E.A. Dupont had been a more or less forgotten figure of the silent period, remembered, if at all, for a single film, *Varieté* (Variety, 1925). The first steps towards an international rediscovery of the director were initiated in the early 1990s with a comprehensive retrospective and conference on the subject in Hamburg, organised by the research centre CineGraph, which resulted in the first book publication on Dupont.[3] The information presented at this event revealed not a one-hit wonder, but a central figure of Wilhelmine and Weimar film culture, and an *auteur* with a remarkably consistent focus on certain themes. While being a down-and-out and by all accounts alcoholic exile in Hollywood, churning out B-movies in the 1930s and 1950s, Dupont could still leave a lasting influence on younger directors. The major coup of the 1991 retrospective was the attendance of American cult *auteur* Samuel Fuller, who had met Dupont in 1949 and who hailed him as a 'Columbus in his field'.[4]

Dupont's influence on German cinema of the 1910s and 1920s was threefold – as a film critic, as a screenwriter and author of filmmaking manuals, and finally as a director. Born in 1891 as the son of the editor-in-chief of the *Berliner Illustrirte Zeitung*, Dupont followed in his father's footsteps and started out as a journalist in 1911. Initially reviewing stage productions and variety shows, he quickly turned his attention to the cinema and eventually established a serious discussion of film in the print media. In a cultural climate where film was primarily regarded as a threat to public morality and a debasement of cultural values,[5] Dupont's approach to the coverage of film in the press was particularly enlightened.

At this time, supporters of the cinema in Germany attempted to raise the medium's prestige by aping legitimate art forms such as the theatre or by attracting respected writers to contribute to films (a strategy that would be known as the *Autorenfilm*, the author's film). Dupont in contrast recognised cinema as an entertainment medium, with its own specific rules and needs. In a screenwriting manual published in book form in 1919, he advised budding authors to always follow public taste, to stay within given economic parameters (a piece of advice he did not always adhere to himself in his own career as a director), and to tell stories visually.[6] Unlike other supporters of cinema, Dupont did not attempt to associate film with highbrow art; instead he pointed to the close relationship of the medium with variety theatre, and this connection informed his own subsequent films, structurally as well as thematically.[7]

In 1912 Dupont penned a lengthy analysis of the relationship between cinematography and performance, again a central nexus in his later films as director.[8] Apart from such general studies, Dupont prolifically discussed individual films. Christiane Heuwinkel has summarised the main characteristics of his film reviews as 'ironic distance, a love for the spectacular, a focus on visual effect and physical presence as surface qualities, and an attention to, almost obsession with, technical detail'.[9]

Perhaps more significant for his later position within the film industry, Dupont's writings displayed an acute understanding of economic contexts. His interventions in matters of film policy and production practices not infrequently caused controversies, for example when he insisted on strictly separating film advertisements and film reviews, when in many newspaper reviews editorial and promotional comments overlapped.[10] In the following years, Dupont became an important mediator between the general public, the print media and the film industry – apart from his own contributions, he was able to persuade major filmmakers to write articles for his column.

Dupont's over-identification with the industry made a switch from critic to filmmaker almost inevitable. His first screenplay during the First World War was for Rudolf Meinert's detective thriller *Mein ist die Rache* (Vengeance Is Mine, 1916). He subsequently wrote other scripts in the same genre for directors including Joe May (*Der Onyxkopf*, The Onyx

Head, 1917), as well as *Durchlaucht Hypochonder* (His Majesty the Hypochondriac, 1917), a comedy for Friedrich Zelnik. That same year, Dupont worked with Richard Oswald on the latter's sex education melodrama serial *Es werde Licht* (Let There Be Light, 1917–18). Increasingly recognised as an expert in detective stories, Dupont debuted as a director with *Europa postlagernd* (Europe poste restante, 1918), followed over the next twelve months by twelve further episodes in this particular serial.

Alkohol (Alcohol, 1919), a film initially started by another director, marked Dupont's first major melodrama, and in its narrative it foreshadows some central aspects of his later work. Indeed the film seems like a first rehearsal of the story of *Varieté*: a respectable middle-class citizen falls for a young woman, both descend into alcoholism, and end up as performers in a variety act. Jealousy leads the man to kill a rival, after which he is sent to prison. The theme is picked up in one of Dupont's next films, *Der weiße Pfau. Tragödie einer Tänzerin* (The White Peacock. Tragedy of a Dancer, 1920), which once again focuses on a tragic love triangle, with a variety theatre as a major setting.

The film provides an interesting comparison with *Piccadilly*. Like the latter, *Der weiße Pfau* is set in London, where an upper-class theatre enthusiast falls for an ethnic other (in this case a Gypsy dancer) who originates from the East End (Whitechapel). As in *Piccadilly*, there is a hint of the Pygmalion myth when the man tries to teach the dancer how to behave and dress. A contemporary reviewer celebrated Dupont's skilful narration, in particular the use of retardation to increase suspense. The following description, which refers to the film's climactic confrontation of the heroine with her lover that ends with her killing him, could equally apply to several scenes in *Piccadilly*:

> The scene in her dressing room is a masterpiece of Dupont's direction. He lets the cast act quite slowly, increasing tension to breaking point. One stops breathing when one recognises how a fateful decision takes shape, and with the simplest means a gripping effect is achieved.[11]

With these early films, a clear pattern was established. Dupont returned to the East End in his next film, *Whitechapel* (1920), which chronicled the activities of London's criminal underworld, contrasted with the glittering lights of yet another variety theatre.

Not all of Dupont's films followed the same formula – *Die Geier-Wally* (Vulture Wally, 1921), one of his most successful films of the early 1920s, was an alpine melodrama, while *Die grüne Manuela* (Green Manuela, 1923) was a Spanish-themed spectacle highly derivative of the story of Bizet and/or Merimée's *Carmen*, telling the story of a Gypsy dancer who gets mixed up with a group of smugglers. The film is particularly important as it marked the first collaboration of Dupont with two technicians who would later work with him in Britain: set designer Alfred Junge and cinematographer Werner Brandes.

Das alte Gesetz (The Ancient Law, 1923) is one of Dupont's most interesting films prior to *Varieté*, and initially seems like a substantial departure from his previous work. Set in a Jewish *shtetl* in the middle of the nineteenth century, it thematises a familiar motif of narratives featuring Jewish characters, the conflict between tradition and religious orthodoxy, on one hand, and assimilation and emancipation on the other. As in the Hollywood film *The Jazz Singer* (1927), the conflict is located in the relationship between a rabbi and his son (Ernst Deutsch) who aspires to and eventually does become a famous actor. By the end of the film, however, the son abandons the stage and returns to the *shtetl*, where he finds happiness not with the Austrian duchess (Henny Porten) who has advanced his career, but with his childhood sweetheart. Dupont's direction and the camerawork by Theodor Sparkuhl (also working in Britain in the late 1920s) found universal critical acclaim, as did Alfred Junge's authentic recreation of the Galician *shtetl*.

On closer inspection, the film's historical framework and its provincial setting show affinities with Dupont's more modern and urban tales. There is the conflict between the world of the stage versus a respectable, 'normal' existence, and the tension between public and private; there is the incompatibility between different cultures; and there are triangulated relationships, played out in claustrophobic settings. S.S. Prawer, who has documented Dupont's careful engagement with Jewish issues in *Das alte Gesetz*, has suggested that Dupont was 'perennially interested in the interplay of different worlds that obeyed strict, initially incompatible rules'.[12]

Seen in the context of his previous films, *Varieté* (1925), despite its international acclaim and status in film history, seems like a variation on a – by then – well-rehearsed theme. As in *Alkohol*, the main anti-hero is a middle-aged former circus artist, 'Boss', who falls for a younger woman, simply referred to as the 'foreign girl' (played by the Hungarian actress Lya de Putti). He leaves his wife, and they join the trapeze act of a variety star. The latter and Boss's lover begin an affair, triggering a jealous rage in the hero. Boss kills his rival and is sent to prison.

Whereas the story was far from new, in its stylistic concentration and profusion of visual effects the film marked a summation of what has come before. As with *Piccadilly*, what particularly strikes a contemporary audience about the film is its intelligent, sophisticated narration, and the modernity and psychological realism of its characterisations. Emil Jannings, an actor generally prone to overacting and sentimentality, and whose performances (for example in *Der blaue Engel*, The Blue Angel, 1930) have generally not aged well, is remarkably matter-of-fact and convincing here, while de Putti's vamp is also wholly believable – both refrain from any typical silent film histrionics. As Thomas Elsaesser has argued:

> What made *Variety* such a success was the blend of a closely observed milieu, indeed sordid naturalism, with a particularly intense, brooding psychological study of male masochism, jealousy, and murderous rage.[13]

Aided by Karl Freund's unchained camera and Oscar Werndorff's atmospheric yet resolutely realist sets, *Varieté* became a showcase for what Weimar cinema was capable of at this particular moment. The film's technical perfection has subsequently made a number of critics suggest that its success should primarily be attributed to producer Erich Pommer's expertise and marketing strategies, or alternatively to Karl Freund's camerawork.[14] Yet, as Elsaesser has pointed out, many of the visual characteristics present in *Varieté* had been rehearsed in some of Dupont's previous films, which he shot with Brandes or Sparkuhl. One can also see a similar approach in Brandes' work on *Piccadilly* (see Kelly Robinson on the cinematography in this film in this volume).

It is certainly true that Pommer's global contacts and Ufa's international reach during this period guaranteed *Varieté* a wider distribution than any of Dupont's earlier films, produced for smaller, independent companies such as Gloria or Terra. Its success also led to Dupont's first sojourn in Hollywood, where he helmed the 'Old Vienna' story *Love Me and the World Is Mine* (1927) as a star vehicle for Mary Philbin. Pointing to similar career developments in the case of other Hollywood émigré directors such as Ernst Lubitsch and Joe May, Thomas Elsaesser has rightly concluded that 'whatever directors had been famous for at home, all that American producers could think about was "Old Vienna"'.[15]

Dupont's subsequent films in Britain, in contrast, seamlessly returned to the main themes he had already covered in Germany. The variety theatre or nightclub once again became a metaphor for social, cultural, ethnic, sexual and generational conflicts in *Moulin Rouge* (1928) and *Piccadilly*. Whereas the former was arguably not yet wholly successful in adapting Dupont's style to a new production context, the latter holds up well in comparison with *Varieté*, and indeed in many respects remains a more rounded film. Whereas *Varieté* – with its kaleidoscopic effects and near constant dazzle – provides pure surface attraction, *Piccadilly* is narratively more complex, less abstract, more 'real', which may in part be due to the naturalist influence of the film's British author, Arnold Bennett.

The juxtaposition of different layers of reality commenting on each other is a common motif of Dupont's films in both Germany and Britain. Werner Sudendorf has argued that 'the illusionist character of the entertainment world, always depicted in a technically perfect way, remains intact, despite its simultaneous deconstruction'.[16] What makes Dupont's films so 'modern' to audiences in the new millennium is not only their naturalist performance style, visual virtuosity or realist sets, but also their self-reflexive gestures, drawing attention to the artificiality of cinematic representation. In *Piccadilly*, classic examples of these can be found in the film's opening sequence, where the credits appear on billboards and advertisements on the sides of buses. Like Dupont's early film reviews, his films combine, and alternate between, ironic distanciation and emotional immersion, as towards the end of *Piccadilly*, where the melodramatic revelation of the circumstances of Wong's death in a courtroom is followed by an abrupt change in tone. An epilogue-like street scene ironically negates the emotional investment the film has built up over the preceding hour, and dismisses the film's story literally as yesterday's news.

Dupont, who in the late 1910s advised screenwriters always to think of the audience, incorporates the audience as a protagonist into his films. The latter are, apart from their specific melodramatic plot lines, narratives about spectatorship and about the spatial hierarchies of the gaze. Comparing Dupont's films with the classic *auteur* cinema for which Weimar is famous, Heide Schlüpmann has argued that while the latter constructs an aesthetic of negation and suppression of cinema's mass industrial origins, Dupont's films instead embrace these in an aesthetic centred on spectacle and display. In these respects, Schlüpmann identifies in Dupont's films a lingering legacy of early cinema's socially progressive potential.[17]

The fact that Dupont's protagonists were often itinerant characters (travelling artists, actors, Spanish dancers, Gypsies, 'foreign girls', Chinese immigrants) made them ideally suited for cosmopolitan narratives that could be told within the framework of any national cinema. However, in his work cosmopolitanism never equalled placelessness. In his German films that took place in foreign locales (including Britain, as in *Whitechapel* or *Der weiße Pfau*), Dupont attempted to imbue his settings with cultural authenticity. Equally, the almost documentary and ethnographic perspective he employed in his depiction of East End pub life in *Piccadilly* demonstrates his (and his collaborators') skills in accurately evoking a particular social milieu.

Most scholars who have written on Dupont seem to agree that *Piccadilly* marked the director's creative peak. Many have followed Lotte Eisner's assessment that he was one of the prominent victims of the transition to sound:

> The sound film affected Dupont much more than it did other film-makers because, though he knew how to place his actors, he did not know how to get them fully express themselves. His strength lay elsewhere.[18]

Although it is true that Dupont's career went into free fall after his second, permanent emigration to Hollywood in 1933, Eisner's evaluation of him as failing the transition to sound needs to be reassessed. As Elsaesser has noted, already at the height of his fame the director made some erratic career choices:

> The question that poses itself ... is why, when arriving in Hollywood in 1926 at the height of his reputation, did he *not* make a film featuring a circus ring or a *ménage-a-trois* (that is, a remake of *Variety*), and instead adapt a popular Austrian novel?[19]

While the answer to this question may indeed have something to do with what US producers expected from European directors, Dupont's fragmented career in the late 1920s and early 1930s poses new questions.

Atlantic (1929), Dupont's first sound film and the follow-up to the dazzling *Piccadilly*, became one of the most expensive productions of its time, and also the first ever multilingual production, shot in three versions. Based on a stage play, it told the story of the last hours on board an ocean liner which is about to hit an iceberg (although obviously modelled on the fate of the *Titanic*, the name of the ship was changed for legal reasons).[20] *Atlantic* largely eschewed grandiose spectacle in the style of later adaptations of the disaster in favour of intimate dialogue scenes between a group of individuals under deck. It is unlikely that the film harmed Dupont's career and position in Britain; indeed, it was overall well received and a box office hit. While this may be the case, one cannot help agreeing with Eisner's retrospective disappointment. Although the film does share certain characteristics with some of Dupont's previous work (the focus on an enclosed and clearly defined environment, the clash of social and cultural differences), it also diverges quite significantly in others.

Whereas in earlier films retardation was a carefully employed tool to raise suspense, *Atlantic* almost grinds to a halt – Jeffrey Richards has commented on the film's 'funereal' pacing.[21] Compared to the sophistication of Anna May Wong's acting in *Piccadilly*, the performances in *Atlantic*, especially in the English version, seem embarrassingly wooden. More crucially, the film lacks the visual fluidity of Dupont's silent films. Charles Rosher's cinematography does include a number of nice touches, like the atmospheric shots of waves, but overall the camera remains static, while Hugh Gee's perfunctory sets are a far cry from Alfred Junge's or Oscar Werndorff's lovingly detailed contributions to Dupont's previous productions.

While *Atlantic* remains a landmark in the history of film technology, far more interesting within the context of Dupont's career overall are his remaining multilingual sound films, *Two Worlds* (1930) and *Cape Forlorn* (1930), not least because they clearly demonstrate that far from being unable to cope with new technology, Dupont was learning rapidly how to overcome the restrictions and limitations that sound imposed on his primarily visual style. *Two Worlds*, as S.S. Prawer has pointed out as a programmatic title for Dupont's films and his career more generally, revisits the Jewish issues of *Das alte Gesetz* with a story set during the First World War on the Eastern front.[22] As in the previous film, the narrative centres on a culture clash, between Russians and Austrians, between Jews and Gentiles, and between two young lovers torn apart by the forces of history. *Two Worlds*, like *Das alte Gesetz*, ends tragically – although Dupont often articulated the possibilities of cultural exchange as a progressive and positive force, and although his own career constituted an exemplar of the same kind of process, his films ultimately deny cultural mixing as a realistic option for their protagonists. *Two Worlds* benefited enormously from Dupont being reunited with Alfred Junge, who once again created impressive sets, and was also supported to a much greater degree by Rosher's (and Mutz Greenbaum's) cinematography.

Cape Forlorn represented a particularly ingenious strategy to deal with the problems of sound recording. The film once again charts a torrid love triangle, in this case between two lighthouse keepers stuck on a desolate island and the nightclub dancer one of the men brings back from a trip to the mainland. As in previous Dupont films, the tension builds up to an accidental murder, inevitably followed by retribution. Except for a few scenes in an exotic harbour nightclub (a grotesquely fetishistic design by Junge that almost caricatures Dupont's well-known predilection for 'leg shots' with prominent columns in the form of women's thighs) and some outdoor footage, the remainder of the narrative is mostly set within the lighthouse's claustrophobic interiors. These serve the story very well, while at the same time the closeness of the set helped to minimise sound recording difficulties. Claude Friese-Greene's cinematography is very inventive, far more fluid than Rosher's in Dupont's previous two films, and highly adaptive to the film's physical and technological environment.

Judging by the stylistic trajectory from *Atlantic* to *Cape Forlorn*, one can only speculate how Dupont might have continued had he stayed in Britain. Andrew Higson has argued that he failed in the British film industry and that there was no space for him once the production of multilingual version films had ceased and the economic boom in the British industry had suffered a significant setback in the early 1930s. Higson also maintains that Dupont's 'reputation for profligacy … would not have gone down well in such a cost-conscious environment'.[23] While this reputation may or may not have been based on fact, the three films Dupont made after the conversion to sound indicate that he was certainly able to modify and adapt his general thematic interests to new production contexts, and *Cape Forlorn* represents the most imaginative solution in this respect.

The main reason Dupont left Britain was because he received an attractive offer to become production manager at Emelka in Munich.[24] Accepting this offer proved a disastrous career choice in hindsight, not only because of the Nazis' policy of expelling Jews from the German industry, which would come into effect less than three years after Dupont's return from Britain. It also proved the wrong decision because the contract collapsed before Dupont could initiate any major production (ironically, this happened because he had fulfilled a last contractual obligation to British International Pictures in completing the German-language version of *Cape Forlorn*). Nonetheless, despite this setback his remaining sound films in Germany comprise at least one further interesting variation on the circus artist theme with *Salto Mortale* (1931), in all but name a sound film remake of *Varieté* and again a box office success; the globetrotting crime comedy *Peter Voss, der Millionendieb* (Peter Voss, Master Thief, 1932); and *Der Läufer von Marathon* (The Marathon Runner, 1933), another love triangle (but with a happy ending), this time among Olympic athletes competing at the Los Angeles Games. The latter film united a number of soon-to-be exiles – cinematographer Eugen Schüfftan would move to France, producer Marcel Hellmann and set designer Ernö Metztner would find work in Britain, while Dupont would go to Hollywood.

In the same way as one can imagine in retrospect Dupont making films in Britain after *Cape Forlorn*, there is no indication that his career in Germany in the early 1930s could not have continued had the Nazis not come into power. Confronted with this tantalisingly unfulfilled potential, Thomas Elsaesser has suggested viewing Dupont primarily as an adventurer: 'To understand the logic of his professional life, it needs to be reviewed as several, rather discrete "slices", happening almost to different individuals'.[25] In my reading of Dupont's career, in contrast, I perceive a remarkable consistency and continuity that links his early career as a critic and supporter of Wilhelmine and later Weimar popular genres, his single contribution to Weimar's art canon with *Varieté*, and his films in Britain (with his career in Hollywood marking indeed a separate, and largely tragic, chapter). I would also qualify Elsaesser's suggestion that for Dupont 'the term émigré director, with its political overtones, is peculiarly inappropriate'.[26] While this is true for Dupont's movements in the mid- to late 1920s, in 1933 he definitively became an exile, and understood himself as such – in the absence of any film work he returned during the war years to his earliest profession as a journalist, writing anti-fascist articles for *The Hollywood Tribune*.[27]

Notes

1. For an extensive discussion on the subject, see Thomas Elsaesser, *Weimar Cinema and After. Germany's Historical Imaginary* (London and New York: Routledge, 2000). The classic reference texts are Siegfried Kracauer, *From Caligari to Hitler. A Psychological History of the German Film* (Princeton: Princeton University Press, 1947) and Lotte H. Eisner, *The Haunted Screen. Expressionism in the German Cinema and the Influence of Max Reinhardt* (Berkeley, Los Angeles and Oxford: University of California Press, 1994).
2. See Andrew Higson, 'Polyglot Films for an International Market: E.A. Dupont, the British Film Industry, and the Idea of a European Cinema 1926–1930', in Andrew Higson and Richard Maltby (eds.), *'Film Europe' and 'Film America': Cinema, Commerce, and Cultural Exchange 1920–1939* (Exeter: University of Exeter Press, 1999), pp. 274–301; Tim Bergfelder, 'Negotiating Exoticism: Hollywood, Film Europe, and the Cultural Reception of Anna May Wong', in Higson and Maltby, *'Film Europe' and 'Film America'*, pp. 302–24; and Karen Leong, 'Anna May Wong and the British Film Industry', *Quarterly Review of Film and Video*, vol. 23, no. 1, January–March 2006, pp. 13–22.
3. See Jürgen Bretschneider (ed.), *Ewald André Dupont. Autor und Regisseur* (Munich: edition text+kritik, 1992).
4. Samuel Fuller, 'He Will Grip You', in Bretschneider, *Ewald André Dupont*, p. 8.
5. For a discussion of the cultural debates concerning film during this period, see Anton Kaes, 'Literary Intellectuals and the Cinema. Charting a Controversy (1909–1929)', *New German Critique*, no. 40, Winter 1987, pp. 7–33. See also Fritz Güttinger (ed.), *Kein Tag ohne Kino. Schriftsteller über den Stummfilm* (Frankfurt am Main: Deutsches Filmmuseum, 1984).

6. See Uli Jung, 'Schreiben und verwerten. Duponts Ratschläge an Drehbuchautoren', in Bretschneider, *Ewald André Dupont*, pp. 15–23.
7. On the connections between film and variety theatre in Germany, see Joseph Garncarz, 'Die Entstehung des Kinos aus dem Varieté: Ein Plädoyer für ein erweitertes Konzept der Intermedialität', in Jörg Helbig (ed.), *Intermedialität: Theorie und Praxis eines interdisziplinären Forschungsgebiets* (Berlin: Erich Schmidt, 1998), pp. 244–56.
8. E.A. Dupont, 'Kinematographie und Darstellungskunst', *Berliner Allgemeine Zeitung*, 17 August 1912.
9. Christiane Heuwinkel, 'Die Metamorphose der Tagespresse. Der Filmkritiker E.A. Dupont', in Bretschneider, *Ewald André Dupont*, p. 29. My translation.
10. Heuwinkel, 'Die Metamorphose der Tagespresse', p. 26.
11. -rd, *Berliner Börsen-Courier*, 15 August 1920. My translation.
12. S.S. Prawer, *Between Two Worlds. The Jewish Presence in German and Austrian Film, 1910–1933* (Oxford and New York: Berghahn, 2005), p. 22.
13. Elsaesser, *Weimar Cinema and After*, p. 376.
14. Kracauer, *From Caligari to Hitler*, p. 127.
15. Elsaesser, *Weimar Cinema and After*, p. 376.
16. Werner Sudendorf, 'E.A. Dupont', in Hans-Michael Bock (ed.), *CineGraph. Lexikon zum deutschsprachigen Film* (Munich: edition text+kritik, 1984–), p. E4. My translation.
17. Heide Schlüpmann, 'Auf dem Wege zur Kulturindustrie. Anmerkungen zur Ästhetik in Filmen Duponts', in Bretschneider (ed.), *Ewald André Dupont*, pp. 49–58.
18. Eisner, *The Haunted Screen*, p. 275.
19. Elsaesser, *Weimar Cinema and After*, p. 378.
20. See Robert Peck, '*Atlantic* – The First Titanic Blockbuster', in Tim Bergfelder and Sarah Street (eds.), *The Titanic in Myth and Memory. Representations in Visual and Literary Culture* (London and New York: I.B. Tauris, 2004), pp. 111–20.
21. Jeffrey Richards, *The Definitive Titanic Film: A Night To Remember* (London and New York: I.B. Tauris, 2003), p. 15.
22. Prawer, *Between Two Worlds*, p. 141.
23. Higson, 'Polyglot Films for an International Market', p. 292.
24. Evelyn Hampicke and Jürgen Bretschneider, 'Biografie', in Bretschneider (ed.), *Ewald André Dupont*, pp. 122–23.
25. Elsaesser, *Weimar Cinema and After*, p. 375.
26. Ibid., p. 376.
27. Hampicke and Bretschneider, 'Biografie', p. 124.

Chapter 3

GEZA VON BOLVARY, ARNOLD RIDLEY AND 'FILM EUROPE'

Lawrence Napper

The Ghost Train, adapted from the British theatrical hit by Arnold Ridley, was directed in 1927 by Geza von Bolvary as part of a production deal between Gainsborough in Britain, and Fellner & Somlo in Germany. The film is interesting for a number of reasons.

First of all, *The Ghost Train* was a European co-production, a collaboration between British and German production interests, with a Hungarian director and a combination of British and German actors – a 'British' film made in Germany. Being an relatively early example of this kind of co-production, many in the British trade press nevertheless regarded the film as having become impractical at the point of its release. Indeed, I hope to demonstrate that *The Ghost Train* is something of an anomaly. Its particular moment of release – just prior to the passing of the Cinematograph Act at the end of 1927 – witnessed a change in the way British-European co-productions were organised. This change – away from the practice of sending British productions abroad, and towards that of attracting European directors and technicians to Britain – to a large extent heralded the golden age of the German-speaking émigré in the British film industry. For *The Ghost Train* this proved to be not so beneficial, and indeed this 'international' film was almost a casualty of that policy shift.

Another interesting fact about *The Ghost Train* is its connection with British theatre, and with Arnold Ridley in particular. Ridley will be familiar to many, mainly in his guise as Private Godfrey in the long-running BBC sitcom *Dad's Army*. If audiences know his work as a playwright at all, though, it will be for *The Ghost Train*, for while he continued to write for the stage, and indeed *The Wrecker* was also adapted by Gainsborough, none of his other plays had anything like the extraordinary success of this one.

It could be argued that the play is a perfect example of the struggle over taste that featured so prominently in British culture, particularly during the interwar years. From its first performance in November 1925 it was roundly despised by critics who dismissed it as 'a mere fifth-rate claptrap spoof!', and ever since it has enjoyed a reputation as a hoary old piece of theatrical hokum, poorly written and ripe for parody.[1] Nevertheless, *The Ghost Train* was a massive commercial success, enjoying over 600 West End performances, and still touring successfully two years later when the film adaptation was released.[2] It entered the national life so successfully that it is alleged that since its premiere not a single day has passed without a staging of *The Ghost Train* somewhere in Britain by either amateurs or professionals.

Bolvary's film adaptation, only the first of many made both in Britain and on the continent, was rewritten as a comedy vehicle for Jack Hulbert in 1931 and again for Arthur Askey in 1941; it also inspired the 1937 Will Hay vehicle *Oh, Mr Porter!* Indeed, the play's mix of humour and horror appears to have appealed to both British and German sensibilities in a way curiously reminiscent of Freddy Frinton's sketch *Dinner for One*, a perennial stalwart of German television.

The Ghost Train's almost totemic plot involves a group of six travellers stranded at a remote train station in the middle of the night. A singularly unhelpful stationmaster refuses to find shelter for them, but warns that they must not remain there. He tells the grisly story of a train wreck in which many died and the sight of which drove others mad. Every year on the anniversary the ghostly apparition of the train reappears speeding to its doom. All who observe it collapse and die of fright.

This story is told verbally in the stage play and the several remakes of the film. But in Bolvary's adaptation it becomes a visually strikingly fluid sequence which returns insistently to the horrified faces of the travellers as they listen, rapt by the unfolding narrative. Among the passengers is a frivolous young man who, to the annoyance of the others, fails to engage in the seriousness of the deadly dilemma they all find themselves in. He is ultimately revealed as a special detective, engaged in foiling a gang of Bolshevik gun-runners who have circulated the ghost train legend to divert attention away from their criminal activities.

In the various later adaptations of the play comedy is emphasised over horror. However, in the original text and in Bolvary's film version, horror and comedy are given equal weight – the deadly potential of the train and its unhinging effect on its observers climaxes in the play in off-stage sound and lighting effects, and in the film in a really extraordinary sequence of fast, associative editing, double exposures and optical effects. Part of the key to its popularity among British and German audiences during the 1920s may be to do with the way *The Ghost Train* both evoked and symbolically resolved traumatic experiences related to the First World War. I will return to this suggestion following an exploration of the film's production history.

European Co-production

Reviewing *The Ghost Train* for *Kinematograph Weekly*, Lionel Collier was almost unable to contain his enthusiasm: 'Undoubtedly this is one of the best "night of scares" pictures ever produced, and it is a definite triumph for its director, G. Bolvary.' Bolvary's direction, he declared, was 'the absolute making of this picture', with its use of 'brilliant camera angles and most telling dissolves … The flash-back, which shows the supposed crash of the express on the viaduct is technically as good as anything America has produced; model work is perfect'. Otto Kanturek's photography was also singled out for praise, his settings and lighting effects described as 'exceptional'. Summing up the film's points of appeal, Collier concluded that 'the success of the play is a big asset in exploiting the film, although the latter is quite capable of standing on its own merits as one of the most amusing thrill-cum-comedy productions made in this country and equal to anything from abroad'.[3]

Collier's review is curious, to say the least. It not only fails to acknowledge, but actively denies, the international nature of *The Ghost Train*'s production. Contrary to his statement, the film *had* in fact been made abroad – in Germany, at the Staaken studios near Berlin. Indeed, although it was an Anglo-German co-production, it would appear that the only creative British input was the presence of Guy Newall in the leading part and the source play by Ridley. The direction and camerawork, which Collier had so admired, were the work of a Hungarian and an Austrian respectively. Both Bolvary and Kanturek would later come to Britain and make a number of films here, starting with Ridley's 'sequel' to *The Ghost Train*, *The Wrecker*, in 1928. But prior to this, they had never worked outside continental Europe.

Gainsborough's forays into Anglo-German co-production in the mid-1920s are well known because of the involvement of Alfred Hitchcock, who was sent to the Emelka studios near Munich, making both *The Pleasure Garden* and *The Mountain Eagle* there around 1926.[4] He was not the first British director to work in Germany: Graham Cutts had already made *The Blackguard* at Ufa early in 1925, and several of his other films of the period were distributed in Germany through an arrangement between Ufa and W&F.

Cutts's *The Queen Was in the Parlour* (1927), adapted from Noel Coward's play and again shot in Germany, appears to have initiated a new arrangement between Gainsborough and the German-based producers Hermann Fellner and Josef Somlo. It was under this arrangement that *The Ghost Train* was produced, followed by three other films, all directed by Bolvary, all bar one shot in Germany, and all bar one based on British theatrical properties – *The Gallant Hussar*, *Number 17* and *The Wrecker*, all released in 1928 (see Table 1 for details).

The three Bolvary films made in Germany under arrangement with Fellner and Somlo can be regarded as part of an established Gainsborough

Table 1

Title	Date	Director	Shooting Location	Star	Source play
The Queen Was in the Parlour	04/1927	Cutts	Germany	Lili Damita	Noel Coward
The Ghost Train	08/1927	Bolvary	Germany	Guy Newall	Arnold Ridley
The Gallant Hussar	10/1928	Bolvary	Germany	Ivor Novello	Orig scen. Bardos/Langen
Number 17	12/1928	Bolvary	Germany	Guy Newall	Jefferson Farjeon
The Wrecker	12/1928	Bolvary	Britain	Joseph Striker	Arnold Ridley

tradition of involvement in Anglo-German co-production – but also as something of a break in that tradition, in that they employ a director already working within the German industry, rather than exporting a British director to Germany.

In his reticence concerning the international origins of the film, Collier was certainly not alone. The *Bioscope* review of *The Ghost Train* also failed to note its production location, conceding only that 'the scenes at the station, taking [*sic*] in England, are very effective' and that the cast supporting Newall were 'unfamiliar'.[5] Production reports, usually abundant for British films in the trade press, are fairly scarce for this one. They only cover the activities of the 'second unit' shooting exteriors with the help of the Southern Railways. The films' advertisements also conveniently overlooked the name and nationality of the director, identifying it only as a 'Gainsborough Production'.[6]

This reticence in acknowledging the European nature of *The Ghost Train* seems surprising. Given the high reputation of German filmmaking and technical achievement at this point, one would expect these aspects to be capitalised on in the marketing of the film, a usual practice with earlier films of a similar provenance. The fact that shooting took place in Germany is taken into account but not made prominent in any way, and one wonders why such a marketing opportunity was rejected.

I would suggest that during the period between the signing of the Fellner and Somlo deal at the beginning of 1927 and the release of *The Ghost Train* in the autumn, British criteria for desirable European co-production had shifted quite decisively away from one where British companies funded production in Europe, and towards one where European personnel came to Britain to work. As the provisions of the Cinematograph Films Bill for the registration of British films were finalised, Gainsborough's deal began to look particularly precarious since, unlike previous arrangements, it included provision for British films made in Germany *with foreign directors*. As a result, it became expedient for the company to downplay the production strategy of *The Ghost Train*, even while other companies played up their European connections. One might in fact suggest that it was partly as a result of this revised model for European co-production that so many German-speaking émigrés can be found working in Britain from the mid- to late 1920s onwards.

Looking at the trade press throughout 1927, it is not difficult to identify reasons for the shift in emphasis. Earlier, Gainsborough had sent productions to Germany because of the technical advantage that Berlin's studios had over the grossly undercapitalised and old-fashioned studios available in Britain, and the variety of economic incentives provided by Germany's weak currency. By 1927, however, the German film industry began to suffer as a result of the end of inflation, culminating in a financial crisis at Ufa caused partly by the spiralling costs for Fritz Lang's *Metropolis* (1927). Meanwhile, a sea change in the British production context was becoming apparent. The Cinematograph Act, while it did not pass into law until December that year, had already had a major effect. The Act would boost the British production industry through the use of a quota scheme which made the showing of a certain percentage of British films on British screens compulsory. In order to benefit from this scheme, of course, such films had to meet the definition of a 'British film' laid down in the Act. Reports of its readings at committee stage dominate *Kinematograph Weekly* throughout the summer, and the boost its anticipation had given to British production was already being felt.

In March 1927 came the announcement of the combining of Gaumont, W&F and Ideal with finance from the Ostrers, and in April a similar announcement about the creation of British International Pictures was made.[7] Both of these schemes involved ambitious production plans, as well as plans for studio-building. British International Pictures' announcement also emphasised plans for 'international' productions, made by arrangement with Carr-Gloria-Dupont – a deal which actually went through various permutations before finally resulting in possibly the best-known series of British contributions to 'Film Europe': E.A. Dupont's *Moulin Rouge* (1928), *Piccadilly* (1929) and *Atlantic* (1929). When the original deal was struck in 1927, though, Carr-Gloria-Dupont were confident enough of the potential appeal of these films to suggest that:

> It is likely that some of these films will come within the quota scheme, but no attempts, however, will be made to hamper the productions by way of casting, simply to satisfy these requirements. Rather the films are to be made big enough to ensure universal showing …[8]

By May 1927 there had been such increased production activity that P.L. Mannock was able to report with satisfaction that:

> What I and most other observers of the British production problem have been expecting for four years has now come to pass – a desperately acute studio shortage. Today it is to all intents and purposes impossible to obtain space on a worthwhile British floor for picture-making.

Mannock hoped that the much discussed proposal to build a studio at Wembley (partly funded through the new Act) would ease the problem, but meanwhile he suggested that 'it would be foolish to blame British producers who go abroad; and the Films Bill definition will be a fatal handicap to native effort if foreign studios are barred'.[9]

The provisions for the definition of a British film under the Act are of course crucial here. As Mannock suggests, if European-co-production was to continue along earlier lines, the Cinematograph Act's definition of a 'British Film' would have to include provision for films made with British money on foreign soil. As the committee readings continued through the summer of 1927, it became increasingly clear that this was not to be the case.

Writing for *Kinematograph Weekly* in July 1927, A. Rosenthal, editor of the German paper *Film-Kurier*, was astute in identifying the implications of this development. Under the headline 'RECIPROCITY: A Problem for Germany and Britain' he admits the importance of the Films Act in fending off the threat of American competition. Rosenthal is, however, much more sceptical about the possibilities of British–German co-productions and suggests that previous attempts under Pommer at Ufa had been largely unsuccessful. Later moves by British companies had resulted, he claims, in 'lawsuits between producers and actors', and the announcement of the Carr–Gloria–Dupont scheme had generated more negative than positive comment. Rosenthal also criticises the British lack of prominence in the European Film Congress at Paris the previous year. His conclusion is to stress the importance of mutual distribution arrangements over co-production ones: 'After all, let us be perfectly frank about it, the German, like the English producer is even more interested in mutual film business between the two countries than in co-operative production.'[10]

Other commentators were less pessimistic about the possibilities of actual co-production arrangements, but it is perfectly clear that, as the provisions of the Films Act emerged, it became far more attractive to bring foreign personnel to Britain than to go in the opposite direction. As they were finally constituted, the criteria for the definition of a British film to be registered under the Act (and to receive its benefits) included the requirement that the film should be made in a British studio (or one within the Empire), that 75 per cent of the labour costs had to be paid to British subjects, and that the scenario writer must also be British. An amendment stipulating that the director must also be a British subject failed. Thus, for a co-production to be registered, it was acceptable to import a foreign director (or indeed producer) as long as the studio work was done in Britain and the film was based on a British story.

Despite their confident assertions in April that 'no attempts will be made … to satisfy these requirements', it is clear that the Carr–Gloria–Dupont project was careful to ensure that their films *did* qualify for British registration. Indeed, their production deal had since been renegotiated so that the three Dupont films were in fact made firmly under the banner of the newly formed British International Pictures, at Elstree, and two of them adapted from scenarios by British writers (Arnold Bennett for *Piccadilly*, Ernest Raymond for *Atlantic*).

For the architects of the Fellner–Somlo–Gainsborough deal the timing was less serendipitous. By the time the criteria for British registration became clear in the autumn of 1927, *The Ghost Train* was ready for release. It premiered before the Act came into force early the following year, but as we have seen, in the face of the Act's provisions, Gainsborough was already keen to downplay its international credentials.

Bolvary's next film made in Germany under the deal, *Number 17*, gained registration under the Act as a British film on its release in 1928, partly due to the fact that it was again adapted from a British stage play (written by Jefferson Farjeon). His follow-up, *The Gallant Hussar*, starring Ivor Novello, based on an original scenario by Hungarian Artur Bárdos and Margarete Langen and set firmly in a 'mittel-European' past populated by Prussian officers and White Russian princesses, however, failed the test of 'Britishness'; it was registered as a foreign film and achieved only minimal distribution as a result.

For the final film of the series, *The Wrecker*, based again on a Ridley play and centred on the railways, Gainsborough took no chances. They brought Bolvary over to Britain to direct it, and following the trend of many German-speaking émigré filmmakers in Britain, he stayed there for a little while, making a couple of Betty Balfour films for British International Pictures – *Bright Eyes* (1929) and *The Vagabond Queen* (1930) – before returning to Germany in the early 1930s, where he worked for the next three decades. Art director Oscar Werndorff, on the other hand, worked permanently in Britain from 1928 onwards, while Kanturek returned to Britain in 1933 and stayed until his death in 1941.

The Ghost Train and the 'War Touch'

During the summer of 1927, the Cinematograph Act and Film Europe were not the only subjects to dominate the pages of the trade press. The editorial of *Kinematograph Weekly* asked:

Is the War Overdone?
'Are we making too many war films?' A fine picture in any setting will attract widely. Whether British producers are relying too much on war subjects is another matter.

> In our long list of new home productions on another page, about 25 per cent
> are war stories, and there is a risk that the public may tire of the eternal battle
> footage, however well done.[11]

It was certainly an apposite question. The glut of British films about the
First World War continued throughout the period from 1927 to the early
1930s. These included romance stories of returning amnesiac soldiers, spy
yarns, a famous series of battle reconstruction films produced by British
Instructional Films, and more subtle narratives dealing with the traumatic
aftermath of war and the effect of its experience, particularly on the male
population during the 1920s. Several such films were produced by
Gainsborough Pictures in the same year as *The Ghost Train*, including
Adrian Brunel's *Blighty* and Maurice Elvey's *Roses of Picardy*.

One might speculate that war stories were rather touchy in the context of
Anglo-German co-production, but this doesn't seem to have been the case.
Some films made great play of the use of German actors reconstructing
their own wartime roles for greater authenticity. *The Battles of Coronel and
Falkland Islands* (Walter Summers, 1927) was especially singled out for
bringing over German naval officers with war service experience to play in
the film and advise the director on 'all questions of German naval routine
and etiquette'.[12] Stark-International's *When Fleet Meets Fleet / Die versunkene
Flotte* (Manfred Noa, Graham Hewett, 1927), about the Battle of Jutland,
features its Anglo-German cast prominently in advertisements.[13]

While *The Ghost Train* clearly is not a film that deals directly with the
war, I would like to conclude by suggesting that for audiences both in
Britain and Germany in the late 1920s it certainly had resonances of what
Michael Williams has described as 'the War Touch'.[14] Placed alongside the
cycle of war dramas and reconstructions I have just described, the film
might be said to contribute to a general culture in which the experience of
war was still being processed on every level. Bolvary himself had seen
action, serving with the Hungarian Army in a mounted regiment. Ridley
had also fought on the Western Front, and had been invalided out of the
Army in 1917 suffering from injuries which still caused him trouble years
later, forcing him to abandon his career as a stage actor.[15] It was thus partly
as a result of his wartime experience that he had turned to writing.

In *The Play Pictorial* B.W. Findon in 1926 made an explicit connection
between the play *The Ghost Train* and wartime experience:

> I had some cold, dreary waits at wayside stations 'somewhere in France' in the
> winter of 1918 and therefore I can sympathise with those unfortunate travellers
> who were doomed to pass the night in the cheerless and fireless waiting-
> room …[16]

Findon was also at pains to point out that the play observed Aristotle's
unities – there are no ellipses of space and time, the action does not shift
from the waiting room in which the characters are trapped while they wait

in horror for the 'ghost train' to arrive. Memoirs of the war commonly cite boredom and terror as the two primary emotions of life in the trenches, and perhaps it is not too fanciful to suggest that the waiting room in *The Ghost Train* might be regarded as a loose metaphor for a Western Front dugout.

The play presents a striking parallel with *Journey's End*, the other blockbusting hit of the 1920s, which received its first performance three years after *The Ghost Train* and was also subject to a film adaptation involving international co-production (although this time with America).[17]

Both plays (and their film adaptations) do not stray from the single setting in which their protagonists are trapped, concentrating on a range of characters and their separate reactions to the psychological strain under which they have been placed. A key element is the sense of an adjacent off-stage space where the actual theatre of horrors takes place, and from which the theatrical space of the dugout/waiting room only affords a temporary respite. Both films largely resist the temptation to stray out of the original setting, providing only brief shots of the landscape over the parapet or out on the platform.

The interdiction against looking delivered by the stationmaster at the beginning of *The Ghost Train* when he suggests that 'the sight of it means death', is strikingly realised at the dramatic climax of the film. Hertha von Walther plays Julia Price, a woman so deranged by her witnessing of the original accident that she gets irresistibly drawn to the sight of its ghostly replay, despite her knowledge that the vision might prove fatal. Bolvary's cut away to the newly-wed couple during Julia's mad scene neatly sums up the compulsion and prohibition around looking and the evocation of traumatic memory – the husband is drawn irresistibly towards the horror show while his wife frantically tries to save him, putting her hand up over his eyes.

This narrative is, after all, dominated by the idea of trauma. The horrific memory which won't disappear, the abhorrent sight which has the power to unhinge, the knowingly illusory belief in a spirit world, are all dominant tropes of the aftermath of wartime experience. The male members of the travelling party are schematically arranged according to responses to this experience – the stoic, the flippant, the brutalised. The fact that the 'ghost train' turns out to be an illusion – a trick to hide criminal activity – does not detract from this central psychological metaphor.

Teddy Deakins, the 'silly ass' who turns out to be a top sleuth from Scotland Yard, is also important in this respect. The comedy of the film revolves centrally around Deakins, contrasting his flippant responses to the range of more serious and frustrated reactions of the other characters. His facetiousness, of course, hides a deadly serious intent, and his complexly masking language of frivolity also has its origins in the trenches.

As George Simmers has argued with reference to the work of Dornford Yates (the popular 'middlebrow' writer of the period), facetiousness was a key mode of discourse for officers in the trenches, a hangover from public-school language, and one which was adopted for use during the war partly because it so effectively effaced the division between the serious and the frivolous, the real and the unreal.[18] Deakins's use of that language evokes that other interwar detective struggling with traumatic wartime memories, Lord Peter Wimsey. As played by Guy Newall in the film, Deakins might be said to be the model for such a figure; with buck teeth, an eyepiece and plus fours, he is the very image of the upper-class twit whose apparent concern for surface appearances – particularly those of dress and manners – is designed to avert attention away from a more serious intent and a more tragic history.

To suggest that German cinema of the 1920s might have a relationship to the traumatic experiences of the First World War is, of course, no great revelation. The twisted sets and psychology of Expressionist works such as *The Cabinet of Dr Caligari* (Robert Wiene, 1920) are regularly understood as metaphors for wartime trauma. Curiously, that suggestion with regard to British cinema of the 1920s is much less familiar. *The Ghost Train*, both German and British, both horror and comedy, both art and 'clap-trap', serves as a warning against assigning neat national categories to either cinema or psychology.

Notes

1. H.M. Walbrook, 'Plays of the Month', *The Play Pictorial*, January 1926, p. x. See also *The Times*, 25 November 1925, p. 14.
2. *Kinematograph Weekly*, 1 September 1927, p. 57.
3. *Kinematograph Weekly*, 15 September 1927, p. 66.
4. Charles Barr, *English Hitchcock* (Moffat: Cameron & Hollis, 1999), pp. 215–17.
5. *The Bioscope*, 15 September 1927, p. 56. The curious construction creates two possible meanings – it may be a misprint for 'taken in England' as some of the exteriors shot by the second unit were, or it could be intended to mean 'taking in England' in the sense of 'showing' or 'displaying' as a tourist might 'take in' various attractions. Either way, the fact that the majority of the film was shot in Germany is obscured.
6. See for instance *Kinematograph Weekly*, 21 April 1927, p. 31, and 1 September 1927.
7. *Kinematograph Weekly*, 24 March 1927, p. 33.
8. *Kinematograph Weekly*, 14 April 1927, p. 34.
9. *Kinematograph Weekly*, 5 May 1927, p. 37.
10. *Kinematograph Weekly*, 21 July 1927, p. 29. Indeed, the importance of pan-European distribution was emphasised by the programme of the newly reorganised Gaumont combine announced in May 1927, which ensured 'German distribution for British films on an unprecedented scale'. *Kinematograph Weekly*, 12 May 1927, p. 39. See also Andrew Higson and Richard Maltby (eds.), *'Film Europe' and 'Film America'* (Exeter: University of Exeter Press, 1999).
11. *Kinematograph Weekly*, 9 June 1927, p. 20.
12. *Kinematograph Weekly*, 5 May 1927, p. 37.
13. *Kinematograph Weekly*, 2 June 1927, p. 9. The German version of the film is presumed lost. See http://www.dhm.de/kino/filme2004_10.html
14. Michael Williams, *Ivor Novello: Screen Idol* (London: BFI, 2003), p. 55.

15. 'Mr Arnold Ridley' (obituary), *The Times*, 14 March 1984, p. 18.
16. B.W. Findon, '*The Ghost Train*', *The Play Pictorial*, February 1926, p. 18.
17. *Journey's End* by R.C. Sheriff premiered in London in December 1928. The film adaptation was directed by James Whale in Hollywood in a co-production deal between Gainsborough Pictures and Tiffany Stahl, and released in 1930.
18. George Simmers, 'Dornford Yates and the Uses of Facetiousness', paper delivered at The First World War and Popular Culture conference, Newcastle upon Tyne, March 2006.

Chapter 4

INSIDE THE ROBOTS' CASTLE:
UFA'S ENGLISH-LANGUAGE VERSIONS
IN THE EARLY 1930S

Chris Wahl

British International Pictures (BIP) – the film company that emerged in 1927 out of British National – is mainly remembered for having produced the first multiple language version film (MLV) worldwide, *Atlantic* (1929), with the aim of establishing the Elstree studios near London as a 'British Hollywood'.[1] The director of *Atlantic* and two other BIP MLVs, *Two Worlds* (1930) and *Cape Forlorn* (1930), E.A. Dupont, belonged to a community of German artists and technicians working in English studios at this time.[2] The *Film-Kurier* described the cooperation thus: 'In Elstree, the British speak broken German, and the Germans speak broken English'.[3] The fact that so many countrymen were contributing to those films made parts of the German press consider the German versions made in England as truly German films.[4] That does not go without saying because, legally, German versions made in foreign countries did not count as German films as from 1932,[5] and the English versions made by Ufa were never treated as English films.[6]

The idea of building a European alliance against Hollywood had been discussed since 1924 and partly been realised in the form of cooperations between distributors and producers. With the advent of sound, it became necessary to create a large continental market, a 'Film-Europe', to be able to compete with the United States where the large monolingual home market guaranteed profitability.[7]

During the first two years of sound film production, MLVs were the predominant method of adapting films for other countries. Films were shot in identical sets, based on the same script, with different casts in several languages. Translating the dialogue also meant making concessions to the presumed taste of different audiences. This process was not entirely new: during the silent era export versions were frequently based on different negatives, leaving out or adding particular elements, such as erotic allusions. MLVs can be considered as an attempt to solve the problems that arose with the coming of sound by applying this approved method. Very soon, however, the latter turned out to be far too expensive, though it still had a very important advantage over dubbing: the MLV guaranteed the unity of body and voice. Today, film historians agree on the assumption that the public of the early 1930s was highly sensitive about that unity and rejected dubbing not because of technical shortcomings but because it felt betrayed. (In the 1930s, only a few had the opportunity of seeing two or more different versions of a film.[8]) In subsequent decades MLVs, regarded as a dead end in film history, were largely neglected. Nowadays it is still difficult to study them because the versions are, if extant at all, scattered across various archives and therefore often hard to locate.

Ufa and MLVs

As Europe's largest film company and the only serious competitor of the American film industry at that time, German Ufa was the most significant producer of MLVs, being involved in around 160 versions of seventy-five films from 1929 to 1939. The majority of those versions were shot in French, but English came in second with eleven films. They comprised *Melody of the Heart* (*Melodie des Herzens*, 1929), *Love-Waltz* (*Liebeswalzer*, 1930), *The Blue Angel* (*Der blaue Engel*, 1930), *The Temporary Widow* (*Hokuspokus*, 1930), *Monte Carlo Madness* (*Bomben auf Monte Carlo*, 1931), *Congress Dances* (*Der Kongress tanzt*, 1931), *Happy Ever After* (*Ein blonder Traum*, 1932), *Early to Bed* (*Ich bei Tag und Du bei Nacht*, 1932), *F.P.1* (*F.P.1 antwortet nicht*, 1933), *The Only Girl* (*Ich und die Kaiserin*, 1933) and *Did I Betray? / Black Roses* (*Schwarze Rosen*, 1935/37).

In this chapter I want to discuss why Ufa stopped making English-language versions in 1933, and why it resumed this activity in 1935, but only for one film. Drawing on observations by Robert Stevenson (the English supervisor of many Ufa English-language versions) and comparing the German and English versions of three Ufa films, I will clarify why the German company was predetermined to produce MLVs, and discuss the difficulties of adapting a film for a foreign public.

Early Attempts at Foreign-language Versions

After the financial debacle of *Metropolis* (1927), producer Erich Pommer moved to Hollywood where he worked briefly for Paramount and M-G-M, but he returned to Ufa in September 1927 as Head of the 'Erich-Pommer-Production-Unit'.[9] During the period when BIP shot *Atlantic* (June/July 1929), Ufa produced *Melodie des Herzens* in a silent version as well as in

German, English, French and Hungarian sound versions. In contrast to the BIP film, where English actors were replaced by German ones in the German version, Pommer made his actors learn their lines phonetically for every single foreign-language version. Afterwards native speakers dubbed them.[10] In adopting this method, he wanted not only to avoid the multi-casting required by different language versions, but also to achieve a better lip sync. Because the results were still not satisfying, Pommer kept on trying other hybrid forms such as *The Blue Angel* or *Love-Waltz*, where the German actors spoke rather simple English as well as German without being dubbed afterwards; their poor mastery of English was motivated by the script and turned the story into some kind of polyglot adventure.[11] With *Hokuspokus/The Temporary Widow* Ufa finally opted for producing 'pure' MLVs, and continued to do so until the late 1930s.

Throughout the early sound period, Pommer was a strict adversary of dubbing and an explicit advocate of MLVs. As he stated,

> A love scene in Berlin, Paris or London has never the same colouring. That's why the sound film shot in three or four versions will always meet the mentality of the distinct countries much better than the silent films ever could.[12]

Out of ten English versions of Ufa productions shot until January 1933, Pommer produced nine.[13] As the only Ufa producer with professional experience in an Anglophone country, his reputation in Britain as a first-class producer could not have been higher. When discussing Ufa's English-language versions, the English press always referred to Pommer as their true creator.

Ufa and Gaumont-British

English-born actress Lilian Harvey starred in five out of Ufa's ten English-language ventures, *Love-Waltz*, *The Temporary Widow*, *Congress Dances*, *Happy Ever After* and *The Only Girl*, and in three of them she appeared in all three (German, English, French) versions.[14] The first of these trilingual productions, *Der Kongress tanzt* (1931), made her a star across Europe. For the French versions of Harvey's films, Ufa cooperated with its subsidiary Alliance Cinématographique Européenne (ACE), and for the four English versions after *Congress Dances* it found a strategic ally in England in Gaumont-British. Rachael Low documents the start of this partnership:

> It was at this time that Isidore Ostrer [chairman of Gaumont-British since June 1931], much struck by the English-language version of the spectacular German musical *Congress Dances*, initiated a policy of Anglo-German co-production between Ufa and Gaumont-British which was announced in May 1932.[15]

The minutes of Ufa's Board of Directors on 31 May 1932 announced that the company had decided to produce four English versions in 1932/33, comprising two Lilian Harvey films, one starring Renate Müller, and the so-called 'super-film' *F.P.1*. The inclusion of a vehicle for Müller made economic sense to Gaumont; the actress had become a star in England with *Sunshine Susie* (1931), Victor Saville's remake/version of Wilhelm Thiele's *Die Privatsekretärin* (1931) – at exactly the same time that Lilian Harvey had her huge success with *Congress Dances*.[16] The two Harvey films were *Ein blonder Traum* and *Ich und die Kaiserin*. Instead of the Müller vehicle, Ufa eventually produced *Ich bei Tag und Du bei Nacht* with Käthe von Nagy in the German version and Heather Angel[17] in the English one.

The agreement between Gaumont and Ufa – which included the clause that Gaumont was supposed to pay 25 per cent of the negative costs of each version[18] – clearly indicates that at the heart of this strategy was the necessity for polyglot stars. The big advantage of stars such as Harvey was that the company could economise on production time and salary costs. In addition, they were already established and integrated into German studio routines. In contrast, the case of Jack Hulbert[19] indicates the difficulty of integrating British actors into the German system. Robert Stevenson, who worked for Gaumont-British in Berlin, recalled that,

> Jack has been very difficult and has upset everybody a bit, which is pretty easy to do as they don't speak our language. The trouble has been partly his way of fussing about on the floor, but more particularly an unfortunate want of punctuality in turning up for his shots.[20]

For its French and English language versions Ufa employed supervisors who monitored every stage of production, from script development to final cut, in order to achieve high quality standards in the adaptation process. To ensure personal continuity, the studio relied upon just two English-version supervisors: the American Carl Winston and the Briton Stevenson. Winston had arrived in Babelsberg in August 1929 – together with his brother Sam, a cutter – as an assistant to Josef von Sternberg for the production of *Der blaue Engel* and was asked by Ufa to stay.[21] His contract stipulated that he had explicitly been hired as an expert for the American market, and his duties were described by Pommer as follows:

> His activity started with the first preparations of the picture, such as working on the manuscript and casting. After that he would be on the set all the time, assisting shooting and selecting rushes. His activity on the picture would finish with the last cuts.[22]

Winston's departure, apparently owing to his being homesick,[23] coincided with Ufa's orientation towards the British market. Michael Balcon, Head of Production at Gaumont-British between 1932 and 1936, sent Stevenson as the studio's representative to Babelsberg where he was to supervise four English-language versions until the end of the cooperation between the two companies.[24]

The End of Ufa's British Ventures

Although most of its first-version films were shot in English, Ufa stopped producing English-language versions after *The Only Girl* (1933). There are several reasons why the partnership with Gaumont did not continue. The year 1933 witnessed significant personnel changes. In January, after completing *Ich und die Kaiserin*, Harvey left for Hollywood, lured by a contract with Fox. Pommer's Ufa contract was terminated on 20 March 1933 as a direct result of the NSDAP (Nazi Party) takeover in Germany, so within months MLVs had lost not only their major star, but also a strong supporter at the studio and a renowned figure in international film business. Even when a film received unfavourable reviews, as in the case of *Monte Carlo Madness*, this could not diminish Pommer's status in Britain. In its review of the film, *Film Pictorial* commented that 'Erich Pommer is a great producer, but in this film he does not live up to his established reputation'.[25] A few months later, the same magazine wrote about Sari Maritza that 'she went to Germany to make *Monte Carlo Madness*, under the *direction* of Erich Pommer'.[26] The director of the film, of course, was Hanns Schwarz, but the magazine's mistake clearly indicates Pommer's standing in Britain at the time.

Horst Claus and Anne Jäckel offer a reasonable explanation for Ufa's initial interest in English versions:

> Unable to place its products through links with 'partners' in the USA, it began to establish or sign agreements with cinemas in areas with large communities of German descent (e.g. in New York). Of the fifteen films planned for 1930/31, the five big budget films were earmarked for English and German versions, while the remaining ten – all with a budget-allocation of 200.000 RM – were first and foremost destined for distribution at home. Ufa's decision to concentrate on English language versions was clearly prompted by the desire to break into the American market.[27]

Seen from this perspective, the end to making English-language versions was a logical conclusion for the economically minded Ufa Board of Directors:

> By 1933 it was clear to them that it would be impossible for their productions to break into the North American distribution network. As the English cinema circuits were generally regarded as the 'least important in Europe' for the German film industry, Ufa, by the end of 1932, had given up making English versions altogether.[28]

Regarding British attitudes towards MLVs, Michael Balcon appears to have played a similarly crucial role to the one Pommer occupied in Germany:

> In later years Balcon was anxious to dissociate himself from these films … He disapproved of co-production, which he later referred to as suicidal, and much preferred the newer policy of buying rights to German films and remaking them in England.[29]

In the letters between Balcon and Stevenson, the latter refers to misunderstandings due to cultural and linguistic differences as well as a lack of consideration of the British mentality by the Germans.[30] In this context, Balcon's shift from producing versions to commissioning remakes is no surprise. Concurrently, Ufa began to think about dubbing its films for the British market. British legislation allowed dubbing with English actors on German soil, but Ufa would have to find a British distributor having films made in Britain at its disposal to comply with the quota.[31] It is partly against this context that there would be a final epilogue to Ufa's British aspirations.

Unable to replicate her European fame in the United States, Harvey returned and in February 1935 signed a contract with BIP in London for three films.[32] The first (and only) result of this alliance was *Invitation to the Waltz* (Paul Merzbach, 1935). Rachael Low summarises the film as 'a light-hearted confection about the romance of a dancer at the time of Napoleon, based on a story by Holt Marvel', but suggests that 'Lilian Harvey, the English girl who had become a star in German films, was slightly disappointing'.[33]

In March 1935 Ufa borrowed Harvey from BIP to make *Capriccio*, meant to be the first in a series of three 'super films' in German, French and English versions to be produced within one year.[34] But in April Ernst Hugo Correll, Head of Production, reported to the Ufa Board that Harvey's contract at BIP had been cancelled by mutual agreement. Ufa now wanted to hire her for further films to be made under the direction of Reinhold Schünzel (these projects never materialised).[35] Although Harvey had originally been assigned to film *Capriccio* (which was eventually shot in 1938, and only in a German version), her first role at Ufa after her sojourns in Hollywood and Britain was *Schwarze Rosen*.[36] Despite the fact that Ufa had just lost ties with its British partner BIP, this film was made not only in a German and a French, but also in an English version (which had its trade show in England in 1937 under the title *Did I Betray?* and was eventually released in 1938 as *Black Roses*).

Ulrich Klaus suggests that Harvey paid for the English version with her own money; unfortunately he does not give a source.[37] In any case, while Harvey may have insisted on shooting in English, for Ufa the venture was economically risky, and indeed the English version turned out to be virtually unmarketable. Originally, it should have premiered before Christmas 1935 – at the same time as the German one.[38] But by February 1936, Ufa was still looking for a British distributor.[39] National Provincial F.D. finally trade-showed *Did I Betray?* in April 1937, but it was universally panned by the British press as too slow for English tastes,[40] while critics also complained about 'poor photography'.[41] The latter assessment, at least, seems rather unfair, as in terms of camera aesthetics (the photography was by Fritz Arno Wagner who had shot Murnau's *Nosferatu*, 1922) the film was highly accomplished.

Film Weekly summarised the prevailing British opinion that 'this film is [only] interesting because it shows us Lillian [*sic*] Harvey once more'.[42] Drawing on its experience with *Black Roses*, the Ufa Board decided in March 1936 that an English version of the next Harvey film would only be considered if a buyer were found beforehand.[43] This never happened: although Harvey continued to work for Ufa until the outbreak of the Second World War, there were no more English versions, and she left Germany in 1939 for France and eventually fled to the USA. By 1936, Ufa apparently could not manage to sell its products in the British market without a long-term British partner.[44]

Stevenson's Views on MLVs

Script supervisor Robert Stevenson emerges as one of the key witnesses and sources for the short-lived Anglo-German cooperation between Gaumont and Ufa.[45] His published comments and informal remarks on the shooting of Ufa's MLV productions are elucidating because only very few first-hand accounts on this topic exist. Most of the personnel involved did not pay much attention to the language versions in their autobiographies. This is surprising because for some of them it must have been a very significant experience, considering the efforts of the polyglot actors and the lengthy and monotonous working days for the whole team. Stevenson describes these conditions in a letter to Balcon:

> For though the German staff are almost all delightful people, by the time they have taken four German takes and four French, they are bored to tears with the shot in question and would like to finish with the English takes in exactly the same way with exactly the same business in the shortest time possible.[46]

After his return to the UK Stevenson in November 1933 gave a paper at the Gaumont-British Theatre in London entitled 'A Year in German Studios', which was then being printed in the *Proceedings of the British Kinematograph Society*.[47] In this lecture he reports at length on the 'goddess of efficiency'[48] and 'the excellence of their [German studios'] engineering and technical departments',[49] dispelling any doubt over Ufa's professionalism and technical superiority. As Stevenson argues, 'You may ask, what is it that makes possible the efficiency of the Ufa? In my opinion, it is the excellent system developed by the Ufa producers.'[50]

During Stevenson's time in Babelsberg there were four distinct production units, each working independently, the most important being Erich Pommer's. Ufa's decentralisation and the efficiency of the unit system were, according to Stevenson, even more developed than in Hollywood:

> This enormous Ufa staff is organised on military principles, each member being responsible to the grade above him; and I must here point out the astonishing military atmosphere of the Ufa studios as a whole.[51]

Stevenson's observation of the inside of the Ufa studios is backed by a description of the outside given by a British reporter visiting Babelsberg in 1932:

> If Herr Hitler ever conquers Germany he will probably turn the Ufa film city, near Berlin, into a fort. It certainly looks like one. When you approach the main studios you expect to be shot at from above, or exterminated by an invisible ray coming through the windowless walls of this Robots' castle.[52]

The military analogy does indeed hold when one recalls that from the porter to the Director, many former soldiers and officers were employed at Babelsberg, still proud of their Prussian heritage. With their help, the system functioned with the precision of a machine, 'but all machines have one weakness – they work too mechanically'.[53]

Alongside the complaint about the production process being too monotonous (or, as he put it more bluntly, 'they are extremely boring to make'[54]), Stevenson enumerates a number of problems inherent in the production of MLVs. One of these is the 'common' language spoken on the set – discussed here with regard to *Happy Ever After*:

> If you imagine what it was like for Cicely Courtneidge[55] to be directed in an allegedly funny scene through a German interpreter by a Jugo Slav [sic] director[56] who could not speak English, you will realise what a monstrous Tower of Babel a multilingual film studio becomes.[57]

Another problem identified by Stevenson concerns the inflexible attitude of German executives towards the adaptation of the films for a British audience. In a letter to Balcon he cites the following example:

> He [Pommer] has however allowed me to voice my protest to Wecksler [sic], a charming young man who is in charge of the production of the English version. He is Pommer's second assistant but not I think of any particular importance. He seems to be convinced that except for Cicely's part, we shall put up with a line-by-line translation of the German ... In view of the difference in cast, it is ridiculous.[58]

Stevenson also points to differences in narrative pace between German and British films, arguing that the German ones are far too slow for British audiences. This was supported by the British press; a reviewer of *Did I Betray?* complained about 'the cardinal German vice of slowness',[59] and another found the movement in *The Only Girl* 'rather slow'.[60] On the other hand, it is doubtful that German films were in general too slow for British tastes, bearing in mind such successes as *Congress Dances*.

Differences in national taste regarding questions of sex and humour also left their mark on the films that the respective country's audiences preferred. Stevenson argues that

> in questions of sex, the Continental story often appears to the English public brutal and ill-mannered, and the romantic lover, whom the Continentals consider a hero, often appears to an English audience a cad.[61]

As regards humour, Jack Hulbert in his autobiography recalls the shooting of *Happy Ever After*: 'The difficulties we had in trying to fit our humour into scenes already established were insuperable.'[62] Differing attitudes to humour and sex had already been the main reason for alterations of export versions in the silent era.

Considering all these differences, Stevenson concludes that the only films adequate to be shot in multiple language versions are super-productions and films with polyglot stars. In the remaining part of this chapter I will discuss his complaints with reference to specific examples of how Ufa adapted its MLVs for English audiences.

Early to Bed and The Only Girl

Ich bei Tag und Du bei Nacht/Early to Bed tells the story of Hans/Carl (Willy Fritsch/Fernand Gravey), a waiter working the night shift, and Grete (Käthe von Nagy/Heather Angel), a manicurist. Living in the apartment of Widow Seidelbast (Amanda Lindner/Lady Tree) they share the same room – he occupies it during the day, and she by night. One day, Grete and Hans, who haven't yet met, get acquainted by coincidence. Unaware of the fact that they are roommates, they fall in love. This quotidian love story is ironically counterpointed by the upper-class romance played out in a parody of an escapist film operetta, shown at the local cinema next door.

In contrast to the former film's modern setting, *Ich und die Kaiserin/The Only Girl* is a historical costume drama, centred on the Marquis de Pontignac (German version: Conrad Veidt, English version: Charles Boyer). A narrative of mistaken identities commences when the Marquis finds a silk garter in the woods. Juliette (Lilian Harvey), a lady-in-waiting, 'borrowed' it from the empress (Mady Christians) and lost it. *Ein blonder Traum*, meanwhile, the German version of *Happy Ever After*, tells the story of two window-cleaners falling in love with the same girl (Harvey again).

It is worth noting that none of the three English film titles provide literal translations of the German title. This is all the more surprising as the equivalent titles of the French versions *are* literal translations.[63] In a letter to Stevenson Michael Balcon refers to the film that was later released as *Happy Ever After* as follows:

[Angus] Mac Phail [Head of the Story Department] suggests *Dolly Daydream* or *Little Dolly Daydream* as the title for the English version of the Lilian Harvey subject. We (including yourself) are all agreed that *A fair dream* is an impossible title and although I do not say that the present suggestion is perfect, my personal opinion is that it is a very good title indeed, particularly as the subject is on musical comedy lines.[64]

It appears that the English co-producers tried to find an original title for the English version not only because a literal translation of the German title would have sounded odd, but rather because they wanted *their* version to stand out clearly against the German one. Certainly, this was not a question of copyright: a film called *I by Day and You by Night* (which is the literal translation of *Ich bei Tag und Du bei Nacht*) had not been released before. *Early to Bed*, however, was the title of a Laurel and Hardy comedy short (1928).

Supervisor Stevenson and his deputy screenwriter John Heygate had to work very fast. Writing to Balcon Stevenson complained: 'At present there is nothing to report, as in spite of copious protests, we have not yet received a translation of the whole of the script (though shooting began yesterday)'.[65] It is thus not surprising that many puns in the original script are not rendered equivalently in the English version. Juliette in *Ich und die Kaiserin* is constantly interrupting tête-à-têtes between the Empress and the Marquis under the pretext of reporting on the empress's nieces. In the German version, the somehow awkward situation is levelled out by adding a play on words with *Nichten – mitnichten – nicht* (nieces – by no means – not),[66] while the English translation does not include any obvious puns. The corresponding sentences ('I thought they were here, but I see they're not' – 'Your nieces want to go to bed' – 'Your nieces don't want to go to bed') fail to achieve the same comical effect.

In other cases, the English script doctors did a remarkable job of improving on the original lines. Grete in *Ich bei Tag und Du bei Nacht* warbles away to herself a song from a film that is being shown in the cinema. As it is early morning and breakfast time, the English Grete is taking a spoonful of jam while singing 'I'm the girl who's looking for jam'. In the German version, she sings 'Auch die nächste Woche ist genauso flau' ('The next week will be just as flat') which does not create a similar correspondence between performance, setting and song lyrics.

In *The Only Girl* as well as *Early to Bed*, the characters bear the same names as in the German versions, except Hans who is now called Carl. By renaming him, the allusion to the fairy tale *Hänsel und Gretel*, present in the original, is eliminated. While we do not know the exact reasons for that decision, in other cases we do. In his paper for the British Kinematograph Society, Stevenson relates the following anecdote from the making of *F.P.1*:

In the German version, the villain who tries to sabotage the island was called Damski. I pointed out that to an English audience this name would suggest

George Robey[67] dressed up with a Russian beard and carrying a bomb, and that therefore for the English version the villain should have a fresh name. I suggested the good, simple name of Hartmann, but the moment this name appeared in the rushes, the whole of the Ufa was up in arms. Hartmann is a *German* name, and apparently the villain of big Ufa pictures must not be a German. He should preferably be a Russian, because Russia has no Ambassador to protest. But it still seemed to me childish to give him a Russian name like Damski, and so for ten days the great Damski controversy went on. I suggested every name I could think of, I offered to give the villain my own name, I did not mind. Ultimately, Pommer lent me his car to travel 200 miles to the Baltic, where in an historical conference on a small island we compromised on the name of Lubin, a name which, since it could be English, American, Polish or Russian, completely satisfied the official patriotisms of the Ufa.[68]

While *Ich bei Tag und Du bei Nacht* featured German idols Willy Fritsch and Käthe von Nagy, *Early to Bed* starred Fernand Gravey and Heather Angel, neither really established in Britain. Consequently, the focus partly shifts to the supporting characters. Famous comedian Sonnie Hale was cast as the projectionist of the local cinema, which contributed to the English version being arguably funnier than the German and French ones; here everyone is fooling about whenever possible; telephone cables and ball-pens are creatively utilised as objects of childish nonsense. Of course, Stevenson and Heygate, together with the actors, could not always succeed in improving on the German original by incorporating British comedy conventions. A reviewer commented on *The Only Girl*: 'The film itself is curiously uneven. I do not know whether it is that Germanic and Anglo-Saxon humour cannot be successfully blended.'[69]

With regard to specifically 'national' cultural or historical references or characteristics, Stevenson and Heygate's approach to adaptation is interesting. In some cases the change was simple. Thus, when widow Seidelbast in *Ich bei Tag und Du bei Nacht* remembers her past as a theatre actress, she enthuses about her performance in Friedrich Schiller's *Don Carlos*. For the English version, Stevenson and Heygate replaced the reference to Schiller with Shakespeare's *Macbeth*. In other instances, the reasons for textual and representational alterations are more difficult to understand in retrospect. While the projectionist in *Ich bei Tag und Du bei Nacht*, for example, eats a bread-and-butter sandwich and carries around a vacuum flask, his English equivalent eats sausages. From a modern perspective, of course, it might seem more natural to attribute the vacuum flask (filled with tea) and the sandwich to the English projectionist, and sausages to the German, yet for some reasons *Early To Bed* confounds expectations in this respect. Incidentally, the related sequence in the film's French version, *À moi le jour, à toi la nuit*, conforms much more to national stereotypes; here the projectionist is presented filing his fingernails, reading a newspaper, and drinking red wine.

Representing historical references, especially those concerning Prussian history, also proved a challenge to the adaptors. Interestingly, British publicity for *Early to Bed* attempted to co-opt Frederick the Great, who has a significant narrative function in a sequence situated in his former palace, Potsdam's Sanssouci.[70] The write-up proposed that Frederick, 'in alliance with England under the great Earl of Chatham, fought the Seven Years War, 1756 to 1763, in the course of which England conquered Canada from the French'. Within one sentence, the Prussian monarch had been 'made British' for a British public.

More often, however, considerable sections of the German version were left out completely where they dealt excessively with political and historical matters, even if they included significant punchlines. For example, in *Ich und die Kaiserin* a sequence was cut where the visit of the Prussian envoy is imminent, and the Chamberlain commands the servants to bring an additional carpet because the Emperor hates the military clicking of the Prussian envoy's boots.

Conclusion

I have argued that the impossibility of conquering the American market was only one of several reasons why Ufa stopped making English versions of their films. There are two other problems Ufa had to face – the loss of two individuals crucial for their English-language films, Erich Pommer and Lilian Harvey, and the lack of a strategic partner for co-production after Gaumont-British had lost interest in English-language versions. The latter aspect in particular is exemplified by the case of *Did I Betray?/Black Roses*, the only English version Ufa shot after January 1933. Robert Stevenson described the Ufa of the early 1930s as a military machine that was predetermined for the production of multiple language versions by the amazing discipline and precision with which every process was being accomplished. He was clearly in favour of resuming the production of multiple language versions in England and named the difficulties that they would have to face when adapting English films to other cultures. However, despite the risks involved it was possible to succeed in creating versions that would appeal to the target public.

Notes

1. See Patricia Warren, *Elstree: The British Hollywood* (London: Elm Tree Books, 1983). The last multiple language version produced by BIP was *Dreyfus* (1931).
2. See Jörg Schöning (ed.), *London Calling. Deutsche im britischen Film der dreißiger Jahre* (Munich: edition text+kritik, 1993).
3. Karl Ritter, 'Die deutschen Filme in Elstree', *Film-Kurier*, 7 June 1930. My translation.

4. 'Nun haben wir den deutschen Sprechfilm' ('Now we have the German talking film'), Ernst Jäger writes in his review of *Atlantic* in *Film-Kurier*, 29 October 1929. And the *Morgenpost* on 30 October 1929 claims, 'Der deutsche Tonfilm ist da!' ('German sound film is here!'). Hans-Michael Bock quotes *Atlantic* (without giving the source) as the 'first 100% German talking picture'. Bock, 'Keine dramatischen Maggiwürfel. Die Einführung des Tonfilms', in Hans-Michael Bock and Michael Töteberg (eds.), *Das Ufa-Buch* (Frankfurt am Main: Zweitausendeins, 1992), p. 257.

5. See Wolfgang Mühl-Benninghaus, *Das Ringen um den Tonfilm. Strategien der Elektro- und der Filmindustrie in den 20er und 30er Jahren* (Düsseldorf: Droste, 1999), pp. 351ff.

6. See Rachael Low, *The History of the British Film 1929–1939. Film Making in 1930s Britain* (London: George Allen & Unwin, 1985), p. 94.

7. See Andrew Higson, 'Film-Europa. Dupont und die britische Filmindustrie', in Jürgen Bretschneider (ed.), *Ewald André Dupont. Autor und Regisseur* (Munich: edition text+kritik, 1992), pp. 95ff.

8. In London, for example, not only the English version of *Atlantic*, but also the German and later the French versions were programmed. See '*Atlantic*. French version for London', *Kinematograph Weekly*, 24 July 1930, p. 28.

9. See Hermann Kappelhoff, 'Lebendiger Rhythmus der Welt. Die Erich-Pommer-Produktion der Ufa', in Bock and Töteberg (eds.), *Das Ufa-Buch*, pp. 208–13.

10. See Michaela Krützen, 'Esperanto für den Tonfilm. Die Produktion von Sprachversionen für den frühen Tonfilm-Markt', in Michael Schaudig (ed.), *Positionen deutscher Filmgeschichte. 100 Jahre Kinematographie. Strukturen, Diskurse, Kontexte* (Munich: Schaudig & Ledig, 1996), p. 149.

11. See Chris Wahl, *Das Sprechen des Spielfilms. Über die Auswirkungen von hörbaren Dialogen auf Produktion und Rezeption, Ästhetik und Internationalität der siebten Kunst* (Trier: Wissenschaftlicher Verlag Trier, 2005), pp. 175–77. *The Blue Angel* was shot with exactly the same cast as the German version whereas in *Love-Waltz* some actors from the German version remained (including the polyglot Lilian Harvey, but also Georg Alexander and Hans Junkermann, who had to work hard on their English lines), and others were replaced by English actors (John Batten plays the part of Willy Fritsch).

12. Erich Pommer, 'Einleitende Worte', in Hans Kahan, *Dramaturgie des Tonfilms* (Berlin: Mattisson, 1930), p. 6. My translation.

13. *The Temporary Widow* was produced by Günther Stapenhorst.

14. *Der Kongress tanzt, Ein blonder Traum* and *Ich und die Kaiserin*.

15. Low, *History of the British Film*, p. 132. The contract between the two companies was signed on 3 May 1932. See *Film-Kurier*, 4 May 1932.

16. See 'Anglo-German Star Exchange. *Sunshine Susie* Coincidence', *The Bioscope*, 2 December 1931, p. 14.

17. Heather Angel had made her first film appearance in *The City of Song* (1931), another production in English and German versions. She played Carmela, a girl from Naples, and looked – according to the film's editor Lars Moën – 'more Italian than the original Carmela' (p. 16), a 'little Italian girl' who was sent away because 'she just hasn't got it in her' (p. 15). Lars Moën, 'On Location with *The City of Song*', *Picturegoer*, March 1931, pp. 14–16.

18. See minutes of Ufa's Board of Directors, Bundesarchiv-Filmarchiv Berlin, BArch, R 109 I, 1028c, Bl. 233.

19. Jack Hulbert is ranked 21st in the chart 'The most popular 100 stars in Britain, 1932–1937', printed in John Sedgwick, *Popular Filmgoing in 1930s Britain. A Choice of Pleasures* (Exeter: University of Exeter Press, 2000), p. 189.

20. Stevenson to Balcon, undated. Aileen and Michael Balcon Collection, BFI Special Collections (MEB/B/57).

21. Winston's first Ufa contract (26 August 1929) is kept in the Carl Winston Collection at the Filmmuseum Berlin – Deutsche Kinemathek.

22. Quoted from Winston's leaving certificate, written by Pommer on 30 December 1931. Carl Winston Collection, Filmmuseum Berlin – Deutsche Kinemathek.

23. Pommer writes in the leaving certificate: 'Mr Winston is leaving Berlin in view of the fact that he has been over here for more than two years and feels that he has to go back to the States in order not to lose contact with his home country'. Carl Winston Collection, Filmmuseum Berlin – Deutsche Kinemathek.

24. *Did I Betray?/Black Roses* seems to have been supervised by John Heygate who had already been working as an assistant (script writer) to Stevenson.

25. *Film Pictorial*, 23 July 1932, p. 18.

26. *Film Pictorial*, 28 January 1933, p. 5 (my emphasis). In the Christmas Yearbook 1932 of *Picturegoer Weekly* an entire page is dedicated to a visit to Erich Pommer's office in Babelsberg. See W.D., 'Erich Pommer Votes for Amusement', *Picturegoer Weekly*, December 1932, p. 62.

27. Horst Claus and Anne Jäckel, '*Der Kongreß tanzt* Revisited', *CINEMA & Cie.*, no. 6, Spring 2005, p. 77.

28. Horst Claus and Anne Jäckel, 'MLVs in a Changing Political Climate', *CINEMA & Cie.*, no. 7, Fall 2005, p. 51.

29. Low, *History of the British Film*, p. 133. In a letter to Robert Stevenson from 2 June 1932, Balcon jokes: 'I cannot imagine anything more trying than these trilingual [German-French-English] versions – please excuse the play on words, it was not intentional.' MEB/B/57.

30. See MEB/B/57.

31. See BArch, R 109 I, 1031a, Bl. 55. The 1927 Cinematograph Films Act specified a quota of British films for distributors and exhibitors. This was placed at 7.5 per cent for distributors and 5 per cent for exhibitors, gradually rising to 20 per cent for both by the end of the Act's ten-year duration. A British film was defined as one in which 75 per cent of salaries went to British subjects including a British writer, and covered production throughout the British Empire.

32. See Uwe Klöckner-Draga, '*Wirf weg, damit du nicht verlierst ...*' *Lilian Harvey – Biographie eines Filmstars* (Berlin: edition q, 1999), p. 199.

33. Low, *History of the British Film*, p. 125.

34. See BArch, R 109 I, 1030a, Bl. 35/36.

35. See BArch, R 109 I, 1030a, Bl. 1.

36. Harvey arrived from London at Tempelhof airport on 19 June 1935. See *Film-Kurier*, 18 June 1935.

37. See Ulrich J. Klaus, *Deutsche Tonfilme, 6. Jahrgang: 1935* (Berlin: Klaus, 1995), p. 167. Harvey's biographer claims the same. See Klöckner-Draga, '*Wirf weg, damit du nicht verlierst ...*', p. 215.

38. See BArch, R 109 I, 1031a, Bl. 82.

39. See BArch, R 109 I, 1031b, Bl. 349.

40. See *The Cinema*, 22 April 1937, p. 12.

41. See *Kinematograph Weekly*, 29 April 1937, p. 43.

42. *Film Weekly*, 11 March 1939, p. 31.

43. See BArch, R 109 I, 1031b, Bl. 331.

44. And it had given up the US market: the 1936 Harvey film *Glückskinder* was set in New York, but Ufa produced only a French – but not an English – version.

45. Today Stevenson is better remembered as a Hollywood director, most prominently of *Mary Poppins* (1964).

46. Stevenson to Balcon, undated. MEB/B/57.

47. See Robert Stevenson, 'A Year in German Studios', *Proceedings of the British Kinematograph Society*, no. 20, 1934, pp. 3–12.

48. Ibid., p. 5. He continues as follows: 'As the result of this new cult, the Ufa is now a magnificent machine, and everything is excellently organised, organised as only Germans *can* organise.'

49. Ibid., p. 7.

50. Ibid., p. 6.

51. Ibid.
52. *Film Pictorial*, 5 March 1932, p. 26.
53. Stevenson, 'A Year in German Studios', p. 5.
54. Ibid., p. 9.
55. Wife of Jack Hulbert and ranked 79th in the chart 'The most popular 100 stars in Britain, 1932–1937', printed in John Sedgwick, *Popular Filmgoing in 1930s Britain*, p. 191.
56. Paul Martin was born in 1899 in then-Hungarian Klausenburg, which is today in Romania.
57. Stevenson, 'A Year in German Studios', p. 9.
58. Stevenson to Balcon, 11 May 1932. MEB/B/57. 'Wecksler' is Fritz Wechsler.
59. *The Cinema*, 22 April 1937, p. 12.
60. *Talkie Magazine*, 16 September 1933, p. 16.
61. Stevenson, 'A Year in German Studios', p. 9.
62. Jack Hulbert, *The Little Woman's Always Right* (London: W.H. Allen, 1975), p. 199.
63. *À moi le jour, à toi la nuit*; *Moi et l'impératrice*; *Un rêve blond*.
64. Balcon to Stevenson, 6 May 1932. MEB/B/57.
65. Stevenson to Balcon, 11 May 1932. MEB/B/57.
66. 'Ich dachte, dass sie hier sind, die *Nichten*. Aber wie ich sehe, sind sie's mit*nichten*.' – 'Die Nichten wollen schlafen gehen.' – 'Jetzt wollen die *Nicht*en wieder *nicht* schlafen gehen.'
67. British music hall star who had a good command of German.
68. Stevenson, 'A Year in German Studios', p. 6.
69. *Talkie Magazine*, 16 September 1933, p. 16.
70. The programme can be found in the Special Collections of the British Film Institute.

Chapter 5

FLAMBOYANT REALISM: WERNER BRANDES AND BRITISH INTERNATIONAL PICTURES IN THE LATE 1920s

Kelly Robinson

In 1929 British International Pictures' (BIP's) market share in Britain was a substantial 36 per cent.[1] Two years after the company's inception in April 1927, the number of productions involving German directors and/or cameramen also peaked; approximately three-quarters of BIP's feature-length films featured German personnel. From its outset until 1936, when the company changed to Associated British Picture Corporation, this quota fluctuated, depending on who was being contracted to the studio. Altogether, BIP used German directors and cinematographers in a quarter of its entire output.[2] In this chapter I will assess the contribution of German cameraman Werner Brandes to the company's formation of an international aesthetic.[3]

BIP's hiring of German personnel was part of a wider phenomenon of cross-cultural exchange that had been taking place between Britain and Germany since the early 1920s. The German film industry in the 1920s proved to be one of the few national cinemas offering any real challenge to Hollywood. The artistry of many of its productions and their filmmakers' technical knowledge were admired in Britain, and some films even became successful in the USA.[4]

In 1928 Sinclair Hill, Managing Director and Chief Producer of Stoll Picture Productions, visited studios in Paris and Berlin, 'accompanied by his chief cameraman D. Dickinson', and was 'strongly impressed' with what he saw there.[5] In particular, he admired how the Germans created spectacle 'without the expenditure of the vast sums of money required by anyone producing on the lines of the big American spectacular pictures'. He added that 'it would be idle to suggest that German influence, which has already made its unmistakable appearance in American productions, will never be seen in British pictures'.[6] John Maxwell, director of BIP from its beginning, sought to attain quality both through aesthetic means and the appropriate industrial infrastructure. He understood that for an efficient business to run smoothly, 'technicians and players must be kept continuously in work'.[7] From tours of production facilities in both the USA and Germany he had learnt about efficient production organisation.[8]

The German studios in the 1920s had a reputation for being impeccably organised, with the production team working together extremely closely. Significantly, considering his status as world-famous filmmaker, the first job German director E.A. Dupont was given at British National Pictures (BNP) – the studio's name before taken over by Maxwell and renamed British International Pictures – was that of overseeing production.[9] Dupont expressed to *Kinematograph Weekly* in January 1927 'his belief that the studios, when completed, would be as well equipped as those of Ufa'. The British reviewer added: 'Young and unassuming, Mr Dupont feels confident that our resources are capable of making films in a steady output of a standard ensuring release.'[10]

Many press reports in the mid to late 1920s observed that the major problem facing producers was the lack of decent studio space and experienced personnel. *Bioscope* asserted retrospectively: 'they [BIP] found themselves faced with a dearth of trade personnel who could use the plant … they had to go abroad for the technical skill they needed'.[11] An article in *Kinematograph Weekly* in January 1927 entitled 'Britain's Hollywood' reported that,

> one of the most interesting and advanced sections of the Elstree scheme will be the electric lighting installation, which will surpass all previous efforts in studio illumination, and even in its incomplete present state is capable of producing the most brilliant effects in artistic camera craft.[12]

The same journal also announced that Helmuth Marx, 'the famous ex-Ufa technical expert, is shortly installing an overhead mobile lighting system, also a grouping frame system of his own' and that BNP had acquired the world rights to the Schüfftan process (outside Canada and the USA).[13] The British film industry sorely lacked the personnel who could use this state-of-the-art equipment, so its hiring of internationally renowned film personnel was a practical as well as a promotional necessity.

In 1929 Maxwell stated: 'At the outset we set for ourselves a standard, and that standard was world quality.'[14] Whereas in the earlier wave of cooperations in the mid-1920s British filmmakers were going to Germany to use their facilities, by the end of the decade the direction was reversed with German personnel coming over to Britain, often to use the newly equipped studios at Elstree, 'Britain's Hollywood'.

The influx of German filmmakers into British studios in the 1920s was not a result of forced exile, as it would commonly be after 1933. Jan-Christopher Horak has discussed some of the difficulties that German-speaking émigrés faced when negotiating the parameters of the Hollywood studio system in the mid-1920s, and Thomas Elsaesser has also highlighted the restrictive impact of the producer-unit system introduced at Ufa in 1927.[15] He argued that 'room for creativity on the part of the cinematographer began to shrink. Opportunities to experiment on the set dwindled; films were more tightly shot according to the shooting script which often specified technical detail (camera movement, shot size).'[16] The mode of production that BIP initially adopted was a director-unit system, similar to Erich Pommer's at Ufa in the mid-1920s, which gave significant freedom to its personnel. In this respect Britain emerged as an attractive alternative to Hollywood's and Ufa's creatively stifling mode of production.

The arrival of German cinematographers in the late 1920s was enthusiastically received by British cameramen such as Jack Cardiff, who was beginning his career at Elstree with *The Informer* (Arthur Robison, 1929).[17] He later explained that 'the Germans were more advanced – it was rather romantic having them there, the same with the Frenchmen'.[18] Sinclair Hill noted the 'psychological difference' between technicians in Germany and Britain: 'I saw for one thing a feverish concentration and picture obsession in the studio rank and file, far greater than I have noticed here. The lowest paid technician is picture mad …'[19] Cardiff, shedding light on the differences between British and German cameramen, provided further evidence of the dedication that the continental cameraman demonstrated. 'There was a cameraman, I forget his name – he was purely British – absolutely adored cricket and belonged to the cricket team at BIP. Cricket and life always came first – lighting came second – just something he did. Whereas with the Germans and French you could tell that lighting was their life.'[20] This lack of commitment manifested itself in much of the British cameramen's photography, which Freddie Young found to be 'pretty crude'.[21] Cardiff also compared British and German approaches to their craft:

> The British approach to lighting was very naïve. They had adopted simple lighting techniques. They often used back lighting which made everything sparkle. Germans were more advanced. They made fantasy with the lighting. When I was a numbers boy I assisted [Heinrich] Gärtner and [Bruno] Mondi – I had to carry all their equipment and there was a lot of it![22]

In other words, the German-speaking cinematographers introduced a degree of quality and artistry to British cinema that was lacking in many of their British counterparts.

Enter Werner Brandes

Felix Bucher in retrospect assessed Werner Brandes as a 'very efficient and busy cameraman'.[23] He had had a long career in Germany before working for BIP, starting out in 1914 with *Die Befreiung der Schweiz und die Sage von*

Wilhelm Tell (Friedrich Feher, 1914) and frequently collaborating with Joe May, shooting six of his films between 1919 and 1921, including the serial *Die Herrin der Welt* (Mistress of the World, 1919) and the hugely successful *Das indische Grabmal* (The Indian Tomb, 1921).[24] Brandes had also worked with Dupont, on *Die grüne Manuela* (1923) and *Der Demütige und die Sängerin* (1925), and he collaborated with some of Germany's most important cameramen, including Günther Krampf, Theodor Sparkuhl and Karl Puth.[25]

Prior to being employed by BIP, Brandes had worked regularly at Ufa studios and therefore would have been familiar with the working practices there and with the latest technological advances and experiments in cinematography. German cameramen in general took their work very seriously. There were specialist publications on cinematography and their technical skills were supplemented by an enthusiasm for other arts as well.[26]

In 1927 Werner Brandes was the first German cameraman to work for BIP. Dupont, who was in a position of authority at BIP at this time, may have demanded to work with a former collaborator, but the studio would willingly have acquiesced anyway – employing a 'star' cameraman was in line with the high standards set for the personnel who worked on their films. Brandes photographed three BIP films at Elstree: Dupont's *Moulin Rouge* (1928) and *Piccadilly* (1929), and *The Informer* (1929) by Arthur Robison, the director of *Schatten* (Warning Shadows, 1923). He also filmed two other films at Elstree, *Tesha* (1928), directed by Victor Saville and produced by Saville's company Burlington Films (which was financed by Maxwell), and the silent version of *White Cargo* (1930), produced by Neo-Art Productions and directed by J.B. Williams. According to the diaries of David Cunynghame, a BIP employee from 1927 to 1929, Brandes left Elstree on 23 June 1929 to fulfil a contract in Germany.[27] Freddie Young took over the shooting of the sound version of *White Cargo*, and Cunynghame observed that he 'appears slow after Brandes'.[28] In the following pages I will focus my attention in particular on Brandes' work on the two Dupont films, and on *The Informer*.

Moulin Rouge and *Piccadilly*

Moulin Rouge was originally planned as a project for Carr–Gloria–Dupont Productions, Ltd., a company formed by Dupont after the termination of his contract with BNP. It was an Anglo-German initiative, yet the contemporary press were keen to point out that Britain had a controlling interest in the company. Dupont was to be the director of a series of nine 'big films, costing some £50,000 each'.[29] The company failed to come to fruition and a few months later it was announced that BIP had signed the director and that his first film for the company would be *Moulin Rouge* – 'characteristic Dupont material'.[30]

Shooting began on location in Paris in September 1927. Shortly afterwards the crew moved to Elstree, where they worked on the interiors until January 1928.[31] The film cost a reputed £100,000.[32] *Piccadilly* was announced as Dupont's next production as shooting for *Moulin Rouge* wrapped up, although the film did not go into production until 13 August.[33]

P.L. Mannock, British Studio Correspondent for *Kinematograph Weekly*, repeatedly visited the sets of both films. He was 'fascinated by the lavish and bold methods of A.E. Dupont [*sic*]'.[34] In an article entitled 'Montmartre, Herts' he was struck by the 'magnificent spectacle' of the huge reproduction of the Boulevard Montmartre in Elstree's studios for *Moulin Rouge*. He noted the

> pavements, cobbles, kerbs and buildings of public amusement, fitted with flashing and undulating electric signs. A large café, also brilliantly lit, was crammed with the most remarkable collection of Paris types imaginable. Dupont does not rely on agents for these special crowds, but chooses all the types himself ... Music, the clatter of glasses, and the passing of cars, all helped the illusion, which only lacked the blended smells of Paris petrol and State-monopoly cigarettes to carry complete conviction.[35]

Mannock thus describes the setting which forms the opening sequence of the film and introduces Paris as the 'City of temptation'. The initial montage of Paris landmarks often filmed from moving vehicles creates a dizzying effect. The following scene inside a café sets up in condensed form the main themes of the film. The camera tracks up the legs of a woman sitting at one of the tables in the café. Dupont cuts to a close-up of her face as she looks off-screen – evidently 'eyeing' a potential suitor. The camera pans promptly to the object of her gaze; a man grins knowingly back at her. The pan continues to a further figure dressed in black with her back to the camera. She eventually turns to look at the man. A series of glances between the characters ensues, resulting in the first woman being rejected by the man in favour of the second.

Sexual intrigue, jealousy and rejection are themes which pervade Dupont's films for BIP. Brandes discloses these tensions through a signature technique. For instance, in *Piccadilly* Mabel Greenfield (Gilda Gray), a star dancer in a club in Piccadilly, establishes that she has a younger rival for both her job and her lover in Shosho (Anna May Wong). Valentine Wilmot (Jameson Thomas), the object of Mabel's affections and also her employer, has asked Shosho to come to his office after seeing her dance in the scullery of his club. As they discuss the terms of her contract, he is distracted by her tattered stockings and draws her portrait on a piece of paper on his desk. Mabel enters the office and immediately tension arises between the three characters. In an attempt to assert her authority, Mabel refers to Shosho's work in the scullery. A swift pan to Shosho registers the latter's visible annoyance, followed by a cut back to a gloating

Mabel. The camera then lingers on the latter as she leans into Valentine to whisper suggestively into his ear.

Moulin Rouge uses special effects in imaginative ways to express character subjectivity. The protagonists Margaret and André go out to dinner to celebrate their engagement. André is unhappy both at the ensuing marriage (as he's in love with her mother Parysia, played by Olga Chekhova) and Margaret's drunkenness. Signalled by a tight forehead shot of André, we literally enter his thoughts when, whilst kissing Margaret, he envisions Parysia. To create this effect, Brandes dissolves between the two images of the women kissing André – the kiss is transformed from one of reluctance to one of passion.

Both *Moulin Rouge* and *Piccadilly* feature melodramatic love triangles. But narrative is secondary to their spectacular visual appeal. *Piccadilly*'s sets fascinated Mannock in their vastness and attention to detail.[36] He reported that an acre of space had been allocated for the lavish club and that it had been six weeks in construction.[37] 'The set, which will be occupied for about two weeks, measures 200ft. in length, is 90 ft. wide and 45 ft. high and has two broad circular staircases at one end leading up to tiered terraces, and a balcony which encircles the entire hall.'[38] Brandes takes advantage of this space, shooting from the balcony, the dining area, the orchestra pit and sweeping the camera along the dance floor as Mabel and her dancer twirl around.[39] To introduce this dance a published score called 'Mabel and Vic' is held in front of the camera. It is abruptly pulled back away from the camera, exposing the orchestra pit where the drummer is hitting the snare in a drum roll. This dynamic shot, which keeps everything in focus, gives an illusion of the camera tracking back. It bears striking resemblance to a shot in Murnau's *Der letzte Mann* (*The Last Laugh*, 1924) where the camera tracks back from a trumpet.

In Germany in the mid-1920s technicians revolutionised scaffolding and crane technology and as a result there was an increased mobility in their films. The *entfesselte Kamera* ('unchained camera') became prevalent at the Ufa studios with such films as *Der letzte Mann* and Dupont's *Varieté* (*Variety*, 1925), both shot by Karl Freund. These films owed the critical plaudits they received in both the USA and Britain mainly to their technical and aesthetic appeal. The appropriation of these techniques by BIP was an attempt to extend this marketable aesthetic.

The camera in *Piccadilly* is rarely still. There is a dissolve from Shosho's address written on a notepad in Valentine's hand to the Chinese restaurant where she lives. A pan searches and locates the restaurant's sign. As Valentine walks towards the front door and pushes it open the camera follows him all along. When he enters the back-room bar a point-of-view shot continues this forward tracking motion; then Dupont cuts back to Valentine again as he approaches the bar. Although there are a series of cuts the fluidity and consistency of the movement gives the illusion of one continual long take.

Moulin Rouge and *Piccadilly* are not solely dominated by Brandes' moving camera. Long, high angle shots also feature – encompassing the spectacular sets by Alfred Junge, thus announcing BIP's high production values. The camera assistant Peter Hopkinson recalled that King Vidor told him that 'in Hollywood the cameraman lights the star, in Europe he lights the set'.[40] German filmmakers were influenced by Hollywood's methods of shooting the star; Brandes often films leading characters with diffused lighting and in close-up – yet he also just as frequently obscures their figures. In a club in *Moulin Rouge* balloons vie for the attention of the camera; in *Piccadilly* he frames Shosho and Valentine through bars at the pub in the Limehouse district of London. In both Dupont films, Brandes also shoots characters through blinds and fabric for beautiful lighting effects. The body, in a variety of ways, is manipulated for artistic purposes, with chiaroscuro lighting frequently forcing the body into a purely compositional element within the frame. In Shosho's bedroom in *Piccadilly* sunlight blazes through the blinds on her windows creating bars of light and shade on her body. At the nightclub, the shadow of her writhing body is projected onto a pool of light on the floor.

The lighting equipment available to Brandes at Elstree was said to equal that of any studio in the world. The lamps included the very latest models from France, Germany and America, 'as well as the best British types … portable switchboards … a generating mobile truck … and trollies and runways, capable of lighting any set with a minimum of delay'.[41] This new equipment at Elstree gave British and German technicians opportunities to experiment with different lighting techniques:

> Banks of 100-watt gasfilled lamps have been successfully used in conjunction with panchromatic stock for close-ups, and there are a number of banks of this particular type of lighting … German electricians have been very ingenious in making up these lamps, and at Elstree are found lamps which will give an imitation candle, hand lamp, billiard lamp, stable lantern, miner's lamp, coach lantern, paraffin lamp, saloon lamp, writing lamp and several other units which can be made up into any conceivable thing that sheds light of any kind.[42]

Whilst visiting the set of *Piccadilly*, Mannock praised the polished floor of the dance hall as being 'remarkably effective in its reflections', and described the lighting equipment available to Brandes at the studios: 'There were four sun arcs of 14,000 candlepower each, fourteen smaller arcs and forty-two domes of 7,000 candle power each, seven large spotlights and hundreds of smaller lights and incandescents.'[43]

During Shosho's dance there is a high-angle long shot that illustrates the extent of these different lighting sources, giving the impression of light emanating from candles around the room and from a giant chandelier hanging on the ceiling. Brandes manipulates the lamps so as to bounce light off various light reflecting surfaces, including Shosho's costume and the four rotating mirror balls that enclose her routine. Even the crystal door knob in Mabel's apartment gets the Brandes treatment. As Valentine turns it from the other side of the door light reflects off its surfaces spectacularly. Unlike in classic Hollywood cinema, lighting in these films rarely works as a neutral element of the *mise en scène*.

The Informer

In September 1928 it was announced in the trade press that BIP had purchased the rights to Liam O'Flaherty's novel *The Informer* and that Arthur Robison had been signed on to direct.[44] *The Informer* was filmed at Elstree during the spring and summer of 1929. Mannock regularly recorded Robison's endeavour for authenticity: his preparatory research included a visit to Ireland to absorb its 'atmosphere'.[45] In his autobiography Jack Cardiff writes about the complete Dublin street, which was 'packed with four hundred extras, and looked splendidly authentic'.[46] Robison's attention to detail is illustrated by a pawnbroker's which 'was crammed with clocks, watches, rings, riding boots, silver cups, hats, golf clubs, cameras – you name it'.[47] This appears fleetingly in the film.

Mannock, whilst visiting the set, was reassured by Robison that there was nothing anti-British in the treatment of Liam O'Flaherty's play centred on the activities of the IRA.[48] Mannock was unnecessarily worried; BIP's internationalist policy would have meant precluding controversial subject matter.[49] Although not quite lacking the historical and geographical specificity of the 'film operetta' genre – a feature of many international productions – like the Paris of *Moulin Rouge* and the London of *Piccadilly*, Robison's 'Ireland' is still a tourist's imaginary, represented by bottles of Guinness and dingy bars.[50] The film had an international cast of stars, including the Hungarian Lya de Putti and the Swede Lars Hanson. BIP's approach to the production of the film was persistently internationalist and this is also reflected in the film's aesthetic qualities.[51]

The scene I want to examine in this respect occurs a little way into the film. Gypo Nolan (Lars Hanson), the film's protagonist, is a member of an unnamed Irish insurgence group. When the police raid their headquarters, his friend Francis McPhillip (Carl Harbord) accidentally kills the Chief of Police and is forced into hiding. He returns briefly to the city to say goodbye to his mother and ask his girlfriend Katie (Lya de Putti) to come to America with him. But whilst Francis was in hiding, Gypo had formed a relationship with Katie. Gypo has been spying on Francis, who he believes has returned to take Katie away from him, unaware that Katie has told Francis she is now in love with Gypo. Convinced the former lovers are reunited, Gypo, in a jealous rage, goes to the police to inform on Francis's return to the city.

Initially, the camera is static and in mid-shot as Gypo contemplates the 'Wanted' poster on the wall. He slowly turns towards the camera; the realisation of how to get his revenge slowly registers on his face. He starts to walk towards the main street as if in a trance, with heavy posturing, arms pulled down and head bent low, but his pace becomes more determined as he heads towards the crowd – here Hanson's performance recalls the Expressionist acting style of the early 1920s. The camera tracks him from behind, speeding up as Gypo's pace gets more urgent. People and traffic cross his path both in front of and behind him. The sequence builds to a hectic climax, as the people on the street, some exiting the cinema, become frustrating obstacles. Gypo pushes through them, the camera now cutting in front of him to show his frustration in close-up. This is followed by a tracking shot, pulling back Gypo's face tightly framed. The scene ends with Gypo entering the police station.

Brandes clearly exploits the studio resources at Elstree and the freedom to experiment. The camera's presence in the scene becomes as noticeable as the action it depicts. The sequence invites comparison with the long tracking shot of the couple walking through the city in Murnau's *Sunrise* (1927). Barry Salt in his 'Statistical Style Analysis' of camera movement from the 1920s to the 1950s discusses the role of the director and the cinematographer and suggests that

> real camera movements are only made when authorised by the director, and further than that they are nearly always called for by him rather than anybody else, so I hope that one day we will see the end to the practice of film reviewers referring to such and such a cameraman's '… fluid and intricate camera movements …' In any case, once a director has decided on a tracking shot, the execution of it is usually supervised by the camera operator rather than the lighting cameraman (i.e. DOP), at any rate in England and America.[52]

Brandes' moving camera, though, contributes to a signature style that one can trace across all his films at BIP.[53] For example, in *The Informer*'s opening sequence where the insurgents sit around the table in their hideout, instead of cutting between characters, Brandes uses the short whip-like pans already seen in the films he shot for Dupont.

The long tracking shot in *The Informer* is not simply an endeavour to represent the psychological tension of its protagonist; it also gives an impression of the length and breadth of the set, the enormity of which featured in much of their publicity material. Through sets and camerawork BIP was attempting to differentiate its product from that of other British studios and, more generally, from the reputation British cinema had acquired in the early 1920s.

If the moving camera is one of the most striking features in the Dupont films, in *The Informer* it is the use of light and shadow. Brandes frequently employs arc lights to produce directional illumination and high contrasts. This lighting anticipates and heightens the drama that unfolds. Believing that Katie is still in love with Francis, Gypo storms out of her apartment and slams the front door behind him. Katie's shadow then appears on the

curtain of the front door. Her head repeatedly tilts back as she calls
frantically after Gypo. As in Robison's *Schatten*, shadows often enter the
frame before the visible body. As Francis looks at the 'Wanted' poster, a
policeman's shadow lurks ominously behind him. In a later sequence, the
police corner Francis on the roof whilst his mother and a gathering crowd
look on from the street below. Robison then cuts between the crowd
framed between walls on the street and Francis on the roof. Prefiguring the
climax of classic film noir *The Big Combo* (1955) by several decades, he is
literally trapped by the spotlight of the police. In the rooftop sequence the
set is dynamically broken up with streams of light and darkness. 'At some
personal peril' Mannock climbed the roof of one of the houses and
observed that 'some striking angles of the crowded thoroughfare from
above had, of course, already occurred to cameraman Brandes.'[54]

Brandes' inspired approach to filmmaking was admired by Mannock:

> At the command of Dr. Arthur Robison's whistle, passed by a typical crowd of
> all kinds and conditions of people, with traffic, including a donkey barrow, a car
> or two, jarveys, bicycles, and lorries. I perceived that this was all behind the
> camera, and that a mirror at the back of the shop window was reflecting the
> passing traffic as a background to the two principals. Presently, a shot was taken
> through the glass from inside the window, with the same traffic in motion.[55]

After Gypo has informed on Francis he meets Katie in the street outside a
clothes shop. She confesses that she had hidden Francis to protect him
from Gypo. In an instance of dramatic irony she says that she'll never see
Francis again. The sequence opens with an establishing shot of the couple
on the busy street; then their conversation is filmed in shot/reverse-shot
alternation. What could be a conventional sequence is made extraordinary
by using the window of the shop and the bodies of the passers-by to add
a further dimension to the image. The shadows of people walking past the
couple sweep over Gypo's face dramatically. Katie, in contrast, is brightly
lit. Centrally positioned, she is framed on one side by the reflections of the
passing traffic in the shop window behind her and, on the other, by an
inanely grinning mannequin, which is seen through the glass in the shop
window. These rather stylised techniques, paradoxically, add greater
realism to the sequence.

In *The Informer* tension is repeatedly conveyed through close-ups of
hands. The film opens with the fist of the insurgents' leader Gallagher
(Warwick Ward) thumping determinedly on the table. Francis, although in
fear of being caught, visits Katie in her apartment to see if she will run
away with him to America. She tells him that things have changed. There
is a fade from a close-up of Francis to Gypo walking happily along the
street holding flowers – suggesting that Francis realises who his rival is.
Robison cuts back to Francis's face and the camera follows his hand as it
moves to stub out his cigarette on the ashtray. Shortly afterwards, Katie has
to hide Francis in the kitchen as Gypo has turned up at her apartment for

their date. Francis tells Katie, 'get me out of here', and she looks off-screen to Gypo in the other room. This is followed by a close-up of a knife being held horizontally – the camera pulls back to reveal that Gypo is about to cut bread. (Both shots are reminiscent of Hitchcock, who would include a similarly evocative knife sequence in his contemporaneous *Blackmail*.) There is now a close-up of Francis's hand as he hangs precariously from the roof of his mother's house just before he falls to his death.

An Excessively Visual Style

Brandes' BIP films present a montage of the modern world: streets, cafés, clubs, bars, cinemas – these are spaces where the crowd congregates. The Dupont films, in particular, are built around spectacle – Kracauer's 'surface distractions'. Close-ups of legs abound, a hallmark of Dupont's films, reflecting the exotic, sensual nature of the worlds the characters inhabit – and an excuse, perhaps, to titillate the audience: '[It's] basically … a "leg" show', *Kinematograph Weekly*'s reviewer remarked upon *Moulin Rouge*.[56] Yet character psychology and narrative are similarly important: Lya de Putti in *The Informer* is shot very differently from Anna May Wong and Olga Chekhova in Dupont's films, as the film downplays her star appeal in favour of her role in a gripping plot of betrayal.

In *The Informer*, Brandes often adopts a more subdued approach to style, which might be indicative of Robison's endeavour for realism. Although form is very often adapted to suit content, his Elstree films provide a virtuoso display of cinematic techniques: superimpositions, double exposures, chiaroscuro lighting effects, long tracking shots, used flamboyantly in Dupont's films, and with more restraint in *The Informer*.

Many contemporary critics delighted in a cinematic spectacle based upon the creative use of the camera's potential. Cinematography in these films is frequently not merely 'denotative' but privileges its own artifice. This style has more in common with the 'cinema of attractions', a term coined by Tom Gunning to describe early cinema's propensity for showmanship and spectacle rather than the effacement and narrative of the 'classic' style which followed it.[57]

This stylistic melange, however, aggravated some critics from the British cultural elite who agreed with Mannock that 'art should conceal art'.[58] Contemporary reviewers repeatedly observed that, although technique was clearly improving, dramatic values were frequently neglected. Lionel Collier, for instance, in a review of *Moulin Rouge* noted that 'technique is remarkable … But plot value is negligible'. He argued that 'even characterisation is swamped in this maelstrom of spectacular appeal'.[59]

Narrative, in these films, is indeed often subservient to an almost purely visual film style. There are sequences that serve no purpose but to show off the spectacular sets and superb lighting effects. This is typical of art cinema modes of production where stylistic developments have always been pushed to greater lengths. And it was this same strategy, developed in the mid-1920s under Pommer at Ufa, which many commentators on the industry in Britain hoped would be a viable commercial alternative to Hollywood in the latter part of the decade.

BIP's breakthrough export techniques were creating in the films a look of 'quality and variety' to which Brandes contributed significantly. His role was recognised as such in contemporary reviews, where he is almost always mentioned by name. 'Few British films have been more artistically set or better photographed. There is nothing freakish about the latter, but it is full of well composed shots with most effectual lighting. The credit for this goes to the German cameraman, Werner Brands [*sic*], who is a very real asset to the BIP studios.'[60] The same reviewer commented on *Piccadilly*: 'So much for the plot. It is not, however, the plot that goes to make the appeal of this picture, it is first and last a cameraman's production. Werner Brandes has given us arresting camerawork which has never been equalled in a British feature.'[61] Even *Close Up*, a journal which frequently criticised the internationalist ambitions of BIP, would write that 'Werner Brandes, at least, achieved something with the camera ...'[62]

BIP's production strategies, at least initially, proved successful. The company, branding its output as big-budget productions of quality and variety, received remarkable publicity for its films. Many of them were released in the USA, and by 1930 critics were often referring to the studio by name.[63] Only eleven of the forty-seven BIP productions that included German personnel did not feature in *Variety*'s review section.

Joe Grossman, one-time production manager at BIP, said of *Piccadilly* that '[It] cost a fabulous sum, but the company took the view that it would be excellent prestige for British films at the time ...'[64] Grossman refers to the artistic flourishes in these films as 'production touches'. But, 'while these "touches" were original and produced prestige, they were extremely costly and boosted up the original estimated costs of his [Dupont's] films beyond all expectations'.[65] The films therefore would have to be guaranteed a market abroad if this strategy was to be a success.

In 1927 a press party had been invited to visit BIP's studios. A journalist reported that 'a rather unusual spectacle will be British, German and American directors working under the same roof ...'[66] BIP was founded along these international lines and its acquisitions were an important part of the films' promotion. On the front page of *Bioscope* in 1927 there is a BIP advertisement which lists the 'first rate directors and stars' then working for the company.[67] The studios were hardly 'a burial ground for Hollywood has-beens',[68] as Paul Rotha and Hugh Castle have argued.[69]

Werner Brandes' contribution to BIP was twofold. His adoption of an international style gave a distinctive edge to BIP's films on the world market and his presence at the studios – the dedication and expertise he demonstrated – influenced a younger generation of British cameramen, who would adopt a similar craftsman-like approach to their own work. In this he contributed more generally to the rejuvenation of the industry in the late 1920s and 1930s.

Notes

1. Sourced from the annual 'In Production' charts in Linda Wood, *British Films 1927–1939* (London: BFI, 1986), p. 124.
2. Figures established from cross-referencing BIP productions with Linda Wood's statistics in *British Films 1927–1939*, Denis Gifford's *The British Film Catalogue, 1895–1985: A Reference Guide* (Newton Abbot, Devon; London: David & Charles, 1986), and the SIFT database at the BFI (which itself utilises these resources). This is supplemented by my own research into BIP's productions.
3. This is part of a larger research project which will look at the contribution of German cinematographers to BIP from 1927 to 1936.
4. 'The English have stood still, if not going backward. They did not seem to even pick up the fundamentals of better picture making from their sparse few that have reached these shores, while the Americans, as admitted, have swiftly advanced, but none have progressed as have the Germans if *Variety*, the picture, may be taken as a model of their current output'. Review of *Varieté* (E.A. Dupont, 1925) in *Variety*, 30 June 1926.
5. Sinclair Hill, 'Continental Studios Today', *Kinematograph Weekly*, 20 September 1928, p. 67. D. Dickinson is presumably Desmond Dickinson (1903–86) who worked as a cameraman for Hill on six films in the late 1920s and early 1930s. See Duncan Petrie, *The British Cinematographer* (London: BFI, 1996), pp. 89–92.
6. Hill, 'Continental Studios Today', p. 67.
7. John Maxwell, 'British Pictures Abroad', *The Times*, 19 March 1929, p. ix.
8. 'British National Strengthened', *Kinematograph Weekly*, 13 January 1927, p. 56.
9. 'Mr E.A. Dupont has been appointed by BNP Ltd., director-general of productions at the new studio at Elstree.' *The Times*, 22 December 1926, p. 10. Kristin Thompson argues that 'Germany's system was closer to the Hollywood mode of production than were those of France or the USSR'. Kristin Thompson, 'Early Alternatives to the Hollywood Mode of Production', *Film History*, vol. 5, 1993, p. 388.
10. 'British National Strengthened', p. 56.
11. '"We Cannot Prey on Exhibitors"', *Bioscope*, 23 January 1929, p. 23.
12. 'Britain's Hollywood', *Kinematograph Weekly*, 13 January 1927, p. 105.
13. 'British National Strengthened', p. 56.
14. '"We Cannot Prey on Exhibitors"', p. 23.
15. See Jan-Christopher Horak, 'Sauerkraut & Sausages with a Little Goulash: Germans in Hollywood, 1927', *Film History*, vol. 17, no. 2/3, 2005, p. 243; Thomas Elsaesser and Michael Wedel (eds.), *The BFI Companion to German Cinema* (London: BFI, 1999), p. 53. Kristin Thompson has noted how in 1927 the German industry had reorganised its approach to production by introducing several 'Produktionsleiter', or 'production chiefs', following the Hollywood model. See Thompson, 'Early Alternatives', p. 395.
16. Elsaesser and Wedel (eds.), *The BFI Companion to German Cinema*, p. 53.
17. Indeed, Sparkuhl, who assisted Brandes on *The Informer*, was the first cameraman to allow Cardiff to crank the camera. This was on the musical *Harmony Heaven* (Thomas Bentley, 1929). See Jack Cardiff, *Magic Hour: The Life of a Cameraman* (London: Faber and Faber, 1996), p. 18.
18. Jack Cardiff, interview with the author, 28 September 2005.
19. Sinclair Hill, 'Continental Studios Today', p. 67.
20. Jack Cardiff, interview with the author, 28 September 2005.

21. Freddie Young, *Seventy Light Years: A Life in the Movies* (London: Faber and Faber, 1999), p. 19.
22. Jack Cardiff, interview with the author, 28 September 2005. Austrian Heinrich Gärtner and German Bruno Mondi were two cameramen working for BIP at Elstree.
23. Felix Bucher, *Germany* (Screen series) (London: A. Zwemmer; New York: A.S. Barnes, 1970), p. 24.
24. *Die Herrin der Welt* was one of the few films to have received proper distribution in the USA by the Hamilton Film Corporation through Paramount in 1921. This followed the success of the Lubitsch films *Madame Dubarry* and *Anna Boleyn* in the United States. See Jan-Christopher Horak, 'Rin-Tin-Tin in Berlin or American Cinema in Weimar', *Film History*, vol. 5, no. 1, 1993, p. 50. For an extensive filmography of Brandes' work in Germany see www.filmportal.de.
25. Brandes worked with Krampf on *Die Legende von der heiligen Simplicia* (Joe May, 1920), with Sparkuhl on *S.O.S. Die Insel der Tränen* (Lothar Mendes, 1923) and with Puth on *Die grüne Manuela*. In Britain, Sparkuhl assisted him on *The Informer* and Puth on *White Cargo*. Sparkuhl would go on to shoot eight films for BIP. David Cunynghame also considered Sparkuhl, whom he saw shooting scenes on *The Informer*, to be 'a quick worker'. David Cunynghame, 'Film Diary', Monday 27 May 1929, The David Cunynghame Collection, held at Special Collections at the British Film Institute. Cunynghame worked in various positions whilst at BIP, including the casting office, the cutting room, as a camera assistant, as a second assistant director and as a member of the sound department. He later became production manager at London Films, where in 1936 he had to defend the company's employment of foreign cameramen. See Kevin Gough-Yates, 'The British Feature Film as a European Concern: Britain and the Émigré Film-Maker, 1933–45', in Günter Berghaus (ed.), *Theatre and Film in Exile. German Artists in Britain, 1933–1945* (Oxford/New York/Munich: Berg, 1989), p. 150.
26. See Elsaesser and Wedel (eds.), *The BFI Companion to German Cinema*, p. 53.
27. Brandes' prolific 1930s output includes German and Austrian films such as *Liebeswalzer/The Love Waltz* (Wilhelm Thiele, 1930), *Emil und die Detektive* (Gerhard Lamprecht, 1931), *G'schichten aus dem Wienerwald* (Georg Jacoby, 1934), *Die Töchter Ihrer Exzellenz* (Reinhold Schünzel, 1934), *Der Herrscher* (Veit Harlan, 1937), and *Finale* (Geza von Bolvary, 1938). In the late 1930s he went to Switzerland, where he worked on a few more films.
28. David Cunynghame, 'Film Diary', Monday 24 June 1929. *White Cargo* was originally shot silent; BIP decided to reshoot certain scenes with sound. Freddie Young confirms that Brandes had by then returned to Germany, and so he was asked to take over the photography. 'We were given a week to complete this, because BIP wanted the studio back to do the sound sequences on *Blackmail*.' Young, *Seventy Light Years*, p. 24. Unfortunately, it shows. The sound version of *White Cargo* has stilted dialogue and unimaginative cinematography.
29. See 'Activity in British Industry', *The Times*, 13 April 1927, p. 12, and 'Anglo-German Films New Production Company', *Kinematograph Weekly*, 14 April 1927, p. 34.
30. 'A Scoop. Dupont Signed. British International's Capture', *Kinematograph Weekly*, 18 August 1927, p. 35.
31. See P.L. Mannock, 'British Production', *Kinematograph Weekly*, 1 September 1927, p. 50, and in the same column on 8 September 1927, p. 66. See also 'The Faculty of Herts', *Kinematograph Weekly*, 10 October, 1927, p. 42, where Mannock observes the filming of Olga Chekhova in close-up by 'G. Brandes [*sic*]'.
32. F.G. Culmer, 'Trade Finance', *Kinematograph Weekly*, 26 January 1928, p. 48: 'Two £100,000 films have been in course of completion – *Moulin Rouge* and *A Little Bit of Fluff*.'
33. Mannock, 'British Production News', *Kinematograph Weekly*, 2 August, 1928, p. 26.
34. Mannock, 'Elstree's Extensions', *Kinematograph Weekly*, 26 January 1928, p. 43.
35. *Ibid*.

36. For the scenes in Chinatown, Dupont had hired a Chinese consultant. 'British Production News', *Kinematograph Weekly*, 4 October 1928, p. 38.
37. Mannock, 'Dupont's Acre', *Kinematograph Weekly*, 13 September 1928, p. 51.
38. Mannock, 'British Production News', *Kinematograph Weekly*, 8 November 1928, p. 36.
39. In contrast, when Shosho dances in the same club the camera is uncharacteristically still, in obedience to the more delicate and refined technique adopted by Shosho.
40. Quoted from Kevin Brownlow's documentary *Cinema Europe: The Other Hollywood* (1996). Arthur Crabtree, cameraman at Gainsborough in the 1930s, also took this position. See Duncan Petrie, 'Innovation and Economy: The Contribution of the Gainsborough Cinematographer', in Pam Cook (ed.), *Gainsborough Pictures* (London/Washington: Cassell, 1997), p. 126.
41. 'British International Pictures: A Year of Remarkable Success', *Kinematograph Weekly*, 3 January 1929, p. 95.
42. 'Elstree: Britain's First Big Scale Enterprise, *Bioscope*, 18 June 1927, p. 70.
43. Mannock, 'British Production News', *Kinematograph Weekly*, 8 November 1928, p. 36.
44. See Mannock, 'British Production News', *Kinematograph Weekly*, 6 September 1928, p. 50. Robison, born in Chicago in 1888, enters the German film industry in the mid-1910s. In 1930 he directs German and French versions of MGM films in Hollywood, then returns to Germany where he dies in 1935.
45. See Mannock, 'British Production News', *Kinematograph Weekly*, 7 March 1929, p. 32. Mannock found Robison to be 'a thoroughly charming personality ... a commanding figure in a black silk dressing gown'. See also 'An Irish Crowd: Big Scale Realism in Robison's Complete Street' in Mannock's 'British Production News', *Kinematograph Weekly*, 18 April 1929, p. 41.
46. Cardiff, *Magic Hour*, p. 15.
47. Ibid.
48. Mannock, 'British Production News', *Kinematograph Weekly*, 7 March 1929, p. 32.
49. 'At this stage, internationalism was seen almost exclusively as a matter of adding qualities to films that would make them attractive beyond the borders of their countries of origin. Such qualities might include subject matter that avoided a strong national identification, the use of expensive or sophisticated techniques and the inclusion of internationally famous stars. Such tactics have remained bulwarks of export-minded European producers ever since.' Kristin Thompson, 'National or International Films? The European Debate during the 1920s', *Film History*, vol. 8, 1996, p. 282.
50. See Tim Bergfelder on the 'film operetta' genre in 'Surface and Distraction: Style and Genre at Gainsborough in the late 1920s and 1930s', in Cook, *Gainsborough Pictures*, pp. 31–46.
51. At the end of May 1929 they started shooting a sound version of the film. Although Mannock reported that 'the accents of the various principals are being successfully burnished into a convincing Hibernian brogue', the final version has English actors speaking the dialogue off-screen. Mannock, 'British Production News', *Kinematograph Weekly*, 30 May 1929, p. 22. *Bioscope* in a review of the sound version was disappointed with the lack of genuine Irish voices and said that 'the film would have been better without dialogue at all'. *Bioscope*, 23 October 1929, p. 37.
52. Barry Salt, *Film Style and Technology: History and Analysis*, second expanded edition (London: Starword, 1992), p. 223.
53. In trying to explain the inconsistent quality of Dupont's films, William K. Everson goes so far as to say that Dupont was not responsible for the artistic achievements of his best films. He believes that in both *Moulin Rouge* and *Piccadilly* Dupont was 'helped by the stylists who still surrounded him'. See Everson, 'Program Notes for the New School for Social Research', *Film History*, vol. 15, no. 3, 2003, p. 332.
54. Mannock, 'British Production News', *Kinematograph Weekly*, 18 April 1929, p. 41.
55. Ibid.
56. Lionel Collier, *Kinematograph Weekly*, 29 March 1928, p. 51.

57. See Tom Gunning, 'The Cinema of Attractions: Early Film, Its Spectator and the Avant-Garde', in Thomas Elsaesser (ed.), *Early Cinema: Space, Frame, Narrative* (London: BFI, 1990), pp. 86–94.

58. Mannock, 'Technique Can Be Overdone', *Journal of the Association of Cine-Technicians*, vol. 1, no. 1, May 1935, p. 60.

59. Lionel Collier, 'Reviews of the Week', *Kinematograph Weekly*, 29 March 1928, p. 49.

60. Lionel Collier, Review of *Tesha*, *Kinematograph Weekly*, 30 August 1928, p. 50. In *Tesha*, Brandes' approach to lighting, although more subtle than in the films under discussion here, is just as meticulously crafted. Light emanates from candles, lamps and fires. Tesha (Maria Corda) meets her soon-to-be lover Lenane on the balcony of a hotel in Southampton. The light source (imitating the moon's glow) creates striking shadows of branches on their faces. Tesha's hesitancy in reciprocating Lenane's advances is suggested in the way the figures move in and out of this darkness.

61. Lionel Collier, *Kinematograph Weekly*, 7 February 1929, p. 55.

62. Hugh Castle, 'The Battle of Wardour Street', *Close Up*, March 1929, p. 14.

63. See *Variety*'s review of Dupont's *Atlantic*, 20 November 1929.

64. Joe Grossman, 'Red Letter Days', in Leslie Banks et al., *The Elstree Story* (London: Clerke and Cockeran, 1949), p. 87.

65. Ibid.

66. 'Talk of the Trade', *Bioscope*, 10 November 1929, p. 35.

67. *Bioscope*, 1 December 1927.

68. Paul Rotha, *The Film Till Now: A Survey of World Cinema* (London: Vision Press Ltd, 1951), p. 545.

69. 'Wardour Street agrees we must be "international". Accordingly it solves our problems by importing played out stars and third-rate directors.' Hugh Castle, 'The Battle of Wardour Street', *Close Up*, March 1929, p. 12. It is worth remembering the international success of *Warning Shadows* and, of course, *Varieté*. Although over six years old, the Robison film was frequently revived at the Avenue Pavillion and included amongst a fortnight of German films in 1929 at the Savoy (which included *Varieté*). See 'Long Shots and Close Ups', *Kinematograph Weekly*, 17 January 1929, p. 26, and 'Result of Avenue Pavilion Film Ballot', *Kinematograph Weekly*, 25 April 1929, p. 23.

Chapter 6

FAMOUSLY UNKNOWN: GÜNTHER KRAMPF'S WORK AS CINEMATOGRAPHER IN BRITISH FILMS

Michael Omasta

Günther Krampf must be considered a phantom of film history. The brilliant reputation as a cinematographer that he enjoyed among his peers is curiously at odds with the scant information on his life.[1] Analyses of his filmic work are equally scarce. In books on British film history Krampf barely features; and where references exist, factual mistakes, speculation and untenable assertions abound. A telling example can be found in Geoff Brown's study on Michael Balcon, one of the few reliable German-language publications on British cinema, which includes a photograph from the set of *Little Friend* (1934). Its caption reads, 'To the left of the camera is Berthold Viertel (in a light-coloured suit)' – the man in the picture, however, his right hand propped on his hip in a gesture of mild impatience, is not the film's director but its cinematographer, Günther Krampf.[2]

In 1931 Krampf photographed his first two British pictures, the quota quickie *The Outsider* and *The Bells*, the latter co-directed by fellow émigré Oscar Werndorff. By this time his most productive years had all but run their term. Krampf's forte being the sophisticated *Zeitfilm* – a genre in German cinema that addressed contemporary social issues – he had repeatedly worked with outspoken, politically progressive artists in Weimar Germany, joining forces with author Carl Zuckmayer and film theorist and screenwriter Béla Balázs. Three times he was behind the camera on Prometheus Film productions, a Berlin company co-founded and for many years co-financed by the German Communist Party. They were based on plays by writers with strong KPD affiliations: *Schinderhannes* (1928, original play and script by Zuckmayer), *Cyankali* (1930, original play by Friedrich Wolf) and *Kuhle Wampe* (1932, original screenplay by Bertolt Brecht).

Krampf was capable of doing the impossible. His last silent film, *Narkose* (1929), may be seen as both pinnacle and sum total of his work until then. Written by Balázs after Stefan Zweig's novella *Letter from an Unknown Woman*,[3] the film, told in flashback, recounts the story of an unhappy love affair, which the film's heroine relives while under anaesthetic during the birth of her child. Krampf's camera portrays the duality of the dreamer, motionless in her sleep but active amid her unfolding dream. All the juxtapositions of scenes and optical effects were apparently done in the camera. According to Balázs, 'there were no cuts at all', because the film's style 'demanded a rhythm of shots blending softly into one another' to convey 'the great epic mood of changing fate in the course of a life'.[4]

Such highlights established Krampf's reputation as one of the eminent cinematographers of the German silent era,[5] an artist of the standing of greats such as Eduard Tissé and Gregg Toland.[6] Famous British art director Edward Carrick commented thus:

Artists like Krampf ... look on their work as an artistic contribution to the film. He used to do something which I have never seen done by any other cameraman: he would decide upon a main source of light and from that point switch on a sun arc, which would cause one mighty set of shadows to be cast across the set. These shadows he would then have recorded upon the set by a painter using a spray gun loaded with a darker colour. It was then possible for him to switch on his other subsidiary lights without ever losing his main directional light.[7]

Somewhat less enthusiastic are the assessments of former colleagues and co-workers of Krampf as a person. 'He was very much German in character', Lionel Banes, who met Günther Krampf in 1936 on the set of *The Amateur Gentleman* and frequently worked as his operator,[8] later remembered. 'I don't think I ever actually talked to him', said Ronald Neame who in 1940 was replaced by Krampf during the shooting of *Convoy*, Britain's famous 'first' Second World War film, at Elstree. 'I believe he used so many gismos in front of his lights that the actors had difficulty getting to their marks. Also he hated the fact that they had to walk around spoiling his perfect lighting.'[9] 'He was elderly, smallish with glasses, not very sociable and the only contact was with work', recalls Manny Yospa who worked with Krampf at Welwyn Garden City Film Studios in the early 1940s. 'I especially remember him because he was insistent on soft photography. He had his own special diffusion filter, slightly chipped, and in addition used the standard diffusers, and with his soft lighting nothing was sharp. I was the focus puller and was told off for not getting it sharp but Gunther was delighted.'[10]

None of Krampf's work – except *Der Student von Prag* (*The Student of Prague*, 1926) and, possibly, *The Ghoul* (1933), whose visuals may be considered as a parody of old German horror films – has anything to do with Expressionism.[11] On the contrary: his most distinguished work on Austrian and German silent films – Robert Wiene's *Orlac's Hände* (*The Hands of Orlac*, 1924), and Pabst's *Die Büchse der Pandora* (*Pandora's Box*, 1928) – provides ample proof of the keen interest he had in naturalism – a slightly exaggerated, but nevertheless *realist* vision of the world.

Krampf's self-conception as a cinematographer went well beyond that of a mere technician; it was that of an artist who feels responsible for all aspects of a film and longs to be involved in its making from the very beginning. In one of his few statements on his work, a text on the advantages and disadvantages of using multiple cameras in sound film, Krampf arrived at the predictable conclusion that it is more practical to use just a single camera, to 'put up with having to move lights' and, moreover, to 'do what was not always done in silent films: in a briefing meeting, director, cameraman and sound engineer go through the script and decide at what points the camera can and will need to switch position.'[12]

Rome Express, the first of six films Krampf photographed for Gaumont-British between 1932 and 1936,[13] may well have suited his preferred way of working. Michael Balcon, Gaumont-British's chief of production at the time, set great store by staff trained in Berlin studios and hired experienced cinematographers such as Otto Kanturek and Mutz Greenbaum, and art directors such as Ernö Metzner and Alfred Junge, from the continent. He 'presented these illustrious talents to his homegrown force as teachers as well as studio colleagues, partly, perhaps, to justify the superior income his émigrés enjoyed; their lessons at any rate, were readily absorbed'.[14]

Krampf played a special role in this context. *Rome Express* was Balcon's first production for Gaumont-British and the first to be filmed in the newly opened Shepherd's Bush studios; purportedly, Krampf acted as a consultant in fitting out the studios and '[m]any of the best ideas of the German studios were thus incorporated'.[15] These included the so-called Schüfftan process, a special-effects technique originally devised in 1923 that was first used in a British production on this streamlined comedy thriller. In *Picturegoer Weekly*, director Walter Forde wrote in some detail about 'How We Made *Rome Express*':

> The rub came when we were faced with the problem of making a film of a moving train against the right scenery, on the right route, with a model which, though true to dimensions, was stationary. The camera staff and myself made the journey from Paris to Rome several times, picking out the most typical and at the same time the most beautiful scenery and photographing it. When we returned, this film by a studio process was photographed again at the same time as the film in the studio and the result is the impression you now have of a train moving rapidly along on the journey from Paris to Rome … Part of the action in the film takes place during the night. Clearly the cameraman who travelled through France and Italy could not photograph after sun-down. On one of the stages, therefore, was assembled a forty-foot model comprising midget stations, farms and houses, advertisements, telegraph poles, trees, fields and hills.

Parallel to the model, which was painted a very dark grey, ran a track carrying a mobile camera. The studio was thrown into complete darkness but for a spotlight fixed to the camera. A strip of board, slotted at intervals, was placed between the spotlight and the model. The effect was to throw a reflection on to the model similar to that produced by a moving train.[16]

Although Forde avoids mentioning Krampf, it becomes obvious that the tremendous success of *Rome Express* had more to do with the advanced technical resources at Shepherd's Bush and the expertise of the cine-technicians than with the story or the direction. The camera keeps the action going, literally – it travels up and down the narrow corridors of the train in front of the actors, speeding up the action by means of short, fast close-ups shot slightly from below. Periodically, Krampf reminds us of the train's speed, either by having one of the passengers open a window, enhancing the rhythmical sound of the express, or by depicting the train rushing along through a tunnel.

Newspaper advertisements promised 'a lifetime of adventure in one night on a train!'[17] From today's point of view, however, Krampf's camerawork is the only major asset of the film – whereas the plot involving 'a runaway wife ... an erring husband ... a famous detective ... a murderer ... a male gossip ... a bored movie star ... a young lover ... men and women from all walks of life'[18] is highly predictable and some of the acting rather hard to bear. Even the film's 'master villain', Conrad Veidt in his British screen debut, looks bored; the only time he does come across as menacing is the scene in which he is about to throw a deceiving accomplice out of the window of the moving train: 'You need the holiday badly, my friend'.

Rome Express was no doubt immensely important for Krampf's British career. Audiences and critics were impressed, and critical voices few and far between. 'Technically, and in a sense intellectually speaking, this film puts Forde into class A1', wrote Basil Wright, articulating a general feeling of unease with such a piece of commercial cinema devoid of all substance. 'I would suggest, however, both to him and Gaumont, that there are in England things more important, more exciting, and no less box office, than the Gare de Lyon and the P.L.M. Railway, on which the vast resources of Shepherd's Bush should be concentrated without a moment's delay.'[19]

What this review addresses applies more generally to Krampf's career in the British film industry. The artistic and political relevance of the approximately thirty-five productions he worked on generally fails to live up to the cinematographer's abilities. Critical praise for Krampf's mostly outstanding achievements behind the camera is usually expressed *ex negativo*. Exceptions such as *Little Friend*, the dream-like story of a small girl, who is distraught at the break-up of her parents' marriage, just serve to prove the rule. Astute critics like Paul Rotha did not fail to notice the film's serious flaws, '[b]ut, and this is the point, it marks a breakaway for Gaumont-British into more worthwhile subjects and for that deserves our recognition'.[20]

The opening paragraph of a review of *The Ghoul* in *Picturegoer Weekly* is both telling and typical: 'Britain's contribution to the thriller cycle is definitely poor, its main asset is the undoubtedly clever and striking photography by Gunther Krampf, the brilliant German cameraman.'[21] Equally noteworthy in this context is the reasoning of the cine-technicians' trade union ACT, which took a similar stance just a few years later, if for only too transparent political motifs. 'When ... the Association of Cinematographic Technicians provided a written statement to the Ministry of Labour on 28 June 1937, on the subject of foreign technicians in the British film industry, it complained that the eminent lighting cameraman Günther Krampf was working on a film not worthy of his talents', Kevin Gough-Yates reports in his seminal essay on émigré filmmakers in Britain. 'It could, the union argued, have been photographed by "a British cameraman".'[22] Krampf himself may well have felt the same. In any case, there is some indication from the mid-1930s onwards that he was not happy with his life and working conditions in the UK. It also seems that he had never intended to stay in the country for good, and allegedly never bothered to learn English.[23]

In the winter of 1934/35 Krampf returned to Nazi Germany to photograph Gustav Ucicky's *Das Mädchen Johanna* (*Joan of Arc*), an anti-British Ufa production that focused on the historical heroine's fanatical love of her fatherland and her fierce battle against the English.[24] It is not without irony that, of all his films, it was this picture that was lavished with praise not only by German critics but also by parts of the British press. 'We experience Günther Krampf's achievement behind the camera full of admiration', applauded the Berlin *Film-Kurier*. 'He vividly paints the horrors of the Plague and the terrors of war, the eerie blaze of the stakes and the glowing promise of the symbols.'[25] This is even surpassed by the British *Life and Letters To-Day* magazine, which favourably compares the Nazi picture with domestic productions: 'The whole film is, indeed, of the period; with a good feeling for armour and none of that parvenu lighting which Korda would have given to the Middle Ages.'[26]

In early 1936, Krampf sued Standard-Film, a short-lived Viennese production outfit, for breach of contract. He had initially been assigned to work on a film called *Mausi* (which never got made), but ultimately the company refused to employ the cinematographer as it had turned out that he was *not* a member of the *Reichsfilmkammer*, a subdivision of Goebbels' Ministry of Propaganda controlling the production of German films and those made in Austria for German distribution. According to a brief report in an Austrian trade paper, the Viennese court had requested information from Berlin, resulting in the advice to 'the Austrian authorities that K. had hitherto neither applied for membership nor had it ever been granted to him'. The court arrived at a typically Viennese verdict: It dismissed 'the cameraman's overall claim – of 10,000 Schilling and 2,000 Reichsmark – but awarded him half the sum'.[27] It remains unclear whether Krampf either had 'forgotten' to apply for membership or simply could not do so because he was possibly of Jewish descent. Be that as it may, one can only speculate how he got a job on the prestigious Nazi production *Das Mädchen Johanna* in the first place.

It is fair to assume that 1935/36 marked a turning point in Krampf's life. Evidently, any chances of the cinematographer finding further work in Germany or Austria had fizzled out during the few months between his Ufa engagement and the above-quoted notification from Berlin. At the same time, Krampf's years at Gaumont-British were coming to an end as well.[28] *The Tunnel* (shot in 1935, released in 1936), his penultimate film for the company, is a production of imposing dimensions, made with an eye to the American market. A big-scale fantasy adventure based on a script by Kurt Siodmak, and with sets designed by fellow émigré Ernö Metzner (see Laurie Ede in this volume), it tells the story of the building of a transatlantic tunnel connecting Britain and the United States. Even its opening scene, a musical soirée to which wheelchair-bound billionaire Lloyd has invited potential financiers of the project, denotes pure luxury. At first, we hear more than we see, being presented with the conductor's back; the camera then slowly travels backwards, opening up our field of vision to reveal, one after another, the orchestra, the hall, and finally the audience. As elaborate as this scene may be, it also highlights the extent to which Krampf is forced to submit to the logic of budget and production values.

It is primarily the more intimate scenes, those *not* dominated by Metzner's outsized sets, that allow Krampf to achieve extraordinary lighting effects and astonishing camerawork, frequently making use of flat focus. The backgrounds are brightly lit, but often slightly out of focus; all our attention is directed on the actors. Ruth (Madge Evans), the neglected wife of the tunnel's architect, McAllan (Richard Dix), has, at the advice of her best friend, taken a job in the tunnel company's sickbay. We have hardly seen her at work in her white nurse's uniform when she suddenly collapses and passes out. Cut, the camera switches over to a subjective perspective, revealing the blurry silhouettes of two doctors approaching, who a few moments ago were discussing the symptoms of the insidious tunnel sickness. Complicated medical tests are not required; a point-of-view shot is more than enough to deliver the diagnosis: Ruth is going blind.

Owing to Krampf, *The Tunnel* succeeds not only as pacifist science fiction in its plot of uniting the people of two continents, but also as melodrama. McAllan, who only lives for his idea, not only sacrifices his marriage to the tunnel but also his son, who dies in the eruption of an underwater volcano. Having broken off all contact with her husband and hiding her illness from him, Ruth retires to the country. The emotional turning point of the film is marked by a scene in which Varlia Lloyd (Helen Vinson), the billionaire's daughter, comes to see Ruth at her country retreat to convince her over a cup of tea to agree to divorce McAllan: 'I can't understand how you can be so careless. Can't you see how he suffers, how he's changed, are you *blind*?' At that moment the music stops. We see a close-up of Ruth, her face in soft focus, framed, Madonna-like, by a halo of blazing light: 'Yes, quite blind.'

With the simplest of means, Krampf here enhances Ruth's dreary reality by literally blanking out anything that might distract us from the essence of the scene. He paints with light. The following passage from an article for *World Film News*, in which he seems to assure himself yet again of his artistic means, reads as if Krampf had this scene in mind:

> Technical devices are certainly important. In the Germany of 1920, there was little money to be spent on pictures, and filmmakers had to be very ingenious. Necessity led to the discovery of panning, trucking and low camera-angle ... In film, truth and sincerity are hard to obtain. There are so many temptations to over-light a set, to avoid dirt and untidiness where they should normally be. Producers will tell you that the cinema public wishes to see things clean, beautiful, glamorous. But I do not believe this to be the case. You can arouse the emotions only by the representation of truth. A white-washed wall for background, with an actor properly directed, well lit and composed, will express this as adequately as an elaborate set, and probably more truthfully. The false economy of methods of production has been largely responsible for many failures ... [T]he tendency is, as in Hollywood, to spend an enormous sum of money on elaborate, artificial scenes with glamour and glitter – scenes which can be simply classified as entertainment. The whole attitude is wrong. The thing of fundamental importance is to tell the story by the picture, to stick closely to the visual effect. In this, the basic principle of movie, film has a language in which to speak to all nationalities. In this, it is an art.[29]

Considering Krampf's familiarity with major productions, this text lends itself to be seen not only as a 'rehashing ... of the old, and, one is tempted to say, never-ending German debate on the film poet',[30] but also, and more importantly, as a surprisingly pithy declaration of an increasingly frustrated artist who has come to realise that he is but a small interchangeable cogwheel in the dynamics of a huge film industry, and wasting his time.

In subsequent years, especially during the Second World War, Krampf had the opportunity to work, as a freelancer, on war and propaganda films produced at the Ealing and Welwyn studios.[31] These films not only allowed him to demonstrate his inventiveness but also forced him to draw on the finesse of his camerawork to compensate for often poor production conditions. A good example in this context is *The Night Has Eyes*, Leslie Arliss's old-dark-house picture of 1942. Two young women set out for the Yorkshire moors in search of a friend who disappeared a year before and was never seen again. They are caught in a storm and seek shelter in a country house owned by a composer and shell-shocked veteran of the Spanish Civil War (played by a young James Mason), who is suspected of being a murderer.

Krampf and art director Duncan Sutherland worked wonders with their limited B-movie resources. The moor was constructed on Welwyn

Studios' small sound stage. Several decades later, when interviewed about the making of the film, Mason recalled:

> In the days when fog was thought to be a necessary ingredient of the British thriller ... our cameraman was a perfectionist, Gunther Krampf. He had to see that the fog remained consistent through every scene of that last exciting sequence. If too thick, the doors of the stage had to be opened to release some of it; if too thin, more waiting while the fog men laid it on with their bellows, Gunther gazing at it steadfastly through his little square of dark glass.[32]

There is one superb shot early on in the film where we first see Mason and the old dark house that stands stark and brooding in silhouette amidst the storm with the single small frame of an open door ominously lit up. Apart from the dramatic effect they created, fog and storm were perfect to cover up the use of miniatures disappearing in the depths of the moor, obviously to great success. 'The film was originally rated "A" by the British censor, then suddenly changed to "H" (for Horrific), making it off-limits to everyone under 16.'[33]

The production conditions Krampf encountered during his work with Alfred Hitchcock were even tighter. *Bon Voyage* and *Aventure Malgache*, two half-hour anti-Nazi films made with French actors and technicians for the Ministry of Information in 1944 and, like *The Night Has Eyes*, shot at the Welwyn Studios, were filmed in five days each. Both employ flashback narratives. In *Bon Voyage*, Dougall, a Scottish RAF pilot, upon the request of officials of Free France reports of his escape through France with an Allied agent named Godowski. Members of the resistance smuggle them from place to place. Tracks are covered up in a train tunnel and supplies and bicycles await them in a barn. In a second flashback Dougall learns that his Polish companion was a Nazi spy who scouted the secret networks of the resistance fighters.

Like everyone else working on these films, Krampf is not credited in either of the two productions. Rather than aiming for propaganda effect, both seem more interested in the suspense they create, an impression further enhanced by their 'noir' look. Striking black and white contrasts, usually absent from Krampf's British films, dominate the flashback sequences and the background story of *Bon Voyage*. During his interrogation, deep shadows ominously cast the wall behind the unsuspecting Sergeant Dougall in a menacing deep black. The whole universe seems to be playing some sort of diabolical trick on him.

It has yet to be conclusively established whether the two films were ever put on general public release at the time. In any case, Duncan Petrie argues that Krampf 'was never able to re-establish himself after the war and consequently his career drew to a close'.[34] Illness may have added to Krampf's problems, as he developed stomach cancer that ultimately led to his death. Krampf's last film of note, *Fame Is the Spur* (Roy Boulting, 1947), is an earnest account of a politician's career loosely based on the life of

Labour leader Ramsay MacDonald. Hamer Radshaw (Michael Redgrave), as the film's anti-hero is renamed, a man of great ability but even greater ambition, gradually, and without even realising it, sacrifices all his ideals. 'Oh yes, Hamer can believe everything he wants to', says his wife Ann (Rosamund John).

Political betrayal and the estrangement of husband and wife are inextricably interwoven. Hamer does not do anything to stop his wife's arrest when she disrupts one of his statesmanlike public speeches with shouts demanding the right to vote for women. The following scene, shot with extreme depth of field, is among the most brutal sequences of the film. We witness how Rachel, one of Ann's comrades-in-arms, is being force-fed while on hunger strike. Doctor and nurses are, menacingly magnified, at work in the foreground, while in the background we can make out a battery of medical instruments and the open door of the cell. Of all the films Krampf photographed during his years in Britain, *Fame Is the Spur* was certainly the most ambitious. A veritable flop at the time of its release, it today counts among the central works of British postwar cinema.[35] It is symptomatic of Krampf's major difficulties in continuing to land interesting jobs as a freelancer after the war that he was no longer first choice as the cinematographer of this film. 'After a few days of shooting', remembers Richard Best, editor of *Fame Is the Spur*, 'the Boultings were not satisfied with the work of the original cameraman they had hired and replaced him with Gunther Krampf – who did a superb job on main photography of the whole picture. I believe Harry Waxman did some second unit. My memories of Gunther are of a very warm and friendly person.'[36]

Günther Krampf died in London on 7 August 1950. The most extensive obituary hardly exceeds forty words: 'Günther Krampf, the well-known cameraman, unexpectedly died in London following of an operation. Krampf, who used to work in Germany, had lived in England for more than ten years; his last film, *Portrait of Clare*, was only premiered a few weeks ago.'[37]

Translation: Christine Wagner.

Acknowledgements

Special thanks for his invaluable help to Roy Fowler (London) who not only researched the actual date of Krampf's death but also contacted some of Krampf's former colleagues and allowed me to quote from emails by Ronald Neame, Emmanuel Yospa and Richard Best.

Notes

1. Krampf's family background remains in the dark: both the year and the place of his birth have as yet to be established. The date of birth usually referred to (8 February 1899) is definitely incorrect; according to the London Family Records Centre, Krampf was already sixty when he died in 1950. A note on the spelling of his first name: Günther Krampf's first name is correctly spelled with an Umlaut, but during his time in Britain he was mostly credited as Gunther. This article retains both forms, but does not use other variations in circulation at the time (such as Gunter or Guenther).

2. Geoff Brown, *Der Produzent – Michael Balcon und der englische Film* (Berlin: Volker Spiess, 1981), p. 66.

3. In 1948 Max Ophüls directed a well-known Hollywood adaptation, *Letter from an Unknown Woman.*

4. Béla Balázs, *Filmkultúra. A film müvészetfilozófiaja* (Budapest: Szikra, 1948), p. 127. Quoted from Joseph Zsuffa, *Béla Balázs. The Man and the Artist* (Berkeley, Los Angeles and London: University of California Press, 1987), p. 161.

5. When I interviewed director Fred Zinnemann in the early 1990s on his work with Karl Freund on *The Seventh Cross* (1944), it transpired that he couldn't stand Freund's Teutonic behaviour and considered three cinematographers of the German silent era to be far superior: Günther Krampf, Curt Courant and Fritz Arno Wagner.

6. See Edward Carrick, *Designing for Films* (London and New York: The Studio Publications, 1941), p. 27.

7. Ibid., pp. 78–79. This passage is accompanied by a photograph from Henrik Galeen's *Der Student von Prag* (*The Student of Prague*, 1926) on which Krampf worked as cinematographer; the only film Carrick and Krampf collaborated on was *The Amateur Gentleman* (1936).

8. Alan Lawson, *Lionel Banes: BECTU Interview* (1992).

9. Email by Ronald Neame, 15 July 2000.

10. Email by Manny (Emmanuel) Yospa, 14 October 2000.

11. A widespread misconception relates to Krampf's alleged work on Murnau's *Nosferatu – Eine Sinfonie des Grauens* (1922). In fact, Krampf was not involved in photographing this German Expressionist classic, although he did shoot the dialogue scenes added to the film's re-release version (and critical disaster), *Die zwölfte Stunde* (1930).

12. 'Was sagen die Techniker? Günther Krampf: Mehrere Kameras für Tonfilme?', *Film-Kurier*, 24 May 1930.

13. Followed by *Sleeping Car* (Anatole Litvak, 1933), *The Ghoul* (T. Hayes Hunter, 1933), *Little Friend* (Berthold Viertel, 1934), *The Tunnel* (Maurice Elvey, 1936) and *Everything is Thunder* (Milton Rosmer, 1936).

14. Geoff Brown, 'A Knight and His Castle', in Brown, *Michael Balcon: The Pursuit of British Cinema* (New York: The Museum of Modern Art, 1984), p. 20.

15. Short, unsigned Krampf biography attached to Gunther Krampf, 'The Curse of Dialogue', *World Film* News, no. 11, February 1937, p. 4.

16. Walter Forde, 'How We Made *Rome Express*', *Picturegoer Weekly*, 17 December 1932, pp. 8–9.

17. *The Galveston Daily News*, 21 May 1933, p. 12.

18. Ibid.

19. B.W., '*Rome Express*', *Cinema Quarterly*, vol. 1, no. 2, Winter 1932, p. 113.

20. Paul Rotha, '*Little Friend*', *Cinema Quarterly*, vol. 3, no. 1, Autumn 1934, p. 52.

21. Lionel Collier, *Picturegoer Weekly*, 14 October 1933, p. 28.

22. Kevin Gough-Yates, 'The British Feature Film as a European Concern. Britain and the Emigré Film-Maker, 1933–45', in Günter Berghaus (ed.), *Theatre and Film in Exile: German Artists in Britain, 1933–1945* (Oxford, New York and Munich: Berg, 1989), p. 141.

23. Lionel Banes, for instance, is convinced that he was made Krampf's operator, a position he was to occupy for many years, because he spoke some German. See Peter Sargent,

Lionel Banes: BECTU Interview Part 2 (1988), quoted from www.screenonline.org.uk/audio/id/952263/index.html. Kevin Gough-Yates also refers to a court case of October 1936 in which Krampf made his statement with the help of an interpreter. Gough-Yates, 'Berthold Viertel at Gaumont-British', in Jeffrey Richards (ed.), *The Unknown 1930s. An Alternative History of the British Cinema, 1929–1939* (London and New York: I.B. Tauris, 1998), p. 256.

24. Krampf was of course not the only well-known later émigré working in the German film industry until the mid- or late 1930s; Anton Walbrook, Reinhold Schünzel, Jan Kiepura and Douglas Sirk are other examples. However, Krampf must have been aware that director Ucicky openly sympathised with the Nazis. In 1933, he already had directed *Morgenrot* and *Flüchtlinge*, both of which promoted the National Socialist movement.

25. Georg Herzberg, *Film-Kurier*, 27 April 1935.

26. *Life and Letters To-Day*, vol. 13, no. 2, December 1935, pp. 185–186.

27. 'Arierparagraph vor dem Wiener Gewerbegericht', *Österreichische Film-Zeitung*, 12 June 1930.

28. Michael Balcon also left Gaumont-British in 1936 to become head of production with MGM British; this might have contributed to Krampf leaving.

29. Gunther Krampf, 'The Curse of Dialogue', *World Film News*, no. 11, February 1937, p. 4.

30. See Thomas Brandlmeier, '"Rationalization first". Deutsche Kameraschule im britischen Film', in Jörg Schöning (ed.), *London Calling. Deutsche im britischen Film der dreißiger Jahre* (Munich: edition text+kritik, 1993), p. 75.

31. Charles Barr's *Ealing Studios* (London: Cameron & Taylor, 1977) offers an excellent overview of the war films produced at Ealing, among them *Convoy* (1940).

32. Clive Hirschhorn, *The Films of James Mason* (London: LSP Books, 1975), pp. 55–56.

33. Kevin Sweeney, *James Mason: A Bio-Bibliography* (Westport/London: Greenwood Press, 1999), p. 102.

34. Duncan Petrie, *The British Cinematographer* (London: BFI, 1996), p. 115.

35. A comprehensive assessment of the significance and reception history of the film is provided by Brian McFarlane, '*Fame Is the Spur:* An Honourable Failure', in Alan Burton, Tim O'Sullivan and Paul Wells (eds.), *The Family Way. The Boulting Brothers and Postwar British Film Culture* (Trowbridge: Flicks Books, 2000), pp. 122–33.

36. Email by Richard Best, 18 January 2001.

37. *Aufbau*, 25 August 1950, p. 12. Although unsigned, the obituary can no doubt be attributed to Paul Marcus. In an issue *of Pem's Personal Bulletins* published a few days earlier, he wrote: '*P.B.B.* regrets to report the death of cameraman Guenther Krampf in London after an operation.' *Pem's Personal Bulletins*, no. 431, 14 August 1950, p. 1. Thanks to Christian Cargnelli for this reference.

Chapter 7

'GERMAN, OR STILL MORE HORRIBLE THOUGHT, RUSSIAN – AT ANY RATE, IT IS UN-ENGLISH!': A WIDE SHOT OF EXILE, EMIGRÉ AND ITINERANT ACTIVITY IN THE BRITISH FILM INDUSTRY IN THE 1930S

Amy Sargeant

In the 1930s, *The Spectator*, among other journals intended for a general audience, frequently discussed the contending merits of the modern versus the ancient home. Its correspondent, Geoffrey Boumphrey, director of the plywood furniture importers Finmar, urged shops to support good design in china, glass, typography and textiles, and encouraged his readers to recognise that modernity is not of necessity foreign. 'How often', he asked in a 1932 article, 'does one hear it urged against modern architecture that it is German or, still more horrible thought, Russian – at any rate, it is un-English!'[1] In 1933 he welcomed the Gorell Report on Art and Industry: 'it is at last dawning on those elusive entities – the Powers that Be and the Man in the Street – that good design is of importance to others beyond artists and the arty – more – that good design may actually be good business.'[2]

The professional press was divided between commentators who promoted modernism (notably Leslie Martin, F.R.S. Yorke, and Philip Morton Shand at the *Architectural Review*, and Nikolaus Pevsner, a German émigré resident in Britain from 1933) and those (including the veteran architect Reginald Blomfield) who reviled it. 'It is essentially continental in its origins and inspiration', ranted Blomfield in 1933. 'It claims as a merit that it is cosmopolitan … as an Englishman and proud of this country, I detest and despise cosmopolitanism.'[3] 'There is such a thing as good manners in architecture', he continues in his 1934 polemic *Modernismus* (extending the grounds of his argument to painting, sculpture, music and literature), 'and what might be endurable in a suburb of Paris or Berlin is quite intolerable in the Chilterns and the English countryside.'[4] Meanwhile, of course, in Nazi Germany official doctrine increasingly dismissed modernism as Bolshevik, Jewish and anti-nationalist (and there was a tendency in Britain, also, to associate modernism with socialism in this period, whether for good or ill), while in Russia it was denounced as bourgeois.

In this chapter I will situate the contribution of German-speaking artists to British cinema in a wider context of émigré activity; establish this within a more general discussion surrounding the origins and aspirations of modernism; and indicate that German-speakers are not necessarily German-born. I am especially interested here in the British work of the Hungarian-born designer, photographer and filmmaker László Moholy-Nagy.

Emigrés contributed to cinema, that most popular of leisure activities, in a number of different ways apart from their obvious roles as producers, directors, designers and performers in 'super features' (big-budget studio productions). The Russian, Komisarjevsky, provided *moderne* (rather than modern) meringue decoration for cinema interiors while Monja (Solomon) Danischewsky organised publicity for Michael Balcon.[5] These contributions need to be placed amongst a broader range of commercial services performed by named artists for a number of public institutions. The work of the architect Charles Holden and the manager Frank Pick (much praised by Pevsner), the typographer Edward Johnston, the weaver and textile designer Marion Dorn and Moholy-Nagy created a corporate identity for London Transport as surely as the architecture and lettering of the 'speed-whiskered' factory of the Odeon cinema (much maligned by the *Architectural Review*) branded the chain as it extended into the suburbs.[6] Moholy-Nagy's posters, including 'Escalators' and 'Pneumatic Doors', combine bold and colourful composition with detailed technical drawings. 'The Underground', enthused Shand in 1929,

> expresses its functions and emphasises their imaginative appeal in a spirit wholly of today, if not tomorrow, which has resolutely put aside all preoccupations with the past. It leads before other commercial undertakings dare to follow. Where they are at best content with being 'up to date' – that is to say, imitating instead of initiating – it originates. It insists that it is impossible to be modern in spirit without being also modern in the letter ... In short, the Underground provides the citizens of London and their country cousins with a gratuitous education in the outward manifestations of the modern spirit. It inculcates a proper pride in our own particular *Zeitgeist*.[7]

With his 1934 Penguin Pool, the Polish architect Berthold Lubetkin (trained in Moscow, Berlin and Warsaw) created an iconic image for Julian Huxley's Regents Park Zoo. Moholy-Nagy was duly commissioned to make a documentary film, *The New Architecture in the London Zoo* (1936), by New York's Museum of Modern Art and Harvard University's

Department of Architecture. The ex-Harrovian Russian architect Serge Chermeyeff filmed new architecture in Stuttgart, Frankfurt and Berlin and provided a commentary for the *Architectural Review*.[8] Moholy-Nagy designed fittings for Simpson, the Piccadilly menswear store, layouts for the *Architectural Review* and, with fellow Hungarian Marcel Breuer, display stands for the textile company Courtaulds.[9] Breuer-style tubular steel chairs mark the contemporary sequences of Victor Saville's 1934 film *Evergreen*, designed by Alfred Junge, as distinctly modern, and Breuer collaborated with Yorke on architectural projects in Britain.[10]

The Bauhaus Ethos

Such contributions to filmmaking, its promotion and exhibition should, I think, be linked to the importation (or derivation) of a Bauhaus ethos into British architecture and design alongside particular personnel. Moholy-Nagy had taught at the Bauhaus in Weimar from 1923 to 1928 with the architect and teacher Walter Gropius, who arrived in Britain in 1934, proclaimed by guru Herbert Read in his *Art and Industry: the Principles of Modern Design* as 'the inspiration and leader of all who possess new vision in industrial art'. Read published paintings by Moholy-Nagy's friend Ben Nicholson alongside taps, cutlery, Breuer chairs and Bauhaus crockery. Moholy-Nagy, who came to London from Amsterdam at Read's invitation, is thanked for practical help in securing photographs and for giving Read 'the necessary impetus to write'.[11] Leslie Martin, in his 1939 *Flat Book*, published textiles by Nicholson and interiors by Chermeyeff and Breuer.[12] Like Boumphrey, Read blamed 'the middleman' for foisting bad design on the public. Meanwhile, the critic John Gloag claimed that the manufacturer 'wants something safe to sell' and that the buyer thinks he knows 'what the public wants and is nervous of trying experiments' but confides that 'the public doesn't know itself what it wants'.[13]

Thus, what we might call a Bauhaus ethos (exemplified by Gropius and Moholy-Nagy) is embraced in Read's commitment to art education, the activity of single artists across disciplines, the collectivisation of effort and in his determination to make good design available to a general public through commercial mechanised mass production. The Bauhaus school acted as a clearing-house for international talent, including the Hungarians Moholy-Nagy and Breuer and the Russian Wassily Kandinsky, much as Ufa's Neubabelsberg studios had in the 1920s for a multilingual film crew.[14]

The GPO

The Empire Marketing Board and the General Post Office (GPO) famously enlisted the talents of filmmakers and artists. Lotte Reiniger's 1938 animation *The HPO* ('A Heavenly Post Office') was scored by Benjamin Britten for piano, adapting themes from Rossini. Unlike her previous black and white shorts and the feature-length *The Adventures of Prince Ahmed* (filmed in Germany in 1926 and exhibited by London's Film Society in the 1930s), this was made in suitably vibrant and joyous Dufaycolor.

Greetings are delivered by white outlined, suitably accoutred cupids, despatched from heaven by a fellow cupid who observes events on earth through a telescope: a baby deposited by a stork upon a welcoming couple; engaged lovers under the shadow of a tree in blossom and the light of a full moon; a child on her birthday presented with a doll and an illuminated cake; and a boxer in the ring receiving congratulations; meanwhile a fisherman under a rainy sky with a meagre catch is consoled. One cupid on a hobby horse meets a fox-hunting party. 'IT'S HEAVEN TO RECEIVE A GREETINGS TELEGRAM. BE AN ANGEL AND SEND ONE!', Reiniger's appropriately abbreviated and capitalised cut-out paper lettering advises.

As Rachael Low and Paul Rotha (himself commissioned by Vickers Armstrong, the Orient Shipping Line and, like Moholy-Nagy, Imperial Airways) noted, many revered 'documentaries' of the decade should be regarded more properly as an advertisement for a particular product or company.[15] Oswell Blakeston, a correspondent for the highbrow film journal *Close Up* and for the *Architectural Review*, commented in 1931 that:

> The commercial cinema is so tied-up with itself that an experimental approach can only be found in the new possibility of the advertising film. Indeed, the advertising film provides the economic basis for all pioneer work at the moment.[16]

The producer John Grierson commended the products of the Hollywood film factory for their vitality, invention and mastery of technique ('the larger imaginative qualities have been lacking, but their achievement is none the less solid and impressive') even while reserving his greatest praise for the example set by Russia and Germany for the British film of the future. American cinema has, he suggested,

> taken its own present and made most positive drama of that. Its railways, its cities, its police, its banditry, its newspapers, its aircraft and its ships, and a great deal of its ordinary life, have been turned into story material.[17]

The reappraisal of film, as J.L. Myres wrote in *The Spectator* in 1932, 'as a powerful instrument of culture, even more than of policy', should be examined in the context of artists working for a mass audience through industry, the valorisation of the aesthetic merits of mechanically produced objects and the appropriation of artisanal labour (rather than mechanised labour) as subject matter for films.[18]

Moholy-Nagy and British Film

Moholy-Nagy's interest in film should be regarded as an integral part of what his daughter Hattula calls his 'holistic' approach to work and his resistance to categorisation and the specialist training increasingly promoted in Germany.[19] In his letter of resignation from the Bauhaus he cited social and artistic considerations:

> Basically one can't object if human power wants to measure itself on the object, the trade. This belongs essentially to the Bauhaus programme. But one must see the danger of losing equilibrium, and meet it. As soon as creating an object becomes a speciality, and work becomes trade, the process of education loses all vitality. There must be room for teaching the basic ideas which keep human content alert and vital. For this we fought and for this we exhausted ourselves. I can no longer keep up with the stronger and stronger tendency toward trade specialisation in the workshops.
>
> We are now in danger of becoming what we as revolutionaries opposed: a vocational training school which evaluates only the final achievement and overlooks the development of the whole man. For him there remains no time, no money, no space, no concession.
>
> The school today swims no longer against the current. It tries to fall in line. This is what weakens the power of the unit. Community spirit is replaced by individual competition, and the question arises whether the existence of a creative group is only possible on the basis of opposition to the *status quo*. It remains to be seen how efficient will be the decision to work only for efficient results. Perhaps there will be a new fruitful period. Perhaps it is the beginning of the end.[20]

During his residency in Britain Moholy-Nagy was invited to produce photographs to illustrate Mary Benedetta's *The Street Markets of London* (1936), Bernard Fergusson's *Eton Portrait* (1937) and John Betjeman's *An Oxford University Chest* (1938).[21] There was much here which recalled Moholy-Nagy's composition, techniques and choice of subjects for his work in Berlin and which anticipated his initial response to America: cropping, acute perspectives of architecture from above and below; a negative image of Trinity College's spiky railings; atmospheric weather; a frontal, flat shot of differently lettered shop signs on the High Street, and Eton's 4th June fireworks reflected in still water.[22] Moholy-Nagy's survey of Oxford extends to 'Motopolis: scenes in the Morris works' and of Eton to the mechanical workshops, drawing school and pottery class. 'Banana Mess: the caviare of Eton' (a round, chipped white dish of bananas, ice cream and wafers, laid on a carpet over angled parallel lines of cast sunlight and shadow) is similar in composition to 'an undergraduate bedroom' in Oxford.

Most of the photographs for Benedetta's gazetteer were taken with an inconspicuous Leica. In his foreword, Moholy-Nagy advised:

The Photographer can scarcely find a more fascinating task than that of providing a pictorial record of modern city life. London's street markets present him with an opportunity of this kind. It is not, however, a task to which the purely aesthetic principle of pictorial composition – which many readers may expect in my work – can be applied, for from its very nature it requires the use of the pictorial sequence and thus of a more effective technique approximating to that of the film. I am convinced that the days of the merely 'beautiful' photograph are numbered and that we shall be increasingly interested in providing a truthful record of objectively determined fact …. The subject is a vast one, comprising problems of history, sociology, economics and town planning. It is approached in this book by means of literary and impressionistic photo-reportage. This method of studying a fragment of present-day reality from a social and economic point of view has a wide general appeal[23]

A man who sells from a suitcase 'a mysterious preparation for making brass fenders look like chromium' is photographed from a balcony directly above him, the sceptical potential buyers circled around him as he demonstrates his wares. Stalls are photographed through hanging lines of narrow solid razor straps or an array of sheer stockings. Another, 'a stall for housewives', is photographed with its foreground display of shiny steelware in sharper focus than the bustling, blurry background. Second-hand and third-hand shoes and coats are shown, and hats for sale laid on newspaper on the ground. There are portrait photos of world-worn types, of various ethnic origins, akin to the uniformed portraits of boys, masters and other staff at Eton – likewise experienced as strange. Sibyl Moholy-Nagy said that her husband shared Voltaire's Anglophilia and that he told his hosts at Eton that he was gratified by Britain's lack of success at the 1936 Olympics – the team's inability to secure medals was understood to demonstrate its merely competing for fun (as if it were no more than the Wall Game of 'Fives').[24]

Moholy-Nagy co-directed (with John Mathias), photographed and edited the 1935 documentary *Lobsters*, accompanied with original music and arrangements of traditional shanties by Arthur Benjamin; the film was partly funded by his fellow Hungarian, the producer Alexander Korda. Like Grierson's *Drifters* and Moholy-Nagy's *Marseille Vieux Port* (both 1929) it traces the progress of an animal from the High Seas to High Table and the lives of fishermen dependent upon it for their livelihood. Similar to Jean Painlevé's poetic documentaries *Crabes et crevettes* (Crabs and Shrimps, 1929) and *L'Hippocampe* (The Sea Horse, 1934), it follows a hidden underwater existence and metamorphosis, a lobster shedding one carapace before growing another (fourteen times in its first three years, we are informed, consuming its old casing in the process, 'a remarkable achievement'). 'A lobster can shed a claw in a fight, then regrow it within a month' (here, photographed in a tank).

Alan Howarth's brisk commentary begins with willows, shown in silhouette wafting against a clear sky, which are then woven into pots made and mended over the winter, 'an ancient craft' in which the young and old (shown in close-up) of six families are involved. In the summer, the fishermen travel twelve miles every day to the reef. Pots are lowered more than seven fathoms deep, emptied and rebaited, across a track laid using a compass salvaged by 'Harry' from a torpedoed French boat. Meanwhile, the lobsters' feelers are 'constantly sweeping for an enemy or even an unfriendly relation'; 'if two gentlemen or ladies meet they are always prepared to have a row'.

The commentary describes the anatomy of a female carrying eggs and the hatching of larvae – scampering on a clear glass plate on a white background in the laboratory, they are said to be 'strange and lively little fellows' whose 'antics are disconcerting'. The lobsters get hauled onboard along with the 'unwelcome whelks' similarly captured by the fishermen's pots, and their claws tied with willow strips. But as fish provide the prey of the lobsters and as the fishermen are the lobsters' adversaries, the sea is the adversary of the men. 'The day's catch must be safely stowed' and Moholy-Nagy uses accelerated sequences to stress the urgency as a storm brews and waves crash over the rim of the boat. 'The rougher the sea, the harder the work ... Rough weather makes the journey home a trying ordeal', and the wind rustles through the willows onshore under an overcast sky. The fishermen's dark sweaters wipe the frame as the crew is dashed across the deck, lifting the ballast. A girl on the jetty looks through a telescope, hoping for a sighting of her nearest and dearest. Moholy-Nagy revels in the patterns of light glinting on calm water as the ketch eventually returns safely to its Sussex port. At the very end of the film, a shiny black lobster claws his way through a white menu written in copperplate on which dishes featuring his fellow crustaceans are listed.

Moholy-Nagy and *Circle*

The 1937 book and exhibition *Circle* inherits from precedents in journals such as *Close Up* (based in Switzerland), *Veshch' Gegenstand Objet* (based in Berlin) and *Das neue Frankfurt* a remit to draw together an international list of collaborators and readers. In these magazines, film is discussed alongside developments in modern art, literature, music, photography and architecture. Moholy-Nagy associated with artists gathered around *Circle* (including Naum Gabo), with Grierson's experimental film group and with a broader community of Hampstead émigrés. The lightweight plexiglas and metal constructions of the Russian brothers Naum Gabo (from 1922 to 1932 in Berlin, from 1939 to 1946 in Britain) and Antoine Pevsner (who had worked in Paris) are echoed in various modernist contraptions in William Cameron Menzies' 1936 film *Things to Come*, produced by Alexander Korda, an adaptation of H.G. Wells's *The Shape of Things to Come*, to which Moholy-Nagy also contributed an abstract film sequence.[25] Sibyl Moholy-Nagy describes the intention behind the abstract constructions designed as settings but not used in the final production:

> The fantastic technology of the Utopian city of the future would, so Moholy dreamed, eliminate solid form. Houses were no longer obstacles to, but receptacles of, man's natural life force, light. There were no walls, but skeletons of steel, screened with glass and plastic sheets. The accent was on perforation and contour, an indication of a new reality rather than reality itself. In its final version the film never lived up to the talent of its originators.[26]

A Moholy-Nagy kinetic sculpture (a variant of his 1925/1930 *Light-Space Modulator* – and 'star' of his 1930 abstract film *Light Play: Black-White-Grey*) constructed from metal rods, mesh, perforated and polished angled discs, filaments and twisted glass, serves as the background to the portentous prologue of Stuart Legg's 1933 documentary *The Coming of the Dial*, produced by Grierson for the GPO. After a triumphant opening blast of Handel's *Trumpet Voluntary*, the narrator informs us:

> Research – the creative power behind the modern world – building the future in the laboratory: the industrial chemist determining a carbon percentage for a safety steel; the physicist analysing coloured light rays for signal lenses; the plant breeder, pollinating selected grasses for mountain pastures – these men are applying the laws of science to everyday problems, and research into the behaviour of electro-magnets has revolutionised the telephone system and introduced the dial.

There follows a routine exposition of tests at Dollis Hill and the humdrum workings of a telephone exchange: 'Once more the laws of science have been applied to an everyday problem and this dial system is a vital contribution to efficiency and speed.'

Emigrés and Modernism

All the above-mentioned peripatetic artists, I would suggest, found themselves temporarily in Britain in the 1930s, by invitation and by circumstance as much as by choice. Moholy-Nagy, Breuer, Gabo, Chermeyeff and Gropius subsequently emigrated to America. The Korda brothers, Conrad Veidt and the Brazilian Alberto Cavalcanti – head of the GPO film unit when the Second World War broke out – also had meandered between European studios and locations (Berlin, Paris and the Victorine in Nice) before winding up in London. Again, I want to stress filmmaking and artistic practice in the late 1920s and 1930s as an intrinsically itinerant practice rather than a specifically located affair, either by intention or necessity – and to set this against the relative stability of Balcon's Ealing 'family business', or 'Academy for Young Gentlemen' (including the thoroughly acclimatised Russian Danischewsky) and the presumed comfortable security of Blomfield's position, employing the solid, heavyweight Classicism of a previous era.

'It is an axiom in furnishing the modern house (no less than in the building of it)', stipulates Boumphrey, 'that nothing is to be present which does not serve a very definite purpose.'[27] Thus far, I have approached Weimar notions of 'Sachlichkeit' (generally denoting healthy 'realism', 'sobriety' and 'objectivity') in film, the applied arts and a method of working from a foreign perspective, terminology that Rotha sought to introduce into his 1931 book *Celluloid: The Film Today*. But Hermann Muthesius, in *Das englische Haus* (1904), had already proclaimed English middle-class Arts and Crafts décor – and, remarkably, plumbing – as 'sachlich' in its utilitarian plainness and simplification. In his 1936 *Pioneers of the Modern Movement*, 1942 *Outline of European Architecture* and 1956 *The Englishness of English Art*, Nikolaus Pevsner similarly attempted to root Bauhaus modernism in Britain. Even while William Morris (a utopian socialist commonly thought irredeemably 'arty-crafty' and unfashionable by the early 1930s) renounced mechanised production, in theory and in practice, he was rendered, in retrospect, as a welcome antecedent: 'Do not have anything in your house which you do not either know to be useful or believe to be beautiful.'[28]

The furniture designer and manufacturer Gordon Russell, in the same series of BBC talks to which Boumphrey and Gloag contributed, quotes Morris with approval: 'This is a good standard to go on', adding 'it is wrong to imagine that experts or art critics only are qualified for this form of scrutiny.'[29] Isambard Kingdom Brunel's Clifton Suspension Bridge (built from 1836) is appreciated by Pevsner alongside medieval European cathedrals (Amiens, Beauvais, Cologne): 'Not one word too much is said, not one compromising form introduced', although he determines that nothing else of significance happened in British architecture for forty years or more.[30] Indeed, the very term 'sachlich', in its various guises, may be rooted in the 'realism' that Pevsner identifies as a recurrent, peculiar aspect of English art. It may be, as Timothy Mowl has suggested, that Pevsner, in thanks to his host nation after 1933, flatteringly discovered 'un-Englishness' by recasting it in an international mould, there again oddly reencountering Blomfield – in other words, he made Britain seem modern in spite of itself. Mowl equally acknowledges the irony of Pevsner imbibing a similar essentialist, nationalist interpretation of artistic criteria to that which had condemned him to exile: a Lutheran convert, he had been purged as a Jew.[31]

Conclusion

I am suggesting that the discussion of individual émigré careers in British cinema be discussed in a broader mapping of cultural concerns and exchange between Britain and Germany, a wider Europe and America. Film should be considered as an example of artists working in industry, setting the practical and political exigencies of émigré, exile and itinerant activity in film against modernist internationalism as an idealist aspiration. A country of domicile may be no more than a strategic, provisional expedient. Moholy-Nagy's brief sojourn in Britain reinforced a growing appreciation of the significance of art and design to industry – including the film industry – and to a design ethos purportedly imported from the Bauhaus. Meanwhile, there is a paradox: while modernism was met with much antagonism in Britain (as internationally), German critics, from Muthesius to Frey to Pevsner, identified Britain as the cradle of modern design in its arts, crafts and engineering.[32]

Notes

1. G.M. Boumphrey, 'This Foreign Stuff', *The Spectator*, 9 December 1932, p. 833.
2. G.M. Boumphrey, 'Design for Modern Life', *The Spectator*, 31 March 1933, p. 465; see also John Betjeman, 'The Gorell Report', *The Architectural Review*, July 1932, pp. 13–14.
3. Reginald Blomfield, 'Is Architecture on the Right Track?', *The Listener*, 2 July 1933, p. 124–25.
4. Reginald Blomfield, *Modernismus* (London: Macmillan, 1934), p. 164.
5. See Paul Rotha, *Celluloid: The Film Today* (London: Longmans, Green and Co., 1933), p. 72; also Monja Danischewsky, *White Russian – Red Face* (London: Victor Gollancz, 1966), pp. 127–35. Danischewsky was a White Russian, brought to Britain by his father in 1919, and became publicity director for Balcon in 1938. He describes Balcon's leadership as 'benevolent paternalism … [Ealing Studios] somehow had the air of a family business'.
6. See Nicholas Bullock, 'Circle and the Constructive Idea in Architecture', in Jeremy Lewison (ed.), *Circle: Constructive Art in Britain 1934–40* (Cambridge: Kettle's Yard, 1982), p. 34.
7. P. Morton Shand, 'Underground', *Architectural Review*, November 1929, pp. 217–24; Shand was also responsible for English translations of Moholy-Nagy's writings in German; see Richard Kostelanetz (ed.), *Moholy-Nagy* (London: Allen Lane, 1971). Pevsner praised Pick and the Underground in similar terms in 1942. See also Simon Loxley, *Type* (London: I.B. Tauris, 2006), pp. 109–22.
8. Serge Chermeyeff, 'Film Shots in Germany', *Architectural Review*, November 1931, pp. 131–33; for Lubetkin's various contributions to the London Zoo, see Peter Coe and Malcolm Reading, *Lubetkin and Tecton: Architecture and Social Commitment* (London: The Arts Council of Great Britain, 1981).
9. See Paul Jobling, *Man Appeal* (Oxford: Berg, 2005), p. 64.
10. See F.R.S. Yorke, *The Modern House* [1934] (London: The Architectural Press, 1962), pp. 148–53, for houses by Gropius, Breuer and Chermeyeff – Chermeyeff and Erich Mendelsohn were also responsible for the famous De la Warr pavilion in Bexhill-on-Sea. Gropius is generally thought to have provided the model for Evelyn Waugh's Professor Otto Silenus in *Decline and Fall* [1928] (Harmondsworth: Penguin, 1980), p. 119: 'He had first attracted Mrs Beste-Chetwynde's attention with the rejected design for a chewing-gum factory which had been produced in a progressive Hungarian quarterly. His only other completed work was the décor for a cinema-film of great length and complexity of plot – a complexity rendered the more inextricable by the producer's austere elimination of all human characters, a fact which had proved fatal to its commercial success.'
11. Herbert Read, *Art and Industry* (London: Faber and Faber, 1934), p. 1. Read is referring to Moholy-Nagy's *The New Vision* (1928), which gave particulars about the educational methods of the Bauhaus; see Moholy-Nagy, *The New Vision and Abstract of an Artist* (New York: George Wittenborn, 1947).

12. Leslie Martin, *The Flat Book* (London: The Architectural Press, 1939).

13. John Gloag (ed.), *Design in Modern Life* [1934] (London: George Allen and Unwin, 1946), p. 17.

14. For personnel at the Bauhaus, see Magdalena Droste, *Bauhaus 1919–1933* (Berlin: Bauhaus- Archiv/Taschen, 1990) and John Willett, *The New Sobriety: Art and Politics in the Weimar Period* (London: Thames and Hudson, 1978), pp. 118–23; see also Michael Balcon, *Michael Balcon Presents ... A Lifetime in Films* (London: Hutchinson, 1969), p. 52, and Monja Danischewsky (ed.), *Michael Balcon's 25 Years in Films* (London: World Film Publications, 1947), p. 11.

15. See Rachael Low, *Documentary and Educational Films of the 1930s* (London: George Allen & Unwin, 1979), pp. 2–4, and Paul Rotha, *Documentary Film* (London: Faber and Faber, 1936), pp. 60–62.

16. Oswell Blakeston, 'The Film and Final Statements', *Architectural Review*, April 1931, p. 137; Blakeston's 'The Still Camera Today', *Architectural Review*, April 1932, pp. 154–57, cites photographs by Moholy-Nagy.

17. John Grierson, 'The Future for British Films', *The Spectator*, 14 May 1932, p. 692.

18. J. L. Myres, 'The Film in National Life', *The Spectator*, 11 June 1932, p. 825.

19. Hattula Moholy-Nagy, 'László Moholy-Nagy: Transnational', in Achim Borchardt-Hume (ed.), *Albers and Moholy-Nagy: from the Bauhaus to the New World* (London: Tate Publishing, 2006), p. 115.

20. Sibyl Moholy-Nagy, *Moholy-Nagy: Experiment in Totality* [1950] (Cambridge Mass.: MIT Press, 1969), pp. 46–47.

21. Mary Benedetta, *The Street Markets of London* (London: John Miles, 1936); Bernard Fergusson, *Eton Portrait* (London: John Miles, 1937); John Betjeman, *An Oxford University Chest* (London: John Miles, 1938); the last of these includes humorous sketches by Osbert Lancaster alongside Moholy-Nagy's photos.

22. For Moholy-Nagy's earlier negative shots see Krisztina Passuth, *Moholy-Nagy* (London: Thames and Hudson, 1985), ills. 99–105, and Moholy-Nagy, *Painting Photography Film* [1925] (London: Lund Humphries, 1967), which also features a section of a Reiniger animation. For his subsequent work in America see Moholy-Nagy, *Vision in Motion* (Chicago: Paul Theobald and Company, 1947).

23. Benedetta, *The Street Markets of London*, p. vii. Sibyl Moholy-Nagy (in *Moholy-Nagy: Experiment in Totality*, p. 82) says that he was met by Billingsgate fish merchants with chunks of ice (a frequent hostile response to intrusive documentary photographers in the 1930s). See also John Taylor, *A Dream of England* (Manchester: Manchester University Press, 1994), pp. 152–81.

24. S. Moholy-Nagy, *Moholy-Nagy: Experiment in Totality*, p. 117.

25. See Teresa Newman, *Naum Gabo* (London: Tate Gallery Publications, 1976), p. 29.

26. S. Moholy-Nagy, *Moholy-Nagy: Experiment in Totality*, p. 129.

27. Boumphrey, 'Pattern', *The Spectator*, 30 December 1932, p. 920.

28. Lionel Cuffe, 'William Morris', *Architectural Review*, April 1931, p. 151.

29. Gordon Russell, 'The Living-Room and Furniture Design', in Gloag, *Design in Modern Life*, p. 43.

30. Nikolaus Pevsner, *Pioneers of Modern Design* [1936] (London: Penguin Books, 1975), p. 128.

31. Timothy Mowl, *Stylistic Cold Wars: Betjeman versus Pevsner* (London: John Murray, 2000), pp. 77–78.

32. Mowl (*Stylistic Cold Wars*, pp. 140–41) notes the significance of Dagobert Frey's 1942 *Englisches Wesen in der bildenden Kunst*, as does Irving Lavin in his introduction to Erwin Panofsky, *Three Essays on Style* (Cambridge, Mass: MIT Press, 1995), pp. 12–13. Panofsky's 1962 essay, 'The Ideological Antecedents of the Rolls Royce Radiator' may be regarded as a rearguard defence of the car's design as more than simply the product of functional engineering.

Chapter 8

EXTENDING FRAMES AND EXPLORING SPACES: ALFRED JUNGE, SET DESIGN AND GENRE IN BRITISH CINEMA[1]

Sarah Street

When Russian émigré set designer Lazare Meerson arrived in Britain at the end of 1935, he complained to a colleague working in Paris that 'complete disorganisation reigns over the studios. In comparison, our poor Epinay looks like a lost Hollywood to me. The technical equipment is completely rudimentary'.[2] His account of an inefficient, chaotic economic infrastructure was also observed by Oswell Blakeston, writing for *Close Up* in 1927. He reported that an art director complained to him that 'the balance of his composition had been completely spoilt. When the carpenters came to execute his design they were compelled to cut the top off his set to make it fit into the studio'.[3] This bleak picture of English backwardness was contrasted with more enlightened German studios when the designs created by Walter Röhrig and Robert Herlth for *The Wonderful Lie of Nina Petrovna* (1929) received effusive praise from Paul Rotha, who wrote that 'art direction such as this does not come your way every day'. He went on to report that the film's British distributors, Gaumont-British, held art direction in such low esteem that they neglected to credit the art directors in the British release print.[4]

Yet by the end of the 1930s things had changed considerably. That decade, especially during the second half, saw a great improvement in conditions for art directors: Denham and Pinewood studios were built with facilities that were heralded as state of the art and Alfred Junge's tenacious and pioneering work at the Gaumont-British Lime Grove Studios at Shepherd's Bush enhanced the status of the art director to such an extent that he exercised unprecedented levels of creative control. Junge first worked as an art director in Britain in the late 1920s, as a member of German director E.A. Dupont's production team when British

International Pictures was keen to introduce 'continental' techniques to British cinema, which they did, particularly, with *Moulin Rouge* (1928) and *Piccadilly* (1929).

Early Days

Junge studied art in Germany and Italy and then served in the First World War. He later recalled that he was 'never a good soldier. I painted and sketched the graves of comrades, or the swallows sitting on telegraph wires … I never fired a shot all through the war and have thus the wonderful feeling of never having killed a man'.[5] Junge started out as a stage scenic designer and painter in his home town of Görlitz in the Stadttheater. After working in a variety of theatres in Gleiwitz, Königsberg, Kattowitz, Lucerne and Zurich, he was hired by the prestigious Staatsoper (State Opera) in Berlin.

After the war he and some friends set up their own design studio, but as the demand for scenic painters fell they were increasingly employed as furniture restorers, apartment decorators and poster designers. Film designer and director Paul Leni introduced Junge to film, and he soon found work with companies including Ufa, Germany's premier production outfit. He went on to design many German films before relocating briefly to France to collaborate with Vincent Korda on the art direction of *Marius* (1931), a film based on Marcel Pagnol's play and set in Marseilles.

Emigrés and 'Total Design'

In 1932 Junge settled more permanently in Britain where he was appointed as supervising art director by Gaumont-British. He worked there until 1937, producing many of his most distinctive designs. Junge applied his skills to many genres, including historical films such as *The Iron Duke* (1934), comedies including *The Good Companions* (1933), musicals, dramas, and Hitchcock thrillers such as *The Man Who Knew Too Much* (1934).[6] Indeed, his efforts are in large part responsible for the advances made in British films during the 1930s, particularly those that were planned for export.

Several other factors contributed to this turnabout: the general stylistic development of British films; changes in film studio organisation to more streamlined modes of production; and, most importantly, the creative input of other celebrated designers, many of whom were émigrés, including Andrei Andreiev, Vincent Korda, Lazare Meerson, Ernö Metzner and Oscar Werndorff. Along with Junge, their influence was noted by a contemporary critic who commented in 1935 on recent British films that they displayed 'a greater extravagance of setting, together with extraordinary predominance in certain quarters of candlesticks and staircases [referring to films such as *The Dictator*, 1935, designed by Andreiev]. This ritualistic sumptuousness seems to derive more from the continental than the American schools'.[7]

As Tim Bergfelder has argued, these artists 'reorganised the concept of *mise en scène* in the British film industry' by aspiring towards 'total design', a concept that emphasised pre-planning the 'look' of a film before shooting began, thus involving designers with key aspects of creative control during the production process.[8] Designers' sketches, drawings, models and built sets provided the essential stylistic mood of a film that was further embellished in collaboration with writers, directors and cinematographers. German artists were a major source of influence on the concept of 'total design'. In the introduction to Edward Carrick's pictorial directory of British art directors, he argued that German cinema was the first to use artists such as Hans Richter to design for films, and the stylistic legacy of Expressionist cinema was legendary for its painterly affinities and for drawing attention to the art of screen design.[9]

Piccadilly

Junge applied many of these German techniques to British cinema, which becomes particularly evident in *Piccadilly*, a film that, while not well received by *Close Up* (the art film magazine that was usually highly critical of British films), nevertheless was noted for its sets.[10] In particular, the cabaret set was singled out as distinctive for its success as a design built for maximum visual impact while at the same time facilitating the work of the camera:

> The design is sumptuous without being gaudy, and, while the general plan is quite simple, the strong curves promise to be more satisfactory to the camera, even, than they are to the eye. As the set is completely enclosed a mobile camera will have the freest scope, and there is hardly a point from which lines and masses do not construct interesting patterns, while still remaining explanatory of the simple ground plan.[11]

Junge achieved this by pushing the boundaries of studio organisation at Elstree, the largest studio in Britain before Denham was built. The set in *Piccadilly* is indicative of design work that is integrated with the concept of the moving image, an essential element of preparatory drawings that anticipated cinematographic fluidity as well as stasis. As Roger Manvell argued, films such as this are 'designed and composed' so that 'always behind the design lies the need to make something which a mobile camera can work into'.[12] The cinematographer for this film was another German émigré, Werner Brandes, who made excellent use of the camera to explore the potential for mobility that was an inherent aspect of Junge's design (see also Kelly Robinson in this volume).

Indeed, when we first see the set of the Piccadilly club the band is enclosed in a circular structure at the top centre of the frame, surrounded by curvilinear staircases with swirling banisters. This pattern is repeated on either side of the frame by curved balconies up above. The dancing couples move in the bottom half of the frame, creating an overall impression of fluidity. After this shot, which is held for a considerable time so that we can admire the scene closely, the camera surveys the spaces of the set in more detail: the guests sitting at tables, up on the balconies and at the bar. This is followed by the reverse shot of the entire set, with the band this time in the foreground, opening up the frame to be dominated even more by the dancers. The cumulative impact contributes to an experience of a space that is opulent, expansive and vibrant, effects created by careful design and composition.

It was Junge who later introduced further innovative techniques to British films, including the use of scaffolding and crane technology to facilitate camera and set mobility.[13] He also famously established the designer's right to fix camera positions for all set-ups.[14] This is a key indicator of the extent to which it gradually became recognised that designers' awareness of 'camera consciousness' was a crucial determinant of mood.[15]

Art Deco and the Moving Image

The rest of this chapter will explore how the British studio genre system enabled Junge to further develop sets that were predicated on the concept of the moving image. He adapted his skills to particular projects and genres, some of which gave scope for designs to be obtrusive, occupying a significant, almost excessive, presence in relation to film narrative. Similar examples have been discussed by Charles and Mirella Affron in their book *Sets in Motion*. They propose a schema of progressively intensive film set designs which may, or may not, relate to the dominant narrative trajectory; in the case of many of Junge's designs the category 'embellishment-artifice' is most appropriate.[16] In the Jessie Matthews musicals, the set can be seen to 'extend the frame', using a term developed by Charles Tashiro. This refers to the ways in which sets, in combination with the camera, can encourage the viewer to look beyond the frame into implied off-screen space.[17]

Junge's work was particularly distinctive for its incorporation of contemporary architectural/design movements, particularly Art Deco. As early as 1932, in *After the Ball* he was creating, as one critic noted, 'exquisite modern settings ... He has used every opportunity of expressing his belief in the beauty of plain surface and simple line, and his designs show a bold, unaffected style, a sense of proportion and an appreciation of the beauty of the material'.[18]

Art Deco was used, to a greater or lesser degree, in *Evergreen* (1934), *It's Love Again* (1936), *Gangway* (1937), *Head Over Heels* (1937), *Sailing Along* (1938) and *Climbing High* (1938), star vehicles for Jessie Matthews, one of Gaumont-British's top female stars in the 1930s. In these films you find many examples of shots that display sets as sites of performance, including the illusion of great depth necessary to accommodate both star performer and Deco set. They are also expansive and spectacular, an effect achieved by use of white, shiny surfaces that are explored by a mobile camera.

Jessie Matthews and the Musical

As Lucy Fischer has pointed out in relation to Hollywood musicals, the aspects which created a particularly close affinity with Deco were the genre's dependence on the female figure and the focus on dance and dance costuming, as well as on the display of design and architecture in spectacular production numbers.[19] Similarly, in the British films there was a connection between Deco motifs, vernacular architecture and the movement of the female figure. Matthews's dances provided Junge with an opportunity to design sets that displayed both a performance and the *moderne* environment in symbiosis. In a metaphorical sense he employed Deco to convey personal transformation, since the sets provide the environment for characters who aspire to be upwardly mobile and successful, in Matthews's case usually as a singer and dancer.

While many science fiction films used *moderne* designs to express ambivalence about progress and new technology, a different slant was evident in the musicals. In *Head Over Heels*, *Gangway*, *Sailing Along* and *Climbing High* the Deco sets are associated with modernity and technology, respectively radio offices; newspaper offices; parts of the house of an eccentric patron who has commissioned a Deco kitchen; and a modelling/advertising agency. Radio, the press and advertising are obvious indicators of the modern, professional, technologically based world of communication.

These are exciting, dynamic spaces, and in the majority of the films no hint of critique emerges except for occasional sarcasm, as when the kitchen in *Sailing Along* is likened by one of the characters to a clinic because of its streamlined, pristine appearance. The sequence in *Climbing High* when a mechanical wind machine gets out of control, causing carnivalesque mayhem because it has been too efficient, represents another exception. An advertising/modelling agency becomes a model of efficient organisation with state-of-the-art technology. It functions much as a contemporary film studio, with areas demarcated for photography, make-up and costume, under the direction of a charismatic disciplinarian who behaves like a film producer. However, the set gets completely wrecked when the machine is accidentally switched to overdrive, and we witness the total destruction of a modern working environment, ironically the victim of one of its most prized machines.

Gangway displays Deco sets most obtrusively in the depiction of the *Daily Journal* offices. Jessie Matthews plays Pat, an assistant film critic who wants to be a singer and dancer. The newspaper offices are a particularly stunning homage to Deco. When we first see Pat she's arriving at the *Daily Journal*: we adopt her point of view as the camera literally follows her into the building. The door opens and she walks into a foyer that is light and spacious, the mobile camera travelling into a space that bombards us with chrome, reflective surfaces, geometric shapes and the bustling activity of a modern enterprise.

In this context Giuliana Bruno's observations about the cinema giving spectators a tactile, 'embodied' experience are particularly apposite.[20] We experience a vicarious tour, sharing with the character a sense of the building's expansive layout and surface glamour. The foyer becomes the occasion for a Jessie Matthews impromptu performance when she sings and dances her way to her office. On the way we see a barrage of Deco objects including glass doors with shiny silver tubular handles across their centres, as well as a bronze wall engraving with an Egyptian motif that was a common Deco fascination. Deco's emphasis on texture, smoothness and form does indeed invite a tactile response: we want to touch the perfect surfaces. The camera's mobility again serves to create a kinetic sense of progress through the corridors until we finally arrive at Pat's office. Junge's surviving drawings demonstrate how this tracking shot was planned at the design stage, as was his distinctive conception of the office space.

The use of sets to display a performer's mobility in a literal and metaphorical sense can also be demonstrated by an example from another Jessie Matthews vehicle, *Evergreen*. Two characters, Tommy and Harriet, are forced to share a house against their will, even though they are romantically attracted to one another. So when they occupy the house it's in a spirit of forbidden desire: they can't act on their mutual attraction because of a deception central to the plot. The house is on two levels separated by two staircases, one of which is spiral, up to the second level which has a landing between the two bedrooms. Junge's drawings reveal the close relationship between the original conception and the final set, as well as how it functions for figure movement since Matthews utilises the various spaces of the house as part of her dance. Her flowing dress constitutes a typical example of how Deco, while representing a modernist shift away from Art Nouveau, nevertheless retained some of the latter style's proclivity for curvaceous, free-flowing female expression. This is also evident in the statue up on the balcony.

Once Tommy has gone to bed, Harriet sits alone at the piano and starts to play and sing. A non-diegetic orchestra can be heard and she looks towards the camera to begin her impromptu performance. The set proves to be perfect for her dance: it is vast and allows us to follow her movements very smoothly. Dressed in a diaphanous nightgown, Jessie Matthews glides over the floor, performing a dance quite classical and flowing in its movement. The performance appears to extend outwards beyond the frame, producing, in Tashiro's terms, an 'open' effect.[21] The hard, clean lines of the décor provide a contrast to her free-flowing movements, forcing us to notice the set as an entity in itself. Unlike the previous scenes, when the couple's distance from each other was represented by entrances and exits, Matthews's dance expresses a longing for the removal of the physical and emotional boundaries which the narrative has placed between Tommy and Harriet.

Enter Hitchcock

Lighting was always an integral aspect of Junge's designs, especially in thrillers. As a contemporary critic noted when commenting on the work of Korda and Junge, the 'perfect' sketch for a film design 'shows style and furnishing, indicates character of dressings, determines lighting'.[22] Art directors frequently had knowledge of painting not possessed by cinematographers, knowledge that proved useful in advising on lighting strategies. This expertise can be traced back to Junge's early career in Germany when he studied electric lighting and the theatres were equipped with modern lighting facilities. Also, when he was in Berlin working for the Staatsoper he attended night classes on painting. As he later remembered in a letter to Carrick, it was in Berlin that he 'developed a great urge to paint and draw'.[23]

Junge's set drawings were sometimes replicated quite faithfully in the films he did with Hitchcock, as, for example, in the mill design from *Young and Innocent* (1937). It also seems quite evident that he anticipated the camera's exploration of space by producing drawings that showed the set from above. While this perspective does not appear in the film, it is important in presenting the geography of the building that would have informed Hitchcock's approach to the use of space in the court scene.

Additionally, details that can be found in drawings were often exaggerated in close-up to produce what we would probably identify as a typical 'Hitchcockian' motif, as illustrated by a comparison of Junge's drawing of the exterior of the dentist's surgery from *The Man Who Knew Too Much*, including its small detail of false teeth above the sign, with the giant teeth in close-up in the final film. Junge's drawing of a man ascending the stairs bears an extremely close resemblance to the final scene in the film, as suspense is created by low-key lighting. The sketches also reveal how the central light that becomes an important element of suspense in the following scene was very much Junge's idea. Indeed, this may have acted as an inspiration for the action as the light becomes an active prop.

From these examples it is evident that the work of the art director was of fundamental importance during pre-production. Junge's knowledge of lighting techniques and his insistence on including light as an integral facet in his drawings reveal how the cinematographer's work was anticipated by the art director. Of course, it is more than likely that final decisions would have been made very much as a process of consultation between art director, cinematographer and director, but even when working with a director such as Hitchcock, who was notorious for claiming total control over his films, Junge's expertise was incorporated and his creative ideas embellished in the final stages of pre-production.

Powell and Pressburger

In 1938 Junge left Gaumont-British and was employed by M-G-M-British to design their two prestigious productions, *The Citadel* (1938; Junge completed the designs that Lazare Meerson had started before his death) and *Goodbye, Mr Chips* (1939). After a period of internment on the Isle of Man during the Second World War, he entered his next distinctive phase as an art director in his collaborations with Michael Powell and Emeric Pressburger. (He had worked with Powell on *The Fire Raisers*, 1933, and *Contraband*, 1940, among others.)

The Life and Death of Colonel Blimp (1943) presented Junge with the challenge of designing for Technicolor cinematography. When he was commissioned by the art periodical *The Artist* in 1944 to write about his craft, he described how *Blimp* gave him the opportunity to grapple with designing three different time frames within the same film (1902, 1918 and 1942) as well as for colour. One set in particular demonstrated how Junge's designs were often inspired by a close study of character. The room kept for Clive Candy (Roger Livesey) in his aunt's house (which later becomes his own on the death of his aunt) was of crucial importance in all three periods covered by the film. A thread that runs through Candy's life is competition and hunting: as a child he wins trophies at school and collects butterflies; as he grows up his 'treasures' become stuffed animals he has shot, hung as trophies of adventure on the wall. Junge's designs for the room include all these carefully planned details, showing other subtle changes in the room as time advances, such as the introduction of electric light instead of paraffin lamps, different furniture, and redecoration. Junge decided not to go overboard on this last aspect because he considered that Candy's character would not favour modern design. He opted for tones of beige for the wallpaper, in order for the mounted stuffed animals' heads to stand out as important symbols of character.

Junge also noted that Technicolor needed very much to be taken into account during the design phase; for example, red colours would appear to be stronger, or furniture near a fire ought not to be too reddish 'as it would attract the eye too much'. Yet he was also concerned to privilege the demands of narrative and character over what might be easiest for Technicolor cinematography. When designing the hall in Candy's house he decided that 'it had to be just right in character with his small staircase leading up to the next floors ... A more square shaped hall would be easier for action and lighting, especially as Technicolor needs stronger and more lamps, but to me we had to overcome all the difficulties to get the proper surrounding for the characters'. Junge had to avoid strong, florid colours and design every set on a lower key than he expected the film to reproduce. Yet the colours nevertheless had to be interesting: 'I had to tempt the camera to make more of my colour scheme than the actual scheme itself did.'[24]

Perhaps Junge's greatest challenge in creating an environment perfectly suited to character, colour and dramatic action was *Black Narcissus* (1947), an adaptation of Rumer Godden's novel, set in the Himalayas. Powell decided against location shooting on the grounds that a studio environment provided greater opportunity to produce a precisely controlled effect: 'The atmosphere in this film is everything, and we must create and control it from the start ... If we went to India and shot a lot of exteriors, according to the usual plan, and then came back to Pinewood and then tried to match them here, you would have two kinds of colour and two kinds of style.'[25] So the Himalayas were recreated at Pinewood and at Leonardslee, a subtropical garden in Horsham, Surrey.

The atmosphere that proves to be so seductive to the English nuns who establish 'The Convent of St Faith' high in the mountains, was suggested by Junge's early drawings of the old palace at Mopu that was converted into St Faith. The key detail of the bell tower symbolises the nuns' attempt to maintain order and time-keeping in a setting that frustrates their ability to do so. It is the site of our first introduction to Sister Ruth (Kathleen Byron) who is most unsettled by the atmosphere at Mopu, as she rings the bell in a lusty, distracted manner. The film's climactic scene also takes place in the tower: Sister Clodagh (Deborah Kerr) struggles for her life with Sister Ruth, who has become mentally unbalanced.

Junge's drawings show the bell near the terrifying precipice that causes Sister Ruth's death when she loses her struggle with Sister Clodagh at the end of the film. The bell was in fact located only a few feet above the ground. The film's deployment of matte painting allowed Junge's original conception to be fully realised in the completed film. Junge also created significant interior details in his designs for the old palace that was formerly used as a harem. The erotic wall paintings that cause the nuns embarrassment, for example, were his idea. They produce a key effect in the film of combining the past with the present while at the same time symbolising the sexual longings experienced by the nuns who are profoundly unsettled throughout their stay at Mopu.[26]

Even though Junge designed some of his most fantastical and ingenious sets for Powell and Pressburger, particularly the dramatic whirlpool sequence that was created in the studio for *I Know Where I'm Going!* (1945) and the grand staircase and celestial court in heaven in *A Matter of Life and Death* (1946), Powell preferred to use Hein Heckroth for *The Red Shoes* (1948). Heckroth had been the costume designer on *Black Narcissus* and Powell felt that he would bring an even greater imaginative touch to *The Red Shoes*, even though he was a great admirer of Junge's work.

Until he retired in 1957, Junge worked for M-G-M-British at Boreham Wood, Elstree. Yet again he was at the forefront of technical development, continuing to experiment with colour (Technicolor and Eastmancolor) and widescreen processes that were introduced in the 1950s. As far as Cinemascope was concerned, he thought it presented technical problems since 'our eyes do not normally span this wide expanse'.[27] In the same 1958 article Junge urges studios to turn to art directors for advice on pictorial composition for widescreen effects so that cameramen and directors can 'visualise accurately how the picture will appear on the Cinemascope screen'.[28] Films designed by Junge for Cinemascope projection include *The Knights of the Round Table* (1953), *Bedevilled* (1955) and *The Adventures of Quentin Durward* (1955).

Some commentators presented Junge as somewhat authoritarian. Edward Carrick, for example, recorded that Junge told him that when asked as a youth by friends or relatives about what he intended to do, his answer was 'I'll be an artist or a Kaiser'.[29] But there is no doubt that his methods revolutionised British art direction by instituting its primacy within the bureaucratic structures of the British studio system. Indeed, Junge proved that creativity could flourish far more decisively within these structures than in the rather haphazard conditions he experienced on his first arrival in Britain. I will let Michael Powell have the last word, since he described Junge as 'the greatest art director that films have ever known … I have never known anyone to touch him, to come near him'.[30]

Notes

1. See also my discussion of Junge in Tim Bergfelder, Sue Harris and Sarah Street, *Film Architecture and the Transnational Imagination. Set Design in 1930s European Cinema* (Amsterdam: Amsterdam University Press, 2007). That book's illustrations include a number of the drawings referred to and described in this chapter.
2. Letter to Georges Lourau of Tobis at Epinay Studios, Paris, 24 November 1935. Filed in Box 9 of the Meerson Papers, Bifi, Paris.
3. Oswell Blakeston, 'Further British Problems', *Close Up*, vol. 1, no. 5, November 1927, p. 51.
4. Paul Rotha, 'Plastic Design', *Close Up*, vol. 5, no. 3, September 1929, p. 228.
5. Junge, letter to Edward Carrick, not dated, Alfred Junge Collection, Harry Ransom Humanities Research Center, University of Texas at Austin.
6. For a comprehensive list of films designed by Junge see Catherine A. Surowiec, *Accent on Design: Four European Art Directors* (London: British Film Institute, 1992), pp. 17–18.

7. A. Vasselo, 'Recent Tendencies in the Cinema', *Design for Today*, May 1935, pp. 170–74. Edward Carrick Collection, Harry Ransom Humanities Research Center, University of Texas at Austin, Box 29.
8. Tim Bergfelder, 'Surface and Distraction: Style and Genre at Gainsborough in the late 1920s and 1930s', in Pam Cook (ed.), *Gainsborough Pictures* (London: Cassell, 1997), p. 36.
9. See Edward Carrick, *Art and Design in the British Film* (London: Dennis Dobson, 1948), pp. 12–14.
10. The negative review was written by Hugh Castle who described *Piccadilly* as 'one of the world's worst' because of the wandering camera and frequent use of close-up. *Close Up*, vol. 5, no. 1, July 1929, p. 45.
11. *Close Up*, vol. 3, no. 5, November 1928, p. 69. It is interesting that this observation *praises* the way in which the set facilitates the mobile camera, while Castle's later review criticised the film precisely for having *too much* mobile camera.
12. Roger Manvell, 'Introduction', in Carrick, *Art and Design in the British Film*, p. 11.
13. See Tim Bergfelder, 'The Production Designer and the *Gesamtkunstwerk*: German Film Technicians in the British Film Industry of the 1930s', in Andrew Higson (ed.), *Dissolving Views. Key Writings on British Cinema* (London and New York: Cassell, 1996), p. 25.
14. See Carrick, *Art and Design in the British Film*, p. 13.
15. The term 'camera consciousness' is used by Edward Carrick, *Designing for Films*, 2nd edn (London and New York: Studio Publications, 1949), p. 24.
16. See Charles and Mirella Affron, *Sets in Motion: Art Direction and Film Narrative* (New Brunswick, NJ: Rutgers University Press, 1995), pp. 82–152.
17. See Charles Tashiro, *Pretty Pictures: Production Design and the History Film* (Austin: University of Texas Press, 1998), p. 45. For an extended discussion of Junge's designs for Jessie Matthews's musicals see Sarah Street, '"Got to Dance my way to Heaven": Jessie Matthews, Art Deco and the British Musical of the 1930s', in *Studies in European Cinema*, vol. 2, no. 1, 2005, pp. 19–30.
18. Carina Carroll, 'Art Direction for Films', *Design for Today*, October 1935, pp. 389–95. Edward Carrick Collection, Box 29.
19. See Lucy Fischer, *Designing Women: Cinema, Art Deco and the Female Form* (New York: Columbia University Press, 2003), p. 126.
20. See Giuliana Bruno, *Atlas of Emotion: Journeys in Art, Architecture and Film* (New York: Verso, 2002), p. 6.
21. For a discussion of 'open' and 'closed' images see Tashiro, *Pretty Pictures*, pp. 41–46.
22. Carroll, 'Art Direction for Films'.
23. Junge, letter to Edward Carrick, not dated, Alfred Junge collection, Harry Ransom Humanities Research Center, University of Texas at Austin.
24. All quotations in this paragraph are taken from Alfred Junge, 'The Art Director and His Work', *The Artist*, parts 2 & 3, April and May 1944.
25. Michael Powell, *A Life in Movies: An Autobiography* (London: Heinemann, 1986), pp. 562–63.
26. For a fuller discussion see Sarah Street, *Black Narcissus* (London: I.B. Tauris, 2005).
27. Alfred Junge, 'Art Direction Yesterday and Today', 1958, typescript for an article commissioned by *Film and TV Technician*, Alfred Junge Collection, Harry Ransom Humanities Research Center, University of Texas at Austin.
28. Ibid.
29. Carrick, *Art and Design in the British Film*, p. 74.
30. Powell, *A Life in Movies*, p. 628.

Chapter 9

LOST IN SIBERIA:
ERNÖ METZNER IN BRITAIN

Laurie N. Ede

Most accounts of British film art direction have offered an idealised picture of European influence. In particular, we have read that European designers – many of them former employees of the German studios – modernised British film design during the 1930s (as Edward Carrick had it, Alfred Junge, Andrei Andreiev and others 'made up our minds for us').[1] This historical orthodoxy has endured for one central reason – it happens to be true. However, this is not to say that all of the émigré art directors exerted equal influence or that they enjoyed similar levels of success. Foreign designers' British careers were particularly susceptible to the vagaries of British film finance. In addition, imported talents had to deal with a range of pressures which were not experienced by their British peers, such as protectionist union regulations (and attendant hostility from British technicians), language difficulties, unfamiliar working practices on the studio floor – and simple loneliness.

The productive British careers of Junge, Andreiev and Vincent Korda were the highlights for European designers during the 1930s. Far less happier times were experienced by the Russian Lazare Meerson and, most notably, by the Hungarian art director Ernö Metzner. This luminary of German studio design was frustrated by second-rate facilities and inappropriate assignments. Metzner believed that he would be a named art director within British studios, a significant player in British films' internationalist production campaign. In the event, he found himself consigned to Gaumont-British's secondary production facilities, the Gainsborough studios at Poole Street, Islington – or 'Siberia', as they were known to British film technicians.

I want to achieve two things with this article. To begin with, I would like to qualify the idealist position on European influence on set design that has come down to us from Carrick. Second – and most importantly – I want to try and unravel why Metzner failed to build a substantial career in Britain.

The Foreign Art Director in Britain

Edward Carrick's untroubled view of foreign design influence was predicated on his own untroubled view of foreign*ness*. Few of his British design peers shared his cosmopolitan outlook. Art directors were comparatively well paid. Also, they cherished their position as influential executive technicians. For both of these reasons, they tended to take a hostile attitude towards the emerging Association of Cinematograph Technicians. (The art directors' union representative Maurice Carter recalled that he turned up to every union meeting merely to 'vote against everything').[2] However, most were four-square behind the ACT in its defining early campaigns against the employment of foreign technicians. An interview by Herbert Wilcox's designer L.P. Williams for *Pearson's Weekly* indicated his critical attitude to foreign design 'aces'. He observed that 'an art director gets from thirty to forty-five pounds a week, but if he is German he gets from sixty to seventy'.[3] Williams also felt that British producers and directors tended to be overimpressed by foreign designers – mainly because of their own insecurities:

> People in British films were very conscious of the fact that they were no bloody good … I think most people, if a foreigner comes along it'd be, 'oh yes, he knows all about it'. English directors [would] fall for it immediately.[4]

But Williams and other artistically progressive British designers of the period (such as Laurence Irving and his protégé John Bryan) were caught in a cleft stick vis-à-vis émigré art directors. On one level, they hoped that outsiders might help to address the reactionary influence of the old school of design (as represented by Clifford Pember and Walter Murton). At the same time, they were acutely aware of their own job insecurity.

During the 1930s, it was evident that the sense of chagrin at design outsiders won out. Foreign designers were usually given the cold shoulder. Junge was friendless for a time following his arrival in 1932. In the same year, Andreiev was dumped by a taxi at Ealing for his first working day in Britain. Werndorff found perennial problems working in British studios from 1929; he lamented to Carrick that 'no-one tells me anything'.[5]

Ernö Metzner Arrives

Metzner's employment in Britain came about as a result of an advertisement which he placed in the cineastes' journal *Close Up* in September 1933. Poignantly, he wrote that he was 'obliged to cease work in Germany [and find] English contacts'. In fact, Metzner had a double 'obligation' to flee Nazi persecution: he was Jewish and he was a left-wing intellectual. He had been closely associated with the left-leaning Neue Sachlichkeit (New Objectivity) movement in German cinema. Moreover, in 1928 Metzner had directed the anti-Nazi short *Dein Schicksal* (Your Fate) for the Social Democratic Party.

As is well known, British film technicians – socialist union officials included – were notably unsentimental in their attitude towards persecuted émigrés (instantly we recall the ACT's early rallying cry 'And still they come!'). Nonetheless, Metzner's advertisement drew a swift response from the Head of Production at the expanding Gaumont-British concern, Michael Balcon. Balcon had good reason to be interested in Metzner. For one thing, as a Film Society member, he knew of Metzner's famous work in Germany. Metzner had an impressive CV, built on his close collaborations with the cineastes' idol G.W. Pabst. At the same time, Balcon – in common with other top level British producers during the 'Klondyke era' of British films (such as Alexander Korda, Basil Dean and Herbert Wilcox) – was desperately short of executive technicians.[6] The *Evening News* reported on 5 August 1935: 'The British film business is finding itself short of everything it requires except money. There are not enough studios, stars, technicians of all sorts.'[7]

In contrast with the nationalistic Wilcox, Balcon had unswerving faith in the superior talent of foreign designers (particularly those who had worked in the revered Ufa studios at Tempelhof and Neubabelsberg). In 1932, he spoke of his desire to create the Gaumont-British art department 'on modern German lines'.[8] Accordingly, he devised the plan of employing Metzner to work alongside the Austrian Oscar Werndorff at Poole Street. Metzner subsequently designed nine British productions, mainly for Gaumont-British at either Islington or its main studios at Lime Grove, Shepherd's Bush. (See Table 2 for a list of his films.)[9]

A few things become immediately apparent as one peruses Metzner's British credits. First, it is a paltry record when compared with the forty-seven productions amassed by Gaumont-British's supervising art director Alfred Junge (who headed the art department at Shepherd's Bush). Second, it seems clear that Balcon's idea of associating Metzner with Islington broke down quickly; certainly, he would have achieved many more credits had he shared Junge's advantage of being a supervising department leader.

Clearly, something went wrong for Metzner. My suggestion is that his British career really floundered on a kind of film culture clash; Metzner's method for art direction was at odds with the demands of the British studios. To understand this, one needs to think about the specific elements of the Metzner method – as developed in the German studios – and see how these were adapted within a British context. This will enable us to evaluate what was lost and what was retained in the journey from Neubabelsberg to London.

Table 2: Ernö Metzner's British Films

Film	Company	Start of production	Studio
Princess Charming	Gainsborough	November 1933	Islington
Chu Chin Chow	Gainsborough	February 1934	Islington
The Robber Symphony	Concordia	January 1935	Elstree Shepperton
The Tunnel	Gaumont-British	July 1935	Shepherd's Bush
Seven Sinners	Gaumont-British	February 1936	Shepherd's Bush
OHMS	Gaumont-British	May 1936	Shepherd's Bush
Strangers on Honeymoon	Gaumont-British	May 1936	Shepherd's Bush
Take My Tip	Gaumont-British	October 1936	Shepherd's Bush
Break the News	Jack Buchanan	September 1937	Pinewood

Metzner in Germany

Metzner's career before Britain occurred almost exclusively in Germany, starting (as a 28-year-old) on Lubitsch's *Sumurun* (1920). He went on to design thirty-four German productions between 1920 and 1933 (as well as creating the costumes for a number of famous films). Of his design assignments, Metzner was known particularly for his six films for Pabst: *Geheimnisse einer Seele* (Secrets of a Soul, 1926), *Tagebuch einer Verlorenen* (Diary of a Lost Girl, 1929), *Westfront 1918* (1930), *Kameradschaft* (Comradeship, 1931), the trilingual production *Die Herrin von Atlantis/ L'Atlantide/The Mystery of Atlantis* (Germany/France/UK, 1931) and *Du haut en bas* (France, 1933).

As I have noted, Pabst was the hero of heroes to the Film Society set. He embodied the early ideal of the self-determined film *auteur*. Equally, he appealed to British cineastes as the champion of a purposeful, authentic commercial cinema. To the savants of the Pavilion Cinema and *Close Up*, Pabst was the guru of the New Objectivity; the great intellectual who could nurture a thinking cinema based on the sober but sensitive rendering of everyday worlds. At the same time, he was valued as the omnipotent film man who built the careers of great technicians.

Metzner revelled in the reflected glory, for a time becoming the European art director of the hour. By the late 1920s, his work was renowned for four tendencies: a mechanical intelligence, texture, realism and (overall) a sense of the defining hand of the *Architekt*. In Germany, Metzner had been known less for the traditional skills of design and dressing than for his ingenious solutions to mechanical problems on the sound stage. He enjoyed thinking about the problems of filmmaking and his projects often demanded that he was as much a special effects man as an artist. This facet of his character was best illustrated by *Kameradschaft*. The tale of French-German unity in the face of a mining disaster called for the development of new techniques. To begin with, Metzner had to find ways to create safe explosions within the studio mine sets. Thereafter, Pabst put him to work finding solutions for specialised photographic problems. During shooting, Metzner invented two new dollies; one with a long tongue for filming in tight mine sets, another in two sections for an elaborate tracking shot up a flight of stairs.[10]

Metzner's highly practical bent for design did not preclude attention to its broad decorative aspects; the films for Pabst demonstrated his alertness to the textural possibilities of art direction. His comment on the design rationale of *Atlantis* held good for a number of the films; he observed that the sets were 'entirely built for the effect of the material, without using any ornament'.[11] Metzner had a strong sense of cinema's world of appearances – he knew instinctively how his sets would appear to the camera lens. This enabled him to derive many of his effects from surfaces, rather than from traditional dressings. Naturally, for Pabst, this gift was placed largely at the service of realism. During the 1920s, Metzner shared his master's devotion to a post-Expressionist, but nonetheless psychologically rooted, sense of filmed reality.

In all respects, and as the above examples indicate, Metzner was far more than merely Pabst's art director – he was a prime interlocutor. In this sense, he embodied the German studio ideal of the *Architekt*: a designer who planned a film in no small part and who also played a fundamental role in devising solutions to the ongoing problems of film production. Of necessity, this made Metzner a film all-rounder. He knew the camera and he knew how to direct (his own experimental short *Überfall* [Accident] confirmed this in 1928). But Metzner's design ideals in Germany were fostered by an indulgent industry; he was thrived within the creative spaces maintained by a range of successful, yet creatively attuned, producers and directors. The tragedy of Metzner's subsequent career was that he expected the same elsewhere.

Metzner in Britain

In Germany, Metzner enjoyed some of the best facilities in Europe, but in Britain he often had to cope with poor or makeshift equipment and buildings. Facilities were particularly poor at Islington. Developed from an old power station, the studios were small and ill-equipped. Initially, Balcon hoped that Poole Street would be an equivalent facility to Shepherd's Bush (indeed, early Metzner British assignments such as the £100,000 *Chu Chin Chow*, made in 1934, testified to this ambition). However, Islington soon became thought of as the poor relation within the Gaumont-British production empire – Junge ventured there only twice during his five years at the company. The workers at Islington knew that they were thought of as the Gaumont technical underclass. The appellation 'Siberia' thus signified not just the desolation of the place, but its function as a place of correction; as the designer Peter Proud recalled, 'you were sent there if you did something wrong'.[12]

Metzner was associated early on with the second-string facilities at Gaumont-British, but he also felt disempowered in more profound ways. Whereas in Germany he had been used to being at the right hand of the director, in Britain he found himself in a subordinate role. Most importantly, Metzner discovered that his mechanical, plastic design style was absolutely out of sympathy with the prevailing ethos of British studios. These are generalised points. In order to truly come to grips with Metzner's British experience, we should turn again to those elements that defined his style and technique at the height of his career.

The evidence suggests that Gaumont-British and his other British producers appreciated that Metzner was at his best in solving specialised, mechanical design issues. The outstanding example was *The Tunnel* (1935). This £150,000 'super production' was closely based on a German film, *Der Tunnel* (1933),[13] but the British remake featured no footage from the original. Metzner therefore had to devise his own ingenious design solutions for this sci-fi yarn about a transatlantic tunnel. The tunnel itself was built on the Gaumont lot at Northolt and modelled on the Mersey tunnel; it was 52 feet at its mouth. Elsewhere, Metzner applied his keen mind to other futuristic elements, such as the 'radium drill', torpedo-shaped cars and 'stratospheric' airplanes. These planes provided the best demonstration of Metzner's logical approach to props. He reasoned that the planes of the future would require thick fuselages and would incorporate reservoirs of compressed air and oxygen. Metzner also devised 'gyroplane' rotary propellers to notionally allow his planes to achieve horizontal roof landings.

Metzner's engineering projects for *The Tunnel* suggested the persistence of his *Kameradschaft* spirit. Other Gaumont projects indicated his continuing preoccupation with texture. Metzner's British sets sometimes had a peculiarly organic sensibility. This was noted in his incorporation of natural motifs. The heroine of *Princess Charming* (1934) slept in a grand bed with a giant shell headboard. Those shells also appeared at times in the sets of *Chu Chin Chow*, but to different effect. Here, Metzner – in consultation with director Walter Forde – seemed intent on creating a sense of ancient Arabia growing out of the sand. Elements from nature –

shell, leaf and tree details – were inscribed into the walls to figure a society which was developing out of the natural world.

Metzner's British assignments demonstrated some continuities with his German work in terms of their mechanical and textural elements. But he was generally undermined by the lack of a coherent aesthetic sensibility to British films and, moreover, by his relative lack of influence over the British studio system. From one perspective, it could be argued that Metzner continued to be a realist art director in Britain. Most of his British projects were based on plausible recreations of the real world, but, of course, this was a depoliticised, banal realism. In socio-political terms, Gaumont-British productions were films from nowhere, their stories generally set in never-never Ruritanian worlds or in the homes of the untouchable upper-middle classes. These must have been anathema to Metzner. Worse still, he came to be employed increasingly in the degraded position of locations art director, frequently on secondary productions. Thus, he was put to work constructing a mock US-Canadian border on location for *Strangers on Honeymoon* (1936) or creating an elaborate Chinese village by the River Avon for *OHMS* (1937). These sets were reasonably impressive – and entirely believable – but they hardly stretched him. Furthermore, Metzner must have been aware of his place within the Gaumont-British studio system. As locations art director, his function was to build in the open air so as to relieve pressure on the overburdened stage space at Shepherd's Bush – and therefore on Alfred Junge. It was little wonder that Proud came to think of Metzner purely as 'Junge's assistant'.[14]

Clearly, Metzner stood little chance in Britain of becoming again the all-powerful *Architekt*. The British studio system suited Junge; in Germany, he had worked on a wide range of productions with scores of directors and photographers drawn from the technical pools at Tempelhof and Neubabelsberg. Conversely, Metzner was used to working closely with photographers and directors. Gaumont's departmentalised studio system prevented such creative alliances. Furthermore, he found that the cramped studios and tight schedules demanded design skills that were far different from those he had used in Germany. Metzner, like Vincent Korda, placed great emphasis on working with his building materials on the studio floor – a chronic and laborious process out of keeping with British methods. Junge's success at Shepherd's Bush was built on his use of definitive, meticulous water colours; these allowed for the quick building and dressing of sets. In contrast – and as his surviving British designs testify – Metzner was a crude sketch artist.

The tensions between Metzner's style and the Gaumont-British ethos were cruelly revealed at Islington during the shooting of *My Old Dutch* (1934). The deployment of Metzner on this routine comedy was mysterious in itself. Support features of this kind were usually farmed out to Junge's assistants and the use of Metzner (rather than Proud or Relph) implied much about Gaumont's declining faith in him. Certainly, the film did Metzner no favours. Early in the production, director Sinclair Hill complained to Balcon that Metzner's drawings were unusable. This ultimately led to a kind of tendering process, whereby the Hungarian's designs were placed in competition against some produced by the tyro Proud. Metzner was humiliated when Balcon and Hill agreed that the 21-year-old should be allowed to proceed with the art direction of *My Old Dutch*.[15]

Proud later averred that Metzner 'couldn't draw'. He also characterised his former superior as a 'supervising art director', but not in the Junge sense of the term. To Proud, Metzner was more akin to Clarence Elder at BIP – he could oversee the efforts of others, but couldn't design in his own right.[16] But Metzner's experiences at Gaumont-British were really to do with a clash of expectations. Gaumont directors – even hacks like Hill – expected designers to come up with detailed visualisations in the Junge manner. For Metzner, it was the completed set that mattered, however this was achieved. Unsurprisingly, the studio view prevailed and the company subsequently made cautious use of the Hungarian art director. Metzner was absorbed into Junge's department, prior to being loaned out to a Hollywood studio in 1936.

Overall, Ernö Metzner's British career provides solid evidence that (contrary to the rhetoric of the ACT and other influential voices) foreign 'aces' did not necessarily enjoy an easy ride within British studios. Sadly, his career did not recover following his time at Gaumont-British. He designed one last film in Britain (*Break the News*, 1938, inherited from the luckless Meerson) before leaving for Hollywood, where he worked on just two further productions.

The Robber Symphony

By any criteria, Metzner's career faltered badly following his removal from the German studios and one can only agree with Paul Rotha's retrospective assessment that his work 'was ... wasted by British and American studios'.[17] However, there is one important exception. As we have seen, Metzner was deemed to be largely surplus to requirements at Shepherd's Bush following the *My Old Dutch* debacle and once again obliged by circumstance to seek work elsewhere. For a short time, he diverted himself by creating a theory for designing in colour, based upon relationships between tones, shades and musical keys.[18] More importantly, Metzner's removal from Gaumont-British gave him the opportunity to become involved in one of the most remarkable films to be made in Britain during the 1930s. Concordia Films' *The Robber Symphony* (1936) was shot at the Sound City studios at Shepperton, but its largely foreign crew imparted a distinctly European aesthetic. Metzner found full expression within this compelling, stateless fairy tale.

It was commonplace throughout the 1930s for film people of all kinds to refer to the 'internationalist' film. The term really had two meanings. Mainly, it was applied to those producers (notably Korda and Balcon) who made big-budget productions for world markets. But the term 'internationalist' was also used, often pejoratively, to describe films which were made by foreign producers and technicians and which were deemed to lack a sense of Britishness. As Graham Greene had it, these were films that suggested alien control of British film culture.[19] Viewed today, famous internationalist productions such as *The Marriage of Corbal* (1936, directed by Karl Grune) and *Southern Roses* (1936, directed by Frederic Zelnik) do seem remarkably insubstantial.[20] But the same could be said of many a wholly British-made film of the period. Moreover, the deployment of foreign technicians allowed for some intriguing moments of cross-pollination.

The point was proven by *The Robber Symphony*, conceived and directed by the Austrian actor/director Friedrich Feher. Feher was mainly known as the man who had played Francis in the Expressionist classic *The Cabinet of Dr Caligari* (1920), but he had serious musical and directorial ambitions. Feher had been a child prodigy in music (he had written a symphony at the age of fifteen) and he formed Concordia Films specifically to indulge his notion of the 'composed' film, i.e. a film where the action would be shot to fit a pre-existing score. Feher was able to persuade a number of financiers – including an ex-attaché to King Karl of Austria and a lady's underwear magnate – to subscribe to his visionary scheme.

Concordia's publicists claimed that Metzner's market set at Shepperton was the 'biggest set yet built in the country'.[21] This was a familiar boast – London Films and Gaumont-British publicists said the same in the 1930s of sets designed by Junge for *Jew Süss* (1934) and by Vincent Korda for *Things to Come* (1936), amongst many others. More importantly, it missed the essential point of Metzner's work on *The Robber Symphony*. Assisted by the resident Sound City art director Douglas Daniels, Metzner was able to produce superbly textured sets which exemplified his maxim that the best design did not rely on set dressings.

Remarkably, Metzner's designs were profoundly Expressionist. Expressionism might have been expected of Feher; he had once directed a film called *Das Haus ohne Tür und Fenster* (The House with No Windows, 1921) on Caligaresque lines. Expressionist intent may also have been anticipated of the photographer of *The Robber Symphony*, Eugen Schüfftan; the famed creator of the 'Schüfftan Process' (a trick photographic effect) was well known for his love of chiaroscuro lighting. But little in Metzner's background spoke of an affinity with Expressionism's vocabulary of distorted geometrical planes and anti-realist perspectives. Nonetheless, he immersed himself fully within the dark psychological universe of *The Robber Symphony*. Strikingly, his design for the major set of the inn featured twisted beams, roughly hewn doorways and the Expressionist staple of stairways that ran in the opposite direction to the major supporting structures. All of these points were carried through to the cat's cradle of a set that lay at the heart of *The Robber Symphony*.[22]

The logic of Expressionism was defined best by the German film and theatre director Leontine Sagan. She wrote that the aesthetic 'wanted to chisel out the physiognomy of the world, to nail down the physiognomy of things'.[23] This romantic ideal of personification was reflected by Feher when he named 'the wind', 'the snow' and 'the rain' (also a donkey, a dog and a piano) amongst the players of *The Robber Symphony*. Of course, Sagan also hinted at the fundamental psychological terrain of Expressionism; the idea was for the artist to express their emotional relationship with objects in the material world. Metzner developed this theme in two further sets of *The Robber Symphony*, the robbers' hideaway and the fortune teller's cottage.

Feher's story was elementary. A gang of robbers led by the 'Black Devil' steals 12,500 ducats from a fortune teller. The gang is subsequently undone by Giannino, the son of a travelling musician (played by Feher's son, Hans).[24] Metzner and Schüfftan were able to impart extraordinary psychological depth to this simple tale. Together, they created an archaic Alpine netherworld where people were never quite what they appeared to be. The hideaway set instigates the theme. Ultimately, it is revealed that the robbers secrete themselves in a large barrel, but we first see this nestling snugly within a curved archway. Helped by Schüfftan's shadows, the whole composition takes on the appearance of a large eye; ominously, the robbers use the barrel as both a hideaway and a lookout. Later on in the film, Metzner personifies the barrel further by giving it three slots; two for eyes and one for a mouth.

The fortune teller's cottage also speaks of the hidden elements of human existence. The textural and architectural elements strongly recall Rotwang's cottage in Fritz Lang's *Metropolis* (1927), for which Schüfftan created the special effects, but Metzner adds some extra spooky elements. The asymmetrical carved pentacle in the door and the crooked railings outside underscore the sense of plastic expressionism. Within the house, Metzner makes effective use of the drapes and dressings; filmed straight on, these create a dizzy Caligaresque pattern. Best of all, Metzner incorporates an imaginative alcove complete with two skeletons.

Appropriately for a film based on music, the overall design scheme of *The Robber Symphony* falls into two broad movements. The first part looms large on Metzner's sets, whilst the second concentrates on outdoor scenes shot in Mer de Glace, Nice and other places on the Cote d'Azur. Metzner was not a fan of location work; he observed that it was 'full of difficulties for him [the art director]'.[25] Nonetheless, the design schemes for Feher's film achieved a strong unity between location and studio. This was helped by the general avoidance of cross-cutting, but Metzner also worked hard to encourage a strong match between the indoor and outdoor worlds of *The Robber Symphony*. The rugged textures of the walls and floors help to create an impression of the village as being not so much man-made as a representation of nature. His incorporation of circular arches and doorways also impart a uniquely organic sensibility to the village scenes which sympathise with the authentic face of nature.

Feher intended *The Robber Symphony* to be a profoundly experimental film; to this end, he was pleased to cast himself as an *auteur* 'fighting the cold commercial attitude of the entire film world'.[26] Sadly, if inevitably, his £80,000 project failed to find an audience, despite its ballyhoo premiere (with the London Symphony Orchestra) at the Palace Theatre. But the film provided some respite for Metzner from his tortuous British career. His loving creations for *The Robber Symphony* demonstrated that he was, for once, amongst friends.

The credits for *The Robber Symphony* stated that Metzner participated 'by arrangement with Gaumont-British Picture Corporation Limited'. It seems obvious that the arrangement suited the company well – it had little use for one of the great theorists of set design. But the deal also provided Metzner with an unexpected opportunity to flourish within a British studio. In November 1929 he had spoken to *Close Up* about his surprising decision to direct a sports adventure film, *Achtung! Liebe! Lebensgefahr!*: 'I like [sic] to make such a film once, but not more than once.'[27] Clearly, Metzner enjoyed no such right to self-determination working within the conventional British studios. Like most of the technicians who fled persecution, he had to accept what he was given. In terms of the British art direction world of the 1930s – and thinking of the contrasting stories of Junge, Korda, Andreiev and Werndorff – Ernö Metzner appears to have been given very little.

Notes

1. Edward Carrick, *Art and Design in the British Film* (London: Dennis Dobson, 1948), p. 15.
2. Sue Harper, 'Interview with Maurice Carter', in Sue Aspinall and Robert Murphy (eds.), *Gainsborough Melodrama* (London: BFI, 1983), p. 56.
3. Lawrence P. Williams in 'Profile of L.P. Williams, Art Director', *Pearson's Weekly*, 7 December 1935.
4. L.P. Williams, interview with the author, 20 February 1993.
5. Edward Carrick, interview with the author, 18 January 1993.
6. The term 'Klondyke [sic] era' was coined by BIP producer John Maxwell to describe British companies' profligate chase after American markets.
7. Cedric Belfrage in the *Evening News*, 5 August 1935.
8. Quote drawn from C.A. Lejeune, 'The Pictures. The Best is Cheapest', 27 November 1932.
9. This table lists Metzner's films in order of their production start dates (rather than release dates). The data has been gleaned from contemporary newspaper and trade paper accounts.
10. Metzner described his technical solutions for Pabst in two self-penned articles for *Close Up*, 'A Mining Film', March 1932, and 'The Travelling Camera', June 1933.
11. Metzner quoted in 'On the Sets of the Film *Atlantis*', *Close Up*, September 1932, p. 159.
12. Peter Proud, interview for the BECTU Oral History Project, 18 November 1987. This is held at the BFI Library in London.
13. The concurrently made French version *Le tunnel* starred Jean Gabin.

14. Proud, interview details in n.12.
15. Details of Metzner's dismissal on *My Old Dutch* (1934) can be gleaned from Proud's BECTU interview.
16. Proud, interview (see above). Before Gaumont-British, Proud had been part of Elder's famously chaotic art department at Elstree.
17. See Paul Rotha's back-page comment in *Films and Filming*, February 1967, p. 66.
18. Metzner explained his ideas to the *Bulletin and Scots Pictorial*. See 'British Colour Expert for Hollywood', 11 November 1936.
19. See Graham Greene, *The Spectator*, 19 June 1936.
20. Both films were produced by Max Schach, the Hungarian who became keenly associated with internationalism and was frequently blamed for the collapse of British film capital in 1937.
21. Press materials for *The Robber Symphony*, held at the BFI Library, London.
22. Metzner's designs for the film are held at the BFI Library in London. They are also reproduced in *Film Dope*, October 1989.
23. Leontine Sagan, 'The Miscellany', *Cinema Quarterly*, Summer 1933.
24. A French version of *The Robber Symphony*, *La symphonie des brigands* (1936), was shot simultaneously with Françoise Rosay playing the role of the fortune teller.
25. Metzner, 'On the Sets of the Film *Atlantis*'.
26. Feher in the *Sunday Times*, 24 May 1936.
27. Metzner quoted in an anonymous review of *Achtung! Liebe! Lebensgefahr!* (Where's Love There's Danger), *Close Up*, November 1929.

Chapter 10

'BE KVITE KVIET, EVERYBODY, *PLEASE!*': PAUL L. STEIN AND BRITISH CINEMA

Christian Cargnelli

In February 1935 the British journalist Edmund G. Cousins visited the set of *Mimi*, a screen version of Henri Murger's novel *Scènes de la vie de bohème* on which Puccini's well-known opera is based. He eavesdropped on director Paul L. Stein, an émigré from Vienna: 'I love to listen to Stein directing. "Be kvite kviet, everybody, *please* – which is the good old Anglo-Saxon vord *shut tup!*"'[1] In this chapter, I will delineate Stein's career in the UK and try to explore the way he constructed images of Austria in his British films. I will also discuss how the latter – and 'foreign' influences in general – were perceived in the popular press in the 1930s and 1940s.

Observations of the kind cited above appear quite frequently in E.G. Cousins's regular column 'On the British sets' in the popular film journal *Picturegoer Weekly* in the 1930s.[2] He prefers to address male continental film personnel as 'Herr', jokes around with their names and makes fun of their language problems. When he notices an actress being nervous before a screen test, he remarks: 'I did not realise why until my friend Herr Eichberg, the director, seeing me there, came over and said, "It is a test ve make, for *Dubarry*, ja, und Anny is nod habby aboud it".'[3] A mixture of admiration and condescension towards foreigners might be the best way to characterise the prevalent attitude of Cousins's reports and the journal as a whole. A close analysis of *Picturegoer Weekly* from 1933 onwards reveals an ambiguous stance especially towards German-speaking émigrés, mirroring a general attitude in the British film industry. Not uncommonly, Central European film personnel were praised for their efforts *and* at the same time made fun of in any one given issue.

On one hand, the technical expertise and quality input brought by the immigrants were welcomed and were of utmost importance to the advance of the hitherto struggling British film industry. On the other hand, their influence was met with irony and scepticism or even straightforward rejection. Comments were sometimes tinged with xenophobic resentment, where 'non-Britishness' in continental stories, genres, visual and acting styles could be detected.[4]

Paul Stein was one of those immigrants. 'I am looking forward with a great deal of interest to *Lily Christine*, Paramount's next production at Elstree', remarks Cousins in early 1932 upon Stein's first British film. *'Lily Christine* is to be directed by Paul Stein, who was responsible for *The Common Law*, *Sin Takes a Holiday*, and other Hollywood successes.' And before introducing a few members of the 'most interesting' cast (including Corinne Griffith and Colin Clive), he adds: 'I have not yet ascertained whether he pronounces his name Steen, Stain, Styne, or Shtyne, although all these forms have their adherents at Elstree.'[5] Thus readers of *Picturegoer Weekly* learn about Paul Stein – before he even sets foot in their country – that he is experienced and successful, having worked in cinema's world capital, and that he comes from foreign, presumably, German lands. *How* experienced he was, and in which way his future efforts could possibly benefit from his private and professional backgrounds, certainly must have been unknown to them.

Beginnings

In 1928 Paul Stein gave this account of his life:

> I am Austrian and was born in Vienna. My father Emil Stein was an actor very well-known in Austria and Germany, so it became quite clear that I was to be trained for the stage, too. I grew up in Vienna, and my education was shared between school and the theatre my father worked in. My progress in dramatic training proved to be so great that my father managed to get me to work with Max Reinhardt, though I was only 17. I stayed with Max Reinhardt for four years and played mostly comical character parts in Shakespeare plays, for instance very often together with Rudolph Schildkraut. Then I went back to Vienna and achieved great success as a Shakespeare actor there, too.[6]

That's impressive – and mostly invented. At least one fact is correct: Stein was indeed born in Vienna in 1892. He grew up there as the son of the Jewish merchant Emanuel Stein and his wife Marie; their address was Obere Donaustraße 87 in Vienna's second district Leopoldstadt, where a large part of Vienna's Jewish population lived.[7] As scholars of the history of mittel-European theatre will assure you with their tongues firmly in their cheeks, everyone at some point worked with famous 'Theatermagier' (theatre magician) Reinhardt. In reality, Stein did not even come close to being a star of the stage. He started out as a student at Reinhardt's acting school at the Deutsches Theater in Berlin, and after humble beginnings in the German provinces he got an engagement at Reinhardt's newly opened Volksbühne (Theater am Bülowplatz) in Berlin for the season 1915/16.

Stein's repertoire included small, sometimes tiny parts; this was not to change during his subsequent stays in Königsberg (under director Leopold Jessner, later also an exile in Britain) and finally, from 1916 to 1919, at the Deutsches Volkstheater in Vienna.[8]

Film: Vienna, Berlin, Hollywood

In 1934 Stein recalled his eventual move from stage to films, talking to Peter Witt, an exiled journalist in London. The director, Witt notes, told him 'how, many years ago he, the most successful actor in Vienna, suddenly and without any real reason, gave up his work and turned his enthusiasm to films'.[9] In reality, Stein's stage career went absolutely nowhere. The films he directed in Vienna in 1919 already indicate his preference for certain genres, thus foreshadowing what was to come: comedies and melodramas. In the comedy *Das kommt davon* (That'll Teach You!), also from 1919, Stein plays a young man with the unmistakably Austrian name Sebastian Flockerl who has his jacket stolen in a popular Viennese open-air pool. 'Bathing scenes excellent', a trade paper noted.[10] The film's director, Rudolf Stiaßny, would work for Stein fifteen years later as location manager in Vienna during the shooting of *Blossom Time* (1934).[11]

In 1919 Stein moved to Berlin and went on to direct no less than twenty-five films in the German capital until 1926, for his outfit Stein-Film and later for Ufa and other companies. In 1920, for instance, Pola Negri starred in three Stein productions: *Das Martyrium* (Martyrdom), *Arme Violetta* (Camille/The Red Peacock) and *Die geschlossene Kette* (Unbroken Chain of Evidence). Stein's German films encompass popular genres of the time: melodramas, society dramas, costume pictures. Only one, *Liebesfeuer* (Flames of Love, 1925), employs a Viennese theme: the joyful life of Austrian hussars on the eve of the First World War.

In 1926 Stein moved to Hollywood, starting to work for Warner Bros. and Cecil B. DeMille. Like a number of other mittel-European film personnel in the 1920s, he was employed in a concerted effort to weaken the European film industries and at the same time enhance the American product by using the experience and the cultural background of film artists trained at renowned German studios like Ufa, preferably in productions with European ambience. The best-known acquisitions included directors Ernst Lubitsch, Michael Kertesz (Curtiz), Friedrich Wilhelm Murnau, Paul Leni and E.A. Dupont, producer Erich Pommer, and actors Emil Jannings and Conrad Veidt.[12] Stein's grandiose 'reinvention' of himself perfectly fit into an established pattern. It seems that the successful Hollywood director did employ the same strategy of self-aggrandising PR that many continental film artists used to their advantage after their arrival in the New World: create a new, shining career in retrospect, a new, more glamorous identity.

Stein's first American film, *My Official Wife* (1926), is set in Vienna, amongst other places. The daughter of a Russian nobleman (Irene Rich) escapes deportation to Siberia by fleeing to the Austrian capital. Here, in the city of music, she enjoys 'a great success as a cabaret singer'. The *Bioscope* review also notes 'brilliant scenes at a Viennese café'[13] – exactly the kind of melodramatic confection Stein was employed to create. The charismatic character villain of the piece was fellow Viennese Gustav von Seyffertitz.

Stein worked in Hollywood until 1932, directing sixteen films altogether: romantic comedies, murder mysteries, spy yarns, domestic dramas. Particularly striking is the number of women dominating on-screen procedures – at first Irene Rich; later Ann Harding, Jeanette MacDonald and Constance Bennett. '"Over there", P.L. Stein has the reputation of being a ladies' director', an Austrian trade paper noted in 1929.[14] Stein's American films are more often than not situated in European or exotic locations: Vienna, Paris, London, Spain, Norway, Arabia. In *A Woman Commands* (1932), for example, Pola Negri, in her first Hollywood feature, loves and suffers in some Ruritanian kingdom.

Settling in Britain

'Let Them *All* Come!' was the title of a *Picturegoer* article in November 1931. The lengthy essay dealt with the internationalisation of British films and explicitly welcomed the influx of foreign film personnel.[15] Whereas a relatively small number of German-speaking film artists had worked here – voluntarily – since the mid-1920s, many more, expelled from Nazi Germany, from 1933 onwards sought refuge in the UK. Paul Stein belongs to the latter category. In 1934 he recounted the days of his forced emigration:

> I wanted to go back to Berlin … there in Berlin I wanted to continue my film work and put to the test the wealth of experience that I had gathered in America. Just as a murderer is always magnetically drawn back to the scene of his crime, so I too was drawn back to Berlin and to the places of my unforgettable years of apprenticeship. But there I was up against the trend of political events. German filmcraft, which has been completely shattered by political experiments, is hardly the basis on which I can work out my ideas.[16]

'Political experiments' meant, of course, that the Nazis had seized power and Stein, of Jewish descent, could not have gone back to Germany without risking his life. We can only speculate whether British readers in 1934 were able to grasp the full meaning of his comments. Stein settled permanently in Britain in 1933 and entered a contract with British International Pictures (BIP). 'It is [sic] very slight and obvious Viennese romance', Lionel Collier mercilessly remarks upon his first BIP effort, *The Song You Gave Me* (1933).[17] This musical comedy, a remake of the German production *Das Lied ist aus* (The Song is Ended, 1930), which was written by later-to-be-émigré Walter Reisch, starred an international cast headed by American Bebe Daniels and Hungarian Victor Varconi. Making no great impression at the time or thereafter, it nevertheless points forward to better, more successful Stein films in the same style and genre: Viennese pictures made in Great Britain.

> The world wants 'Vienna'. This is, for the moment, a completely unpolitical statement. The world I would like to speak about here is the world of theatre, of film, of entertainment and diversion in any form imaginable. A world of appearances. In this world Vienna is a big power of the highest order.[18]

You can hardly put it better than Harry W. Gell, general manager of Fox's Viennese office, does here in the popular film journal *Mein Film*, Vienna's counterpart to *Picturegoer*, in 1934. It is not realism that promises box office success, but the use, recycling and exploitation of those 'timeless' topoi and myths Vienna has always been known and loved for.[19] Not surprisingly, Gell goes on to mention Austrian operettas, plays and novels, composers Lehár, Strauß und Robert Stolz, and actors Elisabeth Bergner, Fritz Kortner and Paul Hörbiger. 'For generations this city has been exporting its surplus of talent to all corners of the world, a talent corresponding with a happy and blessed view of life.'[20]

There is not a word here about the fact that many of those successful and highly gifted individuals, such as Bergner and Kortner, were not allowed to work in Germany any longer – some of them, after their in no way voluntary 'remigration', now living as exiles in Vienna, amongst them actors Peter Lorre and Oscar Homolka. After all, dealing with the Nazified German film industry still meant good business for both Austrian and Hollywood companies.

Stein's next film, *Red Wagon* (1933), an adaptation of Eleanor Smith's eponymous 1930 novel, truly fulfilled *Picturegoer*'s call for foreign talent. 'B.I.P. gathered an international cast', the journal enthused over this 'British movie milestone'. 'It is probably richer in Hollywood "names" than any picture ever made here.'[21] Charles Bickford stars as Joe Prince, an orphan child of circus people, who, after many struggles, achieves his life ambition of owning his own circus. He is torn between Zara, the lion tamer (Swedish-born Greta Nissen), and the Gypsy girl Sheba (Raquel Torres). The most convincing performance, though, a 'brilliant contribution',[22] comes from German exile Paul Graetz, an old friend of Stein since their shared early days with Reinhardt. He excels as Maxi Schultze, the charismatic owner of 'Schultze's Grand Circus' which is flagged with the Union Jack.[23] *Red Wagon* reflects internationalism not only in its cast and crew – German Kurt Schröder worked on it as the musical director – but also, partly, through its narrative. At the start of the film, there are animosities between Americans and Brits when a circus is touring the United States. Joe's father, a trapeze artist, plunges to his death as a result of sabotage, and his girlfriend, Joe's mother, is shot dead; their son and his foster parents move back to Britain. Years later Joe returns from the USA as a star and in a battle of circus bosses defeats his British opponent, Cranley (Francis L. Sullivan).

It is tempting to read the transatlantic angle of *Red Wagon* as a metaphor for the state of Anglo-American film relations at the time, mirroring the struggle for supremacy in British cinema, i.e. the fight against Hollywood's dominance by building up a strong national film industry.[24] A writer in *Picturegoer Weekly* even used war rhetoric in pointing this out: 'It is pleasing to record that another British company – British International, this time – has made a picture far in advance of its usual product. Thus the advance along the Home Front continues all round.'[25]

Not everyone shared this enthusiasm. Seen today, *Red Wagon* deserves attention for its elaboration of internationalism, while not refraining from employing stereotypes such as the good blonde white woman and the dark-haired, treacherous Gypsy girl in the process. One cannot help noticing clumsy storytelling and a rather awkward narrative – shortcomings some contemporary reviewers pointed out:

> It is a story that moves slowly, so slowly that the background of circus and gypsy life is deprived of its full effect. Mr. Paul L. Stein, who directs the film, has a genuine sense of the circus, and he is never more happily inspired than when he has tigers slinking from tub to tub to the cracking of the tamer's whip, 'liberty horses' stepping the musical ride, and trapezists swinging close under the canvas roof. These scenes have the undying charm of a good circus, but when he takes us behind the scenes and tries to show us what manner of men are the clowns, the lion-tamers, the ring-masters, and the rest of them he is not so successful.[26]

When E.G. Cousins visited the set, he, like his *Times* colleague, found himself captivated by the circus atmosphere. But he concluded his report with the observation: 'It's an illuminating fact that the only two directors at present working in the B.I.P. studios at Elstree are Germans: Herren Stein (making this circus film, *The Red Wagon*) and Zelnick [sic] (directing *Happy*).'[27]

Blossom Time

Stein's next film, *Blossom Time* (1934), again for BIP, 'was a major event for the company, costing far more than its other films, with crowd scenes and some large and decorative baroque sets'.[28] Bryan Langley, second cameraman, remembered it as being '*The Sound of Music* of its period'.[29] *Blossom Time*, subtitled 'A Romance to the Music of Franz Schubert', tackles a quintessentially Viennese subject: an episode from the life of the famous composer. It quickly turned into a phenomenal success,[30] certainly owing a great deal to tenor Richard Tauber playing Schubert. This is Stein's real entry into British cinema. Talking to *Mein Film*, he explained:

> Being now about to direct a Viennese film in England which is, of course, also intended for America, I wonder why it should not be possible to shoot such Viennese films for real in Austria. And considering that foreigners should not be shown a film pretending to present an Austria that does not exist, but Austria and Vienna as they really are, I have decided to move the location shooting of the Schubert film to Vienna.[31]

A little 'cheating' certainly didn't hurt: when the young lovers (Jane Baxter and Carl Esmond) pass through the Prater, a large Viennese park, in a horse-drawn carriage while being spotted by a wistful Schubert, they do really cross the park of Laxenburg Castle – because, as British assistant director Frank Cadman explains, in the 'real' Prater 'we could not have avoided anachronisms such as the ubiquitous electric lighting and telephone wires'.[32] Most scenes of the film, though, including the imposing ballroom and the Karlskirche (St Charles's Church) interiors, were shot at Elstree.

In spring 1934, the film crew travelled from London to Vienna separately: Stein, Tauber and cameraman Otto Kanturek made a detour through France and Italy to escape the danger of falling into the Nazis' hands – all three of them had already become exiles in Britain. Cousins reported on another visit to Elstree:

> Gene Gerrard [British actor and director] wandered with me on to the *Blossom Time* set, which represents the interior of Vienna Cathedral a hundred years ago, and remarked to Paul Stein, the director, 'That's the best synagogue I ever saw.' The point of that remark is better appreciated if you realise the number of German nationals who are in our studios because Herr Hitler disapproves of their religion.[33]

Blossom Time, written by Franz Schulz, prolific screenwriter of Weimar cinema who emigrated to the USA in 1934, together with three British colleagues, tells the story of Schubert's unrequited love for Therese Grob (called Vicki Wimpassinger here and played by Jane Baxter) – and provides Richard Tauber, 'BIP's biggest celebrity',[34] presumably the best-known Austrian resident in 1930s Britain, with ample opportunity to sing.

Linz-born tenor Richard Tauber (1891–1948) from the early 1920s had been popular in Germany and Austria, appearing in operas and operettas and enjoying success as a recording artist. His rendition of 'Dein ist mein ganzes Herz' ('You Are My Heart's Delight'), from Franz Lehár's 1929 operetta *Das Land des Lächelns* (Land of Smiles), eventually gained him world-wide fame. Tauber also appeared in a few German-language films and in the early 1930s toured Britain and the USA, becoming a regular event on the London stage.[35]

At the heart of the film, Schubert, after the intended singer's loss of voice, delivers four of his songs himself in front of a packed audience:

'Red Roses' ('Heidenröslein'), 'Faith in Spring' ('Frühlingsglaube') and 'Impatience' ('Ungeduld') in English and the 'Ständchen' in German. One year before, Willi Forst had produced his Schubert biopic *Leise flehen meine Lieder*, starring Hans Jaray, in Vienna. Analysing both leading men's performances, Franz Marksteiner commented:

> Hans Jaray's lovingly restrained performance ... seemingly owes a lot to the kind of naïve respect and admiration Austrian grammar schools conveyed to their pupils. Jaray's way of speaking, owing to its musicality, was to become formative for the Viennese film ... Richard Tauber, whose Schubert is only one among several Viennese characters, in his comical clumsiness sometimes recalls Oliver Hardy. The characters around him are primarily concerned with providing *Tauberschubert* with the best possible entrances ... Where Forst fills up an icon, a character [Schubert] is fitted to Richard Tauber in Stein's picture.'[36]

Ultimately, both must renounce. Tauber's Schubert, at least, actively helps the woman he cannot win for himself to enter the state of matrimony.

From 24 August 1934, *Blossom Time* was shown for the exceptionally long period of seven weeks at London's Regal Cinema (Marble Arch).[37] Critics especially enjoyed the musical elements of the film. *Picturegoer Weekly*, looking back on 1934, commented:

> The most important of the year's musical crop, and the most important film to come out of the British International Studios at Elstree for long enough, was *Blossom Time*, in which the great German tenor Richard Tauber gave both a full-length vocal concert and an excellent imitation of Franz Schubert.[38]

The significance the public attributed to Tauber's British film debut was mirrored in the vast coverage of the film's shooting and its production background. The issue of *Film Weekly* published on the day of the premiere, for instance, devoted a long, very favourable review and four pages of photographs to *Blossom Time*, along with a two-page article in which Stein describes his collaboration with Tauber.[39]

The singer's performance received unanimous praise; the film's plot and set design fared less well. *Blossom Time* suffered from

> a story that is hackneyed and a development that is pedestrian. The singing of the star, however, compensates for a great deal and, despite its faults, the film has a certain gentle charm that has hitherto not often been achieved in British films ... A story of artless simplicity is jumbled with a 'Gay Vienna' atmosphere of sophistication and elaborate, if rather too obviously studio-made, spectacle and settings.[40]

The *Jewish Chronicle* had similar concerns: 'Schubert's music and Tauber's fine voice and superb technique – attractions enough surely; so that it may be churlish to speak of the utterly artificial and sugary little novelette story that forms the plot.'[41] *The Times*, which compared *Blossom Time* unfavourably with *Congress Dances* (1931), the English version of the huge

Ufa success *Der Kongress tanzt* – 'a film which in some particulars it quite obviously imitates' – and criticised the sentimentality and slow pacing, also praised Tauber and the musical arrangements: 'This is really a concert, a very good concert, of Schubert's songs. The music is treated with respect and sung with feeling by Mr. Richard Tauber disguised as the composer, occasionally accompanied by a boys' choir.'[42]

In its short account of the London premiere, German journal *Film-Kurier* moderately praised the film while the names of Stein, Schulz, Kanturek and supporting actor Paul Graetz were not mentioned. Tauber's name still was, and, rather surprisingly, not in a derogatory manner: 'Tauber's portrayal of the great composer Franz Schubert expectedly impressed the premiere audience.'[43]

However, in general the singer was one of the main targets of Nazi propaganda aimed at Jewish entertainers in exile. One of its leading publications, *Der Stürmer*, in the mid-1930s repeatedly and venomously agitated against the 'Operetten-Rundfunkjude' ('Operetta-Radio-Jew') Tauber.[44] Moreover, the tenor found himself – like Kortner, Lorre and Lubitsch – being disparaged and ridiculed in Fritz Hippler's infamous anti-Semitic propaganda picture *Der ewige Jude* (The Eternal Jew, 1940).

In *Mimi* (1935), Tauber was sorely missed: there simply were no singing parts. Puccini without music, Lionel Collier joked, 'is like playing *Hamlet* without the ghost'.[45] The film tells the tragic love story of the title character (Gertrude Lawrence) and aspiring dramatist Rodolphe (Douglas Fairbanks Jr.) in 1850s Paris. '*Mimi* owes much to Miss Doris Zinkeisen's dresses', Graham Greene remarked, 'and to the acting of Mr Douglas Fairbanks Junior, more perhaps than to Miss Gertrude Lawrence's pinched out-of-place charm.'[46] The *Jewish Chronicle*, on the other hand, considered Paul Stein 'to be rather unfortunate in the subjects he is given to direct, but one imagines that he is at least partly responsible for the general high level of acting'.[47] In March 1936, a dubbed and slightly shortened version of *Mimi* was released in Germany. As might be expected, neither the distributor's PR materials nor the reviews include the names of Stein, actor Paul Graetz or co-screenwriter Paul Merzbach, an exile in Britain since 1933. Berlin-based *Der Film*, for example, lists nine cast members, but not Graetz.[48] Other reviews refer to the film's director only by his job title, 'Regisseur'.[49]

Heart's Desire

'We will go to a Heurige', famous tenor Van Straaten (Frank Vosper), who has just appeared at Vienna's State Opera in Bizet's *Carmen*, announces to a young English couple visiting Vienna; they want to contract him for a London engagement. 'A what?' replies Frances Wilson (Leonora Corbett), sister of a London impresario. 'A Heurige, typical Vienna. An old winegarden where the people of Vienna amuse themselves … A few tables under the trees, a little music, everyone's so happy, the new wine, a spring night, a beautiful woman – and that is the Heurige!'

A moment later they find themselves in this very typically Viennese inn. Laughing people are everywhere, some waltzing, others raising their glasses to each other. While the musical quartet – piano, violin, double bass and accordion – is ending its tune amidst thunderous applause, patrons are calling for their local idol. Josef Steidler (Tauber) has another quick drink, walks out into the garden and delivers one of the most classical of Viennese songs: 'Wien, Wien, nur du allein, sollst stets die Stadt meiner Träume sein …' ('Vienna, City of My Dreams').

Heart's Desire (1935), mainly shot at Elstree's BIP studios, is at the heart of the Stein-Tauber collaboration. Though its director, unlike his star, has fallen into total oblivion, this great film is definitely his lasting achievement. *Heart's Desire* negotiates central aspects of exile: rootlessness, alienation, language loss. Unlike Tauber, Josef Steidler is not being expelled to England, but comes here voluntarily – and yet, his story evokes, if not in explicitly political terms, the fate of the exiled individual. The original story of the film is provided by German author Bruno Frank, who in September 1933 had fled to Austria, and later went to Switzerland, France and the UK.[50] Frank's treatments, which are held at the BFI, come pretty close to the finished screenplay credited to him and three British writers, L. du Garde Peach, Roger Burford and Jack Davies.

The Heurigen singer Josef Steidler is discovered by a British socialite and her fiancé, an aspiring composer; she wants him to appear in operettas on the London stage. Before that, though, he has to learn English. His friend and manager Florian (Paul Graetz) is assisting him:

> Florian: Have you a chill or influenza, as the case may be?
> Josef: Hör schon auf! Ich bleibe, wo ich bin!
> Florian: I only understand English!
> Josef: I stay where am I.
> Florian: I am.
> Josef: You are.

The rapport between Tauber and Graetz in this scene is really wonderful – and the very funny dialogue certainly approximated reality, as Tauber's difficulties with the language at the time are well documented.[51]

Josef Steidler loves Vienna where all of his friends live and everyone likes him. But he has fallen for that English lady. At Vienna's Westbahnhof (Western Railway Station) the whole staff of the Heurige bid him farewell in a magnificent ceremony, singing the German folk song, 'Muss i denn, muss i denn zum Städtele hinaus' ('Must I Then, Must I Then, Leave This Little Town') – the Viennese girl who loves him is among them, endlessly sad and crying. 'This is quite a characteristic Austrian custom', it is explained in L. du Garde Peach's script version, 'the singing of a little song before somebody leaves by train – especially amongst the peasants. I have never seen it on the Central Station at Vienna, but I have seen it frequently at village stations.'[52] It seems not unlikely that Bruno Frank added this piece of information.

Heart's Desire finds simple, but impressive images in showing the transition from the familiar to the foreign. Snow-capped Austrian mountains provide the visual background for Josef singing the folk song 'Morgen muss ich fort von hier' (Tomorrow I must leave) in the train compartment. Travellers applaud, plain Austrian food is served – but the English lady intrudes: 'Josef! Lunch, please!' Wistfully he looks out of the train window, and from somewhere, i.e. non-diegetically, 'Wien, Wien, nur du allein', briefly and in an instrumental version, is heard. Dissolve to London, buses in the streets, and swinging urban music on the soundtrack. 'Florian, it is all so strange here. When do we go back to Vienna?'

When Tauber visited Vienna in summer 1935, he talked to *Mein Film* about his role in *Heart's Desire*:

> I play a man whose nature and actions are essentially influenced by his love for his native Vienna and by his homesickness for this city. And it's this kind of emotion I have truly and deeply experienced.[53]

Apart from the fact that Tauber, according to biographical accounts, was not interested in politics and would not have explicitly mentioned topics such as expulsion, emigration or exile, these would have been rather inopportune in *Mein Film* in 1935 anyway. Phrases like 'due to changed circumstances' were usually employed in describing the Nazi takeover in Germany. The journal neutrally reported what was happening in Berlin, Vienna, London or Hollywood at the time, foregrounding Austrian-related film matters; Viennese cinemas screened both Nazi and British films, and Germany was, after all, by far the most important market for Austrian productions.

Heart's Desire presents Vienna, London style: 'In Elstree artists have built old Viennese alleyways and a Heurige amazingly true to life. There is a really typical Viennese atmosphere lingering over this lovely little spot on the banks of the Thames.'[54] Richard Tauber sings three of his own compositions and two songs by Schumann in *Heart's Desire*, and wins acclaim playing a Venetian in the operetta *Venetian Moon* at London's Olympic Theatre. The woman he yearns for, though, he doesn't get. 'Florian, how soon can we be back in Vienna?' And Josef looks towards and into the large panoramic view of the Alps in his dressing-room – and the photograph instantly dissolves into the Alpine panorama behind the train on its way back to Vienna. 'I never realised that Austria was so beautiful!' Florian replies, 'Isn't it great to be home!' Josef: 'Home! Back in our old world!'

In the film's climax London and Vienna, English and Viennese, are united quite miraculously. Josef Steidler enters the garden of the Heurige and again sings 'Wien, Wien, nur du allein' – but this time it is the English version, 'Vienna, City of My Dreams'. Finally, it seems, he has managed to bring with him something useful from foreign lands after all, and now returns it to a British audience. The *Palestine Post* commented on the film's Anglo-Viennese angle:

> The author [possibly Bruno Frank], together with the producer Stein, composed an attractive film over and above the singing, in which sentimental Vienna is amusingly opposed to the more serious character of London. Two worlds are sharply contrasted and then united. This film also has interesting points, by way of language, being alternatively in German and in English. Realism in the surroundings was aimed at, and so the atmosphere of 'new wine in Vienna' was not robbed of its racy dialect.[55]

Almost sixty years later German film historian Frieda Grafe elaborated on cinematographic realism:

> Authentically Viennese films were produced extraterritorially, somewhere else – after the concept of authenticity had been changed by cinema. Whether they are derived from real Viennese experience or from covetous ideas brought about by foreigners, makes no difference. Either way, Viennese is always close to cliché. The filmic image, then, is directly close by.[56]

It is exactly this kind of 'authenticity', based on cinematographic concepts of realism, that *Heart's Desire* strives for, eschewing naturalistic portrayals, instead employing and at the same time transcending Viennese clichés.

Into the War

Paul Stein became a British citizen in 1938.[57] He went on to direct sixteen more films until his death in 1951. They included musical romances, spy dramas, comedies and murder mysteries. In May 1937 he wrote to his friend Paul Kohner in Hollywood, a legendary agent and an exile himself:

> There is no film industry here in England. Still, it remains a fact that some people are making pictures. So don't regret the fact that you are still stuck over there and even if life seems to be very monotonous sometimes, it doesn't matter – you are far away from Europe where, one day, not in the near future, political troubles will start which will end in a war … You know how much I love Europe, you know how much I enjoy travelling around in France, in Switzerland, in Austria and in Czechoslovakia, but, frankly, in the depths of my heart I am longing to go back to the States, to Hollywood, maybe to settle down there and try to get a little peace after all these years of excitement.[58]

In March 1938, a few days before the 'Anschluss', he told Kohner he wanted to go to Hollywood but was afraid of having to start all over again. 'But on the other hand I wish to be as far away from the Continent as possible, because one day there will be trouble.'[59]

The *Film-Kurier* issue of 24 February 1939 includes a long review of Stein's *The Outsider* (1939), starring George Sanders as a villainous osteopath, a remake of Harry Lachman's eponymous 1931 film (both were based on Dorothy Brandon's popular play). That Stein's name gets mentioned here might appear surprising, at least at first glance – on the other hand, his directorial efforts are slated:

> Nonetheless, the film is not short of certain dramatic moments, especially at the end when the female patient rises in front of a physicians' panel and, instead of walking, collapses. But this breakdown is played out much too broadly by the director (Paul Stein), and repeated without good reason, so that the audience cannot help being embarrassed … the director should really have avoided depicting the doctors in the film as a flock of stupid ignorants.[60]

In summer 1939 Stein shot the crime drama *Poison Pen*, which, especially in hindsight, gains particular poignancy. The film is set in a small, peaceful English town where the rector's sister (Flora Robson), by writing anonymous letters, causes the suicide of a young woman and the murder of a man. The girl who kills herself does so after being hounded by the villagers, who pin the guilt for the letter-writing on her, primarily because she came to the village as a 'foreigner', i.e. from another part of the country.

Poison Pen had its premiere in January 1940. Its depiction of a spiteful community evidently did not fit in easily with the national effort to stand together and fight the enemy. 'This rather sordid drama', *Picturegoer* remarked,

> is heavy-going for a wartime audience. It is very well done; characters are exceptionally well drawn and the development is logical and tragic, but with major issues impending it seems to cast a gloom which is unwelcome in times of crisis.[61]

Too English – or not English enough – as the film seemed to Graham Greene, who found it 'a deplorable example of an English film which tries to create an English atmosphere … The background of the picture is as quaint and false as a Broadway teashop'.[62] In 1941 Stein contributed an entry to the RKO's 'The Saint' series, *The Saint Meets the Tiger*. 'It is an involved story', according to *Picturegoer*, 'but has plenty of action and picturesque Cornish settings.'[63]

The war years limited Stein's output. In 1944 he directed the comedy *Kiss the Bride Goodbye*, starring Patricia Medina who is goaded by her mother to become engaged to her employer while her lover (Jimmy Hanley) is fighting in Burma; and the melodrama *Twilight Hour* in which an amnesiac major (Mervyn Johns) eventually recognises the fiancée of his employer's son as his daughter. 'In spite of the worn-out central theme, leading to the usual sort of jokes', *Monthly Film Bulletin* noted on the former, 'this is a well-acted and directed comedy.'[64]

The war was touched upon in a Christmas telegram Stein had sent to his friend Kohner in 1942; it clearly hints at the difficult living conditions he was experiencing at the time: 'Convey our season greetings to Dieterle, Freund, Blanke, Lubitsch and your family and thank them for food parcels.'[65]

Vienna, Again

Stein recreated gay old Vienna one last time in 1945 when British cinema was being dominated by other genres than operettas (melodramas, in particular). 'Once upon a time, in old Vienna, the Waltz was considered a naughty and immoral dance …', are the first lines of the prologue of the aptly titled *Waltz Time* (1945) – and immediately a Gypsy troubadour and his female partner, parading through the streets of Vienna built at Elstree,[66] burst into song with the infectious title tune, 'Waltz Time in Vienna', written by Viennese-born composer Hans May, in British exile since 1934 (see Geoff Brown's essay in this volume).

The film revolves around young Empress Maria (Carol Raye) and her yearning for Count Franz von Hofer (Peter Graves), and also, paralleling it along the lines of classical stage operetta, tells the love story of prime minister's daughter Cenci (Patricia Medina) and a dashing young officer. There are the usual plot intricacies, a fair deal of masquerade and a lot of songs – and finally the Empress proclaims the waltz, formerly considered a frowned-on kind of amusement, the official court dance. In a splendid wedding ceremony she gets married to her beloved Count. Richard Tauber, dressed in white vestment, is standing in the pulpit amongst his choirboys and they perform 'Break of Day' – which closely resembles a scene in *Blossom Time*, when he, accompanied by his school class, delivers a song in the St Charles church during the wedding of Vicki and Count von Hohenberg. Tauber appears as a guest star in *Waltz Time*, playing a shepherd. Before the finale he has already sung the same song in his hut when the Empress passed by in a horse-drawn carriage; he is, though, not integrated in the plot itself. But Tauber's name, emphasised in the film's opening credits, undoubtedly contributed to this recycling of Viennese motifs, helping it to become a big success. 'In my opinion the film stinks', Stein wrote to Kohner, 'but the public is always right'.[67]

After the War

From the correspondence with Kohner we derive a lively picture of the difficult economic situation in England in the immediate postwar era. 'Every food parcel from California is more than welcomed!!'[68] Stein writes in autumn 1945. Kohner sends him food on a regular basis. 'Your last parcel arrived safely', Stein notes in spring 1947, '… the salami is very good – but no more during the summer I am afraid.'[69]

'Whereas a number of formerly German directors, now successful abroad, are avoiding employing emigrated Germans', New York exile paper *Aufbau* comments on Stein's arguably most interesting postwar film, *Counterblast* (1948), 'Paul Ludwig Stein, working on his new picture ... in London, is a notable exception. Amongst those employed are Hans May as the composer, Sybilla Binder, Karl Stepanek, Karl Jaffe, Martin Miller and F. Schiller.'[70] *Counterblast* is a topical anti-Nazi film, reflecting postwar fears of enemies attacking Britain from within. Dr Bruckner (Mervyn Johns), the 'Beast of Ravensbruck', a ruthless Nazi scientist, escapes from a POW camp, kills an English colleague and assumes his identity. He works on a formula to immunise Germans against the plague with which the Nazis intend to wage the next war against England. Their plans come to nothing in the end, of course, also owing to Bruckner's growing affection for his British assistant whom he is not able to kill at a crucial moment.

This might be 'not very convincing and is definitely theatrical',[71] but it certainly deserves interest for its depiction of a Nazi organisation working secretly in London, comprising German *and* British members, headed by a German psychoanalyst nicely named Professor Inman. The latter is played by émigré Karel Stepanek, a very familiar face in numerous villainous parts – Nazi, Soviet or other – over four decades of British and international films. The one really memorable performance, however, comes from Viennese-born actress Sybilla Binder as Martha Lert, a Nazi spy sent to watch over Bruckner's proceedings. 'Guten Abend, Herr Doktor Bruckner', are her first words upon arrival, and she instantly – through her voice and a well-modulated German accent – manages to convey an atmosphere of menace and terror without having to draw on any histrionics. While critical of certain, indeed undeniable, shortcomings, *Monthly Film Bulletin* still conceded that the story 'is not only topical but ... also seems rather disturbingly plausible'.[72]

Gone – But Not Forgotten?

Paul L. Stein died in London in May 1951. There were no detailed obituaries or appreciations. One gets the impression that the British public had forgotten this versatile, reliable, successful director who for almost two decades contributed significantly to British cinema. In a letter to the trade paper *The Cinema*, Arthur Dent, Managing Director of the leading 1930s British distributor Wardour Films (which, amongst others, had brought *Blossom Time* and *Heart's Desire* into cinema theatres), remembered his professional companion:

> So Paul Stein is dead. The man who did more in blending successfully art and industry in entertainment films than anyone I know is no more. His *Blossom Time* was a landmark in the industry and Paul will always be associated with it. It was a stroke of genius to bring Richard Tauber over for the leading role and

Paul was able to bring the film in to schedule … His charm of manner and good temper were proverbial – in fact it was said of him that his manner could almost charm a bird off a tree.[73]

– just what a real Viennese, in a way, is all about. Charm alone, however, will not get you anywhere if you are a director; experience, especially in working with actors, meticulous casting, organisational skills – in one word, craftsmanship – certainly will. In his British films Paul Stein continued to do what he had previously, and successfully, done in Germany and Hollywood: he tried to bring out the best in his actors. Working within an essentially commercial, popular framework, he gave the likes of Richard Tauber, Paul Graetz and Sybilla Binder ample opportunity to shine. His most satisfying effort, *Heart's Desire*, combines this ability with an evocative narrative of the émigré experience – a genuinely international cinema Paul Stein should definitely be remembered for.

Notes

1. E.G. Cousins, *Picturegoer Weekly*, 16 February 1935, p. 26.
2. In January 1936 the column changed to 'We Cover the British Studios'; then later to 'E.G. Cousins Covers the British Studios', amongst others.
3. *Picturegoer Weekly*, 30 December 1933, p. 26. Cousins reported this in retrospect; German actress Anny Ahlers died soon afterwards and the film came to nothing. Later Paul Stein was announced as the director. See '*Dubarry* for B.I.P. Paul Stein to Direct', *Kinematograph Weekly*, 7 December 1933, p. 39. In the end, neither German-born Richard Eichberg nor Stein took charge of the film, which premiered as late as 1936, retitled *I Give My Heart* and directed by Austrian-born exile Friedrich Zelnik.
4. Probably the best-known example of xenophobic resentment is Graham Greene's infamous review of the émigré production *The Marriage of Corbal* (1936), produced by Max Schach, directed by Karl Grune and photographed by Otto Kanturek. See *The Spectator*, 5 June 1936, reprinted in David Parkinson (ed.), *Mornings in the Dark. The Graham Greene Film Reader* (Manchester: Carcanet, 1993), pp. 107–9. The Association of Cine-Technicians (ACT) played an important role in this context. Founded as a proper trade union in June 1933 with the aim of improving the bad working conditions of cameramen, editors and other studio technicians, it came under pressure with the increasing number of refugees from Nazi Germany. Though soundly left-wing and in no way anti-Semitic, the ACT in 1935 nonetheless established a committee to check the number of foreign film personnel working in Britain. As Tim Bergfelder put it, 'the tension between political idealism and economic imperatives must have been nearly impossible to balance'. Bergfelder, 'The Production Designer and the *Gesamtkunstwerk*: German Film Technicians in the British Film Industry of the 1930s', in Andrew Higson (ed.), *Dissolving Views. Key Writings on British Cinema* (London/New York: Cassell, 1996), p. 33.
5. E.G. Cousins, *Picturegoer Weekly*, 20 February 1932, p. 24. *Sin Takes a Holiday* (1930) and *The Common Law* (1931), both starring Constance Bennett, are dramas with a strong female angle that are situated in Paris and the USA.
6. Hermann Treuner (ed.), *Filmkünstler. Wir über uns selbst* (Berlin: Sibyllen, 1928), unpaginated. My translation.
7. Birth certificate 'Paul Ludwig Stein'. Reg. no. 275/1892, Israelitische Kultusgemeinde Wien (Jewish Community of Vienna). Stein's strategy obviously worked: in a 1934 film

journal's 'character study' of the director, his early days are depicted exactly the way he related them in 1928. See Hubert Cole, 'A Mercurial Maker of Stars', *Film Weekly*, 17 August 1934, p. 7.

8. For detailed information on Stein's work in the theatre see *Neuer Theater-Almanach* (1913f.), *Deutsches Bühnen-Jahrbuch* (1915ff.) and the programme notes of the Deutsches Volkstheater Vienna.

9. Paul Stein, 'Heading for British Supremacy', *Picturegoer Weekly*, 3 March 1934, p. 10.

10. *Paimann's Filmlisten*, no. 150 (31 January to 6 February 1919). My translation.

11. Hans Taussig, 'Sommertagstraum in Laxenburg', *Mein Film*, no. 440 (June 1934), p. 11.

12. See Thomas Elsaesser, 'Heavy Traffic. Perspektive Hollywood: Emigranten oder Vagabunden?', in Jörg Schöning (ed.), *London Calling. Deutsche im britischen Film der dreißiger Jahre* (Munich: edition text+kritik, 1993); Elsaesser, *Weimar Cinema and After. Germany's Historical Imaginary* (London: Routledge, 2000), pp. 361ff.; Graham Petrie, *Hollywood Destinies. European Directors in America, 1922–1931*, rev. edn. (Detroit: Wayne State University Press, 2002); Jan-Christopher Horak, 'Sauerkraut & Sausages with a Little Goulash: Germans in Hollywood, 1927', *Film History*, vol. 17, no. 2/3 (2005).

13. *Bioscope*, 21 October 1926, p. 55.

14. *Das Kino-Journal*, 29 June 1929, p. 12. The sentence reads better in German: 'P.L. Stein steht "drüben" in dem Ruf ein Damen-Regisseur zu sein.' See also 'A Director of Women', *Film Weekly*, 13 February 1932, pp. 7 and 17.

15. John K. Newnham, 'Let Them *All* Come!', *Picturegoer Weekly*, 7 November 1931, p. 7.

16. Stein, 'Heading for British Supremacy', p. 10.

17. Lionel Collier, *Picturegoer Weekly*, 13 January 1934, p. 27.

18. Harry W. Gell, 'Die Welt will "Wien"', *Mein Film*, no. 442 (June 1934), p. 24. My translation.

19. See Elsaesser, 'Heavy Traffic. Perspektive Hollywood: Emigranten oder Vagabunden?', pp. 33–34.

20. Gell, 'Die Welt will "Wien"', p. 24. My translation.

21. Lionel Collier, *Picturegoer Weekly*, 18 August 1934, p. 24.

22. Ibid.

23. One of Berlin's best-loved character comedians and cabaret performers before he was forced to flee to England, Graetz enriched a number of British productions from 1933 onwards, for instance *Jew Süss* (Lothar Mendes, 1934), *Mimi*, and two other films by Stein, *Blossom Time* and *Heart's Desire*. In 1936 he moved to Hollywood, but, after having appeared in only four Warner Bros. B pictures, died in early 1937. Pem (= Paul Marcus), exiled journalist in London, wrote in his obituary in the émigré paper *Pariser Tageszeitung* (19 February 1937): 'Paul Graetz, who once played with Reinhardt and was one of the founders of the second "Schall und Rauch" [a famous Berlin cabaret], was the incarnation of the most genuine Berlin spirit.' My translation.

24. The screenplay originated with three British writers: Roger Burford, Arthur B. Woods and New York-born, cosmopolitan Edward Knoblock.

25. M.B.Y., *Picturegoer Weekly*, 23 December 1933, p. 20.

26. Anonymous review in *The Times*, 7 December 1933.

27. *Picturegoer Weekly*, 11 November 1933, p. 32. *Happy*, a 'lighthearted musical about three "lads"… seeking their fortunes in the streets and bistros of London', is a 'good example of the confused sense of national identity and locale to which this form of production was subject. Despite its cheap sets and perfunctory production it has a bizarre charm, but it is pervaded by an uneasy placeless feeling.' Rachael Low, *The History of the British Film 1929–1939* (London: George Allen & Unwin, 1985), p. 93.

28. Low, *History of the British Film 1929–1939*, p. 123.

29. Bryan Langley's Photo-Diary. Number Two: 1934. British Film Institute, Special Collections.

30. This success extended beyond the UK. See, for instance, '*Blossom Time*'s Paris Triumph', *Kinematograph Weekly*, 27 September 1934, and '*Blossom Time* in Australia. Sweeping

Success of B.I.P. Musical', *Kinematograph Weekly*, 29 November 1934. As late as June 1935, the film was used in a magazine advertisement for the skin cream Snowfire Cream, showing a photograph of leading stars Jane Baxter and Carl Esmond under the heading 'We're in Love'. See *Picturegoer Weekly*, 29 June 1935, p. 3.

31. Paul Ludwig Stein, 'Amerika-Film für Europa', *Mein Film*, no. 428 (March 1934), p. 4. My translation.

32. Taussig, 'Sommertagstraum in Laxenburg'. My translation.

33. E.G. Cousins, *'Blossom Time* at Elstree', *Picturegoer Weekly*, 2 June 1934, p. 30.

34. Low, *History of the British Film 1929–1939*, p. 123.

35. For more information on Tauber, see Michael Jürgs, *Gern hab' ich die Frau'n geküßt. Die Richard-Tauber-Biographie* (Munich: List, 2000).

36. Franz Marksteiner, 'Schubert heiß ich. Bin ich Schubert?', in Christian Cargnelli and Michael Omasta (eds.), *Aufbruch ins Ungewisse. Österreichische Filmschaffende in der Emigration vor 1945* (Vienna: Wespennest, 1993), pp. 85 and 82. My translation.

37. Originally scheduled to run for three weeks, 'the terrific reception it received from London picturegoers resulted in its being retained week after week'. See 'Great B.I.P. Success. *Blossom Time* – Record Seven Weeks' Run', *Kinematograph Weekly*, 11 October 1934, p. 34. A number of other interesting productions similarly characterised by émigré involvement also premiered that autumn, which supports the notion of the paramount importance of exile cinema in Britain: Paul Czinner's *Catherine the Great* starring Elisabeth Bergner; *Chu Chin Chow* starring Fritz Kortner (photographed by Mutz Greenbaum, sets by Ernö Metzner); Berthold Viertel's *Little Friend* with Kortner (photographed by Günther Krampf, sets by Alfred Junge); *Evensong* with Kortner and Carl Esmond, aka Willy Eichberger (photographed by Greenbaum, sets by Junge); Lothar Mendes' *Jew Süss* starring Conrad Veidt and Paul Graetz (sets by Junge); and Alexander Korda's *The Private Life of Don Juan*, written by Lajos Biro, with a score by Ernst Toch.

38. E.G. Cousins, 'The Year on the British Sets', *Picturegoer Xmas Annual* (December 1934), p. 16.

39. Paul L. Stein, 'How We Made Richard Tauber's First British Film', *Film Weekly*, 24 August 1934, pp. 8–9.

40. M.D.P. (= Malcolm D. Phillips), 'Richard Tauber's British Debut', *Picturegoer Weekly*, 28 July 1934, p. 16.

41. *Jewish Chronicle*, 24 August 1934, p. 34.

42. *The Times*, 27 August 1934, p. 8.

43. 'Der Schubert-Film von B.I.P.', *Film-Kurier*, 13 July 1934. My translation.

44. 'Der emigrierte Richard Tauber', *Der Stürmer*, vol. 14, no. 15 (April 1936).

45. Lionel Collier, *Picturegoer Weekly*, 10 August 1935, p. 25.

46. *The Spectator*, 2 August 1935.

47. *Jewish Chronicle*, 26 July 1935, p. 43.

48. See 'Deutsche Fassung von *Mimi* reichszensiert', *Der Film*, 15 February 1936.

49. See, for instance, the review in *Film-Kurier*, 28 March 1936.

50. Frank's exile novel *Der Reisepaß* was first published in Amsterdam in 1937 and came out as *Closed Frontiers* in London that same year.

51. See Stein, 'How We Made Richard Tauber's First British Film', pp. 8–9; Jürgs, *Gern hab' ich die Frau'n geküßt*, passim.

52. 'Tauber Film'. Revised script by L. du Garde Peach, 11 April 1935, p. 54. BFI, Richard Tauber Collection.

53. 'Richard Tauber auf der Durchreise …', *Mein Film*, no. 498 (July 1935), p. 5. My translation.

54. C.T.J., 'Heurigenfilm mit Richard Tauber', *Mein Film*, no. 488 (May 1935), p. 8. My translation. The way British magazines described this atmosphere sometimes failed to catch the Viennese spirit: the Heurige is referred to as 'Austrian beer-garden', 'Viennese Biergarten', 'Viennese beer garden' or just 'biergarten'. See *Picturegoer Weekly*, 1 June 1935, p. 30; *Monthly Film Bulletin*, August 1935, p. 133; *Film Weekly*, 18 October 1935, p. 32; *Jewish Chronicle*, 18 October 1935, p. 48.

55. 'German [*sic*] Singer in a British Film', *Palestine Post*, 29 November 1935, p. 10.
56. Frieda Grafe, 'Wiener Beiträge zu einer wahren Geschichte des Kinos', in Christian Cargnelli and Michael Omasta (eds.), *Aufbruch ins Ungewisse. Österreichische Filmschaffende in der Emigration vor 1945* (Vienna: Wespennest, 1993), p. 227. My translation.
57. *Pem's Privat-Berichte*, 14 September 1938, p. 55.
58. Letter from Paul L. Stein to Paul Kohner, 21 May 1937. Paul Kohner Collection, Filmmuseum Berlin – Deutsche Kinemathek.
59. Letter Stein to Kohner, 7 March 1938. Paul Kohner Collection, Filmmuseum Berlin – Deutsche Kinemathek.
60. H.M., 'Londoner Filmbrief', *Film-Kurier*, 24 February 1939. My translation.
61. Lionel Collier, *Picturegoer and Film Weekly*, 25 November 1939, p. 28.
62. Graham Greene, *The Spectator*, 10 November 1939.
63. Lionel Collier, *Picturegoer*, 29 November 1941, p. 13.
64. V.M.C.D., *Monthly Film Bulletin*, 31 October 1944, p. 113.
65. Western Union, 25 December 1942. Paul Kohner Collection, Filmmuseum Berlin – Deutsche Kinemathek. German-born Wilhelm Dieterle, in Hollywood since 1930, started out directing German-language versions and subsequently changed to prestigious biopics such as *The Life of Emile Zola* (1937) and *Juarez* (1939). Highly active in anti-Nazi causes, he was one of the most active members of the European Film Fund that supported European refugees. Cameraman Karl Freund, of *The Last Laugh* and *Metropolis* fame, lived in Hollywood since 1930. German-born Henry Blanke came to Hollywood with Lubitsch in the 1920s and advanced to become a powerful producer for Warner Bros. during the following decades, also working with Dieterle, and supervising numerous film classics, among them many Bette Davis vehicles. More detailed information on Stein's activities during the war years has yet to be established.
66. For an account of the improvisational skills in building the film's sets, see 'Building a Set inside a Set – and Saving Time', *Kinematograph Weekly*, 22 March 1945, p. 47.
67. Letter Stein to Kohner, 15 September 1945. Paul Kohner Collection, Filmmuseum Berlin – Deutsche Kinemathek. Lionel Collier, on the contrary, a critic not known for being carried away easily, had nothing but praise: 'This delightful British picture takes us back to the days when stage musical comedies provided us with so much lilting and tuneful music. It is not only excellent entertainment but a positive relief from the ever-prevalent swing.' *Picturegoer*, 4 August 1945, p. 13.
68. Letter Stein to Kohner, 15 September 1945.
69. Letter Stein to Kohner, 30 April 1947. Paul Kohner Collection, Filmmuseum Berlin – Deutsche Kinemathek.
70. -z, 'Wie wir hören', *Aufbau*, 16 July 1948, p. 19. My translation. Binder, Stepanek, Jaffe, Miller and Frederick Schiller are Austrian, Czech or German-born émigré actors.
71. Lionel Collier, *Picturegoer*, 3 July 1948, p. 12.
72. *Monthly Film Bulletin*, 31 July 1948, p. 91.
73. Arthur Dent, 'To Paul Stein', *The Cinema. News and Property Gazette*, 9 May 1951, p. 27.

Chapter 11

ALLEGORIES OF DISPLACEMENT: CONRAD VEIDT'S BRITISH FILMS

Gerd Gemünden

I

In the 1935 Gaumont-British film *The Passing of the Third Floor Back* Conrad Veidt plays a stranger who mysteriously appears one day in a London boarding house, where he rents a room. During his brief stay the lives of the lodgers are disrupted and dramatically altered by their interaction with this extraordinary figure. Thus, in some form or other, the stranger redeems the various stock characters who inhabit the house, ranging from an abject kitchen help (René Ray) through an embittered woman on the wrong side of thirty (Beatrix Lehmann), a bankrupt retired military man too proud to take a job in sales (John Turnbull), and his poor daughter (Anna Lee) willing to accept a marriage of convenience, to the self-important (and ironically named) Mr Wright (Frank Cellier) who, though quite obviously an evil and oppositional figure to the stranger's goodness, still arouses his compassion. When at the conclusion of his stay, with Mr Wright dead and all tensions resolved, the stranger is asked by one of the boarders how he was able to have such an impact on everybody's life, he simply declares: 'I am a stranger to you. And because of that I am able to see you all a little more clearly than you see yourselves.'

The outsider status ascribed to Veidt's charismatic character has obvious religious undertones, but it is also clear that the very fact of being a stranger, someone who does not belong, has provided this figure with a privileged vantage point from which to comprehend the psychological make-up and social position of each individual in the house as well as the dynamics of their interaction. The position of the stranger is presented as one that brings with it insights other figures do not possess – presumably because they are too close to their own predicament – as well as the respect and authority afforded only to those who can claim to be unbiased. At the same time, he must remain an outsider to the community he has so positively affected during his brief stay. Significantly, he remains unnamed, and at the end departs as suddenly and mysteriously as he had entered.

With its emphasis on types rather than full-fledged characters, a parable-like narrative strongly foregrounding a moral message, and a setting exemplifying a slice-of-life approach, *The Passing of the Third Floor Back* is a highly allegorical film that teaches viewers – through the learning process of the boarders – about their own complicity in creating and upholding everyday misery. On a more general level, the film can also serve as an allegory for the role exiles play within a host country. As Anton Kaes and myself have argued elsewhere, research on exiled artists has long emphasised the significance of the disabling, paralysing, and traumatic dimension of exile, but has mostly neglected to consider the more productive dimension that forced displacement and disorientation can create.[1] While exile is certainly an experience of loss and estrangement, as Adorno has powerfully shown, it also provides opportunities for self-examination and social critique, triggering innovation, creativity and originality.[2]

Kaes has used the figure of the stranger in the house to describe the conflicted position of exile filmmakers in Hollywood, understanding their position as simultaneously insider and outsider, characterised by both limited interaction and marginality as well as by having access to privileged, enabling perspectives.[3] Leading a double life and displaying multiple affiliations, both of descent and consent, exiles live, to use Edward Said's term, in a median state of existence.[4] The films they make or are involved in are predominantly about the host country, but anchored in the reality of the experience of expulsion. Since very few films in which exiles were involved revolve around this experience on a thematic level, reading for exile in these productions means reading for their political unconscious. As I want to show in what follows, Conrad Veidt's career in the UK, particularly his roles in *The Passing of the Third Floor Back* and *Jew Süss* (1934), invite a reading that highlights how the scripted roles and Veidt's interpretation of them are allegories of the larger political, social and psychological displacement he and his fellow exiles experienced.

II

Among the estimated 2,000 German-language film professionals who were forced into exile during the Third Reich – about 400 of whom at one point or another were employed in the UK – actors and actresses faced the strongest obstacles to continuing their careers, because their accents curtailed the roles available to them. The fate of being typecast, most commonly as some form of stranger, is one that few of them were able to escape. Veidt's role in *Passing* certainly fits this picture, but among exiled actors he nevertheless occupies a special place. Not only is his international success a stark contrast to the hardship and relative obscurity the majority of exiled actors experienced, but his career path was, from the outset, also marked by a strong international and even transnational dimension that is unusual even among accomplished actors. This dimension consists of more than working in one's native country, followed by a sojourn in the USA, followed by a return home. Veidt appeared in English- and French-language productions in Germany, was employed in the UK after the coming of sound but prior to being ostracised in Germany, made another film in Germany while already living in the UK, worked in France while living in the UK, and subsequently had a second Hollywood career in the early 1940s. In all these different contexts, Veidt's star persona had something extraterritorial to it, not just exotic, as many foreigners were cast in Hollywood, rather it had a sense of not belonging to one particular country, maybe not even of this world.

From the start of his career in 1917, Veidt's acting style and roles displayed what one might call a dimension of deterritorialisation. His work in the various industries in which he found employment – Germany during the First World War and the Weimar Republic, Britain between 1932 and 1939, a French interlude of 1937/38, and Hollywood before the transition to sound and then again in the early years of the Second World War – features him in roles that have as a common denominator, despite all disparity, the marginal, the duplicitous, the uncanny and the despotic. Veidt's characters defy the norms of a stable identity, be it in terms of the sexual, the psychological, the social or the political.

This deliberate ambivalence also informs his career path. Although he began, like many of his peers, in the theatre, he transitioned back and forth between screen and stage much longer than would be expected of someone who established world-wide fame and a star persona very early in his film career. The advent of sound terminated Veidt's Hollywood career, yet he remained an international star, starring in the English-language versions of several important early German sound productions, including *F.P. 1* (1932) and *Der Kongreß tanzt* (Congress Dances, 1931), in which he also appeared in the French-language version.

Veidt's role as the stranger in *The Passing of the Third Floor Back* thus draws on this established star persona, but it should also be noted that it underwent significant changes with his entry into the British film industry. After leaving Weimar cinema, his repertoire of expressionist characters and mannerisms so powerfully displayed in *The Cabinet of Dr Caligari* (1920), *Waxworks* (1924), *The Hands of Orlac* (1924) and *The Student of Prague* (1926) was replaced with different forms of exoticism. Veidt shifted from representing deviant characters to figures who are on the margins of society, and thus the meaning of his roles changed as well. If in his Weimar films his roles expressed inner tensions, made visible by jagged facial expressions and asymmetrical handling of his body, in his British films we now find balanced composure in his many spy figures. Commandant Oberaertz (*I Was a Spy*, 1933), Convict 83 (*King of the Damned*, 1935), Baron Karl von Marwitz (*Dark Journey*, 1937) and Captain Ernst Hardt (*The Spy in Black*, 1939) provide battlegrounds for external or social conflicts – most often that between loyalty to one's cause or country and sexual desire – but these respective protagonists bear them with stoicism, often as a mixture of Prussianism and British stiff upper lip.

These extraordinary changes in Veidt's roles and also his star persona, which was widely discussed in the British trade press in the mid-1930s, stand out in a profession in which a given screen image is often very hard to shake off.[5] Peter Lorre is a case in point. His success in Fritz Lang's *M*, where he plays a deranged child murderer, would haunt him throughout his more than seventy films and also determine the two roles he played in the UK for Hitchcock in *The Man Who Knew Too Much* (1934) and *Secret Agent* (1936).[6] The respective British careers of Oscar Homolka, Paul Henreid, Dolly Haas and Fritz Kortner proved to be similarly short and frustrating, but are of course much more representative of the experience of the exiled actor than the success story of Conrad Veidt.

The differences in Veidt's roles encompassed changes in his appearance. Sue Harper has remarked upon the alterations in his posture, facial expression and actual build – a radically different *Haltung* (stance/posture) which she attributes to the teachings of F.M. Alexander. She observes that by the mid-1930s Veidt's 'skeletal alignment had altered completely, such that the muscle tone was symmetrically distributed and the head and neck were loose and free'.[7] Veidt's acting style in *Passing* is also distinctly different from the rest of the cast as well as from his earlier British roles: minimalist, almost static. His face appears ambiguous and becomes a projection screen of other people's desires. The gaze is fixed, movements are restrained but resonant with meaning. Veidt himself commented on this minimalism in 1942: '[This was] the most difficult role I ever undertook. There was ever the danger of going too far. If for an instant it were made insincere, the part would fall to pieces.'[8]

III

Veidt's role and acting style were part of the overall aesthetics of *The Passing of the Third Floor Back* and thus in harmony with the set design, the cinematography, the music, and the changes the script introduced from the play by Jerome K. Jerome on which it was based. These changes have to be attributed to the fact that the film was very much an émigré production. Apart from Veidt and director Berthold Viertel, contributors included set designer Oscar Friedrich Werndorff and cameraman Curt Courant. Producer Ivor Montagu, a friend of Eisenstein and Hitchcock's producer, spoke Russian and German fluently and was a valuable link between the frequently foreign staff at Gaumont-British and management, as Kevin Gough-Yates has noted.[9]

Under Viertel's direction, screenwriters Michael Hogan and Alma Reville made considerable changes from Jerome's play as well as the very popular silent film adaptation by Herbert Brenon from 1918. While in the play notions of human agency were somewhat obscure, Hogan and Reville put a stronger emphasis on class issues among the lodgers, certainly also attributable to the Marxist leanings of Viertel. No longer a supernatural appearance, the stranger in the 1935 version challenges the lodgers to acknowledge not only the misery of their everyday desires, but also their complicity in upholding it. The inequities of the social system are indicted, while the stranger facilitates self-improvement, bringing out the best in each of the characters he meets. Ultimately, he is not a *deus ex machina*, but an expression of their inner selves. As he states, 'I came because you wanted me.'

The effectiveness of Veidt's acting has been attributed to a careful integration of his gestures, body movement and facial expression into the overall *mise en scène*, particularly sets and lighting. Cesare's languid movements, for example, follow the zigzag lines of the sets of *The Cabinet of Dr Caligari*, into which he blends seamlessly. Director Paul Leni created his own set designs for *Waxworks*, in which the suspicious and superstitious despot Ivan the Terrible dwells in a cave-like fortification, driven to madness in front of a huge hourglass, with the oval forms emphasising circularity and feeling trapped.

For *The Passing of the Third Floor Back*, Werndorff built sets that throw Veidt's performance into relief in very different ways. The composition around him is always symmetrical, and the lighting serves as a metaphor for his power. In the very first shot of him, for example, when he suddenly appears at the boarding house, a church archway behind him perfectly frames his upper body, and as he steps inside his face is surrounded by a glow (a shot that is repeated when he exits at the end). For the first time (apart from the credit sequence) we hear non-diegetic music, further highlighting the significance of his arrival. Veidt himself commented on the different function of light used in an earlier version of the film:

> In the silent film ... a light shone from behind the stranger's head. In the current production, there is no such mumbo-jumbo. I am just a stranger, human, natural, benevolent ... When the stranger was shown in his room, he took a flower from his coat and put it into a glass of water, then opened the blind to let in a gleam of sunlight. It was the simplicity of beauty you can make out of nothing ... fantastic in a spiritual way.[10]

While Brenon's film (1918) was tailored around the performance of Sir Johnston Forbes-Robertson and considered a one-man show, in Viertel's version, as contemporary reviewers noted, 'Veidt's sensitive and restrained performance' allows the ensemble to shine.[11] The figure of the stranger itself is conceived of differently in the sound film. Whereas

Forbes-Robertson appeared in a long, black coat, Veidt avoids all theatricality, wearing a grey suit and carrying a suitcase like a travelling salesman. Courant's soft-focus shots of Veidt further exemplify his privileged status among the lodgers, who are shot in more realist, almost stage-like lighting. The lighting thus conveys what would otherwise be communicated by dialogue, allowing Veidt to be mostly a bystander, someone who sees and hears but rarely speaks.

Only the final sequence breaks with the structuring aesthetics of the film: a storm rages and each character is shown alone in their own room, wrestling with the decision either to be good and to resist temptation by Mr Wright, or to give in and corrupt oneself in one form or another. It is in this sequence that Veidt's character takes on the more demonic connotations known from Weimar's haunted screen, his face suddenly lit by lightning as he ascends a dark stairway, shot at somewhat obtuse angles. Here he also changes from quiet listener and observer to all-commanding judge, even displaying powers of omniscience.

As shown above, the film strongly foregrounds the motif of the stranger in the house, and the kind of catalytic conversion he can effect amidst the 'natives'. However, it does so by undermining the binary opposition between insider and outsider, between those who belong and those who intrude. On one hand, the transitoriness of the stranger contrasts with the fixity of the lodgers, who seem to be locked into their existences in the boarding house. Yet on another level, they too are without real homes, whether because of monetary problems or because they do not have families, making the boarding house not just the usual symbol for a slice of society, but also one of displacement and non-belonging. This is a transitory space typical of exile cinema (others would be airports, train stations or border crossings) and in keeping with a plot that revolves around arrival and departure.[12] Casting Veidt in a role that emphasises non-intervention, observation and silence adds a layer to his star persona that builds on his previous outsider roles in significantly different ways. This particular outsider is much more a projection screen for the lodgers in which they recognise themselves for what they are – a screen that is created by virtue of Veidt's uncharacteristic minimalist acting, supported by cinematography and set design.

IV

By the time *The Passing of the Third Floor Back* was made, Veidt had been in the United Kingdom for more than two years, having settled permanently there in the spring of 1933.[13] That date did not mark the beginning of a far-reaching wave of emigration to England, but only an intensification of a process that dates back to the 1920s. The relatively smooth transition that German film professionals experienced when they entered the respective film industries of their host countries – be they England, France, or the United States – was made possible by an internationalisation in which competitiveness also ensured compatibility. Veidt's career is ample proof of the strong international connection of film professionals between various European countries and America, just as his permanent emigration to England had been prepared by his prior work there (notably *Rome Express*, made at Gaumont-British in 1932). Yet by 1935, Veidt's position within the British film industry (as well as Viertel's) had clearly changed due to political circumstances in Germany, making a return to Germany undesirable if not impossible.

This status as an exile, and not just an émigré, had been cemented through two films in which Veidt starred prior to *The Passing of the Third Floor Back*; in both of these he played a Jewish character explicitly written to elicit the sympathy of the audience: *The Wandering Jew* (1933) and *Jew Süss*. Both films recast Veidt's previous roles as suffering outsider in particularly radical terms, investing his socially marginal figures with dignity and power, and in the case of the latter, furthermore, establishing clear parallels with the persecution of Jews in the past and the rampant anti-Semitism within Nazi Germany. It was these sympathetic portrayals of the Jew that made Veidt persona non grata in Germany and, according to Allen, led to his detention there in 1934 when working on *Wilhelm Tell*, only to be released through the intervention of Gaumont-British and the British Foreign Office; he subsequently never set foot in Germany again.[14]

The episodic feature *The Wandering Jew*, directed by Maurice Elvey, traced the various historic incarnations of protagonist Matathias (Conrad Veidt) from the times of the crucifixion of Jesus to the Spanish Inquisition and provided an allegory of the fate of the Jewish people without overt reference to the present. The Gaumont-British production *Jew Süss*, meanwhile, can be seen as a direct response to developments in Nazi Germany.[15] The film was directed by Lothar Mendes, a German Jew from Berlin and naturalized American citizen who had come to Hollywood in the 1920s, following his friend and colleague Ernst Lubitsch, and would work in England until 1941. It was based on Lion Feuchtwanger's 1925 novel of the same title, an international bestseller published in England in 1926 that by 1930 boasted translations into fifteen languages. Plans for adapting the book for the British screen with Veidt in the title role date back to 1928, as Billie (later: Billy) Wilder reported for Berlin publication *Tempo*.[16] While events from 1933 onwards obviously gave the story more political urgency, Feuchtwanger's novel itself had already been conceived of as a response to the historical circumstances of his time, namely the rise of anti-Semitism in Germany following the defeat in the First World War and the concomitant search for a scapegoat.

Mendes' film was originally planned as a big-budget historical drama that would rival Hollywood by cashing in on the popularity of the bestselling book as well as on the star power of Veidt.[17] Even though *Jew*

Süss was not a box office success, it did become an early and remarkable document portraying German Jews in a sympathetic light. A calculated response to the antisemitic measures introduced by the Nazis, it did not fail to provoke the ire of Goebbels, leading to the consequences mentioned above for Veidt, as well as Goebbels' efforts for a German cinematic 'response', which would be realised as *Jud Süß* in 1940 under the direction of Veit Harlan.[18]

The Süss figure Mendes and his screenwriters A.R. Rawlinson and Dorothy Farnum created was a larger-than-life character who foregoes friendship, love and his own well-being in order to win power and help the cause of the Jewish people. As such, the film was devoid of the contradictions of the novel, let alone its layered narrative structure; indeed, it took serious liberties with the historical figure of Joseph Oppenheimer which Feuchtwanger had carefully studied.[19] Yet both novel and film show Süss's desire for assimilation to be informed by the larger Enlightenment idea of opening the ghetto, not by personal gain (as Harlan's film later would); thus, much is made of Süss's explaining to the Duke their mutual affinity which is based on 'a mysterious knowledge, an infallible and unshakeable instinct that my fate is linked to yours, unconditionally and completely with all that I have and all that I possess. Just as I am bound to you, so you are bound to me, Karl Alexander'. When Süss plots the Duke's downfall, in revenge for his daughter's death, he does so fully aware that his fall from power will follow the Duke's.

It may be worthwhile to recall that the historical Oppenheimer was the son of a wealthy Heidelberg merchant and not born in the ghetto (which did not then exist in that city). A real-life mixture of Lessing's Nathan and Shakespeare's Shylock, his demise was brought on as much by his own ambition and lack of judgement as by the fact that he was caught in the middle of various tensions: those between a Catholic ruler, Karl Alexander, and a predominantly Protestant state, Württemberg, as well as between Alexander's absolutist style of governance and the resistance of the state representatives. Apparently, Oppenheimer repeatedly sought to be relieved from his service to the Duke, but his appeals for resignation were dismissed. Oppenheimer's chance to become a gentile came through the Duke (not a mysterious gentile father), who appealed to the Emperor to ennoble Süss, but the appeal was not granted because Süss was not willing to convert to Christianity.[20]

Admittedly, the historical Oppenheimer's behaviour at court as womaniser and benefactor of nepotism is to some degree more accurately captured in Harlan's portrait than in Mendes', whose image of Süss is very much shaped by present concerns to create sympathy for German Jews. Yet, even though the Süss figure loses some of these historical contradictions in Mendes' streamlined and somewhat melodramatic narrative, Veidt's interpretation of the role recovers, at least to a certain extent, its psychological and historical complexity.

The opening shots introduce Süss as a worldly man aware of his professional achievements and his charisma vis-à-vis women, both of which he realises are closely bound to his outer appearance, as we repeatedly watch him spend a good amount of time in front of the mirror or calculate how to most advantageously use his dress, posture, or good looks. His professed intent is to open the doors of the ghetto for the Jews (a motif underscored repeatedly by shots of doors, doorways or gates), yet, time and again, the camera isolates him, framing him as a solitary figure not only at court but also within the Jewish community. Clearly separated from the other Jews by appearance, tone of voice and professional ambition, he also remains 'the Jew' at court, tolerated because needed; and significantly he is the only character (apart from Landauer) to speak with a German accent in a film entirely set in Germany.

Süss's singularity and isolation is underscored by the fact that he is surrounded by types: Landauer (Paul Graetz, a German Reinhardt actor who played in many silent and early sound films) as the fearful and meek inhabitant of the ghetto; Rabbi Gabriel (Cedric Hardwicke) as wise elder who mysteriously enters and exits; and most notably Karl Alexander, played by Frank Vosper as a plumpish caricature, loud-mouthed, lecherous and often drunk. Clearly, this Duke is no real match for Veidt's subtle and complex Süss, not a player but a mere pawn in his strategising (as is made amply clear at the end of the film when Süss thwarts the Duke's plan to have him arrested and instead creates a predicament so shocking to the Duke that he suffers a fatal heart attack). Even though Süss may be seen as a mere imitator of the behaviour and social role of Karl Alexander – his open display of attraction to women, his vanity, his enjoyment of power and luxury – he knows that such imitation is his only weapon, possible only at court and under the protection of the Duke. The fact that Süss keeps a parrot – a fact ridiculed by Landauer asking 'what does a Jew want with a parrot?' – indicates that he is aware not only of the lack of originality that bespeaks copying but also of the fact that it comes at the price of a golden cage.

Veidt's acting style, his facial expression, gestures, hair style and hair colour that shape his role as much as dress and lighting, powerfully convey Süss's changing identity in the course of the film. When first introduced at the beginning, he is a meticulously groomed and well-dressed man who exerts considerable charm over women, recognised as a Jew only when Landauer appears at his side. After the death of his daughter, for which he holds the Duke responsible, he realises that the price of assimilation in his quest for 'position, respect, power' has been too high; the inner change from loyal but calculating servant to avenging (but still calculating) adversary is clearly marked: his clothes are now predominantly dark; gone is the wig, and we see in his dark hair a grey streak as testimony to his traumatic loss. Gone also are the scenes of brightly lit interiors and high rooms at court, replaced by candlelit, cave-like enclosures.

When Süss prompts the Duke to dare a *coup d'état* (which he knows will lead to the latter's downfall), he is shown whispering in the Duke's ear in extreme close-up, giving the shot a grotesque feel unmatched by any other in the film. The scheming and demonic Veidt, well-known from Weimar cinema, comes through in full force when Süss enlightens the Duke, paralysed after his stroke and only able to move his eyes, about his true motives, showing the Duke as the immobile puppet that he always was to Süss. Yet Süss knows all too well that without this puppet the puppeteer is equally useless, and accepts his imprisonment and death sentence. In the lengthy execution scene, Süss becomes again the orthodox Jew he once was, reuniting with his community in his death. Veidt now sheds the tears that he did not allow himself even after his daughter's death, showing the vulnerable and human part of his psyche for which his 'slaving and scheming' left no room.

V

In hindsight, it becomes clear that Veidt's two prominent roles as Jew also cast the association of Jewishness over many of his later British roles as outsider, particularly the stranger in *The Passing of the Third Floor Back*. How unusual his career in the United Kingdom really was is brought into relief through the nine films he subsequently made in the United States between October 1940 and May 1943: *Escape* (Mervyn LeRoy, 1940); *The Thief of Bagdad* (Michael Powell and Ludwig Berger, 1940); *A Woman's Face* (George Cukor, 1941); *Whistling in the Dark* (S. Sylvan Simon, 1941); *The Men in Her Life* (Gregory Ratoff, 1941); *Nazi Agent* (Jules Dassin, 1942); *All Through the Night* (Vincent Sherman, 1942); *Casablanca* (Michael Curtiz, 1942); and *Above Suspicion* (Richard Thorpe, 1943). Veidt's roles in these include a haughty German aristocrat, a suave satanic playboy, a sinister head of a cult, a famous elderly dancer, a ringleader of Nazi sympathisers, and, most famously, 'Major Heinrich Strasser of the Third Reich' who leads the efforts to thwart the escape plans of a renowned resistance fighter in *Casablanca*.

Only in his very last film, *Above Suspicion*, which he did not live to see premiered, was he able to shed the typecasting of tight-lipped villain and portray an Austrian sabotaging the Gestapo. What is striking even at a cursory glance is the price Veidt paid for his full-time employment in Hollywood (where in less than three years he made more films than in his eight years in England), namely a return (if not a regression) to narrowly defined roles as outsiders, demons and villains that contain none of the complexity and layers that he found in the roles the British film industry offered him – not to speak of the impossibility of challenging Hollywood's taboos about representing what political reasons or ethnic origins may turn people into outsiders in the first place.

The M-G-M spy thriller *Nazi Agent*, directed by Jules Dassin and co-written by Lothar Mendes, is a case in point. Though in many ways very similar to most US films cited above, Veidt's typecasting here is particularly instructive. He plays the dual role of the upright German bookseller and philatelist Otto Becker, a refugee from Nazi Germany, and his twin brother Baron Hugo von Detner, a German Consul in New York secretly working for the Nazi fifth columnists. Hugo seeks to blackmail Otto, who has illegally entered the country, into using his bookstore as a front for orchestrating sabotage acts against the British army. When Otto defies his brother, Hugo sets out to kill him, but in the struggle between the two siblings the baron falls dead. Otto now needs to assume the identity of his dead brother in order to infiltrate the Nazi supporters. In the most intriguing part of this otherwise rather genre-driven plot we witness how Otto frantically familiarises himself with Hugo's hotel rooms, office, staff, contacts and duties – a veritable crash course in transforming one's identity from politically innocent bystander into cunning and manipulative powermonger.

Casting Veidt in the dual role of genetically identical but otherwise completely different twins was a reprise of the 1926 *Die Brüder Schellenberg*, directed by Karl Grune. Indeed, performing *doppelgänger* (as in the 1926 version of *The Student of Prague*) or multiple roles in one film (as in the American *The Man Who Laughs* from 1927 where he plays both the mutilated Gwynplaine and his father, or in the episodic film *Unheimliche Geschichten*, 1919) must be seen as a staple of Veidt's career. But what began as Weimar cinema's fascination with the psychological dimension of split identities and uncanny doubles takes on a more pronounced political dimension in *Nazi Agent*. Thus, the student Balduin in *The Student of Prague*, haunted by his mirror image, and Wenzel Schellenberg, unequal brother of Michael, are examples of a human psyche driven to self-destruction for reasons that can only be attributed to their tormented souls.

Nazi Agent gives this allegorical dimension a rather original twist: portraying the split political alliances between pro- and anti-Nazi Germans within the same German family, it stages this very predicament as an allegory of Veidt's own career outside of Nazi Germany. Just as Otto, the good German, has to learn how to think and act like his evil Nazi twin in order to be effective in his fight against the Third Reich, the staunch anti-Nazi Veidt, too, had to accept roles that cast him out of character, so to speak, in order to play the roles as Teutonic military that M-G-M and other studios offered him. Veidt's effectiveness in his roles as Nazi villain in *Escape*, *Casablanca* and *All Through the Night* was essential for convincing the American public of the worthiness of the US and Allied war effort, and it was premised on successfully obliterating any reference to Veidt's off-screen activities supporting the fight against Nazi Germany. And just as Veidt and many of his Jewish fellow émigrés and refugees had to hide their victim-status in order to successfully portray their perpetrators, so

Otto Becker, too, cannot ever reveal his true identity if his fight against the Nazi infiltrators is to succeed. Ironically, not even death allows him to resume his old identity: when the Germans finally do catch on to him, they blackmail him into returning to Nazi Germany in the role of his brother, the Baron, so that he can be presented as traitor to the Reich and executed. Whereas Veidt's British films allowed him to connect his roles with larger political concerns of the exiled artist, *Nazi Agent* shows the price of success in Hollywood. Only the complete disappearance into the role allows Veidt to create a successful allegory of displacement; only by rendering displacement illegible can the actor claim to have articulated it successfully.

Notes

1. Gerd Gemünden and Anton Kaes, 'Introduction', *New German Critique* 89 (2003), pp. 3–8. (Special issue on film and exile.)
2. Theodor W. Adorno, *Minima Moralia: Reflections from Damaged Life*, trans. E.F.N. Jephcott (New York: Verso, 1978).
3. Anton Kaes, 'A Stranger in the House: Fritz Lang's *Fury* and the Cinema of Exile', *New German Critique* 89 (2003), pp. 33–58.
4. Edward Said, *Reflections on Exile and Other Essays* (Cambridge, Mass.: Harvard University Press, 2000). The terms 'descent' and 'consent' are used by Werner Sollors in *Beyond Ethnicity: Consent and Descent in American Culture* (New York: Oxford University Press, 1986). He argues that descent relationships are defined by 'substance' (blood or nature; law or marriage); they emphasise hereditary qualities, liabilities, and entitlements. Consent stresses our abilities as mature, free agents, 'architects of our own fate' (choosing spouses, destinies, political systems). Culture is made up of a tension between consent and descent relationships; it requires careful negotiations.
5. Veidt's image in England at the time is aptly described by Michael Powell, with whom he subsequently collaborated on three films: 'I had been longing to get my hands on Conrad Veidt ever since he came to England. He was such an overpowering personality that directors were afraid of him. He was tall, over six feet two inches, lean and bony. He had magnetic blue eyes, black hair and eyebrows, beautiful strong hands, and a mouth with sardonic, not to say satanic, lines to it. He used an eye-glass. He was the show-off of all time.' Powell, *A Life in Movies: An Autobiography* (New York: Knopf, 1987), p. 272.
6. See my essay 'From "Mr. M" to "Mr. Murder": Peter Lorre and the Actor in Exile', in Randall Halle and Margaret McCarthy (eds.), *Light Motives. Popular German Cinema in Perspective* (Detroit: Wayne State University Press, 2003), pp. 85–107.
7. Sue Harper, '"Thinking Forward and Up": The British Films of Conrad Veidt', in Jeffrey Richards (ed.), *The Unknown 1930s: An Alternative History of the British Cinema 1929–39* (London: I.B. Tauris, 1998), p. 124. Harper's thorough account provides a detailed survey of Veidt's career in the UK, as does Daniela Sannwald in her essay 'Continental Stranger: Conrad Veidt und seine britischen Filme', in Jörg Schöning (ed.), *London Calling: Deutsche im britischen Film der dreißiger Jahre* (Munich: edition text+kritik, 1993), pp. 89–97.
8. Veidt quoted in John T. Soister, *Conrad Veidt on Screen* (London: McFarland, 2002), p. 271.
9. Kevin Gough-Yates, 'Berthold Viertel at Gaumont-British', in Richards (ed.), *The Unknown 1930s*, p. 209. The tension-ridden interactions between Viertel and his English producers surrounding a film made the year before, *Little Friend*, are the source of Christopher Isherwood's famous short novel *Prater Violet*, first published in 1945, which with deft precision conveys Viertel's precarious status as exile in the British film industry.

10. Veidt quoted in Soister, *Conrad Veidt on Screen*, p. 271.
11. Frank S. Nugent, *New York Times*, 29 April 1936.
12. Transitory spaces are spaces that underscore arrival and departures but not dwelling. Hamid Naficy refers to them extensively in *An Accented Cinema: Exilic and Diasporic Filmmaking* (Princeton: Princeton University Press, 2001).
13. According to his biographer Jerry C. Allen, Veidt decided to settle permanently in the UK in December 1932, applied for permission to emigrate, which he eventually received, and departed from Germany in late April 1933. He returned to Germany for the filming of *Wilhelm Tell* at the end of 1933. See Allen, *Conrad Veidt: From Caligari to California* (Pacific Grove, Cal.: Boxwood, 1993), pp. 194–95.
14. According to Allen, Veidt and his family were forbidden ever to return to Germany. See *Conrad Veidt: From Caligari to California*, p. 220. However, Michael Powell writes in his autobiography that despite attacks on Veidt in *Der Stürmer* and other anti-Semitic publications, Goebbels 'made many efforts to tempt him [Veidt] back' (Powell, *A Life in Movies*, p. 319). These efforts by Goebbels are also in line with his continued efforts to lure Marlene Dietrich back to Germany.
15. Both the *Observer* and the *Sunday Express* faulted the film for not setting a final episode in Nazi Germany. See Richard Falcon, 'No Politics! "German Affairs" im Spionage- und Kostümfilm', in Schöning (ed.), *London Calling*, p. 86.
16. Billie Wilder, 'Der erste Heimkehrer aus Hollywood', *Tempo* no. 50, 28 November 1928.
17. It was reportedly the most expensive film to date made by a British production company.
18. Goebbels apparently studied Mendes' film carefully before assigning Harlan to direct an overtly anti-Semitic production of the same title. Harlan's film was primarily based on Wilhelm Hauff's novella and only used some characters from Feuchtwanger's novel. It is an ironic twist of fate that the title role also had far-reaching consequences for the actor who played it in that version, Ferdinand Marian. As his biographer Friedrich Knilli states, Marian never forgave himself for accepting the role, and after the war became an alcoholic who died in a car crash in 1946. See Knilli, *Ich war Jud Süss: Die Geschichte des Filmstars Ferdinand Marian* (Berlin: Henschel, 2000).
19. Feuchtwanger himself allegedly called Mendes' film both 'ein prächtiger Film' as well as 'ein Scheissfilm'; it is significant that in a 1941 open letter to seven actors appearing in Harlan's film – among them Eugen Klöpfer, who had played Süss in Feuchtwanger's play of the same title – Feuchtwanger makes no mention of the British film, even though he would have had an obvious opportunity to do so, had he appreciated the film. See Alfons Arns, 'Fatale Korrespondenzen: Die Jud-Süß-Filme von Lothar Mendes und Veit Harlan im Vergleich' in Cilly Kugelmann and Fritz Backhaus (eds.), *Jüdische Figuren in Film und Karikatur* (Sigmaringen: Thorbecke, 1996), p. 111.
20. The most recent and detailed biography is Hellmut G. Haasis, *Joseph Süß Oppenheimer, genannt Jud Süß: Finanzier, Freidenker, Justizopfer* (Reinbek: Rowohlt, 1998). Shortly after Feuchtwanger's novel, and presumably in reponse to its popular success, Selma Stern published a biography which for a long time was considered the definite account of Oppenheimer's life: *Jud Süss: Ein Beitrag zur deutschen und zur jüdischen Geschichte* (Berlin: Akademie Verlag, 1929).

Chapter 12

Anton Walbrook:
The Continental Consort

Michael Williams

In 1937 Viennese actor Anton Walbrook became an international star.[1] While he had had a successful career in Europe, his Austrian and German films had received limited circulation in the UK and America, and it was the success of his Hollywood debut, *The Soldier and the Lady* (UK title: *Michael Strogoff*), directed by George Nicholls Jr., in the summer of that year that consolidated his international profile.[2] The role that really secured Walbrook's film career and fashioned his star persona for at least the next decade was that of Albert, the Prince Consort, in Herbert Wilcox's historical biopic *Victoria the Great* and its Technicolor sequel, *Sixty Glorious Years* (1938).

Seemingly emerging from the European shadows, Walbrook's first British role found him festooned over the covers of the film's publicity brochures, themselves aping the style of royal souvenirs, to promulgate ubiquitous comparisons between the actor and Albert. The film opened to almost unanimous critical acclaim, hailed by the *Monthly Film Bulletin* as 'unquestionably one of the finest pictures yet made in this country', becoming the most popular British film in the UK of 1937.[3] He even had the honour of being a pin-up centrefold alongside the film's female star, Anna Neagle, for the 1938 *Picture Show* calendar, an image to remind audiences throughout the year that this film was 'one which anyone would be proud to call British'.[4]

This chapter will explore the ways in which Walbrook's émigré biography resonated with contemporary issues of national identity, nostalgia and landscape that can be seen to inform his films at this time. Walbrook's later work, including his celebrated anti-Nazi parts in Powell and Pressburger's *49th Parallel* (1941) and *The Life and Death of Colonel Blimp* (1943), is, of course, crucial to these issues, but here I wish to focus primarily on his pivotal, but relatively less well-known work of 1937–40.

Walbrook's presence in these films, as a star with international appeal and associations with artistic quality was strategic, for from 1935 Wilcox had been pursuing an 'internationalist' policy to produce films that appealed to both British and American audiences.[5] A lucrative deal with RKO-Radio for his new Imperator company helped finance and distribute *Victoria the Great*, which would, as *Today's Cinema* frankly observed, 'be made with an eye to the world market', the first film of a ten-year deal, which included its sequel and *The Rat* (Jack Raymond, 1937), a remake of the 1925 Ivor Novello vehicle.[6]

'The Continental Star'

Born in Vienna in 1896, Walbrook fled Berlin during the 1936 Olympiad, ostensibly to take up an invitation from America to film *Michael Strogoff*. By this time he had established himself as a noted star in Europe, particularly in Germany, having already played in both the German and French language versions of *Strogoff*, *Der Kurier des Zaren* and *Michel Strogoff. Le courrier du tzar* (directed by Richard Eichberg and Jacques de Baroncelli in 1935 and 1936 respectively).[7] At Hollywood's insistence, and to his mother's great chagrin, it was here that Adolf Anton Wilhelm Wohlbrück became Anton Walbrook. While Walbrook claimed in 1937 that the studio felt that the name Adolf was 'unromantic' or that the change aided pronunciation, his 1940 understated observation to fan magazine *Picturegoer* that Adolf was 'not a very popular name now' was probably nearer the mark.[8] Every press feature stressed the actor's language skills, dwelling on his considerable stage experience across Austria and Germany, particularly the ubiquitous, almost-mythical, fact of his having come from a 250-year line of actors in his family, broken only by his father, who was a clown.

Walbrook found Hollywood a cosmopolitan place, as he told *Picture Show*: 'I don't think you could call Hollywood America. It is the most cosmopolitan city in the world. I met every sort of nationality over there you could mention, but no Americans.'[9] However, his three-week stay was not a happy one and left him with a resolve to travel to Britain and, as he told the magazine, to learn English without an American accent and, as if to make clear his intention to assimilate, to play cricket.[10] Here, Walbrook is already alluding to his desire to become a naturalised Englishman, or to be 'more English than the English', as *Picturegoer* related in 1940, quoting Walbrook that 'ever since I came here I've tried so hard to lose my accent, but I've still got it, you see!'[11] While this comment contradicts *Film Weekly*'s observation that he 'deliberately preserved his soft, attractive Viennese accent', and another interview where he states that he would 'never attempt to play an English role', noting the fortune that Albert and the Rat 'both call for a foreign accent', it does indicate the significance of voice in his films.[12] Indeed, reviews of *Michael Strogoff* singled out Walbrook and Russian actor Akim Tamiroff as the only actors who conveyed anything other than the 'ludicrous' British or American accents of the rest of the cast, a matter also discussed by an American educational pamphlet.[13]

Walbrook's voice affirms his émigré status as if in a minor key across his work, especially given the prominence of music in his film roles, as I shall discuss below – conveying a sense of loss and yearning through his presence, as well as, of course, the enduring 'foreignness' of his accent.[14] As Andrew Moor suggests, he modulated the tone for dramatic effect, but without his accent Walbrook's persona would be drastically different, losing the crucial continental touch *Picturegoer* described in 1937 as 'the pleasant soft accent of the *cultured* Austrian'.[15]

By 1938 Walbrook was, as Leonard Wallace asserted in *Film Weekly*, 'the first truly cosmopolitan star of the screen':

> He has already French, German, Viennese, English and American films to his credit; and there is no reason why he should not do what no player before has quite succeeded in doing: become equally popular in several countries, and able to make films in each of them with equal facility.[16]

Moor has observed that 'charming' is a word strongly associated with Walbrook, evoking his ability to 'cast a spell, to bewitch and captivate'.[17] Indeed, argued *Film Weekly*, 'Walbrook has a charm of his own that is, perhaps, not unlike that of the Prince Consort'.[18] We should add to that 'Continental', for in his transitional phase of 1937/38 it is rare to find reference to him without the prefix 'the Continental star' or 'the Continental actor'.[19] More than merely being from mainland Europe, being 'continental' implies sophistication, but also hints at a touch of decadence that can assume a less than innocent connotation. It thus easily turns into a rather sneering term, adopting a faux-quaint perspective on liberal 'continental' mores, especially of sexuality, and at the extreme, a continental visitor's social 'mis-placement' is something to evoke suspicion, fuelling the sadism of characterisations such as that of Walbrook in *Gaslight* (Thorold Dickinson, 1940) or the 'misanthropic sense of alienation', as Moor puts it, in *The Rat*.[20]

Walbrook was perfectly cast as Albert, as a 1937 issue of *Film Weekly* proposed:

> It was a lucky break for Walbrook as far as his career in Anglo-American films was concerned. For it took the inspired casting of him as Albert to show the English-speaking world that there was in existence a great actor it hadn't met.[21]

Early press reports, following the cue of the press-books, noted the striking physical resemblance between the build and features of Albert and Walbrook, that he had the right accent and was even the same age as the Prince Consort when he met Victoria.[22] His handsomeness did not go unnoticed, of course, Edith Nepean noting in her *Picture Show* column that

'I have a shrewd suspicion that this very handsome, talented actor will make the ladies' hearts flutter more than a little.'[23]

The pairing of the quintessentially English Neagle with the complex internationalism of Walbrook was an expedient move in British cinema. His keenness to become English is seemingly at odds with the centrality of his non-Englishness to his star persona, although he did portray Englishmen in two German films directed by Reinhold Schünzel, *Viktor und Viktoria* (1933), ironically playing it straight in a drama of gender deception and masquerade, and *Die englische Heirat* (1934). And roles aside, the emphasis on the continental or cosmopolitan in his interviews means that he often doesn't seem to be Austrian either.

Indeed, he is continental, his nationality dispersed across imaginative European landscapes, or rather *bridging* its divides; perhaps evidencing that, at historically uncertain times, according to Richard Dyer, a star can expose what's 'uncertain, unstable and ambiguous' about a particular historical period.[24] Sarah Street notes that the timing of *Victoria the Great's* release, only months after the abdication crisis of November 1936, is hardly coincidental.[25] And indeed, *Picture Show* reported in July 1937 that the portrayal of the monarch had only been made possible due to the Lord Chamberlain's lifting of a ban on the depictions of royalty on stage and screen in June that year.[26]

The film's contribution to the reputation of British cinema did not go unnoticed either. 'By producing *Victoria the Great* at the time he did', wrote *Film Weekly's* editorial, 'by bringing out of the crisis itself a picture which is likely to do more for the prestige of British films than any since *The Private Life of Henry VIII*, Wilcox has earned the gratitude of everybody connected with the British film industry'.[27] The two films' national profile as heritage works dealing with the relationship between Britain and Germany – and, off-screen, British cinema and Hollywood – is thus considerable, and Walbrook's role as Albert significant, playing an émigré who had considerable influence in shaping Victorian England without ever truly becoming part of it.

'How can one live happily in a country that is so difficult to get to?'

From the outset, it is clear that *Victoria the Great* is speaking to a much wider historical context than that of Victoria's reign. The prospective royal couple are presented as comically mismatched. She, attending the theatre, dismisses her cousin, Prince Albert of Saxe-Coburg and Gotha, as 'straight-laced, bookish' and 'self-willed', while he, seen at his English lessons at home in Rosenau Castle, reads about a beetle from a book as his thoughts turn to Victoria: 'The female usually devours her mate immediately after the wedding night – I shall not marry.'

Albert's journey to the UK is given different emphasis in the two *Victoria* films. While *Sixty Glorious Years* foregrounds the lush green countryside to which Albert is saying farewell, nostalgically lingering on what he has left behind, *Victoria the Great* deals only with his arrival. Here, the sound of a howling gale is heard as the screen fades in on a stormy sea at Dover, where Albert's delayed steamship approaches the harbour. On board, as Albert and his elder brother Ernst (fellow émigré Walter Rilla) cling to the rigging, Albert asks: 'How can one live happily in a country that is so difficult to get to?' Having arrived, Walbrook is dishevelled in hat and formal coat, his hair hanging down over his face, telling his brother in broken English that they will go 'home, home at once', back to their 'own dear German on the first occasion'. 'Across *that* ocean again', Ernst adds wearily, still swaying from the journey, underscoring the many barriers that prevent Albert's return. But a different Albert swiftly emerges as Victoria arrives in a carriage, to receive the princes in a drawing room. Now he is draped in full military costume, and Victoria is visibly taken aback by the masculine figure before her, and swiftly contrives an intimacy with the line: 'Courage, cousin, I'm not going to eat you!'

Two sides of Walbrook's 'foreignness' are being articulated here: the sophisticated Continental Consort, attractive, exotic and cultured; and a more socially and sexually uncomfortable figure. Read contextually, one might connect Albert's apprehension at the 'devouring' political power of Victoria with the German humiliation after the Treaty of Versailles, something which his character in *Blimp* famously critiqued. Both films quite effectively align themselves with Albert's outsider's point of view in order to explore contemporary Anglo-German relations. These cultural differences are thus mostly displaced into comic interplay between Albert and Victoria. She thinks he's too serious, he thinks she's frivolous and the English are unromantic – spluttering in exasperation at one point: 'Sentiment is a plant that will not grow in England. If an Englishman will find himself growing sentimental, he – he goes outside and shoots himself.' The apotheosis of a quarrel between the pair is reached as Albert, who has been banned from smoking, is discovered rebelliously smoking an exaggeratedly Germanic pipe by his wife, who wafts away the smoke with a fan. The iconic character of the prop was underscored when *Picture Show* magazine ran a competition for its readers to win it.[28]

Props and costumes are key to marrying period detail with sexuality; of particular importance in this context is the dressing gown. In *Victoria the Great*, Albert wears a distinctly shabby one, tied at the waist with string (Ernst's is overly floral), which he had been forced to wear after losing his clothes overboard on the way to Dover. The brothers are thus rendered sartorially, as well as socially, at sea, and fall foul of the crime of not having the right clothes, and finding it even more difficult to fit in.[29] The dressing gown by nature provides only a thin veil of decency, rendering one neither nude nor properly clothed and, as interior-wear of film and literature, can label one as rather decadent, or even degenerate, by metaphorically disdaining the sport and physical culture associated with the outdoors.[30] Emblematic of Wildean dandyism – particularly of the Wagner-loving aesthete Dorian Gray, whose 'elaborate dressing-gown of silk-embroidered cashmere' bespeaks as much about his demi-monde inclinations as anything else – all but the plainest dressing gowns can function in literary and cinematic representations as a sign of equivocal sexuality, if not homosexuality itself.[31]

Extended further, the almost 'orientalised' foreignness – in terms of the way the ambiguous otherness of his sexuality, nationality and appearance produce a figure of fear or suspicion as well as attraction – would be exploited in Walbrook's later work, including his role as a criminal maniac bigamist in *Gaslight*, a man who, as *Kinematograph Weekly* put it, 'wages a war of nerves on his wife'.[32] Having changed his name, Bauer appears as a doppelganger to the police officer who previously investigated this 'foreigner', who merely remarks on his resemblance to the 'ghost of a man out of my past'. This estranged stranger resides with his new bride in a house suffocating with conspicuous excess of late Victorian décor beyond even the taste of Albert. Walbrook's Bauer is found recumbent on a chaise longue, fingers pressed together, enunciating every syllable with unnerving overdeliberation from behind the fronds of drawing-room palms, or else strutting about with preternatural rigidity. There is something uncomfortable, or unhomely (*unheimlich* in its Freudian sense), about Walbrook in these settings: an uncanniness that begins with his not-quite defined foreignness and elaborated through an equally ill-determined sexuality, with vicissitudes between sadism and camp affectation.

Walbrook was seen again in a dressing-gown in *The Red Shoes* (Powell and Pressburger, 1948) as ballet impresario Boris Lermontov, whose aesthetic obsession with dancer Victoria Page merely reaffirms his implied homosexuality; in one scene he is seen wearing a teal-grey gown of oriental design, while picking at grapes with disdain. Lermontov's Machiavellian personality is embellished by Walbrook's ability to transform charm into a sneer, like the smile he holds for just too long in *Gaslight*, as the film continues to display him as if a gargoyle perched in his opera house office. He is framed under the rising arch of the window behind, like one of the winged statues seen outside, or else masked by shadow or, on the Mediterranean, wearing the kind of dark sunshades later adopted by Dirk Bogarde's Aschenbach in *Death in Venice* (Visconti, 1971).

While I share Andrew Moor's caution at making such readings in hindsight, I would argue that Walbrook's own homosexuality, while not directly addressed, implicitly fuelled the social and emotional complexity of his performance.[33] This engine of suspicion might echo what I have described in my discussion of Hitchcock's exploitation of Ivor Novello's camp performance style in the 1920s. In *The Lodger* (1926), for example, the combination of Novello's alternately neurotic and ambiguously sexual performance was a means of layering further suspicion that his character was equally 'duplicitous' in harbouring a secret murderous identity.[34]

As I will argue later in relation to the remake of Novello's *The Rat*, I do not suggest that Walbrook's performance can so easily be read as being as camp as Novello's. Moreover, Walbrook's private life was more sequestered than Novello's, and his national identity and accent more significant factors in his charismatic otherness than his sexuality. Yet there does seem to be a performative connection here between an ambiguous sexuality and what Moor describes as Walbrook's 'always present, but generally veiled, tendency towards mania'.[35] It is striking that several contemporary interviews also hint at something unspoken about the star's private life. As the 1937 *Film Pictorial* article 'Vienna's Idol Follows in Ivor Novello's Footsteps' put it, 'he is a mercurial character, sometimes moody, sometimes gay ... he is always considerate and courteous – yet with a faint aura of reserve about him'.[36] One 1940 interviewer even relates how they discovered the actor in a moment of (hetero)sexual reticence that could have been taken from any one of these films. Arriving at his apartment, they find him standing 'belligerently' in the doorway with hands 'thrust into the pockets of his rather disreputable-looking dressing gown', 'politely distrustful' in fear that the interviewer might have been another ardent feminine visitor.[37]

'Authentic Backgrounds'

As I have suggested previously, Walbrook's continental charms fitted *Victoria the Great*'s ethos of authenticity. Titles peppered throughout both films boast of actual locations unseen before on the screen, of dialogue appropriated from real speeches and diaries, which Wilcox explained in detail to the press.[38] Meanwhile, a whole series of *tableaux vivants* recreated famous scenes or rather settings for the viewer, something which the regal, deferential format of the souvenir brochures extended beyond the frame of the film itself.[39] The *Photoplay Studies* guide to the film went so far as to include a two-page comparison between fine-art representation of the characters and settings and stills from the film.[40]

Not all critics, however, found the film's pretence to verisimilitude entirely convincing. James Agate was singularly contemptuous of, as he calls it, 'Victoria the Little':

> The present film in its early part presents Victoria as being arch after the way of the servants' hall and uppish in the manner of a housemaid on her Sunday out ... And then there is the film star's accent, overlaid by layer after layer of the best suburban refinement. At any moment we expect Miss Neagle to toss her pretty head and say: 'I hope it keeps fine for you, Albert!' ... One feels that Mr Anton Walbrook's Albert, who is gentleman as well as Prince, would have

declined the proposal and gone back to Germany murmuring the German equivalent for 'baggage!'[41]

The Spectator chimed in, considering Neagle's 'dimpled aseptic coquetry is a bit out of place under a crown', while the *New Statesman* was a little bemused by Albert's 'nice, almost Lubitschian sense of humour' in the second film, but largely perplexed at the sweeping deference of critics to a drama it considered a 'travesty' of a historical document.[42] In this respect Walbrook's own recent journey from Germany, and evolving persona as a charming Continental, gave him an aura of authenticity that facilitated the grounding of the film overall in the very real socio-political context of the 1930s. Furthermore, what was described in the press as his 'sensitive and extremely natural portrayal of the much misunderstood Albert', interrogated the spectacular excesses of the film, such as the film's Technicolor final reel and Neagle's increasingly camp tantrums and costume as Victoria (the sense of empty pageant increases after Albert's death).[43] Indeed, Agate described the whole of *Victoria the Great* as something of a kitsch bauble:

> At the end it breaks into colour, with an effect like that of a picture book on which a six-year-old has been messing about with a box of paints. The result is to make the last half-hour of the picture look like something enamelled on pottery and marked 'A Present from Blackpool'.[44]

Marcia Landy argues that *Victoria* is self-conscious about its technical virtuosity, and through 'allusions to photography, the film calls attention to itself as the recorder of events'.[45] Wilcox does indeed take his subject seriously, on the whole, but I would argue that the self-consciousness of the film's pictorial imagery does foreground its artifice as a nostalgic treatment of history. Moreover, the presence (and later structuring absence) of Walbrook's Albert acts as a chorus to these staged and restaged public and private events, and his relationship to the English landscape and privileged places in the film is marked by the themes of distance, separation and travel, and of course, memory and loss.

As mentioned above, within a few minutes of arriving in England, Albert speaks wistfully of 'home' and how matters of state prevent him from returning, a memory that haunts him through both films. In the second, not only has the textual and contextual notion of Albert's home changed (given that 1937 has elapsed into 1938, and with the annexation of Walbrook's Austria in the intervening period), but this has also brought about the added emphasis on foreign affairs and military conflict observed by *Film Weekly*: 'A keener sense of great events. You are conscious of powerful social upheavals disturbing the people of England.'[46] Neagle's autobiography echoes this, noting of the premiere of *Sixty Glorious Years* in October 1938, attended by Queen Mary: 'Autumn 1938 was not the happiest moment to release a film depicting the glories of the Empire's past … there was an uneasiness in the atmosphere.'[47]

Thus, where in the first film Victoria was shown as the main impulse behind the repeal of the Corn Laws, in order to appease civil unrest, there is a move in *Sixty Glorious Years* to present the German Albert as the greater catalyst for change and a peace-keeper and force for good. The Crimean War is also used to implicitly map European political anxieties of the past over the present – an intertitle portends that 'the clouds of war gathered' as the designs of the Czar upon Turkey threatened to involve England. But it would not do for the mood to be too negative and, after all, Wilcox's project was to accentuate the positive to sell his product at home and abroad; thus he would, no doubt, be gratified by such claims as that of the *Monthly Film Bulletin* that 'if any doubted it they would find it hard after seeing the film not to be convinced that ours is "a good heritage"'.[48]

The Munich Agreement of 29 September 1938 had, of course, been signed just weeks before the premiere of *Sixty Glorious Years*, and tensions were high, with the circulation of millions of gas masks throughout Britain in September and October, so Anglo-German relations, and efforts to avoid another war, had been very much on the agenda. The policy of appeasement had been fully supported by the Foreign Secretary since February that year, and one cannot help but detect echoes in the film's treatment of the royal couple's policy of conciliation towards Imperial Russia, and particularly in the privileging in both films of Albert's intervention in a political incident during the American Civil War, which would have brought war between the nations.

The film industry aside, building Anglo-American relations became crucial over the next few years, and Albert's diplomacy had particular connotations for the late 1930s. In general, *Sixty Glorious Years* is (expediently) ambivalent in its attitude to politics, and most of all to the figure of Albert. While he is praised as a force for good, providing restraint and consolidating the imagination of Victoria and her parliament, Walbrook imbues him with a lingering sense of the outsider. He becomes an affable man whose endeavours largely remain unrecognised and, like Walbrook himself, is someone who seeks, but never quite receives, the full embrace of his adopted country. As Victoria's Scottish 'gillie' John Brown sagely observes: 'The English, aye, they can be a cold stand-offish lot if they want to be – they never took him to their hearts ...' A souvenir programme for *Victoria* neatly merges actor with part:

> As the romantic and wise Prince Albert – the man who was not only the Queen's Consort but who became her greatest and most powerful adviser – who was termed a 'foreigner' by her ministers and who by astute statesmanship, saved the country of his adoption from what might have been the worst catastrophe of its history – Anton Walbrook will stir the peoples of the entire world.[49]

It is the English landscape that most induces Albert's feeling of both separation and connection to home. In *Victoria the Great*, one scene finds

Victoria showing Albert a photograph of the English countryside, asking whether there is a 'very great difference between England and Germany' and whether he 'could ever feel at home here'. By the time *Sixty Glorious Years* was released, because of the *Anschluss* there was no going back for Walbrook to his native Austria. Now we hear Albert remark mournfully when travelling through a German forest on his way to Britain: 'I'm glad, Ernst, to have the final parting over, the whole journey has been one long farewell – every field and every hill and every valley seems to be bidding me to say goodbye.' Later, we find the couple taking tea at Balmoral, immediately after the Battle of Sebastopol, and Albert likens the landscape outside the window to that of Coburg. Looking at their daughter Victoria and Prince Frederick of Prussia, another political marriage is envisioned as Albert observes: 'Through those two children, so much can be done for the peace of the future.' The careful positioning of Walbrook's Albert in the metonymic British landscape makes a contemporary intervention into a nineteenth-century view.

Impossible History

Walbrook's relationship to landscape is twofold in these films. He inhabits a space of pastoral reassurance that nonetheless reminds one of something lost, and, at the same time, he occupies (or even displaces) the vicarious position of the tourist by being granted a temporary gaze in picturesque settings where one doesn't quite belong or yet feel at home. But this stance is complicated by his status as an émigré for whom the notion of returning home afterwards becomes problematic, and thus the spectacle of landscape evolves into a powerful metonym for loss and longing. The cinematic performance of memory is frequently enacted through music (and visually through the dissolve), and for the émigré, as Kevin Gough-Yates has observed, music can often express a 'form of resistance', an expression of the past that can be aurally superimposed over the present.[50] This resonates with the kind of nostalgic memory which, as Pam Cook has shown, longs for something known to be irretrievable but is sought anyway, thus making a performative intervention in history.[51]

In the Victoria films, Albert is frequently associated with music, seen at the piano or organ, and this corresponds to a musical sensibility across many of Walbrook's roles. Though this element may be minor, for example playing the piano or singing in *Gaslight* or *La Ronde* (Ophuls, 1950), it is instrumental in *Dangerous Moonlight* (Brian Desmond Hurst, 1940), where Walbrook plays Stefan Radetzky, an amnesiac Polish composer in a complex wartime narrative of trauma, nostalgia and music. The film opens with Radetzky seated at a piano in a London hospital; a close-up of his hands, bashing discordantly at the keys, gives way to a shot of his face. Gardens are visible through the French windows behind, before being obscured from view as the blackout curtains are drawn. Landscape, music and Walbrook are thus deeply linked, but the connections have been temporarily severed, most specifically by the traumatic plane crash that blocks Radetzky's memory of 'home' and his *Warsaw Concerto* through which these elements are united and performed. 'Perhaps that music will bring back a lot of things', one of the nurses observes. Suddenly, Radetzky stumbles upon the right notes, as a superimposition upon Walbrook's pensive face introduces flashing explosions, rubble and screams as he is drawn back to the destruction of his beloved Warsaw. We share his flashback of events as he is forced to leave, experienced in the present tense. The film here illustrates the symptoms of Post Traumatic Shock Disorder, where traumatic memories resurface as if for the first time, as Cathy Caruth explains in her study of PTSD: 'The Traumatised we might say, carry an impossible history within them, or they become themselves the symptom of a history that they cannot entirely possess.'[52]

There is a strong sense that Radetzky is a recorder and messenger of history through his music and that, being a composer, he is 'not like the others'. Once again, taking into account the sexual ambivalence of Walbrook's screen persona, it is worth noting that the artistic, and particularly musical, temperament sometimes serves as code for the homosexual. The hospital staff observe that if Radetzky's memory is returned then 'we'd done something for the world'; his Air Force superiors surreptitiously spare him from a suicide mission because of his ability to communicate through music; and even his best friend jokes at one point that if he cuts his sweeping mane of hair he might even pass for 'an ordinary human being'. His memory, and the Warsaw it represents, is thus important and he, as an artist, rises above and beyond the destruction that surrounds him. His recollection functions also as a key to the restoration of his relationship with American journalist Carol (Sally Gray), which had begun to fail because she could not understand his desire to return to the war – and to Warsaw, through his repeated phrase, 'I'll be back one day'.

In one scene Carol snaps at him for being 'miserable with your funny continental ways'. Walbrook gently politicises the situation, delivering an interventionist message to the American (in this pre-Pearl Harbor context): 'How soon you seem to have forgotten what is happening in the world', he retorts, a new weight to his voice. The camera closes in on Walbrook's face, catching the glint of moisture forming in his eyes as he relates abstractly to Carol the otherworldly experience of being near the stars while flying: 'You feel like being with them, you almost forgot that you are fighting the war. It seems far away, miles and miles below you.' Carol replies 'I'm cold ...' with resignation, as the historical politics embodied by Radetzky undercuts the romance of this ostensibly domestic scene, his wearing another dressing gown underscoring the incongruity.

Landscape is also central to *Blimp*, as the German Theo (Walbrook), getting lost on his way to Berlin, recalls that 'suddenly the landscape became so familiar to me', as he imagines himself back at the Yorkshire prisoner-of-war camp where, amid the green lawns and ornamental lake, he was held after the First World War. As in *Sixty Glorious Years*, the landscapes become blurred through nostalgia, and it is worth noting that Walbrook had himself been a prisoner during that war.[53]

Walbrook's voice was eminently suited to such reverie, hence his success as the narrator in *La Ronde*, recounting in waltz-time the lost world of *fin de siècle* Vienna – 'so much more restful than the present ... so much more reliable than the future'. In interviews, he would often drift back to Old Vienna, as in a 1940 *Picturegoer* portrait by Sylvia Terry-Smith delightfully phonetically titled 'I am s-ee-k to Death of Albert', in which he discussed, 'with a faraway haze in his eyes', his plan to gain naturalisation in Britain:

> And as this young man with the earnest, dark-blue eyes, went on without a pause, I found myself swept up in his almost reverent enthusiasm, into another world, a world without politics, the old, gay Vienna of thirty, forty, fifty years ago ...[54]

Indeed, while much of the *Victoria* soundtracks consist of patriotic dirges, it is the playfulness of the waltz that awakens mutual ardour in Albert and Victoria and formalises their relationship in the public space of a dance, conducted by Johann Strauß himself. In the first film, after she corrects Albert's pronunciation of the German 'walzer' instead of the Anglicised 'waltz', and he mutters about preferring Beethoven, Victoria announces that the waltz is 'rather shocking, but very pleasant', and it becomes their motif. In *Sixty Glorious Years* Victoria, now festooned with a bright blue gown, asks, 'Do you remember the evening we danced the new waltz by Mr Strauss?', referring back to events only seen in the first film, an act of memory also prompted by the *Cinegram* souvenir magazine.[55]

It is during the waltz that the film draws close to the Viennese/ Ruritanian form of musicals popular until the late 1930s, often produced by émigré filmmakers. As Stephen Guy has demonstrated, the genre presented a pseudo-historical world of romance, sophistication and castles.[56] Walbrook himself appeared in German features such as *Walzerkrieg* (*Waltz Time in Vienna*, Ludwig Berger, 1933), while Wilcox made four of these musical films in the UK, starting with *Good-night Vienna* starring Neagle in 1932.

By 1938, the subgenre was waning, giving way to more 'realistic' settings, and perhaps displaced into texts such as the Victoria films. Indeed, *The Rat* (1937) was a deliberate attempt to market Walbrook in a more 'realistic', even gritty setting and, significantly, the press-book and several reviews advised audiences to see the Albert and Rat films together in order to fully appreciate Walbrook's talents. However, the more 'realistic' approach of the latter arguably creates a greater social and political displacement. Thus while the re-edited Wilcox films were found to resonate with the war context in 1942. When re-released the following year, the trade press found that *The Rat* 'provides ideal escapist material to offset the present state of war films'.[57]

Walbrook brought to Jack Raymond's 1937 *The Rat* a much more forceful physical presence than Novello's 1925 original, presenting a sinewy physique in costumes which accentuate his forearms and biceps for promotional as well as aesthetic purposes. Where Novello's dishevelment brought pathos, Walbrook's intensity suggested that *his* ruffled hair means he has been up to something. *Kinematograph Weekly* thus credited Walbrook with 'effectively suggesting the brute strength' of the Rat in a way that would be unthinkable for a Novello vehicle.[58] Novello's Rat alternates between mischievous grin and doleful melancholy, Walbrook's has a broad and engaging smile, capped by a quizzical eyebrow, and a broader physical frame that brings some very convincing, table-smashing fight scenes. As Edith Nepean wrote in *Picture Show*: 'I have never before seen a more bloodthirsty fight take place.'[59] To stress the realism, studio publicity even encouraged American exhibitors to 'obtain from the police photographic heads and notices of rewards for criminals whose custody is sought by them. These may be mounted for a display under the heading THESE RATS ARE WANTED', along with other police paraphernalia such as handcuffs, grenades and tear-gas.[60] Indeed, the influence of the gangster genre can be seen in the film, tempered by the Rat now being more of a cat burglar and jewel-thief, perhaps more suited to the continental charms of Walbrook.

Despite its overtures towards urban realism, there are two sequences in *The Rat* that seek to place Walbrook at the centre of touristic or romantic spectacle. One presents him consorting with the vamp Zelia (Ruth Chatterton) in a dialogue-free montage sequence across Paris's most cosmopolitan gardens, terraces and palm court cafés – any one of which could have 'Wish You Were Here' scrawled across them, and none of which were the underworld apache's natural milieu. The other is a trip with the young Odile (René Ray) to the French countryside. This is an addition to the 1925 version but does, intriguingly, draw on references to Novello's stage play and also the novelisation of that film: a distinctly melancholy journey during an 'immortal spring' to Fontainebleau that implicitly references, as I have argued elsewhere, the lost youth of the First World War.[61]

While the 1937 film is less subtle – a less passive Rat now strides past picturesque farm machinery before collapsing into a convenient pile of hay with Odile – there is something strangely enigmatic about the sequence. The Rat exclaims that he 'didn't know anything could be so beautiful' as the forest and, upon arriving back in Paris, that he will 'never forget'. Both city and country landscapes here are narratively displaced, and distinct in being shot on location, and both are swiftly consigned to the past as sites of remembrance, what they represent (social fluidity, romance) barely sustainable in the overwhelmingly hostile environs depicted in Montmartre.

Conclusion

While overwhelmingly embraced by the press and film-going public, Walbrook's persona presented him as the perennial foreigner, which afforded him a unique, almost stately, position within British culture. There were occasional glimpses of unpleasant attitudes, as in the bizarre incident of his reported engagement to an 18-year-old chorus girl named Maude Courtney in 1938. An engagement was announced by Miss Courtney, then withdrawn, and within hours announced again. One unkind newspaper commented: 'Anton has been finding that the course of true love does not run smooth, not when you're a German with a Jewish grandmother.' Miss Courtney's mother, meanwhile, stated that 'the idea of her daughter being married to a subject of Herr Hitler, and a refugee at that, appalled her'.[62] The only comment forthcoming from Walbrook's home was that he was 'out of town', in more ways than one. The whole unlikely incident sounds like a publicity stunt, the timing coinciding as it did with the release of *Sixty Glorious Years*, not to mention Walbrook's forthcoming stage appearance as a bisexual painter in Noël Coward's play *Design For Living*. Nationality and sexuality are thus bound together once more, and once again displaced.

As I have indicated, *Sixty Glorious Years'* emphasis on British foreign policy found a new turn in the deployment of Walbrook's persona that would evolve into the articulate and humanitarian anti-Nazi characters in *49th Parallel* and particularly *Blimp*, where Walbrook's name, in the film's credits sequence, is literally, as well as metaphorically, woven into the fabric of Britain as part of a tapestry bearing a regal crest. While, as Sue Harper has observed, the typical female protagonist in Wilcox's films is 'combative and inventive, but … finally returned to a status quo which she herself had reinvigorated', the same cannot be said for Walbrook's Albert. Like the majority of his roles, Walbrook was never *fully* assimilated into the establishment.[63] Though he became a British citizen and very much part of British culture, his persona continued as the insider/outsider, a consort star, indeed, whose presence implicitly challenged national boundaries and identities.

Walbrook later spoke of his regret at the limited range of roles he and fellow émigré Conrad Veidt were offered in the early years: 'The trouble with the British is they think they are the only people in the world who have a sense of humour. All they wanted me to do was make them cry; as the dying Albert they thought I was perfectly in character. Still, I was making money, so …'[64] Luckily, unlike the Prince Consort, the British did take to Anton.

Notes

1. Though Viennese, Walbrook identified as German: 'I am German. I was born in Vienna, and my mother was Viennese, but my father was German.' R. Quilter Vincent, 'For Mr. Walbrook It's All in the Stars', October 1955, www.powell-pressburger.org/reviews/anton/anton55.html
2. 'Looking Back on 1937', *Picture Show*, 1 January 1938, p. 7.
3. *Monthly Film Bulletin*, September 1937, p. 191; 'Top 50 British Films, 1932–37', Jeffrey Richards (ed.), *The Unknown 1930s: An Alternative History of the British Cinema, 1929–1939* (London: I.B. Tauris, 1998), p. 34.
4. '1938 Calendar', *Picture Show*, 25 December 1937, pp. 16–17; quote from review on p. 19.
5. See Sarah Street, *Transatlantic Crossings: British Feature Films in the USA* (London: Continuum, 2002), p. 74.
6. *Today's Cinema*, 15 April 1937, p. 1.
7. Walbrook's version of *The Student of Prague* (Arthur Robison, Germany 1935) is also said to have been the first film broadcast on BBC television on 14 August 1938. See for instance: http://www.terramedia.co.uk/Chronomedia/years/1938.htm
8. Max Breen, 'Acting Is in His Blood', *Picturegoer Weekly*, 25 September 1937, p. 17; Sylvia Terry-Smith, 'I am s-ee-k to Death of Albert, says Anton Walbrook', *Picturegoer and Film Weekly*, 27 April 1940, p. 11.
9. O. Bristol, 'Anton Walbrook', *Picture Show*, 14 August 1937, p. 12.
10. In interviews, Walbrook often spoke of his affinity for Britain: '"And oh, how drab and grey and miserable are the manufacturing towns … [but] the simple people make you feel at home at once, but not the highbrows. I don't like them". He wrinkled his nose and screwed up his eyes in disgust.' Terry-Smith, 'I am s-ee-k to Death of Albert, says Anton Walbrook'.
11. Ibid.
12. Leonard Wallace, 'Meet Anton Walbrook', *Film Weekly*, 7 August 1937, p. 14; Breen, 'Acting Is in His Blood'.
13. *Monthly Film Bulletin*, March 1937, p. 60. The American pamphlet, prepared by an instructor in Motion Pictures at Columbia University, raised the following questions: 'Do you consider that an actor speaking broken English creates the illusion of a foreigner?' and 'Did it annoy you that Strogoff and Ogareff talked like foreigners while Nadia and Zangarra, also supposed to be Russian, were English-speaking actresses?' Frances Taylor Patterson, '*The Soldier and The Lady*', *Photoplay Studies*, Educational and Recreational Guides, Inc., February 1937, p. 12.
14. Jonathan Munby has observed that accent proved a significant intervention to the gangster genre in America, where the voice of 'hyphenated American' actors such as the Austrian Paul Muni underscored the liminal social status of the protagonists. See Munby: 'The Enemy Goes Public. Voicing The Cultural Other in the Early 1930s Talking Gangster Film', in his *Public Enemies, Public Heroes. Screening the Gangster from Little Caesar to Touch of Evil* (Chicago: University of Chicago Press, 1999), pp. 39–65.
15. Andrew Moor, 'Dangerous Limelight: Anton Walbrook and the Seduction of the English', in Bruce Babington (ed.), *British Stars and Stardom – from Alma Taylor to Sean Connery*, (Manchester: Manchester University Press, 2001), p. 83; Breen, 'Acting Is in His Blood'.
16. Wallace, 'Meet Anton Walbrook'.
17. Moor, 'Dangerous Limelight', p. 85.
18. 'And Don't Forget Walbrook', *Film Weekly*, 25 September 1937, p. 8.
19. 'A Glimpse of *The Rat*', *Picture Show*, 22 January 1938, p. 2; Tom Dysart, 'Anton Walbrook', *Film Weekly*, 26 December 1937, p. 21.
20. Moor, 'Dangerous Limelight', p. 88.
21. Dysart, 'Anton Walbrook'.
22. Bristol, 'Anton Walbrook'.
23. Edith Nepean, 'My Friends in British Studios', *Picture Show*, 9 October 1937, p. 6.

24. Richard Dyer, 'Charisma', in Christine Gledhill (ed.), *Stardom: Industry of Desire* (London: Routledge, 1991), p. 58.
25. Street, *Transatlantic Crossings*, p. 74.
26. The film was also made on the 100th anniversary of Victoria's accession, apparently at the Duke of Windsor's request, although Neagle claims it to have been Mrs Simpson's idea, after she had seen Housman's play *Victoria Regina*, on which the film was based, in New York. See 'Sense and the Censor', *Picture Show*, 31 July 1937, p. 9; Anna Neagle, *Anna Neagle Says 'There's Always Tomorrow'. An Autobiography* (London: W.H. Allen, 1974), p. 88.
27. 'Hero and Heroine', *Film Weekly*, 25 September 1937, p. 7.
28. '*Picture Show* Invites You to WIN Anna Neagle's *Victoria* Sunshade … or Anton Walbrook's Pipe!', *Picture Show*, 22 January 1938, p. 4.
29. This incident is evidently based on Queen Victoria's own recollection of events. On 12 October 1839 she wrote to her uncle Leopold that 'having no clothes … they could not appear at dinner but nevertheless débutéd after dinner in their négligé'. A.C. Benson and Lord Esher (eds.), *The Letters of Queen Victoria*, vol. 1 (1907), p. 237, quoted in Stanley Weintraub, 'Albert [Prince Albert of Saxe-Coburg and Gotha] (1819–1861)', *Oxford Dictionary of National Biography* (Oxford University Press, 2004). [http://www.oxforddnb.com/view/article/274]
30. One remembers here the *objet d'art*-cluttered apartment of Clifton Webb's Waldo Lydecker in *Laura* (Preminger, 1944), played by another 'virtually "out"' actor, of course, as Dyer put it, incongruously climbing out of his bath before Dana Andrews's detective, who hands him a robe before pointedly playing on a pocket game of baseball, seen in extreme close-up to announce his heterosexuality by contrast. Dyer, 'Postscript: Queers and Women in Film Noir', in E. Ann Kaplan (ed.), *Women and Film Noir*, rev. edn. (London: BFI, 1998), p. 123. The role of Lydecker, intriguingly, became one of Walbrook's last roles, in the German television version of 1962 (dir. by Franz Josef Wild).
31. Oscar Wilde, *The Picture of Dorian Gray* (London: Penguin, 1985), p. 122.
32. *Kinematograph Weekly*, 30 May 1940, p. 20.
33. Moor, 'Dangerous Limelight', p. 86.
34. See Michael Williams, *Ivor Novello: Screen Idol* (London: BFI, 2003), pp. 27ff.
35. Moor, 'Dangerous Limelight', p. 82.
36. *Film Pictorial*, 14 August 1937, pp. 12–13.
37. Terry-Smith, 'I am s-ee-k to Death of Albert, says Anton Walbrook', p. 10.
38. Herbert Wilcox, 'How We Made *Victoria*', *Film Weekly*, 25 December 1937, p. 20.
39. See for example, the *Victoria the Great* souvenir brochure of the Polytechnic Theatre, London, where the film was showing, coincidentally, across the road from the London Hippodrome, where Neagle was playing the lead in the pantomime *Peter Pan*.
40. H.E. Fowler, '*Victoria the Great*', *Photoplay Studies*, Educational and Recreational Guides, Inc., August 1937, pp. 8–9.
41. James Agate, 'Victoria the Little', 29 September 1937, from *The Tatler*, quoted from James Agate, *Around Cinemas* (London: Home & Van Thal, 1946), p. 185.
42. *Sixty Glorious Years* review, *The Spectator*, 4 November 1938; P. Galway, 'The Movies', *New Statesman*, 22 October 1938 (both unpaginated clippings, BFI library).
43. *Victoria the Great* review, *Kinematograph Weekly*, 23 September 1937, p. 24.
44. Agate, 'Victoria the Little'. The *Spectator* agreed, archly opining of *Sixty Glorious Years* that 'the film is in Technicolor, which is to say that the river-beds of the Highlands are filled with violet ink. They are certainly Sixty Highly Coloured Years'. *The Spectator*, 4 November 1938.
45. Marcia Landy, *British Genres: Cinema and Society, 1930–1960* (Princeton, NJ: Princeton University Press, 1991), p. 69.
46. *Film Weekly*, 22 October 1938, p. 27.
47. Neagle, *Autobiography*, p. 109.
48. *Monthly Film Bulletin*, October 1938, p. 237.

49. 'Polytechnic Theatre Presents *Victoria the Great*', 1937, p. 3.
50. Kevin Gough-Yates, 'Unresolved Questions of Film Exile in Britain after 1928', paper at 'German-speaking Émigrés in British Cinema, 1925–1950', an international conference at the University of Southampton, 15 July 2005.
51. Pam Cook, *Screening the Past: Memory and Nostalgia in Cinema* (London: Routledge, 2005), p. 3.
52. Cathy Caruth (ed.), *Trauma: Explorations in Memory* (Baltimore, London: Johns Hopkins University Press, 1995), p. 5.
53. Walbrook was a prisoner of war in France during the First World War, having been commissioned as a lieutenant in a regiment of guards, and is said to have organised a drama group while held captive. Donald Roy, 'Walbrook, (Adolf Wilhelm) Anton (1896–1967)', *Oxford Dictionary of National Biography* (Oxford University Press, 2004). [http://www.oxforddnb.com/view/article/60815]
54. Terry-Smith, 'I am s-ee-k to Death of Albert, says Anton Walbrook', p. 11.
55. *Cinegram* no. 39: '*Sixty Glorious Years*', 1938.
56. See Stephen Guy, 'Calling All Stars: Musical Films in a Musical Decade' in Richards, *The Unknown 1930s*, pp. 99–120.
57. *Kinematograph Weekly*, 9 December 1943, p. 38.
58. '*The Rat*' (review), *Kinematograph Weekly*, 18 November 1937. Of Walbrook's performance in that film, Novello apparently conceded: 'He gave a much better performance than I would have done.' Peter Noble, *Ivor Novello* (London: White Lion Publishers, 1975), p. 192.
59. Nepean, 'My Friends in British Studios', p. 6.
60. 'Ballyhoos-Stunts: Tie-ups with the Police Department', from *The Rat*, American Pressbook, BFI Library.
61. Williams, *Ivor Novello*, p. 92.
62. 'Anton Walbrook', unattributed clipping from 22 November 1938, BFI Library.
63. Sue Harper, 'From *Holiday Camp* to High Camp: Women in British Feature Films, 1945–1951', in Andrew Higson (ed.), *Dissolving Views: Key Writings on British Cinema* (London: Cassell, 1996), p. 99.
64. R. Quilter Vincent, see endnote 1.

Chapter 13

FROM 'ALIEN PERSON' TO 'DARLING LILLI': LILLI PALMER'S ROLES IN BRITISH CINEMA

Barbara Ziereis

Lilli Palmer left Britain for the USA in 1945, after having lived in London for ten years, as an established screen and stage actress. Before her arrival in Britain she was a talented but largely unknown continental actress and singer who had become a refugee from Nazi Germany. However, by 1945 'Darling Lilli' (as the tabloid press came to call her) had become a British star. She was an integrated and popular member of British society, partly through her marriage to British actor Rex Harrison, with whom she had a son. She had a British passport and lived surrounded by a great circle of friends and family. During her time in Britain, Palmer appeared in sixteen films. In Hollywood and later on Broadway she seamlessly continued with her success.

In retrospect, Palmer's rise to stardom in these times and under these historical conditions appears amazing. Her success in finding safety from Nazi persecution in Britain, which many German Jews failed to find, is a remarkable achievement in its own right. Her professional success as an actress in England, meanwhile, contrasts with the fate of many actors from the continent, who were vainly attempting to establish themselves in the British film industry. Among fellow émigré actors in Britain in the 1930s and 1940s, only Elisabeth Bergner, Anton Walbrook and Conrad Veidt can be seen to have matched or surpassed Palmer's success.

This chapter seeks to answer how Palmer coped with her exile situation, with immigration, assimilation and integration. It also deals with the representation of national identity, exile and immigration in Palmer's films, specifically regarding the characters she played.[1] My arguments are based on the following examples: *Sunset in Vienna* (1937), directed by Norman Walker, *A Girl Must Live* (1939), directed by Carol Reed, Leslie Howard's *The Gentle Sex* (1943), and *The Rake's Progress* (1945), directed by Sidney Gilliat. I want to analyse in particular how these films reflect either directly or indirectly

Britain's immigration policy of the time and its consequences for the situation of Jewish refugees in Britain. Palmer's own biography is instructive in this context, as her trajectory can stand as an example of a successful immigration. Before I concentrate on the filmic case studies, I shall briefly outline the key dates of Palmer's life and her migration to Britain.[2]

Lilli Palmer was born in Posen, now Polish Poznan, in 1914 as Lilli Marie Peiser. She grew up in an open-minded, assimilated, middle-class Jewish family in Berlin. Her father was a surgeon at the Charité hospital and her mother had been an actress before her marriage. After her *Abitur* she studied acting under Ilka Grüning and Lucie Höflich in Berlin. In 1933 her first engagement led Palmer to Darmstadt. There local SA-men disrupted her performances, and after the first season her contract was terminated. She could no longer work in Germany and left for Paris, where she performed with her sister Irene (later also a film actress under the name Irene Prador) as the singing and dancing *Soeurs viennoises* in nightclubs – but without success. It was in Paris that she met the producer Alexander Korda. According to Palmer's autobiography, Korda's first comment to her was: 'Do you know what I think? You'll look a lot better in ten years' time.'[3] Nevertheless he invited her to London for screen tests. Although these did not lead to a contract with Korda, and she had to leave Britain due to problems getting a work permit, Palmer's initial journey to Britain nevertheless had an important outcome: she was signed to the reputable talent agency of Myron Selznick.

While waiting in France, her agent negotiated a first film deal for her. In 1935 she played the female lead opposite British actor Esmond Knight in the B-picture *Crime Unlimited*, produced by Warner Bros. as a quota quickie at Teddington Studios, and directed by the American Ralph Ince. The Home Office issued Palmer with a work permit for eight months. After this film she had to leave Britain again, on condition that she did not come back. Ignoring this condition, she did return and in 1936 signed an optional contract for seven years with Gaumont-British, the most significant British film production firm at the time. The company dealt with the Home Office, stating in a letter that 'Alien Miss Palmer would unquestionably be "a valuable asset to the British film industry".'[4] Finally, she received a work permit – and this marked the start of her career in Britain.

During her early years at Gaumont-British Palmer appeared in a range of different productions, both in leading roles and supporting parts. In her autobiography she claimed that they were not of high quality, and said that she could not remember any of them.[5] Some of these films were produced by Gaumont-British, such as Alfred Hitchcock's *Secret Agent* in 1936, in which she appeared opposite a fellow émigré, Peter Lorre. Another early film was *First Offence* (1936), the British remake of Billy Wilder's French exile production *Mauvaise Graine* (1934), in which Palmer's male partner was the young John Mills. For some films Palmer was loaned out to other production companies – the Herbert Wilcox production *Sunset in Vienna* is one of them.[6] In this musical war drama Lilli Palmer plays the main female part of Gelda, a young Viennese woman who marries Italian officer Tony (Tullio Carminati) on the eve of the First World War and moves to Italy with him. Gelda is initially introduced as chubby-faced, naive and romantic, but soon has to adapt to the war's events and demands. She is torn between her family and her husband, between her old homeland Austria and her new country. The marriage breaks up when Tony shoots at her brother (who is working as an Austrian spy). The emotional happy ending only occurs after long suffering, and after both lovers having lost most of their possessions and innocence (Gelda has become the mistress of an American playboy, Tony has become penniless). The couple are finally reunited after the war in an Egyptian nightclub where Tony works as a singer.

As this brief plot synopsis indicates, *Sunset in Vienna* is a typical melodrama; the settings are not realistic, the characters are rarely more than stereotypes. The film draws heavily on markers of national identity. Foreignness is represented as exotic, and expressed through set design and costume as much as through the behaviour of the characters. Tony and Gelda first meet in a typical Viennese wine tavern called 'Beim Heurigen'. Later on, when they move to Italy, the landscape is visually coded as Northern Italy. Folkloristic practices further help to locate the film's action: Gelda is wearing supposedly regional costumes and is working in the vineyards, with the village community singing all of the time. Tony in particular seems almost a national cliché – he speaks with a strong Italian accent and wins the heart of his love by singing her romantic songs, a supposedly Italian way of courtship.[7] In contrast, Gelda's representation comes across as a more implicit embodiment of foreignness and exile. A lonely character throughout most of the film, she is portrayed in isolation, with no friends or family in Italy, with only her husband by her side. The film addresses overtly problems of mixed marriages in wartime. Gelda's efforts to join an Italian aid organisation, for example, are rebuked by the other women in the village.

Sunset in Vienna deals with divided loyalties. In terms of overall message the film suggests that the boundaries of national identity impede the lovers in their pursuit of happiness. As the case of Gelda shows, leaving one's home country leads to loneliness for the exile and to divisions and hostilities in the host country. The lovers can only find equality and resolution once they have become homeless and encounter each other again in an extraterritorial space (the Egyptian nightclub).

Palmer played a foreigner again in the musical comedy *A Girl Must Live* – Clythie Divine, a 'tough Hungarian chorus girl'.[8] By this time Palmer had established herself on the London stage as well as through her film work. The quality of her film roles began to be noticed and remarked upon in the press.[9] Although her residence permit had to be renewed every third month for years to come, the contract with Gaumont-British gave her security.

Shrewish and arrogant as well as elegant, Palmer's character in *A Girl Must Live* is a far cry from the wide-eyed innocent Gelda in *Sunset in Vienna*. The film's female lead is Margaret Lockwood, who plays Leslie, a young English upper-class woman who runs away from a Swiss boarding school to work on the London stage. It is here that Lockwood encounters Clythie (Palmer) and another chorus girl, the Irish Gloria Lind, played by Renée Houston. By the end of the film Leslie ends up with a young, rich and charming nobleman. Meanwhile, Clythie and Gloria, the two gold-diggers, continue to quarrel and search for potential rich husbands. A comic climax of the film is a sort of catfight between Clythie and Gloria, where they convert 'every conceivable item into a weapon'.[10]

As in *Sunset in Vienna*, national stereotypes are drawn upon to make comic use of the ethnic as well as class differences which separate the three female characters – Clythie the immigrant, Gloria the Irish working-class girl and Leslie as a member of the British upper-middle class. These differences become encoded through accent and language, general demeanour, and the notion of sexual experience. The women's behaviour is significant: Leslie is demure, well educated and polite whereas the two others are loud, childish, emotional, quarrelsome and egotistic. There is also a moral divide between the three – while Leslie as a pupil from a Swiss boarding school is clearly a virgin, Clythie and Gloria are introduced as women with male friends and their jewellery and suggestive dresses indicate former lovers. The fact that Leslie triumphs over Clythie and Gloria is crucial. English modesty and honesty mark her out as attractive, despite her temporary disguise as a showgirl. While the film offers her character social mobility, it denies it to the other two women. As such, the film can be seen to reflect the actual structure of British society at the time and offers what Jeffrey Richards has referred to as a consensus solution.[11]

There are no explicit references to matters of immigration in *A Girl Must Live*. Yet it is possible to read a subtext into the story of the two gold-digging chorus girls so desperately trying to find a husband, especially given the fact that one of them is explicitly introduced as a foreigner. Owing to severe economic depression and high unemployment in the 1930s, the Home Office actively worked to reduce competition for British employees in the British job market. Foreigners who came to Britain during this period faced severe restrictions. As Palmer's own early experiences demonstrate, foreigners could only hope for temporary residence, had to show a will to assimilate and could only work if it was necessary for the British economy.[12] Marrying a British citizen was one of the few ways to stay legally in Britain. Seen against this context, Clythie's story in the film can be read not simply as that of a morally dubious social climber who looks for her luck by nearly all means, but as a metaphor for the condition of exile in Britain.

For Palmer herself the situation was somewhat different, although she too eventually acquired British citizenship through marriage. Prior to the

Second World War, she got a permanent residence permit and was safe in Britain. However, the outbreak of war changed her situation again: her contract with Gaumont-British was dissolved. Theatres in London were closed, but the companies performed in the provinces. During one of these tours she met her first husband, the actor Rex Harrison whom she married in 1943.

After the war had started, the British film industry adapted to the requirements of wartime, and began with the production of propaganda films.[13] It is no surprise that Palmer, as a refugee from Nazism herself, but equally importantly as someone who had established herself in British films playing foreigners, would appear in several of these productions. Perhaps her most notable contribution to the war effort was *The Gentle Sex*.[14] The film was one of the box office hits of its year[15] and widely praised for its documentary style.[16] Palmer portrays 'sad eyed' and 'lonely'[17] Erna Debruski, a Czech refugee among seven girls who join the ATS to work as lorry drivers on a dangerous convoy and in an anti-aircraft unit on the British home front during the Second World War. Accompanied by a voiceover commentary (provided by the film's director, Leslie Howard), *The Gentle Sex* attempts to present a cross-section of British women of the time, encompassing different regions and classes. Included are Maggie Fraser, a Scottish woman (Rosamund John); Anne, the daughter of a major (Joyce Howard); Dot Hopkins (Jean Gillie), an emancipated and glamorous city girl; ambitious and reserved Joan Simpson (Barbara Waring); working-class Gwen Haydon (Joan Gates); and Betty Miller (Joan Greenwood), the youngest, who has never been away from home.

The Gentle Sex campaigns for women's participation in the war effort, but it addresses both men and women. On the one hand, the film encourages the male population to accept and admire the female contribution to the war, dispelling fears of changes in gender hierarchies. As the voiceover insists, the employment of women in so-called male professions is to be understood to be a temporary necessity. On the other hand, *The Gentle Sex* is clearly meant as a recruitment aid for women to join the ATS. Otherwise the film's narrative is structured like a typical war film in its promotion of camaraderie and unity: different individuals come together in a unit, and despite initial differences, they are successful in their effort and become friends.

Life in the ATS camp is presented as an adult variant of a boarding school. Every character has her individual reason for joining the voluntary service. Erna Debruski's motivation is her experience as a victim of the Nazis and as a Czech refugee. *The Gentle Sex* here refers directly to the admission of 6,000 political Czech refugees, who were admitted to come to Britain after the occupation of Czechoslovakia.[18] For Erna, joining the ATS provides her with the opportunity to retaliate against the Nazis for occupying her country, torturing her brother and killing her father and fiancé. She is shown to enjoy the life and the camaraderie in the ATS; she deeply appreciates the regular meals, the uniform which keeps her warm, the chance to feel at home in the company of other women. Erna is the only one who praises the first meal at ATS as 'absolutely delicious'. Lost in thought, she runs her hand over her coat when she wears it the first time. She expresses shy gratitude when another girl hands her a sweet.

Throughout the narrative Erna serves to articulate the moral duty to fight the Nazis and to justify military actions such as air raids on German-occupied French cities. As she tells her female companions: 'In France the French cheer over British bombs because they know a bomb is beautiful. They cry: Bomb us, blast us to dust as long as you blow the dust in the Nazis' eyes! Kill us as long as you kill them!' What becomes clear in scenes such as this is Erna's emotional involvement, her hatred of the Nazis and her thirst for revenge. When the tail of a German plane is shot off, her face – presented in close-up – displays grim satisfaction. Erna's conviction and determination are marked as positive, and serve to rally the other women when they show momentary signs of indifference or apathy towards the war effort.

The women in *The Gentle Sex* are clearly meant to represent the national community more generally. Foreigners and émigrés – such as Erna – are part of this community if they fight on the side of Britain. In this respect, the film offers an extended and inclusive version of British nationhood, at least for the time of war. The representation of Erna reflects the change in attitude towards immigrants during the Second World War, when political refugees from occupied Europe were welcomed as combatants against the enemy. Erna presents an idealised embodiment of the exile, a traumatised victim and at the same time a responsible and reliable person, an effective combatant and a refugee who wants to assimilate and become part of British society.

Palmer's first postwar release, and her first international success, *The Rake's Progress*, revisits the issue of refugees, but from a somewhat different perspective. The episodic film follows the story of Vivian Kenway (Palmer's husband Rex Harrison), a charming, but irresponsible rogue, from his early days at Oxford through various exploits until a final act of heroism during the war that costs him his life. Palmer plays a young Austrian Jew, Rikki Krausner, whom Kenway meets in Vienna, and who offers to pay his debts if he marries her. He agrees and Rikki is able to leave Vienna just after Austria's annexation to the Third Reich. Rikki falls in love with Vivian, who cannot commit and who toys with her. The situation escalates when Rikki witnesses Vivian beginning an affair with his father's secretary. She tries to drown herself, but is rescued. The audience later learns that Rikki divorced Vivian. At the end Vivian, who acted irresponsibly nearly all his life, joins the army and dies as a hero in action. The film discusses the question of whether the efforts in war counterbalance a person's past misdeeds. Moreover, it directly refers to Britain's prewar immigration policy. Marriage seems the only way to rescue Rikki from Nazi persecution and –

as Rikki is introduced as Jewish – from the Holocaust. *The Rake's Progress* shows compassion and understanding for Rikki's motives in pursuing a marriage of convenience, presented as a legitimate attempt to rescue oneself from Nazi terror. Marrying Rikki is one of the few positive deeds the film concedes Vivian, even though he will cause Rikki a lot of personal damage later on.

The film's sympathy towards the refugee character, while at the same time condemning the relationship of Vivian with a foreign girl, reflects the variety of attitudes in Britain towards refugees during the last years of the war. In her study about British immigration policy towards Jews from 1933 to 1948, Louise London describes the attitude of the British government in this matter as being governed by self-interest.[19] Although Britain had the most liberal admission laws in Europe, there were plans to prohibit permanent immigration, especially of Jews. The reasoning behind that was the Home Office's fear of anti-Semitism in Britain. Until 1937 Jewish refugees who wanted to come to Britain were treated as ordinary visitors. Permission to enter the country depended on the individual's assets and the assurance that applicants would leave the country after their allocated period of stay. This explains why it was easier for Jewish children and women to enter Britain than for men of working age, who were suspected of aspiring to permanent residency. While the stay had to be declared as a temporary one, migrants also needed to demonstrate the will to assimilate. After Austria's annexation to the German Reich entry restrictions were tightened. After the occupation of the Sudetenland in October 1938 and the November pogroms in Germany and Austria, entry was facilitated for explicitly political refugees, while fugitives persecuted for racial reasons were still excluded.[20]

After the outbreak of war, frontiers were closed. Although the Home Office was pressured to open the borders after 1942 (when knowledge of the concentration camps started to spread more widely), refugee policy did not change until 1944. Seen against this context, Lilli Palmer's immigration into Britain appears to be typical for Nazi refugees who were allowed into Britain before 1938 – as I have documented before, she entered twice with a visitor's visa. Palmer's on-screen roles as refugees (to which one might also add her role as ghostly refugee in *Thunder Rock*, 1942) also reflected wider patterns and political attitudes towards immigration. While she was never cast as a British character during her career in the UK, Palmer interestingly also never played a German. For a long time she did not portray explicitly Jewish characters either, initially impersonating more diffuse versions of 'continentals' – in her British films she was, inter alia, a Swiss chambermaid, an Austrian aristocrat, a Swedish translator, and, as we have seen, a Czech refugee and a Hungarian showgirl. This blurring of national markers extended to the public perception of Palmer. Not only did she not play German characters, she also erased her own origins. Since her beginnings as a *soeur viennoise* in the nightclubs of Paris, she was perceived as Austrian and encouraged people to believe this myth. Publicity material for *A Girl Must Live*, for instance, referred to her as an Austrian actress. Several serious theatre encyclopaedias of the 1940s and 1950s do the same, and argue that she was born in Austria.[21]

Ultimately, in her British films Lilli Palmer represented the 'good foreigner'. Unlike her one-time co-star Peter Lorre who became typecast in villainous parts, Palmer's image went in the opposite direction. The differences in the representation of the non-British characters she portrayed, in the four films analysed, illustrate the changes and developments in how the (European) 'other' was perceived in British society from the mid-1930s to the end of the Second World War. Her film roles gave Palmer the opportunity to actively promote tolerance of foreigners, of refugees and finally of Jews who fled from Nazism. In this regard she also fought for her own acceptance.

Notes

1. For introductions to film exile in Great Britain see Günter Berghaus (ed.), *Theatre and Film in Exile. German Artists in Britain, 1933–1945* (Oxford, New York and Munich: Berg, 1989); Jörg Schöning (ed.), *London Calling. Deutsche im britischen Film der dreißiger Jahre* (Munich: edition text+kritik, 1993). Regarding film and national identity see Mette Hjort and Scott MacKenzie (eds.), *Cinema and Nation* (London and New York: Routledge, 2000).
2. For biographical information see Lilli Palmer, *Change Lobsters – and Dance* (London: W.H. Allen, 1974); Hans-Michael Bock (ed.), *CineGraph, Lexikon zum deutschsprachigen Film* (Munich: edition text+kritik, 1984–); Michael O. Huebner, *Lilli Palmer. Ihre Filme – ihr Leben* (Munich: Heyne, 1986); Joachim Weno, *Lilli Palmer* (Berlin: Rembrandt, 1957).
3. Palmer, *Change Lobsters – and Dance*, p. 80.
4. Ibid., p. 93.
5. Ibid., p. 94.
6. *Picturegoer Weekly*, 17 December 1938, p. 4.
7. For stereotypes of Italians in US films see Klaus Rieser-Wohlfarter, *Filmische Passagen in die neue Welt. Entwürfe ethno-amerikanischer Kulturen im Migrationsfilm* (Trier: Wissenschaftlicher Verlag Trier, 1996), p. 142.
8. *News from Gaumont-British-Gainsborough Studios*. Booklet, unpaginated, undated, BFI National Library.
9. *Picturegoer Weekly*, 17 December 1938, p. 4.
10. Robert F. Moss, *The Films of Carol Reed* (Basingstoke: Macmillan, 1987), p. 104.
11. Regarding political consensus in film see Jeffrey Richards, 'National Identity in British Wartime Films', in Philip M. Taylor (ed.), *Britain and the Cinema in the Second World War* (Basingstoke: Macmillan, 1988), pp. 42–61, esp. p. 59.
12. See Colin Holmes, *John Bull's Island. Immigration and British Society 1871–1971* (Basingstoke: Macmillan, 1988).
13. See Taylor, *Britain and the Cinema in the Second World War*; Andrew Higson, 'Addressing the Nation. Five Films', in Geoff Hurd (ed.), *National Fictions. World War Two in British Films and Television* (London: BFI, 1984), pp. 22–26.
14. For different approaches to the presentation of women in this film see Antonia Lant, *Blackout. Reinventing Women for Wartime British Cinema* (Princeton: Princeton University Press, 1991), pp. 89–99; Marcia Landy, 'Melodrama and Femininity in World War Two

British Cinema', in Robert Murphy (ed.), *The British Cinema Book* (London: BFI, 1997), pp. 79–89.

15. Lant, *Blackout*, p. 231.
16. *Observer*, 4 April 1943; *Sunday Times*, 11 April 1943.
17. *The Star*, 10 April 1943.
18. See Gerhard Hirschfeld, 'Great Britain and the Emigration from Nazi Germany: An Historical Overview', in Berghaus, *Theatre and Film in Exile*, p. 7.
19. See Louise London, *Whitehall and the Jews, 1933–1948. British Immigration Policy, Jewish Refugees and the Holocaust* (Cambridge: Cambridge University Press, 2000).
20. See ibid., p. 81.
21. See John Parker (ed.), *Who's Who in the Theatre. A Biographical Record of the Contemporary Stage*, 11th edn. (London: Pitman, 1952); Peter Noble (ed.), *The British Film Yearbook* (London: British Yearbooks, 1946); Peter Noble, *British Theatre* (London: British Yearbooks, 1946).

Chapter 14

'YOU CALL US "GERMANS", YOU CALL US "BROTHERS" – BUT WE ARE NOT YOUR BROTHERS!': BRITISH ANTI-NAZI FILMS AND GERMAN-SPEAKING ÉMIGRÉS

Tobias Hochscherf

At the outbreak of the Second World War the British Board of Film Censors (BBFC) eased some of its more stringent regulations, and the newly set-up Films Division of the wartime Ministry of Information (MoI) began to play a key role in the production of films. The combination of entertainment with a political message led to a boom in British cinema – both in terms of both creativity and popularity.[1] Hitherto, this success has often been celebrated as a genuine national achievement. Charles Barr, for instance, argues that 'by the end of the war, a positive reading of "mainstream" British cinema for the first time became convincingly available, both in Britain and abroad. It was a cinema unproblematically British in personnel (after a decade of foreign infiltration that was resented by many)'.[2]

This chapter challenges the marginalisation of émigrés in previous critical accounts of British wartime films[3] and proposes to redraw the boundaries of puristically defined concepts of national cinema. Rooted in Homi K. Bhabha's recognition of an 'anti-nationalist, ambivalent nation-space [that] becomes the crossroads to a new transnational culture',[4] my analysis draws special attention to the various contributions by German-speaking émigrés to British propaganda films or films with an implicit political message.[5]

Covering the period from 1939 to 1945, I want to address whether émigrés were able to influence the style and content of such films or if they were primarily forced to act out Teutonic clichés in what Thomas Elsaesser has labelled a 'mimicry of survival'.[6] Émigré identities have been eclipsed in many accounts of wartime cinema in favour of examinations of English national identity.[7] In contrast, my chapter suggests a different reading that shifts the representation of foreign characters to the centre of attention. In doing so, exile cinema must be regarded as a multifaceted phenomenon that touches upon wider issues such as ethnicity, national identity and otherness; this takes into account a recent paradigm shift in exile studies from biographical approaches 'to a more dynamic scenario of intercultural tension and negotiation', as outlined by Gerd Gemünden and Anton Kaes.[8]

By challenging Barthes' notion of the 'death of the author', Hamid Naficy's work on exilic and diasporic filmmaking has convincingly suggested that the presence of émigré filmmakers can be shown in both the style and content of their work.[9] Following his lead, I suggest that the contribution by many German-speaking immigrants to British wartime cinema can help to explain the nuanced depictions of Germans and foreigners in British films. Through their roles, German-speaking actors such as Conrad Veidt, Lilli Palmer and Anton Walbrook were able to diversify the views on enemies and allies, foreigners and Britons. The situation of German-speaking émigrés in Britain was characterised by artistic and economic constraint and shaped by hostility on the part of the trade unions and important public figures.[10] However, film exile should not be described solely in terms of trauma, estrangement and paranoia, but also as 'productive encounter and active engagement with a new culture'.[11] As Gemünden and Kaes have argued, displacement and disorientation function 'as (admittedly forced) opportunities for self-examination and social critique'.[12]

'What a difference a war makes':[13] German-speaking Emigrés and Wartime Cinema

The boom period of British film production from 1933 to 1937 facilitated a conducive economic environment for German-speaking film personnel coming to Britain after Hitler seized power in 1933. As Andrew Higson has suggested, judging by the cast and credits of films made during these years, they could still relatively easily find a job within the film business[14] – notwithstanding strict immigration control and fierce opposition on the part of the trade union ACT. At times, most of the senior staff involved in the production of a single British film consisted of German-speaking refugees. The financial crisis in the British film industry in 1936/37 and the mass purge of film personnel from Austria after the *Anschluss* in 1938, however, made the situation more difficult, as more people competed for fewer jobs. Consequently, a significant number of émigrés, among them Friedrich Feher, Erich Pommer, Eugen Schüfftan and Berthold Viertel, moved to Hollywood because of better employment opportunities.[15]

When war broke out the situation for German-speaking exiles in Britain was exacerbated. In a climate of xenophobia and fear of fifth-columnists

Westminster resolved to intern thousands of German and Austrian exiles. Although the authorities sought to detain enemy aliens only, many of the internees were Jews and/or anti-Nazi activists who had fled Germany to escape persecution[16] – among them a notable number of film personnel. Besides the actors Annemarie Haase, Margarete Hruby and Gerard Heinz (Gerhard Hinze), the case of set designer Hein Heckroth exemplifies the tragedy of many interned émigrés and the drastic actions by the British government. Although he had no sympathies for fascism – his paintings were removed by the Nazis from galleries – Heckroth was arrested and shipped overseas on 10 July 1940 to be interned in Australia.[17]

Other interned film practitioners included author and director Rudolph Katscher (Cartier), cinematographer Carl Kayser, actor and director Erich Freund, scriptwriters Emeric Pressburger and Heinrich Fraenkel, and set designer Alfred Junge.[18] After their eventual release many émigrés remained under surveillance[19] and found it difficult to be granted work permits, as cinema was seen as a vital and sensitive medium in the fight against Nazi Germany. Regarding Katscher's naturalisation and authorisation to work in the film industry, one Whitehall official explicitly stated on 28 July 1944: 'We ought look very carefully at the establishment of aliens as directors of film companies.'[20]

Despite such adversities two developments benefited the film exiles. First, the relaxation of censorship prompted the production of anti-Nazi films such as the formerly rejected *Pastor Hall* (Roy Boulting, 1940), and thus offered new opportunities. Second, the MoI's imperative to maintain a private 'flourishing British film industry, busy for the most part in producing, not propaganda films, but the normal entertainment film, produced, distributed, and exhibited through the ordinary commercial channels of the Industry',[21] helped German-speaking émigrés to retain their position within British studios. Otto Kanturek, for instance, was working as chief lighting cameraman at Elstree before his death in a plane crash while filming *A Yank in the R.A.F.* in 1941. Other examples include the cameramen Mutz Greenbaum (Ealing and Denham Studios – among others for RKO Radio British Productions, British National and Herbert Wilcox Productions) and Günther Krampf (Associated British and Ealing Studios), and the scriptwriter Wolfgang Wilhelm (Denham Studios – among others for Two Cities Films and RKO Radio British Productions).[22]

Many émigrés became actively involved in British propaganda in order to prove their allegiance to the British war effort – a decisive criterion in the re-evaluation of their alien status and work permit claims. Michael Powell recalled in retrospect that Anton Walbrook, for example, was one of the first stars to agree to appear in his *49th Parallel* (1941), because he was an enemy alien and wanted to state which side he was on.[23]

Like exiled actors in other countries of refuge, almost all of their counterparts in Britain, including Walbrook, Veidt, Palmer, Fritz Kortner, Oscar Homolka, Frederick Valk, Carl Jaffé and Elisabeth Bergner, were determined by their accent – despite language coaches and a growing fluency in English.[24] Their foreign parts can be categorised into three main groups: 'enemy aliens', 'friendly foreigners' and 'good Germans'.

'Enemy Aliens' and 'Friendly Foreigners'

Shortly after his assumption of office, the second director of the MoI Films Division, Kenneth Clark, outlined principles for the production of wartime films in *Kinematograph Weekly*:

> What we are fighting for must be 'put over' on the world by indirect methods … We do not want 'blah' of jingoism … [F]irstly, no film is good propaganda unless it is good entertainment. A bad film transfers boredom to the cause it advocates. Secondly, it must be realised that the essence of successful propaganda is that people should not be aware of it. If you make people 'think' propaganda, their resistance to it is increased.[25]

Producers pursued various ways of combining a political message with entertainment. Such hybrid films corresponded to a change in cinema-goers' preferences. As the critic C.A. Lejeune argued, 'the public couldn't sit through the ordinary talkie-talkie-tea-table picture. [People] wanted action, movement, colour, music, comedy – some sort of proxy release from our pent-up emotions'.[26] Emigrés who had mainly been cast in costume pictures, spy thrillers, musical comedies and melodramas in the 1930s became increasingly involved in films that added elements of action pictures and combat films to peacetime entertainment formulas.

A number of émigrés were repeatedly – and in some cases exclusively – cast as Nazi villains. This holds true for those supporting and character actors who were less well-known by British cinema-goers. Carl Jaffé, for instance, played a Gestapo chief in *Gasbags* (Marcel Varnel, 1941), a Colonel in the Luftwaffe in *Squadron Leader X* (Lance Comfort, 1943), the German Count von Biebrich in occupied Holland in *The Night Invader* (Herbert Mason, 1943), and a German general in *The Man From Morocco* (Max Greene, 1945). The British roles of Albert Lieven show a similar pattern as he frequently appeared in SS and Wehrmacht uniforms. It was a cruel paradox that the persecuted actor had to play the role of the persecutor – a situation Thomas Elsaesser has appropriately referred to as a 'two-fold estrangement',[27] a separation of émigrés from both their homelands and from the attitudes of their host country towards them. On the other hand, their accent and otherness offered them job opportunities and even fame in difficult times.

However, while Jaffé and Lieven were habitually cast as villains, other, better-known German-speaking actors appeared in a variety of roles and were not solely typecast as fascists. Frederick Valk, for instance, did play Nazis but had a far wider repertoire, ranging from the Allied captain of a

Polish bomber crew in *Dangerous Moonlight* (Brian Desmond Hurst, 1941) to an Austrian doctor expelled from his home country in 1849 in *Thunder Rock* (Roy Boulting, 1942). The same can be said about the German-speaking stars in British cinema, such as Veidt, Walbrook and Palmer, who repeatedly appeared as friendly foreigners – in *Contraband* (Michael Powell, 1940), for instance, Veidt plays Captain Andersen, a sympathetic Dane who successfully tracks down German infiltrators in London during the war.

Dangerous Moonlight sympathises with the Central European victims of Nazi oppression. Walbrook plays Polish star pianist Stefan Radetzky, who escapes from Warsaw when the Nazis attack Poland and falls in love with an American heiress. The film calls on an international audience to join in the war against the Third Reich. In one scene, Radetzky's manager Mike leaves America to fight alongside the British. When he is questioned as to why he, as an Irishman, wants to do so after everything the English have done to his ancestors, his answer, 'that doesn't count when somebody else butts in', is a statement which implies that one has to leave all old animosities or doubts aside when fighting Nazism.

After having performed the lushly emotional *Warsaw Concerto*, composed especially for the film by Richard Addinsell, Radetzky decides to fight actively in the Battle of Britain in a Polish division of the RAF, despite his happy marriage and great success as a concert pianist in America. The moving score by Addinsell and an uncredited Mischa Spoliansky makes Radetzky remember the plight of his people and his desire to return to his home country. In one of Walbrook's moving showpiece performances he explains to his wife (and the cinema audience) that avoiding war against Hitler was not an option, as not to fight would mean that 'there would be no art, no music left that would be worth fighting for'.

Walbrook's sensitive, yet passionate acting style and refined screen persona add an interesting nuance to the perception of foreigners in British films. From his performances as the sympathetic Prince Albert in Herbert Wilcox's *Victoria the Great* (1937) to the celebrated musician in *Dangerous Moonlight*, Walbrook repeatedly played charmingly melancholic outsiders. Rather than indulging in swift action, he appears as a taciturn if not introvert character that is repeatedly framed by close-ups of his facial expressions (see also Michael Williams's chapter in this volume). Whenever Walbrook speaks he does so very slowly, giving emphasis and depth to every single word. Andrew Moor pointedly describes his voice as 'subtly modulated and rhythmed tenor, tightening in moments of urgency into a guttural, strangulated rasp'.[28] In contrast with stereotypes of the uncouth 'strange other' speaking loudly with a thick accent, he appears fragile, receptive, cultured, eloquent, and elegant. At variance with other German or Austrian male stars in the 1930s and early 1940s, such as the salt-of-the-earth Richard Tauber or the sinister Veidt, Walbrook is deeply emotional and even cries at the end of the film when he finds a letter from his wife in the belongings of his best friend who was killed in action.

In the context of wartime cinema, *Dangerous Moonlight* is an example of the MoI's increasing support of the incorporation of 'friendly foreigners' into feature film projects. In its endeavour to propagate the conflict with Nazi Germany as the 'People's War' in which all strands of British society are united in the fight against the common enemy,[29] 'friendly foreigners' became valuable allies (see also Barbara Ziereis on Lilli Palmer in this volume).

The 'Good German'

In addition to the 'friendly foreigner', British films also more specifically featured representations of 'good Germans'. For example, *Pastor Hall*, *49th Parallel* and *The Life and Death of Colonel Blimp* (Powell and Pressburger, 1943) all include sympathetic German protagonists who oppose the Nazis. Avoiding the 'xenophobic chauvinism'[30] which had characterised the First World War, 'good Germans' were no longer an oxymoron in wartime discourses. In an article on the situation of immigrants in Britain for the New York-based exile publication *Aufbau*, German émigré Paul Marcus, for instance, reported that English newspapers were calling for a clear distinction between German refugees and Nazis.[31]

Positioning themselves against racist hatred in any form, many émigré feature films of the era accentuate the fact that a significant number of Germans were themselves victims of Nazism. *Pastor Hall* is a case in point. Based upon a play by Ernst Toller, a well-known German-Jewish pacifist playwright expelled by the Nazis, the film's plot revolves around the persecution and martyrdom of the German pastor Martin Niemöller, who was sent to Dachau concentration camp.[32] Although Niemöller had fought for Germany as a U-boat captain in the First World War, he was eventually interned after his religious beliefs had led him to preach regularly against Hitler and the Nazi movement.

Having been banned before the war by the BBFC on the grounds that the film's 'exhibition at the present time would be inexpedient',[33] *Pastor Hall* was rushed into production shortly after the beginning of war. It depicts how German fascists deal with dissident voices within the Third Reich. The violence of the concentration camp scenes, showing the whipping of Pastor Hall and the penning of inmates into small damp cells like animals, anticipate the Allied postwar footage of the Nazi death mills. Not least because of its topicality and the 'artistic validity of Ernst Toller's play on which the screen-script is based, ... *Pastor Hall*', in the judgement of exile Klaus Mann, 'surpasses the American output in intellectual seriousness and moral authority'.[34] Likewise, Minister of Information Duff Cooper wrote to the film's distributor: 'I believe that *Pastor Hall* is a great film showing the nature of our present struggle. I hope it will be widely seen.'[35]

The opening scenes of the film depict an idyllic rural community in Southern Germany; the imagery resembles that of many popular British prewar musical comedies (e.g. *Heart's Desire*, 1935, see Christian Cargnelli in this volume), which also presented a nostalgic and serene view of Alpine life. However, the Nazis soon destroy the harmonious atmosphere. The film conveys this visually, through military uniforms that do not fit the peaceful village life, and through sound, as the cheerful melody that accompanied the beginning of the film gives way to the military tunes of storm troopers marching through the streets. The gloomy cinematography by Mutz Greenbaum identifies the National Socialists as unemotional and blunt characters while Pastor Hall, played by Wilfrid Lawson, appears as a warm and caring father figure. The images convey the cold and claustrophobic atmosphere generated by the Nazi intruders.

Greenbaum, a prominent lighting expert, particularly relied on the creation of chiaroscuro effects through tones of black and white as a means of infusing settings with a specific mood. This becomes particularly evident in his striking juxtaposition of scenes that depict Pastor Hall amongst his family and friends, using flat lighting to create a homely feeling through an even distribution of light and shade, with sequences featuring Nazi characters that employ low-key lighting to evoke a menacing ambience. The cinematography thus underlines the immanent threat emanating from the storm troopers who are, among other things, responsible for the suicide of a village girl who is pregnant by a young Nazi who has no intention of marrying her, and also for the death of a village boy as the result of an internal Nazi power struggle.

Apart from the high contrast that characterises sequences like the conversation of Hall with the storm-trooper leader in the pastor's study prior to his internment, Greenbaum also employs other forms of symbolism as a means of visual characterisation. He frames Nazi insignia throughout the film and, very strikingly, applies back lighting to place objects such as the barbed wire or the prison bars of the concentration camp in silhouette. When Pastor Hall is trying to calm the pregnant girl, he is shot in close-up, holding her head gently leaned to his shoulder and shielding her with his hand, while the back lighting through the lattice windows of her room throws a cage-like shadow on the wall, emphasising her hopeless situation.

Throughout the film the victimisation of 'good Germans' invites audiences to sympathise and identify with the oppressed community, above all with Pastor Hall who seeks to comfort the villagers. When he preaches against Nazi ideology for the last time in the final scene of the film, and the camera position changes from that of the congregation below to a straight-on angle, Hall seems to talk directly to cinema-goers rather than to the fictional characters. Identification with the oppressed villagers is also achieved by means of commonalities that establish links between the German village and British audiences. The *mise en scène* of the picturesque rural locale, for instance, shares many characteristics with the English pastoral tradition – a tradition that was central to wartime representations of Britain.[36] The fact that the protagonist is a Protestant priest, while Southern Germany has always been traditionally Catholic, also smoothes the process of associating an English audience with the religious village community and its pastor.

By engaging the audience's empathy for the German victims of Nazism, *Pastor Hall* adheres to a general pattern of émigré propaganda films: that the fight against Nazism is not a fight against a people, but rather a fight against an ideology. Consequently, a new Germany after the war is deemed possible – a belief emphasised by the title sequence, which explicitly dedicates the film 'to the day when it may be shown in Germany'. Through the character of Heinrich Degan, played by Bernard Miles, the film suggests that there are Germans who were seduced into National Socialism rather than staunch supporters of Hitler's ideology, and could thus be re-educated. Degan, who joins the SS because he has been unemployed for a long time, gets shot while he helps Pastor Hall to escape from the concentration camp.

Two German-speaking film émigrés engaged in the production of *Pastor Hall* appear in the film's credits under an alias: using the surname Reiner, Anna Gmeyner co-wrote the script, and the composer Hans May is billed as 'Mac Adams'. It remains difficult to reconstruct their contributions in detail, owing to the paucity of primary sources regarding the production process. What can be ascertained from contemporary newspaper reviews, however, is that Gmeyner added '"little bits"'[37] to Toller's original play, accentuating the brutalisation of concentration camp detainees.[38]

Besides its strong anti-Nazi message, *Pastor Hall* discusses exile as a way to evade Nazi persecution, which seems rather surprising at the beginning of the war when the topic of refugees was still seen as very problematic. In a climate of mass internment and amidst fears of foreign infiltration, partly stimulated by newspapers such as the *Daily Sketch* or the *Sunday Express* that polarised public opinion,[39] the government and the BBFC were generally determined not to add fuel to the fire by allowing films to treat the controversial issue; it is only because *Pastor Hall* refrains from discussing emigration in connection with Britain that it becomes palatable. The possibility of migration seems to be restricted to France and, above all, to the United States, described by Hall as a 'great and free country' where one can build a life without interference. Yet, the film also refers to the hardships of exile. In a concentration camp scene a Jew tells the other inmates why he is in the camp after having already been safe in exile in France:

> Every morning in Paris I went for a walk ... One morning in April I saw birds on the branches of a tree, everything smelt of spring and everybody was

laughing and happy for their reason. And I, I don't know why, suddenly I felt homesick. I couldn't bear the thought of everybody speaking in a foreign language.

As an important statement the Jewish refugee in *Pastor Hall* personalises the plight of Nazi opponents and sympathises with the fate of exiles.

In order to change public opinion in the United States and end its isolationist policy, the MoI directly supported another émigré anti-Nazi film: *49th Parallel*.[40] Written by Emeric Pressburger, it tells the story of a stranded Nazi U-boat crew trying to make their way to the United States via Canada after their submarine has sunk. A key sequence illustrates the difference between Germans and Nazis. After the peaceful and hospitable Hutterite community has offered the Nazi crew at large food and accommodation – being neither aware of their identity nor their intentions – the Nazi leader tries to convince the settlement of the Third Reich's cause. In his speech, which not coincidentally resembles the way Hitler addressed the public, he praises 'the greatest idea in history, the supremacy of a Nordic race' and asserts a shared German culture by calling the Hutterites 'brothers'. The Hutterites, however, refrain from joining the submarine crew in paying tribute to the Führer by shouting 'Heil Hitler!' In an emotional speech written specifically for him by Pressburger, Walbrook, who plays the Hutterites' leader, stresses the difference between celebrating German cultural heritage and being a Nazi – representing not only the Hutterite settlement in Canada, but also the whole German-speaking émigré community:

> You call us 'Germans', you call us 'brothers'. Yes, most of us are Germans, our names are German, our tongue is German, our old handwritten books are in German script, but we are not your brothers. Our Germany is dead. However hard this may be for some of us older people, it's a blessing for our children. Our children grow up against new backgrounds, new horizons, and they are free … No, we are not your brothers.

49th Parallel stresses the multinational and multifaceted character of anti-Nazi resistance. By contrasting the Nazis with open-mindedness and freedom of speech (represented through the academic aesthete played by Leslie Howard), religious liberalism and brotherliness (the Hutterite community) and equality (Inuit and Franco-Canadians), the film argues that German fascism is a threat not only to specific groups but also to Western democracy and Christian society as such.

Another classic wartime Powell and Pressburger production is *The Life and Death of Colonel Blimp*. Again, it owes much to the émigré filmmakers involved – above all Pressburger, whose collaboration with Powell concerned all stages of production; a special position reflected by that unique credit 'written, produced, and directed by Michael Powell and Emeric Pressburger'. Under the umbrella of the Rank Organisation, their independent production outfit The Archers was allowed a greater degree of artistic licence than most mainstream wartime companies, giving the émigrés involved the opportunity to exert an influence on their films. The leading role of Theo Kretschmar-Schuldorff was, as Powell recalls in his memoirs, especially written for Walbrook,[41] whilst Alfred Junge was responsible for the lavish sets (see Sarah Street's chapter in this volume). Other German-speaking personnel involved in the production include costume designer Joseph Bato and actors Carl Jaffé, Albert Lieven and Ferdy Mayne.

Some of the dialogue is in German without any translation or subtitles, giving the picture a sense of authenticity. By telling the story of a cross-national friendship between a British (Clive Candy, the Colonel Blimp of the title) and a Prussian officer (Theo Kretschmar-Schuldorff) from around 1900 to the Second World War, the film deals with the problem of how a civilised European country could unconditionally follow Hitler's inhumane ideology. The view expressed by Clive Candy's wife while she and her husband are visiting Theo in a First World War prisoner-of-war camp in Britain can be seen as a *leitmotif* of the film and one of the main questions German-speaking émigrés asked themselves:

> I was thinking how odd they [the Germans] are, queer, for years and years they are writing and dreaming beautiful music and poetry – all of a sudden they start a war. They sink undefended ships, shoot innocent hostages and bomb and destroy whole streets in London, killing little children. And then they sit down in the same butcher's uniform and listen to Mendelssohn and Schubert.

In many respects Pressburger, who wrote an original script early in 1942,[42] had his own life and career in mind when he invented this story about a man who comes to Britain as a refugee from Nazi Germany. Set designer Alfred Junge was interned as an 'enemy alien' at the beginning of the war and had just been released from a camp in Huyton near Liverpool when filming started.[43] The odd mix of claustrophobia and lively cultural activity that marks the POW camp in *Blimp* thus, one might argue, would not coincidentally resemble the experiences of many German-speaking émigrés who were classified as 'enemy aliens' and set up theatre groups and organised concerts and lectures in internment camps.[44] Given all the émigré-related issues dealt with in the film (border-crossings, immigration tribunals, internment, cross-cultural friendships, diasporic life), Paul Marcus rhetorically asked whether it was a coincidence that his old Berlin acquaintances Pressburger and the composer Allan Gray (see K.J. Donnelly's chapter in this volume) were involved in the production.[45]

The Life and Death of Colonel Blimp, by and large, avoids one-dimensional characterisations of Germans. Notwithstanding the unwelcoming interrogation by the immigration officer and his own previous internment, Kretschmar-Schuldorff leaves no room for doubt about his allegiance to Britain; he even wants to enlist in the armed forces. However, unlike Radetzky in *Dangerous Moonlight*, he is refused on account of his alien status.

Meant to epitomise the determination and beliefs of German-speaking refugees in the immediate aftermath of xenophobic hysteria and internment, the more balanced view of émigrés in *Blimp* owes much to Pressburger's dramatis personae. Having modelled many sequences in the film on his own experiences, he commented in 1970:

> I who lived for quite a while in Germany and had German friends, I wanted to express this feeling of mine that though my mother had died in a concentration camp and I was preconditioned about the whole thing, I always believed … that there were good Germans … who didn't have to go away from Germany but chose to go away.[46]

Kretschmar-Schuldorff is exactly this kind of a good German who chooses to leave Germany behind. Walbrook's own émigré status once again contributes to the authenticity of his performance. Among other scenes this is particularly evident when he is interrogated at the immigration tribunal. The film sympathises with the refugee rather than with Her Majesty's officer – this is achieved through the interaction of Pressburger's script, Junge's set design, Bato's make-up and Walbrook's acting style that lends itself to present a victim of the once energetic and proud Kretschmar-Schuldorff. While he is standing in front of the immigration officer, who sits behind an elevated desk barely looking at him, grey-haired Theo appears bowed and fragile. In a similar way to his performance in *Dangerous Moonlight*, Walbrook brings forward his case very slowly and wearily as he explains in detail how the Nazis have ruined his life and family.

Stressing the centrality of his long speeches, the *Manchester Guardian* praised the 'gentle pathos and charm' with which they are delivered by Walbrook.[47] In *Blimp* he underlines the fact that the display of conflicting national identities, inflicting recollections of one's home country, disorientation, assimilation and failed cultural adaptation is a common phenomenon of exile cinema. Thus, the findings of Gemünden's analysis of Peter Lorre's performances in American films are applicable to German-speaking émigrés in Britain. He argues that the performances of émigré actors 'are not so much about mimicking as about mimicry – not a simple imitation of a dominant acting style but a blurred copy that always retains the traces of forced assimilation while at the same time mocking the coerciveness of acculturation'.[48]

Conclusion

In British wartime films German and Austrian exiles underwent a significant transition from enemy alien to foreign ally. So it does not come as a surprise that it is a refugee who in *Blimp* informs the British audience about the serious threat posed by Hitler: 'This is not a gentleman's war. This time you are fighting for your existence against the most devilish idea ever concocted by the human brain – Nazism! And if you lose there won't be a return match next year, perhaps not even for a hundred years!' The box office success of films such as *49th Parallel*, *Dangerous Moonlight* and *The Life and Death of Colonel Blimp* suggests that contemporary British audiences did not prefer simplicity to ambiguity. It is important to point out that ambiguous does not mean anti-propagandist. Although many émigré films deal with shades of grey and offer nuanced depictions, they never call into question the brutality of Nazi policies or that the war was justified by a good cause. In fact, through 'good' Germans who themselves opposed the Third Reich the films gain authenticity and, in doing so, support the British war effort.

Through fictional characters émigrés aided in warning against the Nazi threat and in promoting ideas of democracy and freedom as fundamental British values. Consequently, what Andrew Moor says about Anton Walbrook holds true for other émigré film personnel as well: 'In wartime Walbrook can be identified as an ally, his persona partly assimilated into British culture. Yet this is accompanied by a constant awareness of his foreign origins. He remains an outsider, but, with Nazism reserved as the only significant "other", he becomes unthreateningly different.'[49] Moor proposes that the British films made by émigrés 'interrogate nationhood rather than simplistically celebrate it'.[50] The narratives of British exile films, at variance with other British productions, combine otherness with Britishness and thereby depict a hybrid émigré identity in which different traditions and influences collide.

Notes

1. See Philip M. Taylor, 'Introduction', in Taylor (ed.), *Britain and the Cinema in the Second World War* (New York: St Martin's Press, 1988), p. 6.
2. Charles Barr, 'Introduction: Amnesia and Schizophrenia', in Barr (ed.), *All Our Yesterdays: 90 Years of British Cinema* (London: BFI, 1986), pp. 10–11.
3. See, for instance, Barr, *All Our Yesterdays*; Taylor, *Britain and the Cinema in the Second World War*; and Anthony Aldgate and Jeffrey Richards, *Best of British: Cinema and Society from 1930 to the Present* (London and New York: I.B. Tauris, 1999), pp. 57–93.
4. Homi K. Bhabha, 'Introduction', in Bhabha (ed.), *Nation and Narration* (London: Routledge, 1990), p. 4.
5. The term 'propaganda' will be used throughout this article 'not in the popular pejorative sense, but as a specific term to describe the act of mass persuasion', Nicholas John Cull, *Selling War: The British Propaganda Campaign Against American 'Neutrality' in First World War I* (New York and Oxford: Oxford University Press, 1995), p. xi. For a comprehensive discussion of propaganda see, for instance, Garth S. Jowett and Victoria O'Donnell, *Propaganda and Persuasion*, 2nd edn (Newbury Park, Cal., London and New Delhi: Sage, 1992); Robert Jackall (ed.), *Propaganda* (Basingstoke: Macmillan, 1995).
6. Thomas Elsaesser, 'Das Vermächtnis des Dr. Caligari: Film noir und deutscher Einfluß', in Christian Cargnelli and Michael Omasta (eds.), *Schatten. Exil. Europäische Emigranten im Film noir* (Vienna: PVS Verleger, 1997), p. 44.
7. See, for example, Jeffrey Richards, 'National Identities in British Wartime Films', in Taylor, *Britain and the Cinema in the Second World War*, pp. 42–61, and Richards, *Films and*

British National Identity: From Dickens to Dad's Army (Manchester: Manchester University Press, 1997), pp. 85–127.

8. Gerd Gemünden and Anton Kaes, 'Introduction', *New German Critique* 89 (Spring/Summer 2003), p. 4.

9. See Hamid Naficy, *An Accented Cinema: Exilic and Diasporic Filmmaking* (Princeton, NJ: Princeton University Press, 2001).

10. See, for instance, Kevin Gough-Yates, 'The British Feature Film as a European Concern: Britain and the Emigré Film-maker, 1933–45', in Günter Berghaus (ed.), *Theatre and Film in Exile. German Artists in Britain, 1933–1945* (Oxford, New York and Munich: Berg, 1989), pp. 135–66, and Gough-Yates, 'Jews and Exiles in British Cinema', *Leo Baeck Yearbook* 37 (1992), p. 517.

11. Gemünden and Kaes, 'Introduction', p. 3.

12. Ibid., pp. 3–4.

13. *Sunday Pictorial*, 1 June 1941, cited in Jeffrey Richards, 'British Film Censorship', in Robert Murphy (ed.), *The British Cinema Book*, 2nd edn (London: BFI, 2001), p. 158.

14. See Andrew Higson, '"A Film League of Nations": Gainsborough, Gaumont-British and "Film Europe"', in Pam Cook (ed.), *Gainsborough Pictures* (London: Cassell, 1997), pp. 75–77.

15. See Kevin Gough-Yates, 'The European Film Maker in Exile in Britain 1933–1945', unpublished doctoral thesis (Open University, 1991), p. 218.

16. See Louise London, *Whitehall and the Jews, 1933–1948: British Immigration Policy, Jewish Refugees and the Holocaust* (Cambridge: Cambridge University Press, 2000). On the internment of 'enemy aliens' see, for example, Peter Gillman and Leni Gillman, *'Collar the Lot!': How Britain Interned and Expelled its Wartime Refugees* (London: Quartet, 1980); Ronald Stent, *A Bespattered Page: The Internment of 'His Majesty's Most Loyal Enemy Aliens'* (London: Andre Deutsch, 1980); Richard Dove (ed.), *'Totally un-English?': Britain's Internment of 'Enemy Aliens' in Two World Wars* (Amsterdam and New York: Rodopi, 2005).

17. See François Lafitte, *The Internment of Aliens* (1940; London: Libris, 1988), p. 79, and Gough-Yates, 'The European Film Maker in Exile in Britain 1933–1945', p. 420.

18. See Tim Bergfelder, 'The Production Designer and the *Gesamtkunstwerk*: German Film Technicians in the British Film Industry of the 1930s', in Andrew Higson (ed.), *Dissolving Views: Key Writings on British Cinema* (London: Cassell, 1996), p. 31; and Kevin Gough-Yates, 'The European Film Maker in Exile in Britain 1933–1945', pp. 411 and 425. On Heinrich Fraenkel, see the file in the Public Record Office: PRO HO 405/12865.

19. See, for instance, the Public Record Office files on Katscher/Cartier (HO 405/26875), Rudolf Bernauer (HO 405/2616), Lajos Biro (HO 405/2074) and Paul Czinner (HO 405/7511). All files were opened by the Home Office upon the author's request.

20. Handwritten note from 28 July 1944. PRO HO 405/26875.

21. Note on MoI film policy, 3 October 1939, PRO INF 1/194.

22. Among other sources the émigré involvement in wartime productions can be found in the 'Who's Where in Film Production' section that appeared regularly in the wartime issues of the ACT trade journal *The Cine-Technician*, published every other month.

23. Michael Powell in an interview with Kevin Gough-Yates on 22 September 1970. Gough-Yates, *Michael Powell in Collaboration with Emeric Pressburger* (London: NFTA, 1971), unpaginated.

24. See Kevin Gough-Yates, 'Exiles and British Cinema', in Murphy (ed.), *The British Cinema Book*, p. 173.

25. *Kinematograph Weekly*, 11 January 1940, p. C4.

26. C.A. Lejeune, 'A Filmgoer's Diary', cited in Guy Morgan (ed.), *Red Roses Every Night* (London: Quality Press, 1948), p. 69.

27. Elsaesser, 'Ethnicity, Authenticity, and Exile: A Counterfeit Trade? German Filmmakers and Hollywood', in Hamid Naficy (ed.), *Home, Exile, Homeland: Film, Media, and the Politics of Place* (New York and London: Routledge, 1999), p. 113.

28. Andrew Moor, 'Dangerous Limelight: Anton Walbrook and the Seduction of the English', in Bruce Babington (ed.), *British Stars and Stardom – from Alma Taylor to Sean Connery* (Manchester and New York: Manchester University Press, 2001), p. 83.

29. On the 'People's War' as a promoted wartime ethos see Sonya Rose, *Which People's War? National Identity and Citizenship in Wartime Britain, 1939–1945* (Oxford: Oxford University Press, 2003).

30. Robert Murphy, *Realism and Tinsel: Cinema and Society in Britain, 1939–49* (1989; London and New York: Routledge, 1992), p. 9.

31. PEM [= Paul Marcus], 'Die Situation der Emigranten in England', *Aufbau*, 1 November 1939, p. 12.

32. A comprehensive summary of the plot can be found in James C. Robertson, *The Hidden Cinema: British Film Censorship in Action, 1913–1975* (London and NewYork: Routledge, 1993), pp. 74–78.

33. Cited in Jeffrey Richards, 'The British Board of Film Censors and Content Control in the 1930s: Foreign Affairs', *Historical Journal of Film, Radio and Television*, vol. 2, no. 1 (1982), p. 42.

34. Klaus Mann, 'What's Wrong With Anti-Nazi Films?', *Decision* (August 1941). My quote is from the reprint in *New German Critique* 89 (Spring/Summer 2003), p. 177.

35. Cited in Robertson, *The Hidden Cinema*, p. 77.

36. See Jeffrey Richards, 'National Identity in British Wartime Films', in Taylor, *Britain and the Cinema in the Second World War*, pp. 45–46.

37. C. A. Lejeune, '*Pastor Hall*: A British Picture', *The Observer*, 21 January 1940.

38. See James Chapman, 'Why We Fight: *Pastor Hall* and *Thunder Rock*', in Alan Burton, Tim O'Sullivan and Paul Wells (eds.), *The Family Way: The Boulting Brothers and British Film Culture* (Trowbridge: Flicks Books, 2000), p. 84.

39. See Lafitte, *The Internment of Aliens*, pp. 67–68.

40. The amount of financial support given by the MoI varies. Most sources state the figure of £60,000, while the other half of the £120,000 film budget was provided by J. Arthur Rank's General Film Distributors. See James Chapman, '"The true business of the British movie"? *A Matter of Life and Death* and British Film Culture', *Screen*, vol. 46, no. 1 (Spring 2005), p. 34.

41. See Powell, *A Life in Films: An Autobiography* (1986; London: Faber & Faber, 2000), p. 406.

42. See Ian Christie, '*Blimp*, Churchill and the State', in Christie (ed.), *Powell, Pressburger and Others* (London: BFI, 1978), p. 105.

43. See Michael Powell in an interview with Kevin Gough-Yates, see n.15.

44. See Alan Clarke, 'Theatre Behind the Wire: German Refugee Theatre in British Internment', in Günter Berghaus (ed.), *Theatre and Film in Exile: German Artists in Britain, 1933–1945* (Oxford: Berg, 1989), pp. 189–222; and Georg W. Brandt, 'Thespis Behind the Wire, or Entertainment in Internment: A Personal Recollection', in Berghaus (ed.), *Theatre and Film in Exile*, pp. 223–29.

45. PEM, 'Leben und Tod des Colonel Blimp', *Aufbau*, 16 July 1943, p. 12.

46. Emeric Pressburger in an interview with Kevin Gough-Yates, in Gough-Yates, 'The British Feature Film as a European Concern', p. 156.

47. Review of *The Life and Death of Colonel Blimp*, *Manchester Guardian*, 1943 (undated press clipping, BFI Library).

48. Gerd Gemünden, 'From "Mr. M" to "Mr. Murder": Peter Lorre and the Actor in Exile', in Randall Halle and Margaret McCarthy (eds.), *Light Motives: German Popular Film in Perspective* (Detroit: Wayne State University Press, 2003), p. 99.

49. Moor, 'Dangerous Limelight', p. 84.

50. Moor, 'No Place Like Home: Powell, Pressburger and Utopia', in Murphy (ed.), *The British Cinema Book*, p. 109.

Chapter 15

CARL MAYER:
YEARS OF EXILE IN LONDON

Brigitte Mayr

Elisabeth Bergner's memoirs contain an unforgettable description of the virtually hopeless situation faced by immigrants in London. Though finally safe, they were forced to sit idly, waiting to see whether and how those who were most in need of lifesaving aid might receive it.[1] In Carl Mayer's case, this period of uneasy waiting lasted almost two full years before Bergner and Paul Czinner finally managed to obtain the necessary papers so their friend could enter the country. Czinner and Bergner, a director and star duo who later married, had worked together on German films since 1924. From 1929 onward, 'Meyerlein' (Bergner's affectionate nickname for Carl Mayer, which is consistently misspelled in her memoirs) was a permanent fixture in this successful team's work, on such classics as *Fräulein Else* (1929), *Ariane* (1931), *Der träumende Mund* (1932), *As You Like It* (1936) and *Dreaming Lips* (1937). Apart from these collaborations, Mayer (born 1894 in Graz) had been among the most influential screenwriters of Weimar cinema's Golden Age, as the co-writer of *Das Cabinet des Dr. Caligari* (*The Cabinet of Dr Caligari*, 1920), and through his creative partnership with director F.W. Murnau on films including *Der letzte Mann* (*The Last Laugh*, 1924), *Tartüff* (*Tartuffe*, 1925) and *Sunrise: A Song of Two Humans* (1927).

While Czinner was making *Der träumende Mund* and its French-language version *Mélo* in Paris, producer Alexander Korda visited the studio and made the director and Bergner an attractive offer: they could select their own material for a film for his new production company in London. A contract was signed, and late in November 1932 the search for a good story began. 'All kinds of material were suggested, but they had to be right for both England and Germany. The German distribution agreement is what made our work for Korda's new company so interesting.'[2] Therefore, knowing an experienced screenwriter who knew exactly what the audience wanted was perfect. Mayer arrived in London, and not only for professional reasons: he was to be a witness when, on 9 January 1933, 'Mr. Paul Czinner, single, writer, 42 years of age, residing at the Ritz Hotel, and the single woman Elisabeth Bergner, 33 years of age, became man and wife.'[3]

While this presumably registered as the happiest day in Bergner and Czinner's private life, January 1933 was more than depressing professionally. When the German distribution agreement Korda was counting on was terminated, he was forced to either break the contract with the star, then unknown in England, or take the risk of hiring Bergner anyway without any financial support. Korda chose the latter course of action, and fate seemed to smile upon these involuntary immigrants. Mayer, however, apparently did not plan to leave Germany for good like Bergner and Czinner, and he returned against all better judgement. What he went through in the terrible year of 1933 remains a mystery.

Czinner first heard from Mayer after almost twelve months, from Prague.[4] The latter wrote that he was working on a screenplay based on an excellent Czech novel and expressed 'regret that I am not able to realise my intentions, that is, to come visit you, my dear Paul'. Between the lines, quietly and subtly, was an urgent cry for help: Mayer wanted him to do something to aid his old friend get to England and escape the hell he euphemistically tried to play down with empty phrases, 'because I thought, literally day after day, that I could tell you something definite, that is how long some negotiations were being drawn out here'. Despite the note of concern, the letter ends optimistically with a prediction, 'well, I believe that we will meet again, one way or another, either here or there'.

The precise date of Mayer's arrival in Britain is not known, but 18 Kempley Road in London NW3, located between Hampstead and Swiss Cottage, was his first address in his new country. 'This area was a gathering place for German-speaking intellectuals, mostly Jewish or those whom Hitler had turned into Jews, people whose lives were no longer safe in Berlin, Vienna or Prague.'[5] Rents in the south of Hampstead were relatively affordable. The colony of German speakers, which numbered around 25,000, represented over one third of the area's total residents. Immigrant organisations opened offices here, such as the Freie Deutsche Kulturbund (Free German League of Culture) and Club 43, which chose the Belsize Square synagogue for its meetings. The Austrian cabaret group Laterndl put on their shows in the adjacent Swiss Cottage, and even closer to Hyde Park was the Austrian Centre, made familiar by Austrian writers Theodor Kramer and Erich Fried. The Mount Royal Hotel near Marble Arch was the residence of Robert Neumann, initiator of the Austrian PEN Club in exile, and Alfred Kerr, at the time the London correspondent of the *Pariser Tageblatt*.

Mayer was forty-one years of age when he arrived in London – humiliated, burnt out, ruined. The life of an exile meant being out of work, out of money and out of luck. For a writer, it entails the loss of 'the most important tool',[6] namely language. A writer's career depends on it directly, and poor English presented the greatest barrier for actors and writers. With the exception of isolated cases such as Bergner, few German-speaking theatrical stars were successful, and even she was forced to learn her lines phonetically. Journalists and other writers had to work with translators, as there was neither a newspaper nor publishing house for exiles in England. What was to be done without the tools required to get a job, make money and survive? Did Mayer work on strategies to deal with this situation? And, most importantly – was he able to write at all in the face of these deplorable conditions?

'Script by Carl Mayer not made – 1937?' is the terse entry in the Cinémathèque Française's archive in Paris for a screenplay in English, *sans titre*. Attributing the carbon copy's sixty-eight numbered pages to its author is possible only because the final scenes were published under the title *A Film Poem by Carl Mayer* in the January 1939 issue of *Lilliput*. 'The Pocket Magazine for Everyone'[7] was founded by the former editor-in-chief of the *Münchner Illustrierte Presse*, Stefan Lorant, who emigrated to England in 1934. This periodical became an important forum for German-speaking exiles, printing articles by Feuchtwanger, Heartfield, Koestler, Polgar, Roth and Viertel. Mayer's film poem is a condensation of all the things he was most interested in: powerful and at the same time delicate melodrama, this time set in the slums of London's East End; serious conflicts between two people who feel affection for each other; violent emotions and their unfortunate consequences; heartache, sacrifice and sorrow involving two unhappy lovers who are unable to come together, with the Salvation Army in the background. This melancholic script, *East End and the Salvation Army*, which Mayer presumably wrote in 1937, suffered the same unhappy fate as the tragic poet's other projects which were never made. Herbert G. Luft claimed that Mayer 'wrote at least five screenplays that were never produced: *The Ghost Ship, The Iron Maid, The Danube, East End and the Salvation Army*, and *She Stoops to Conquer*. The first three were for German, the last two for British producers'.[8] A first edition of Oliver Goldsmith's *She Stoops to Conquer*, 'bound in fine leather', was mentioned by Paul Rotha who claimed he found it in Mayer's last flat after his death.[9] Whether this book was really the basis of a screenplay he apparently took seriously is doubtful, although Rotha also wrote of 'Carl's passion to make a script of the famous eighteenth century British play' and that he had discussed it with Mayer frequently. Unfortunately however, they were never able to interest an English producer in the material.[10]

It seemed that only work Mayer did in collaboration with others came to fruition in these difficult years. The Bergner-Czinners had recently founded Inter-Allied Film Producers together with C.B. Cochran and Joseph M. Schenck. Cochran, a London producer of musicals, and Schenck, in the same business in Hollywood, intended with Bergner's help to kill two birds with one stone, attracting both theatre-goers and the movie-going public by reviving the most successful roles of German stage and film stars for English viewers. *As You Like It*, based on Shakespeare's play and made according to a screenplay by Robert J. Cullen and Carl Mayer, used the androgynous figures Bergner played in Berlin, where she had her breakthrough at the Lessing-Theater as Rosalinde in 1923. *Dreaming Lips*, based on Bernstein's *Mélo* and a script by Margaret Kennedy, Mayer and Cynthia Asquith, was a remake of *Der träumende Mund* and featured Bergner's unforgettable appearance in the sad swan song of Weimar cinema. Gabriel Pascal, a producer and director from Hungary, helped Mayer with his film adaptation of two plays by G.B. Shaw, *Pygmalion* (1938) and *Major Barbara* (1940/41), both starring the marvellous Wendy Hiller. Pascal praised his script supervisor, whom he consulted on all 'Shaw plays I contemplated to the screen [*sic*]',[11] as 'a true source of inspiration', calling him a 'dear friend'.[12] He was in fact one of Mayer's few friends whom he needed more and more in exile, and who became increasingly scarce.

In 1936, the pioneer of documentary film, Robert J. Flaherty, introduced Mayer to a man named Paul Rotha, who was just twenty-nine at the time. The up-and-coming young executive producer of the Strand Film Company was quite familiar with many of the German silent films Mayer had worked on, having visited Ufa and met Erich Pommer in the late 1920s with the intention of writing a book about cinema,[13] but Rotha and Mayer had never happened to meet before. According to Rotha, they hit it off immediately: 'I have never met a man who saw everyone and everything in filmic terms, through the eye of the camera. He exudes enthusiasm for this thing called movie. Ten minutes talk and you realise that he has the background, the feeling, the smell of the medium for which so many people have worked and sacrificed. Karl [*sic*] Mayer is one of those few who sacrificed.'[14] In fact, the two new friends did work together shortly before the Second World War broke out on *The Fourth Estate*, a film on a (fictitious) day in the life of *The Times* newspaper. Being involved in documentaries as script supervisor represented an entirely new challenge for Mayer – apart from providing the original idea for Ruttmann's avant-garde collage *Berlin. Die Sinfonie der Großstadt* (Germany 1927), he had never worked in this area before.

By that time Rotha had hired a great deal of young talent for his own film unit, including Michael Orrom and Frank Gysin, who were later his co-directors on *The World Is Rich* (1947) and *A City Speaks* (1947), and Yvonne Fletcher, who directed *World of Plenty* (1943) together with Rotha and became one of Mayer's good friends. Mayer visited the studio's offices on Soho Square almost daily.

> He loved life with a happiness you do not normally find among film-makers. He loved all films and could find something to talk about in the worst of pictures. Above all, he loved people – the people he met in cafés and trains and

parks. He seldom read books, and possessed but a dozen connected with subjects on which he was working. He devoured newspapers.[15]

Although he reportedly never was seen without a newspaper, political topics and other people's opinions about war and suffering seemed not to interest him. 'In all our talks over the years', claimed Paul Rotha, 'I never heard Carl express a political opinion.'[16] Mayer presumably preferred to take walks. In the cold winters of the war years, most people lived from hand to mouth, while some had it even worse. For that reason Anglican priest John Groser ran a mobile soup kitchen in London's East End late in the autumn of 1940, as the Blitz was raging. Rotha helped out, and Groser's tales possibly inspired Mayer to write his *Film Poem*.

London at war. Rotha and his team, including Mayer, who had been permanently hired as a consultant, were at the time working for the British Ministry of Information, making entertaining 'educational films' about the most serious problems of the day. For example, *World of Plenty* dealt with global nutrition's terrible state of affairs. Rotha had assembled a first-rate crew: Yvonne Fletcher, cameramen Wolfgang Suschitzky and Peter Hennessy, and also the experts from Oxford's Isotype Institute, who supplied powerful graphics from the workshop of Viennese immigrant Otto Neurath, and thus made a decisive contribution to its success. A huge swastika spanning the skies dominates a small patch of Earth on the lower edge of the picture, obviously representing Hitler and Europe. Eric Knight, a friend of Rotha's for many years,[17] narrated and collaborated with him on the screenplay. Knight and his wife Jere invited Fletcher, Rotha and Mayer to their home in Christmas 1942 for a 'memorable christmas [*sic*] lunch' and to relax, presumably because the three had spent many nights debating the film's editing:

> Carl worked closely with me at the nights on the editing ... he had not worked on the script because there really was no script in the accepted meaning of the word. It was really a series of dialogues between five persons, none of whom met or even knew each other until I joined their voices on sound-track in the cutting room. But Carl would give ideas on timing and the use of the visual pictures which I obtained from many places. He was very happy with the success of the film.[18]

And he could be proud also: when the film was shown at the World Food Conference in Hot Springs, the following telegram was sent from the British Information Services in America to the Ministry of Information in London: '*World of Plenty* was shown to a full house of three hundred delegates and pressmen stop it was received with prolonged applause and excited much comment and enthusiasm stop the film happens to summarise and set forth pictorially some of the most important conclusions of the conference and is therefore particularly timely.'[19]

In 1940, the situation of émigrés in England became even more difficult. 'Enemy aliens' were divided into categories, and many of them put in internment camps on the Isle of Man. Rotha was able to protect Mayer from this fate: 'I immediately placed him on the permanent staff of my film unit and used my "influence", such as it was, to see that so long as he came to my office once every day, he did not have to report to the police. Carl did occasional consultancy work on some of the scripts for which I paid him a fee.'[20] From then on the new employee in fact visited the film unit's office almost daily to discuss manuscripts, rushes, editing or the rough cut. According to Michael Orrom, 'Carl was quietly around Rotha's unit, sitting at a desk, by a desk, in a pub – helping someone with a script. Always gentle, never pushing, and quite sparing in his comments, but invariably to the point.'[21] Conscientious, and never condescending. A close platonic relationship developed between the grey-haired man with the fine features and Yvonne Fletcher, and the two could often be seen sitting on a bench in the Soho park, which was not far from their workplace, intently discussing their latest film. This was the fruit of long, tiring days of work, and Carl's own special way of thanking his friend Paul for the wonderful gift of freedom and being spared internment. In return, Rotha gave Mayer and his crew his full trust along with night-long discussions about literature and film, and life in general.

Number 46 Albany Street, London NW1, near Euston Road, was Mayer's new address, a rented flat in a small terraced house, the rear of which bordered on Regent's Park. The park exercised little attraction during those days, as Mayer normally spent the majority of his time walking in the direction of the City. On these walks, he got to know a city wounded by war, the streets filled with hungry people, the shops empty. Hundreds of buildings had been destroyed, and ashes and dust covered everything. Mayer struggled to make ends meet, like everyone else. Money was in short supply, as were food, fuel and suitable clothing. Consequently, his appearance was simply terrible: a ragged suit, tattered collar, threadbare sleeves, neither hat nor scarf to keep him warm – but Mayer always wore a smile which made up for everything else. Was he thinking about what this bleak world needed most? Some kind of practical invention, for example? Possibly for people forced to do a great deal of walking, who were constantly wearing out their shoes, or at least the soles? He had his idea of simply pulling a new sole over the old worn-out one patented.[22] Necessity is, after all, the mother of invention.

But back to film, his real domain – this time with a proper contract, from Filippo del Giudice, the head of Two Cities Films Ltd., a subsidiary of the Rank Organisation. Mayer was to receive a salary of £25 per week for consulting services regarding material and production, and for 'script conferences'. That was the term being used for meetings at which people discussed their work. Despite all the resulting happiness – 'it was wonderful to be at work again, under such conditions',[23] as he said to his new friend Godfrey Winn, whom he met at a sanatorium in northern Wales – one question remains unanswered: was this September 1943 contract merely pro forma, an act of sympathy for a poor, ill and suffering man?

Carl Mayer had experienced poverty before over the past forty years; that was certainly not enough to faze him. Every now and again friends helped him out, for example Emeric Pressburger, who wrote in his diary on 7 January 1941: 'At about 11 Carl Mayer comes up asking for £2.00. I write a cheque for £5. He is so nice and so helpless.'[24] Or 'the very nice Stefan Lorant', who published his *Film Poem*. On a postcard from London's Fine Art Studio, Mayer wrote the touching line 'in possession of a soothing 10 guineas, I would like to thank you most sincerely – Yours, C.M'.[25] He was much more upset when, unexpectedly during a script conference, a sharp pain shot through his body. 'Then the pain started, here in my side. I could not eat', as he told Godfrey Winn in the Ruthin Castle sanatorium which he entered in the spring of 1944. By that time, Mayer had gone through the tortures of many hospital stays, innumerable wild guesses at diagnoses, delicate operations, dubious prescriptions and hazardous treatments, which lasted from July 1943 at London's University College Hospital until March 1944 at the sanatorium in northern Wales, and finally St John's and St Elizabeth's Hospital in St John's Wood, NW3, in June.[26] The diagnosis: pancreatic cancer.

Exhausted and drained, he repeatedly returned to his flat at 18 Hanover Court for a few days at a time. While the name of that part of London, the City of Westminster, may sound grand,[27] the small room was very modest – it contained hardly any furniture, no possessions, nothing one would be sorry to part with. Actually, it had already been cleared out and cleaned for the next tenant, who was able to get it ready when Mayer was transferred to St John's Hospital in June 1944. On the morning of 1 July, Rotha, who had left his name and address, received a call informing him that the 50-year-old patient was dying. By the time he reached the room that noon, Mayer had already passed away, all alone.

On the Saturday of the following week, 8 July 1944, a small group gathered at Highgate's Eastern Cemetery in northwest London. A few of his friends and acquaintances – Wolfgang Wilhelm, Yvonne Fletcher, Dr Theo Markowicz, Rodney Ackland, Hans Nieter, Edfried Mayer, Andor Kraszna-Krausz, Bernard Miles, Emeric Pressburger, Alfred Junge and Paul Rotha – stood next to a grave freshly dug for the simple wooden coffin, which had an engraved brass plaque with the words 'He Loved Life'.[28] The funeral proceeded quickly, though it was contemplative rather than rushed. Father John Groser of the East End spoke the eulogy.

Three years after Mayer's death, Rotha put on a memorial service in his honour at the Scala Theatre, screening clips from the films *Das Cabinet des Dr. Caligari*, *Vanina* (1922), *Sylvester* (1923) and *Sunrise*; *Der letzte Mann* was shown in its entirety. A memorial programme was printed in which those who had known and worked with Mayer, such as Erich Pommer, Rotha,

Ivor Montagu, Karl Freund, Anthony Asquith and Gabriel Pascal, expressed their admiration. As was noted on the last page, the proceeds were used for 'settling the estate of Carl Mayer and erecting a suitable memorial stone to him at Highgate Cemetery'. The man who had entered their lives so quietly, leaving such a deep and lasting impression in their hearts, is remembered to this day by an inscription on the stone slab: 'Carl Mayer 1894–1944. Pioneer in the art of the cinema. Erected by his friends and fellow workers.'

Translation: Steve Wilder

Notes

1. Elisabeth Bergner, *Bewundert viel und viel gescholten. Unordentliche Erinnerungen* (Munich: C. Bertelsmann, 1978), p. 115.
2. See ibid, pp. 98, 100 and 113.
3. 'Elisabeth Bergner's wedding. To film director Paul Czinner. Telegram from our correspondent.' *Die Presse*, 10 January 1933.
4. Letters Carl Mayer wrote from Prague to Paul Czinner in London, dated 6 December 1933 and 22 December 1933 (Elisabeth Bergner archive), in possession of the archive of Berlin's Academy of Art. The address Bercley Street is not correct (the name of the street in Mayfair is spelled Berkeley), and the hotel was located on the corner of Stratton Street. Evidence that Mayer was in Prague is also provided by writer Hans Sahl, *Memoiren eines Moralisten. Das Exil im Exil* (Hamburg: Luchterhand, 1990), p. 189.
5. The following descriptions of the situation of exiles in London were taken from Steffen Pross's book *'In London treffen wir uns wieder'. Vier Spaziergänge durch ein vergessenes Kapitel deutscher Kulturgeschichte nach 1933* (Berlin: Eichborn, 2000).
6. Uwe Soukup, *Ich bin nun mal Deutscher. Sebastian Haffner. Eine Biographie* (Berlin: Aufbau, 2001), pp. 64 ff.
7. See Pross, *'In London treffen wir uns wieder'*, p. 37. The final scene of the *Film Poem* was printed on p. 204 of *Carl Mayer, Scenar[t]ist. Ein Script von ihm war schon ein Film • A Script by Carl Mayer Was Already a Film*, edited by Michael Omasta, Brigitte Mayr and Christian Cargnelli (Vienna: SYNEMA, 2003).
8. See Herbert G. Luft, 'Carl Mayer. Film Scriptwriter Extraordinary of Post-World War I Germany', *Films in Review*, vol. 23, no. 9, p. 526.
9. Paul Rotha, *Carl Mayer in England*, typed manuscript in the archive of the Stiftung Deutsche Kinemathek, Berlin, p. 12.
10. Ibid., p. 15.
11. Gabriel Pascal, *A Tribute to Carl Mayer 1894–1944* (London 1947), p. 12. Pascal's wording – 'any Shaw play' – suggests that Mayer did 'advisory script work' on Pascal's adaptation of Shaw's *Caesar and Cleopatra* (1945); see Carsten Schneider, 'Carl Mayers Spätwerk', in Bernhard Frankfurter (ed.), *Carl Mayer: Im Spiegelkabinett des Dr. Caligari* (Vienna: Promedia, 1997), p. 130.
12. Rotha (*Carl Mayer in England*, p. 6) plays down the friendship between Pascal and Mayer somewhat: 'He [Mayer] did not discuss this work for Pascal with me and I had the impression that he did not like the arrangement. Nevertheless, he helped Carl with money.'
13. Paul Marris (ed.), *Paul Rotha* (London 1982), p. 90. (BFI Dossier 16).
14. Paul Rotha, 'It's in the Script', *World Film News*, vol. 3, no. 5, September 1938, p. 204.
15. Paul Rotha, 'Carl Mayer – An Appreciation by Paul Rotha', *A Tribute to Carl Mayer 1894–1944* (London 1947), p. 7.

16. Rotha, *Carl Mayer in England*, p. 4.
17. Eric Knight died in a plane crash before *World of Plenty* was completed. Concerning this friendship see Paul Rotha (ed.), *Portrait of a Flying Yorkshireman. Letters from Eric Knight in the United States to Paul Rotha in England* (London: Chapman & Hall, 1952).
18. Rotha (ed.), *Portrait*, pp. 122–23.
19. Ibid.
20. Cf. Rotha, *Carl Mayer in England*, pp. 6–8, 14.
21. Michael Orrom, documentary filmmaker, remembers his work with Paul Rotha. From an unpublished interview with Michael Orrom, conducted by Norman Swallow and Alan Lawson for the BECTU Oral History Project: File No. 244, March 1992 (original audiotape archived at the BFI, London).
22. Rotha, *Carl Mayer in England*, p. 15: 'He had invented, so he told me, a heel which clipped onto a man's shoe to provide a new one instead of having the shoe repaired at a shop. He never showed me a model which he made. He actually took out a patent for it at the British Patent Office.'
23. See Godfrey Winn, *The Bend of the River. A Journey in Ten Stages* (London: Hutchinson, 1949), p. 66.
24. See Kevin Macdonald, *Emeric Pressburger: The Life and Death of a Screenwriter* (London and Boston: Faber and Faber, 1994), p. 173.
25. See the copy of the reverse of this postcard in the archive of the Stiftung Deutsche Kinemathek, Berlin. Unfortunately the obverse, whether a photograph or an illustration, is not shown. Ten guineas are approximately equal to 11 British pounds.
26. See Rotha, *Carl Mayer in England*, pp. 8–10, 14.
27. See ibid., p. 12.
28. Rotha (*Carl Mayer in England*, p. 13) describes the individuals present at the funeral as follows: 'His nephew, Edfried, in Pioneer Corps battledress; Wolfgang Wilhelm (a "refugee" script-writer who worked on several of my films); Yvonne Fletcher (swollen eyed); Dr Theo Markowicz [Mayer's doctor], Rodney Ackland (English script-writer); Hans Nieter (documentary film-maker), Andor Kraszna-Krausz (a "refugee", once a well known avant-garde critic in Berlin and now a publisher in London); Bernard Miles, the actor; Edgar Anstey (documentary filmmaker); Emeric Pressburger (Hungarian journalist and script-writer, who represented the Screenwriters Guild); Alfred Junge (distinguished film designer first in Berlin and later in England) and a few others I do not remember.'

Chapter 16

MUSIC FOR THE PEOPLE: ESCAPISM AND SOCIAL COMMENT IN THE WORK OF HANS MAY AND ERNST MEYER

Geoff Brown

In January 1935 subscribers to the scholarly British magazine *Music and Letters* could read an essay by one William Saunders entitled 'Songs of the German Revolution'. Using song texts, musical examples, and his own selective experiences travelling in Germany, Saunders painted an extraordinarily benign view of the lyric output in Germany following Hitler's election victory in 1933. 'Wherever the Storm Troops may be, and that is everywhere throughout modern Germany, there is to be heard the sound of singing,' he writes. He identifies the 'flag-song' as a genre, followed by the 'shirt-song': 'The Germans dearly love a uniform and consequently these are tremendously popular.' On and on, until he remarks on the final page that the German lyric impulse, 'stimulated by the Nazi revolution, has transformed the entire Reich into a veritable nest of singing birds'. He concludes: 'A nation that can sing, as Germany is doing all through her triumphs and troubles, has little to fear, even from her own so-called rulers and dictators.'[1]

Six million Jews would disagree there, were they alive to do so. Even at the time, such talk was offensive. By 1935 many of Germany's best singing birds, whether singers themselves, composers or musicians, had already flown the nest, to the supposed safety of Austria, or further afield – including this essay's two subjects. By January 1935 Hans May (born Johannes Mayer) had been busy in Britain's film industry for one year. He had supplied musical material for one Sound City quota quickie, *How's Chances?*, and three British International Pictures (BIP) features at Elstree, *Give Her a Ring*, *My Song Goes Round the World* and *Radio Parade of 1935* (all from 1934). Two from this total, *How's Chances?* and *My Song Goes Round the World*, were English remakes of the light-hearted film musicals May had composed in Germany and Austria. Ernst Hermann Meyer, nineteen years his junior, had been living in the country since the summer of 1933, scraping around in odd jobs – German-language teacher, swimming teacher, music copier – while continuing his researches into British and European instrumental music of the seventeenth century, begun at universities in Berlin and Heidelberg. *Music and Letters* published an essay by Meyer himself later in 1935, in October. Its title posed a question of attribution, prompted by Meyer's study of photocopied music manuscripts at the British Museum's Library: 'Has Handel Written Works for Two Flutes without a Bass?' The answer, unfortunately or not, was no.

Even from this brief sally it is obvious that these were two men with very different work experiences and creative personalities. Let me draw out the differences a little more. May was born on 11 July 1886 in Vienna, into a Jewish musical family; he was the brother of another, lesser, film composer, Karl M. May, active in the early 1930s, but stifled in exile. As a true child of Vienna, Hans May's default mode as a composer was always the melodic, the charming, the sentimental. He studied piano at the Vienna Music Academy with Anton Door, and composition with Richard Heuberger, composer of the once-popular operetta *Der Opernball*. May at first worked in the operetta sphere himself, both as a conductor and composer, and never stopped regarding music as something emollient, a means of escape. Meyer, born in Berlin on 8 December 1905, was the child of middle-class intellectuals: his father was a doctor with a strong interest in art, like his mother, who painted. At the Friedrich-Wilhelm University, Berlin, he studied musicology with teachers such as Arnold Schering, Erich von Hornbostel and Curt Sachs; he also took composition lessons with Hindemith, Max Butting and, more informally, Hanns Eisler. He joined the Communist Party as a student, and in varying degrees came to regard all his future musical activities as tools for reflecting revolutionary struggles and aspirations.

In Britain, May contributed to some fifty-six feature films and a handful of shorts, and he worked at the commercial centre of the film industry, just as he had in Berlin before his emigration. In the 1940s, he composed music for Gainsborough melodramas, including *Madonna of the Seven Moons* (1944) and *The Wicked Lady* (1945). He also composed for British National productions, where he held the position of music director; for the Boulting Brothers' *Thunder Rock* (1942) and – not a sequel, of course – *Brighton Rock* (1947). In the 1930s, besides his BIP work, he wrote music for five of the nineteen films put out by the companies managed by Max Schach and Isidore Goldsmith before the banks' money vanished; *The Stars Look Down* in 1939, a project initially intended for Karl Grune but finally directed by Carol Reed, was the last and best of these.[2] Meyer, by contrast, worked entirely on the industry fringes. He composed for no fiction features in Britain; his area was documentaries and instructional films, for the GPO and Realist Film Units, and Halas and Batchelor, and he became particularly known for what he called 'orchestrated sound', an imaginative blend of sound effects and music. Overall, some forty-five titles are known. For this work he won specialist acclaim, but there is still something poignant about a published photograph taken in 1938, showing Meyer out in the country beside a road junction's signpost. One sign points to 'Elstree and Barnet' and the A 434; another signals 'London, A 5083'. Was this the closest to Elstree studios that he came?[3]

The clinching proof of the pair's differences might be their activities in 1948. It is a pivotal year for them both. Blessed with financial backing from the multi-millionaire Lady Yule, co-founder of the British National company, May in that year enjoys the successful West End production of his first wholly British stage musical, *Carissima*, an old-fashioned, escapist, lilting story, set in Venice and New York, about a perfume manufacturer and a gondolier who is not all he seems. The lavish if cumbersome sets are designed by Ernst Stern, veteran collaborator with Reinhardt, Lubitsch and Erik Charell. This paves the way for other stage musicals by May; in 1949 *Waltz Time*, already produced in 1945 as a British National film; in 1954, *Wedding in Paris*, with another prominent émigré, Anton Walbrook, and Evelyn Laye – a show carrying a slightly more modern accent, but with much of its appeal still based on old-style European elegance and romance. His film career will dwindle in the 1950s, but when he dies in the early minutes of 1959 at La Reserve Hotel, Beaulieu-sur-Mer, May is still a well-placed figure, with a comfortable Park Lane address.[4]

Meyer in 1948 pursues a pipe dream of a different kind. He returns to Berlin in Soviet-occupied eastern Germany, where he is appointed Professor of the Sociology of Music at Humboldt University, a position held until his retirement in 1970. Through teaching, composition and writing he will play a significant role in developing the official musical ideology of the German Democratic Republic (established in 1949). Forget perfume, forget waltzes: Meyer sets to writing the *Mansfeld Oratorio*, one hour and forty-five intermittently stirring minutes of proletarian struggle, written to celebrate the 750th anniversary of Mansfeld's copper slate mining industry. The work becomes the GDR's first major example of social realism in music – a style firmly stamped with Communist approval in Moscow in January 1948 at the Central Committee of the All-Union Communist Party's Conference of Musicians. Cinema occupies him occasionally, but he chiefly fulfils his duty with songs, cantatas and symphonic works, mostly for concert hall use, and dies in East Berlin, well respected, on 8 October 1988 – just thirteen months too soon to see the Berlin Wall fall and his own country expire.[5]

As figures, then, May and Meyer seem almost diametrically – you could also say dialectically – opposed. The conservative and the revolutionary. The escape artist and the social realist. Yet matters are not quite so simple. The more you investigate, the more you find them slipping out of their pigeon-holes and poking around in each other's. Both of these composers in very different ways planned on writing, in that convenient phrase, 'music for the people'. But which of the two really succeeded? I will pocket this question for later.

For now, let me consider Hans May. A 1998 issue of *Filmexil* magazine gives a fascinating snapshot of May in the late 1930s in correspondence with an old friend, the émigré producer and agent Paul Kohner, then based in America. Eagerly hoping that Kohner's new agency could engineer jobs for him in Hollywood – jobs that never came – May sweepingly mentions the twenty-one English, French and Viennese films he has composed since leaving Germany. 'But what good is all this in this sick Europe,' he adds in this letter written on New Year's Day, 1938. He encloses a biographical sketch cum publicity blurb, which concludes with a brief artistic credo, stating that Hans May 'is Viennese-born and unites in his music the charm of Viennese music with the rhythm of today'.[6] There is truth in this, at least the truth of intention. The music for *Ein Lied geht um die Welt* (1933) and his other vehicles for the diminutive singing sensation Joseph Schmidt, composed both in Germany and in exile, may well be awash with three-quarter time – fast waltzes, slow waltzes; but elsewhere he made more determined efforts to marry sweet melodies with foxtrot rhythms and turn himself into a composer *à la mode*. The major hit from his score for *Wien, du Stadt der Lieder* (1930) was not the lilting title duet, for instance, nor the old Viennese and Berlin songs grafted in, but the perky 'Ich habe kein' Auto', delivered by Max Hansen and Luigi Bernauer, then reprised solely as a jazz orchestra number.

May's flexibility as a film composer, audible in much of his British work, perhaps had its roots in the 1920s when he contributed music to Giuseppe Becce's *Kinothek*, published in Berlin: twelve volumes of multifarious mood pieces, arranged or newly composed for use in live accompaniments. Following the final *Kinothek* volume in 1927, he issued two similar portfolios himself, *Kino-Lexikon* and *Cinema Collection*, the last published in 1929, when the new sound film technology was just beginning to make such collections irrelevant. May also took part in Berlin's cabaret scene, serving with Paul Leni as co-artistic director of the cabaret *Die Gondel* during its three years of existence (1923–26), where his musical activities included setting the satirical verses of 'Theobald Tiger' (Kurt Tucholsky). But his cinema assignments multiplied when he took command of musical accompaniments at the Alhambra cinema, close by on Potsdamer Platz, work that often spilled over into other Berlin venues. One early triumph in 1925 was a witty compilation score for Hans Neumann's production of *Ein Sommernachtstraum*. Many films were frivolous, but he also conducted Edmund Meisel's score for some performances of the Berlin sensation of 1926, *Battleship Potemkin*. This was not a film that the communist Ernst Meyer, as far as one knows, ever professionally mingled with – though his score for the GPO Film Unit's *Roadways* (1937) shows some signs of Meisel's influence.[7]

When sound films arrived in Germany, May quickly adapted to the new technology. In 1929 he contributed to Richard Eichberg's farcical *Wer wird denn weinen, wenn man auseinandergeht,* one in a series of German productions mounted with British International Pictures, eager to advance its European profile. The film was shot silent, then garnished with synchronised talk, music and sound effects. During the summer of 1929 Eichberg signed a new BIP contract for multilingual sound films, to be made at Elstree. Over an eighteen-month period from late 1929 to the spring of 1931 three were shot in English and German, with altered casts: an exotic Anna May Wong melodrama, *The Flame of Love* (1930; *Hai-Tang* in German, also in French, but a success in none of its languages); a detective drama, *Night Birds* (1930, popular as *Der Greifer*); and a genial musical comedy, *Let's Love and Laugh* (*Die Bräutigamswitwe*, 1931). May composed music and songs for them all, but there is no evidence that he was ever physically in England.

He was certainly in the country by the beginning of 1934. His run of German films – comedies and musicals, mostly, several with Eichberg's new star, Marta Eggerth – had ended with the trite but popular *Ein Lied geht um die Welt,* released on 9 May 1933. With Hitler in power, the film's principal Jewish personnel – May, Schmidt, scriptwriter and lyricist Ernst Neubach, director Richard Oswald – had swiftly relocated to Austria, where May scored two further vehicles for Schmidt, *Wenn du jung bist, gehört dir die Welt* (1934) and *Ein Stern fällt vom Himmel* (1934).[8] He also squeezed in two productions in France, and a side job in Portugal. Arriving in Britain, he made little attempt to mould himself to suit any local musical habits: the Viennese lilt obstinately remained. *My Song Goes Round the World*, BIP's remake of *Ein Lied geht um die Welt,* went before the cameras in June 1934. *A Star Fell from Heaven,* a remake of *Ein Stern fällt vom Himmel,* followed in 1936. 'A delightful musical score,' trilled the reviewer in *Kinematograph Weekly,* 'set in a pseudo-Continental atmosphere of captivating picture postcard prettiness … Light as a cloud, yet rich in bouquet, the film gives all that is best in screen operetta.'[9] Did this enthusiastic trade response actually match the public reaction? In the mid-1930s there were certainly plenty of 'picture postcard' British-made film operettas, pretty or not: the Schmidt vehicles; the Richard Tauber vehicles; May's own 1937 rehash of Charles Cuvillier's musical comedy *The Lilac Domino,* which went creaking before the cameras for producer Max Schach, whose film subjects and key employees were often heavily continental. Audiences, I suspect, enjoyed any star and singing power on offer, as they did in West End theatres, where continental-flavoured operettas hung on at Drury Lane through the 1940s with the Ruritanian romances devised by, and for, Ivor Novello. It is harder to imagine the 1930s cinema public giving thumbs up when the settings were tawdry, the direction stilted, and the singing insufficient: the case certainly with the appalling *Domino,* where critical responses were at best cool, at worst dismissive.[10] Only in 1939 with Goldsmith's Grafton production of A.J. Cronin's novel *The Stars Look Down* did May get the chance to work on more muscular and intentionally realistic film material, predominantly British in origin. The need for a change in tone obviously increased with the Second World War; no British film was going to fight Hitler with apple blossoms and *lederhosen*.

As with many émigrés, inside and outside the film industry, assimilation for May proved difficult: music has its foreign accent as well as speech. At first he met the challenge fitfully. Repeatedly in his scores, which he orchestrated himself (his remarks to Kohner were no empty boast), you hear strings sweeping or sighing sentimentally, often accompanied by harp arpeggios. Listen to *The Stars Look Down* as Michael Redgrave's mother packs his suitcase for university or Margaret Lockwood intimates her love: these cues, tender to the point of mawkishness, clearly fell from the composer more easily than the film's oppressive, brass-heavy 'drudgery' theme, introduced during the main titles. Sometimes the romantic European accent in the films is comical. Judging by the opening music in the Boultings' adaptation of *Thunder Rock*, you would think the lighthouse in Robert Ardrey's original play was in the middle of the River Danube, not on Lake Michigan, northeast of Racine. A solo violin strikes up with a glutinous theme; the harp tinkles, accompanied by a vibraphone halo. All extremely sweet-toothed, and not very good music.[11]

But alongside the sweet and the cosy, May also developed a surprisingly experimental range of musical moods and colours for use in the more extravagant plot situations. For sequences featuring otherworldly apparitions or your average crazed Gainsborough heroine, he would often apply the eerie wavering sounds of the musical saw. You hear this initially some twenty-three minutes into *Thunder Rock* as the shipwrecked characters of 1849 first impress themselves upon Redgrave's mind. The saw plays a bigger role in May's score for Gainsborough's *Madonna of the Seven Moons*, where it is always associated with Phyllis Calvert's schizophrenia and often deployed on an arc-shaped phrase, first heard against tremolo strings as Calvert receives Patricia Roc's gift of earrings. Expectedly, the instrument is also never far away in British National's heavily comic *The Ghosts of Berkeley Square* (1947), where one of its obsessions is the nursery tune of 'Rockabye Baby'.[12]

May also developed a knack for letting brass instruments hover about, dislocated, strangely adrift: another ingredient in scenes featuring emotional turmoil. There is a particularly striking example in his other major Gainsborough melodrama, *The Wicked Lady*. Had he been offered the composing job, Ernst Meyer the seventeenth-century scholar could no doubt have pointed this tale of 1683 towards the authentic, virile music of the period, displacing May's drooping pastiches: this is not one of the composer's strongest scores. But after some sixty-six minutes the music track leaps into imaginative life when Margaret Lockwood's Barbara, at her most wicked, poisons Felix Aylmer's principled Hogarth, then finishes him off with a pillow. Sombre brass chords wander about in extreme harmonic distress, in a manner almost Bernard Herrmann-esque; a strain of writing that intermittently but fruitfully continues for the rest of the film.

But the best example of May's 'advanced' streak remains *Brighton Rock*, one of his most convincing and subtlest British scores. The principal theme is an angular four-note motif, usually issued on the brass, and initially answered by a striding string motif set against a jarring trumpet. Variations and metamorphoses of the four-note motif thread cunningly through the film, always well integrated with the action, as in the extended early chase, building in tension and dynamics as Alan Wheatley is pursued through Brighton's streets. And May's instrumental resources are often unusual. We might have guessed a brass shriek as Richard Attenborough's Pinkie helps Wylie Watson's character fall to his death through a banister. But not the menacing aftermath: a tremulous double bass, with a quiet drum roll underneath. And for once with May, sentimentality overload is avoided. When the focus shifts to Carol Marsh's character, the music becomes 'feminised' and tender (note the strings, solo violin and harp as she tends to Attenborough after the race track fracas) but never schmaltzy.[13]

Overall, May's mature scores of the mid-1940s are an uneven jumble: often mediocre when the melodic material is straightforwardly lyrical; often imaginative and effective when he aims for expressionist tonal colours. Though his techniques and resources had grown more sophisticated, perhaps deep down May never stopped being the silent cinema veteran of the 1920s who loosely stitched mood music together in chameleonic compilations. And no matter how exotic and adventurous the passing sounds, you always know where May's heart really lay. As soon as the war eased and then ended, out came May's European romances again in *Waltz Time*, *The Laughing Lady* (1946), *Spring Song* (1946): old-fashioned musicals which, *Waltz Time* aside, were considerably less popular with the movie public than Anna Neagle's more authentically British entertainments. Listen to the song titles: 'Love Again', 'Love is the Key', 'Magical Moonlight', 'You Will Return to Vienna'. Return to Vienna? Spiritually at least, Hans May had never really left.[14]

Let us now switch to our other singing bird, Ernst Meyer. His arrival on the British scene was in marked contrast to May's. As a known communist as well as a Jew – he was editor of the journal *Kampfmusik*, a writer for *Die Rote Fahne*, and a director of workers' choirs – Meyer had a particularly urgent need to escape Berlin in 1933. At first he fled to Heidelberg; then academic contacts made during his university research gave him the means to leave Germany altogether. Officially, he arrived in England to attend an international musicological conference held at Cambridge that summer; unofficially, he was coming for the duration. His prior experience of composing for films consisted of one year's worth of study with Hindemith at the Hochschule für Musik, Charlottenburg, Berlin, where the lessons included principles of soundtrack instrumentation and composing in counterpoint to the images. He had also taken courses in experimental composition for the radio with another exploratory musical spirit, Max Butting.[15]

In 1934 Meyer's doctoral thesis on seventeenth-century European instrumental music was published in Switzerland, and his first reputation in Britain was as a musicologist, especially in the field of English consort music, then little explored. He organised a pioneering BBC radio series of performances in 1935, and spent much time head down among manuscripts at the British Museum and other collections: work that culminated in the publication in 1946 of a seminal book, *English Chamber Music*, written in fluent English, mostly at the height of the London Blitz.[16] Meyer also established personal roots in Britain, as did May. During his years of emigration he became divorced from his first German wife and married a British citizen. May married in England as well; in fact, he married his agent, Rita Cave. But only Meyer, inside and outside cinema, took genuine sustenance from English musical history. The biggest concert work of his émigré years, the powerful *Symphony for String Orchestra*, completed in its first version in 1947, acknowledges English traditions in its choice of medium and several modal cadences inflected with English folk song. Other aspects of English musical culture feature in his documentary and instructional soundtracks. English eighteenth-century classical pastiche dominates the opening of the Realist Film Unit's *The Londoners* (1939), an ambitious commemoration of the London County Council's fiftieth anniversary. Elsewhere, traditional songs appear. A fragment of 'Hearts of Oak' flickers up in the Halas-Batchelor cartoon *Dustbin Parade* (1942); 'Sing a Song of Sixpence' plays a major part in Len Lye's filmed recipe for a vegetable pie, *When the Pie Was Opened* (1941). And it is Meyer, not May, who writes the music for a docile little film, *British Made*, produced like Humphrey Jennings's *Spare Time* for display at the New York World's Fair during the summer of 1939. Meyer related later that an MP of the time asked in Parliament how it was that a gentleman named Ernst Hermann Meyer had composed the music for something called *British Made*: an exchange, alas, not documented in the official record of parliamentary business, Hansard.[17]

Aside from musical researches and odd jobs, Meyer continued the political activities he had pursued in pre-Hitler Berlin. He conducted amateur and workers' choirs; he allied himself with the Workers' Music Association, founded in 1936, and, more crucially, the Freie Deutsche Kulturbund (Free German League of Culture), a key political and cultural nexus for German émigrés in London, which he helped to establish in December 1938. In Communist Party circles he rubbed shoulders for a time with Michael Tippett, who wrote with displeasure in his autobiography about Meyer's fervent hatred of all things German in the wake of Hitler's ascent: 'He exuded a bitterness and bile that I found intolerable.' There were also aspects of British life that Meyer disliked, principally capitalism and the country's class system. Yet from his later perch in East Germany he wrote and spoke about England with genuine gratitude, both for its cultural life and for simply being 'the country which gave me shelter from fascist persecution'; a shelter also extended to a sister and brother, though not his eldest brother Ulrich, who later perished with their parents in Nazi concentration camps.[18]

And any bitterness Meyer expressed was not caused by any persistent lack of worthwhile British employment. By the end of 1938 he had already established his reputation in documentary films. The GPO Film Unit's *Roadways*, a mosaic portrait of life on Britain's roads, was unveiled in the autumn of 1937. The steps that led to this first film assignment are not now clear: perhaps political contacts; perhaps the Unit's producer Cavalcanti, the employer too of Britten and Auden, dedicated to exploring new talent and finding new ways of blending sound and image. In the instrumentation you hear the fruits of Hindemith's film classes: trumpet and bright woodwind sounds prevail, ideal for the microphone, and there is no big cushion of strings. Economic reasons in any case made that unlikely. Already Meyer is mixing sound effects with music: right at the opening, drum taps and piano crunches bleed into the sound of cars and car hooters, building up to a squeal of applied brakes. For a scene reconstructing nineteenth-century driving conditions, a parlour piano chestnut is resurrected, with impish wrong notes. When twentieth-century traffic turns hectic, the music turns angular, dissonant and aggressive – one more mode in a pungent, kaleidoscopic score.[19] Meyer's soundtrack for the Shell Film Unit's *Oil from the Earth* (1938) furthered his experimental agenda, with edited sound effects of clinking pipelines blending in with the rhythm of work and the preceding instrumental music.

His other prominent early score, for the GPO Unit's *North Sea* (1938), is less inventive, but won Meyer more exposure: Harry Watt's story film about North Sea trawlermen saved from a storm by their radio link was deliberately made to prove that documentaries could have commercial appeal, and was widely praised and distributed on the circuits. To Robert Flaherty, writing in *Sight and Sound*, it was 'one of the most significant short films that has ever been made'.[20] For the communist Meyer this was the perfect assignment: a film about working people cast entirely from working people; and a film moreover where he was given the chance to research his subject on the spot off the coast of Aberdeen. 'I went to sea with the trawlers,' he told John Huntley, 'then I wrote the music from life, from what I had seen and heard … It was the music of reality and gave me a chance to break away from the isolated vacuum into which modern serious music is tending to go.'[21]

We hear a Sunday hymn being sung, 'For Those In Peril on the Sea', and, among the footsteps and dialogue, atmospheric snatches of song from the streets. When the trawlermen wrestle with the choked pump that is stalling their ship, Meyer's music reflects stress and struggle, with cymbal clashes and drum tattoos, after the percussive manner of *Roadworks*. But the score's most noteworthy feature is the number of cues marked by pastiche nineteenth-century gestures, scored for a generous-sized chamber orchestra, with melodic material suggesting diluted Beethoven or, as the ship initially sets out to sea, Schubert's mellifluous, rolling gait. Later in the GDR, in lectures, books and music congresses Beethoven was officially enthroned by the cultural élite as one of the few past German composers whose life and music could plausibly fulfil the communists' need for political correctness; Meyer himself wrote at least five papers on the topic. Perhaps by wrapping these Scottish trawlermen with heroic, quasi-Beethovenian sounds, Meyer was in a humble way preparing the path for the composer's coronation.

Along with his trips to the North Sea, Meyer valued the documentary companies for their collective spirit. This was particularly evident at the Realist Film Unit in the 1940s, where among routine wisps of music contributed to straight instructional films – *Keeping Rabbits* (1942), *Storing Vegetables Indoors* (1942) – Meyer achieved some of his most innovative work in the manipulation of sound effects. Realist was a true co-operative: all seventeen staff members were paid the same (a modest £10 a week), and films were presented as team efforts in the credits. Meyer frequently worked in collaboration with the exuberant mixed-media maverick Len Lye, an association stretching back to 1938, when Meyer replaced Jack Ellitt as Lye's sound editor. One of their films, the live-action *Newspaper Train* (1941), became the first, perhaps only, vehicle for a soundtrack invention developed by Meyer, Lye and others at Realist, involving the printing of two sound strips side by side on the soundtrack, one for dialogue, one for effects, in pursuit of greater clarity and a better balance during projection. As a showcase, *Newspaper Train* proved too ambitious: dialogue battled to be heard against squealing breaks, exploding bombs, and other war sounds as the train, packed with the morning papers, made its way out of central London. Seeking to benefit the entire industry, the Realist Unit persuaded the technicians' union, the Association of Cine-Technicians (ACT), to take out a provisional patent on their behalf, but lack of investment plus the need for alert cinema projectionists to raise their usual sound levels at screenings put paid to the invention's development.[22]

Meyer's sound experiments achieved greater artistic success with the brilliant simplicity of the trailer-length *Mobilise Your Scrap* (1942), made for Films of Great Britain, where the propaganda point is driven home with a soundtrack of factory sounds edited to fit the speech rhythm of the title slogan. But the peak was reached with Lye's *When the Pie Was Opened*. The challenge of making a film recipe for a vegetable pie seems to have inspired everyone. Little purely instrumental music is used; instead Meyer mixes multifarious effects, edited to images with surreal mischief and precise comic timing. Vegetables are summoned for pie duty to the calls from an army parade ground. The pie-crust is indented and cut to the noises of sawing wood and hammering. When mother carries the pie from the oven to the family table, a steam train starts up, the puffs accelerating with each of the mother's steps. The sound mix also includes Louis Armstrong's trumpet ('In My Solitude'), children at play, children singing, each layer woven in and out with a magician's hand. But faced with this aural carnival, did any spectator actually absorb enough of the recipe to cook the pie at home?

Another strand of Meyer's work appears in the descriptive writing for conventional instruments in his Halas and Batchelor cartoons. 'I tried to work with all nationalities involved in the war,' Halas told Paul Wells in the 1990s. Much music was put in the hands of Halas's fellow Hungarian, the inquisitive, chameleonic Mátyás Seiber (see Florian Scheding's chapter in this volume), or the Romanian-born, French-trained Francis Chagrin; but Meyer, the German, also proved his mettle in a range of films from non-commercial instructional features for the Admiralty and the Fire Brigade to *Dustbin Parade* and *Filling the Gap* (1942) – humorous cinema exhortations in the drive for salvage and home productivity.[23] Vegetables, a bone, a toothpaste tube, a spinning top, a tin can: each is given life and character through Meyer's brief phrases for solo instruments (flute, clarinet, violin, cello, etc.), tightly synchronised to the animation.

Speaking in the 1970s about his British film career, Meyer underlined the experience gained in incisive character depiction and the exploitation of modest instrumental forces. Available evidence, however, suggests that his scattered GDR film soundtracks offered limited opportunities to exploit these skills imaginatively; in artistic terms the household junk of *Dustbin Parade* received a better deal than Walter Ulbricht, the GDR's first President, in the flatulent 1953 documentary *Walter Ulbricht*.[24] In his GDR features and documentaries there would have been even less chance to further experiments in orchestrated sound; and Britain itself in the 1950s quickly forgot Meyer's soundtracks among the general diminishment of adventure and creativity in the cinema documentary field. Isolated from the West in East Berlin, Meyer became an easy figure to forget, though his reputation among, and friendship with, British musicological and communist friends continued.

So there in capsule form are May and Meyer: two singing birds, two film composers, yet so different in their careers. Did the two know each other? In the world beyond that signpost towards Elstree, Meyer certainly knew British feature film staff, if only from his extensive connections at the Free German League of Culture, where he headed the music section and served as its first President. At the League he shared a talk about cinema life behind the scenes with the writer Fritz Gottfurcht (Frederic Gotfurt), later scenario editor for Associated British; he also wrote musical material for the League revue *My Goodness – My Alibi!* (1944), one of several written with input from Gottfurcht. The composer Allan Gray was also prominent in League activities and wrote the music for another significant revue, *Mr*

Gulliver Goes to School (1942).[25] But Hans May? As an Austrian, he had his own émigré centre to turn to, should he have wished; but even without that national division, I expect the pair moved in entirely different circles.

Yet there is one place where the two seem to rub together, in spirit if not in body, and that is in Meyer's book *Musik im Zeitgeschehen*, published in 1952, and intended – and for the most part accepted – as a key building-block in the construction of a musical aesthetic in the GDR. Much of the thinking in the book followed lines of enquiry established earlier in a lecture Meyer gave in May 1945 about Germany's musical future, and his book on English consort music, where his musical analyses were consistently inflected with a Marxist-Leninist interpretation of history. But there is now a new and swingeing exuberance about Meyer's arguments, and one of the victims of his vitriol is exactly Hans May's brand of music: mass-produced, light entertainment music, or, as Meyer terms it, *schlagerkitsch*. This music, he blasts (and I summarise), has the appearance of pseudo-art. But it is not art at all. It's so repetitive as to be banal. It never moves forwards, only stagnates. It appeals to the lowliest instinct in people, and summons only false feelings. It's an expression of imperial decadence, and spiritual and mental non-productivity, and is a typical result of mass production in the era of capitalistic monopoly. So there![26]

There are numerous ironies in this attack, but I will draw attention to just two. In the GDR, a socialist country created not from any popular revolution by its inhabitants, evidence indicates that, left unprodded by the authorities, the majority of the common people, the working people, actually preferred *schlagerkitsch*, the sentimental ballads, the escapist songs and musicals. What they didn't particularly want were the officially sanctioned cantatas, patriotic songs, and heroic concertos by Meyer and others – music supposed to bind and uplift the new communist nation. Even in this 'official' music, however craftsmanlike and well-intentioned, some listeners detected kitsch: Bertolt Brecht, never as settled within the GDR establishment as Meyer, once referred to the style of Meyer's Social Realist monument, the *Mansfeld Oratorio*, as 'schmaltz surrogate and artificial honey'.[27]

The second, deeper irony returns us to the question raised earlier. Which of this pair in their British work, in their escapist features and socially useful documentaries, actually delivered 'music for the people'? Neither of them probably could claim to have achieved with their British soundtracks the goals for poetry proposed in the late 1940s by Semyon Kirsanov to Soviet Russia's young poetic spark Yevgeni Yevtushenko: 'Poetry, if it's genuine, is not a racing car rushing senselessly round and round a closed track, it is an ambulance rushing to someone's aid.'[28] But May's films, if never rushing ambulances, certainly saw more patients. His music caressed James Mason, Margaret Lockwood, Patricia Roc and Phyllis Calvert – among the 1940s' most popular British stars; *The Wicked Lady* was pronounced by *Kinematograph Weekly* as Britain's top box office attraction of 1946.[29] Even his more anaemic films were distributed widely through the British circuits. His musical responses, as I have suggested, were not always inured in schmaltz and kitsch, though their strains were never far away. You could even argue that by articulating through his music the heated emotions rampant in Gainsborough melodramas, May, however unconsciously, was doing his bit to further these films' implicit commentary on sexual repressions, female empowerment, social breakdown and other contemporary signs of the times. Schmaltz and kitsch acknowledged, there seems no need now to blast him with Meyer's artillery. And in general terms, no-one's personal or professional allegiance to the light Viennese touch should automatically be a disqualification from harbouring a political conscience. Paul Dessau, another major musical figure in the GDR, worked on Tauber film musicals in the early 1930s, and had an operetta writer in the family (Jean Gilbert, his cousin). Tauber himself scarcely lived in the clouds, as the writers Eric Maschwitz and Armin Robinson discovered when they proposed the germ of the *Carissima* musical in 1939. Apart from gargling, he only wanted to talk about the prospects of a European war.[30]

Meyer, for his part, never aimed in films for wide popular success. It is hard to imagine him following May and writing to Paul Kohner for that big Hollywood break: in *Musik im Zeitgeschehen* America's jazz and boogie-woogie is excoriated as much as schmaltz, even though jazz recordings played a dominant part in his sound compilations for Len Lye. But in Meyer's own documentary sphere in Britain he achieved much that was socially useful, artistically adventurous, and fulfilling for himself. *North Sea* brought him face to face with working conditions among fishermen and pointed towards the documentary-fiction fusion actively developed by film companies during the Second World War. *The Londoners* showcased improvements in urban living standards. Many films pitched into the Home Front battle against Hitler with imagination and vigour, not always the case with May's few excursions into the field. On the technical side, Meyer's work on orchestrated sounds was important and pioneering, and deserves reappraisal. Yet *North Sea* apart, his British films, by their very nature, were tucked away in cinema programmes alongside newsreels, advertisements, and other Ministry of Information exhortations – and given the bombardment, likely to be absorbed and remembered by the relatively few. These were not, in Kirsanov's terms, ambulances rushing to people's aid; they were more like notices on a crowded bulletin board.

So which was the composer most engaged with his public: the revolutionary Ernst Meyer, or the conservative-minded Hans May? The social realist, or the escape artist? I will not answer that question directly. The reader may reach his or her own conclusions, even about the validity of the question. But bear in mind the opening sentence in George Mikes's astute comic guide to émigré behaviour in Britain, *How to Be an Alien*, first published in 1946: 'In England everything is the other way round.'[31]

Notes

1. William Saunders, 'Songs of the German Revolution', *Music and Letters*, vol.16, no.1, January 1935, pp. 50–57.

2. The biographical entry in John Huntley, *British Film Music* (London: Skelton Robinson, 1947), p. 216, lists most of May's work in Britain. His last credited British film score was for *The Gypsy and the Gentleman* (1957).

3. For a catalogue of Meyer film scores and their manuscripts see Mathias Hansen (ed.), *Ernst Hermann Meyer: Das kompositorische und theoretische Werk* (Leipzig: Deutscher Verlag für Musik, 1976). Also see his biographical entry in Huntley, *British Film Music*, p. 217. The signpost photograph is included in Konrad Niemann, *Ernst Hermann Meyer: Für Sie porträtiert* (Leipzig: Deutscher Verlag für Musik, 1971), p. 34.

4. *Carissima* ran for 466 performances at the Palace Theatre, London, from 10 March 1948 to 23 April 1949. The libretto was by Eric Maschwitz, from a story by Armin Robinson, the Austrian publisher and co-author of the 1930 operetta *Im weißen Rößl*. Robinson's participation dates back to 1939, when he hatched a closely related plot with Maschwitz and hoped to lure Richard Tauber into a production. See Eric Maschwitz, *No Chips on My Shoulder* (London: Herbert Jenkins, 1957), pp. 125–6; also Kurt Gänzl, *The British Musical Theatre* (London: Macmillan, 1986). Probate details list May's last London address as Flat 172, 55 Park Lane, W1; the amount of money left after his death was £7996,15/-.

5. *Mansfelder Oratorium* was first performed on 2 September 1950; the libretto was by Stephan Hermlin. The work propelled Meyer towards the National Prize of the GDR, awarded in 1950; also awarded to Meyer in 1952 and 1963. For a useful English-language overview of GDR musical culture, and Meyer's place within it, see Jost Hermand, 'Attempts to Establish a Socialist Music Culture in the Soviet Occupation Zone and the Early German Democratic Republic, 1945–1965' in Edward Larkey (ed.), *A Sound Legacy? Music and Politics in East Germany* (Washington, DC: American Institute for Contemporary German Studies, 2000) [also www.aicgs.org/Publications/PDF/gdrmusic.pdf].

6. Habakuk Traber, 'Hollywood rief nicht: Der Filmkomponist Hans May in seiner Korrespondenz mit Paul Kohner', *Filmexil* no.10, May 1998, pp. 24, 28.

7. May's *Kino-Lexikon* and *Cinema Collection* are mentioned in Traber, 'Hollywood rief nicht', p. 23. For his work with Tucholsky at *Die Gondel*, see Helga Bemmann, *In mein' Verein bin ich hineingetreten: Kurt Tucholsky als Chanson- und Liederdichter* (Berlin: Lied der Zeit, 1989), pp. 73–77. The cabaret's theatre space was designed by Ernst Stern – May's future collaborator, in another world, on his postwar British musical *Carissima*. In the issue of 27 May 1925 the Berlin reviewer for *Variety*, 'Trask', gives an interesting account of *Ein Sommernachtstraum* as performed at the Nollendorf-Platz Theatre, where May's chameleonic music and arrangements, 'played by Eric Borchard's American jazz band', are singled out for special mention: 'At one moment Wagner is being seriously interpreted and the next the latest from "Tin Pan Alley" … And how the boys did play it, the classical as well as the bluest of the blue. When they got hot they just tore the roof off the joint.'

8. A score for Schmidt's last Austrian vehicle, *Heut' ist der schönste Tag in meinem Leben* (1936), followed once May had moved to England.

9. *Kinematograph Weekly*, 18 June 1936, p. 32. *Ein Stern fällt von Himmel* was directed by Max Neufeld; for the British remake, another BIP émigré, the scriptwriter and director Paul Merzbach, took command. Both *Ein Lied geht um die Welt* and its Elstree remake were directed by Richard Oswald.

10. 'In every detail a rubber-stamp film … devoid of the slightest pretence of realism,' groaned the *Monthly Film Bulletin* reviewer, July 1937, p. 142. Also see the *Kinematograph Weekly* review, 15 July 1937. May himself ventured into London's continental stage musical sphere in April 1935 with *The Dancing City*, a musical celebration of Vienna. The German-language original, *Die tanzende Stadt*, was produced in Vienna in October 1935, four months after its English adaptation, produced by André Charlot, had disappeared from the Coliseum.

11. Another, less saccharine European dimension is provided by Mutz Greenbaum's lighting inside the lighthouse as the century-old shipwreck ghosts make their presence felt: wall shadows, tilted angles – the old German tricks for conveying distorted reality.

12. K.J. Donnelly, in a pioneering essay, calls May's *Madonna* soundtrack 'one of the most impressive Gainsborough scores'. See 'Wicked Sounds and Magic Melodies' in Pam Cook (ed.), *Gainsborough Pictures* (London: Cassell, 1997), p.163. That is not quite how I hear it, but its eclectic textures and dramatic juxtapositions do gain in quality over time and help offset the limited melodic interest.

13. To some extent the absence of schmaltz goes against the grain of the references to popular sentimental music in Graham Greene's original novel, neatly analysed in Bernard Bergonzi, *Reading the Thirties: Texts and Contexts* (London: Macmillan, 1978), pp. 119–22. Hearing sentimental dross in the dance hall, Greene's Pinkie wants to 'wrap it up in cellophane … put it in silver paper'. In the cinema he visits, the hero's song prompts weeping: 'He shut his eyes to hold in his tears, but the music went on – it was like a vision of release to an imprisoned man.'

14. Critics swung both ways on *Waltz Time*, set at the Habsburg court in Old Vienna, and directed by Paul Stein. Some praised the absence of 'bandleader din' (*Daily Herald*, 8 July 1945); Lionel Collier in *Picturegoer* (4 August 1945) pronounced it a 'delightful British picture'. Others reached for the knives, most eloquently Helen Fletcher in *Time and Tide* (14 July 1945), who referred to Richard Tauber – featured in two cameo appearances as a singing shepherd with sheep and smock – as 'the rabbit the Elstree python just can't swallow'. The larger success of Neagle's far glossier 'London' series – *The Courtneys of Curzon Street* was the biggest box office attraction of 1947 (*Kinematograph Weekly*, 18 December 1947) – suggests that tuneful escapism was still widely welcomed if the packaging was slick and the film's accent British. Ironically, the director of photography on Neagle's 'London' films was German émigré Mutz Greenbaum, working under his Anglicised name of Max Greene.

15. Meyer recalls his classes in *Kontraste, Konflikte: Erinnerungen, Gespräche, Kommentare* (Berlin: Verlag Neue Musik, 1979), pp. 62–64. By this point, both Hindemith and Butting had practical experience in writing film music. In 1921, Butting had composed a chamber score to accompany the premiere of Walther Ruttmann's first abstract film, *Lichtspiel Opus 1*. Hindemith in 1927 had written a player piano score for a Felix the cat cartoon, presented in the context of the Deutsche Kammermusik festival at Baden-Baden; during the same festival Eisler, another of Meyer's Berlin teachers, presented a score for *Ruttmann Opus III*, a Ruttmann abstract film originally premiered in 1925. A further Hindemith score accompanied the premiere of Hans Richter's *Vormittags-Spuk* at the 1928 festival. Butting's radio explorations in the late 1920s were considerable: at the Hochschule für Musik he created a studio for radio music performance, and wrote pieces himself specifically designed for broadcast. See R. Raven-Hart, 'Composing for Radio', *The Musical Quarterly*, January 1930, pp. 133–39.

16. *English Chamber Music: The History of a Great Art from the Middle Ages to Purcell* (London: Lawrence & Wishart, 1946). Revised editions were published in 1951 and, as *Early English Chamber Music*, in 1982.

17. The MP's query is mentioned in *Kontraste, Konflikte*, p. 160. Meyer mentions that he aimed to give the music an English colouring, but in the National Film and Television Archive's print the few cues, written in nineteenth-century pastiche style to match the film's emphasis on traditional craftsmanship, give no suggestion of this. The film's director was the silent film veteran George Pearson.

18. See Meyer's preface to *Early English Chamber Music* (1982), also *Kontraste, Konflikte*, pp. 136 and 190. Tippett's recollection is found in his autobiography *Those Twentieth Century Blues* (London: Hutchinson, 1992). Aside from *Kontraste, Konflikte*, Jutta Raab Hansen's *NS-verfolgte Musiker in England: Spuren deutscher und österreichischer Flüchtlinge in der britischen Musikkultur* (Hamburg: von Bockel Verlag, 1996) is also invaluable for its coverage of Meyer's English activities.

19. Portions of this soundtrack score, along with others, were worked into a six-movement suite for two trumpets, two pianos and percussion, dedicated to Cavalcanti, first performed at an all-Meyer concert at Adolf Tuck Hall, London,19 April 1944. The Unit's need for economy in musical resources was obvious; but William Alwyn's comments in Manvell and Huntley's *The Technique of Film Music* (London: Focal Press, 1967, pp. 161–162) about a composer being 'literally forced to produce his "airs on a shoe string"' can lead us astray. Some Meyer scores employed fifteen players or more; many used between eight and ten. Britten's GPO scores from the 1930s used similar compact forces, but still found room for added choirs and exotic percussion.

20. Robert Flaherty, 'North Sea', *Sight and Sound*, Summer 1938, p. 62.

21. Huntley, *British Film Music*, p. 162. The ship's interior scenes were shot in the GPO Unit's Blackheath studio in London; all other material was captured on location.

22. See 'A.C.T.'s First Patent', *The Cine-Technician*, November 1941–January 1942, p. 129; also *Kontraste, Konflikte*, p. 167. The film's poor fortune in cinemas is charted in Jeffrey Richards and Dorothy Sheridan (eds.), *Mass-Observation at the Movies* (London: Routledge & Kegan Paul, 1987), pp. 445–55. Meyer's films with Lye are treated in Roger Horrocks's biography *Len Lye* (Auckland: Auckland University Press, 2001).

23. Halas's comment is in Paul Wells, 'Dustbins, Democracy and Defence: Halas and Batchelor and the Animated Film in Britain 1940–1947', in Pat Kirkham and David Thoms (eds.), *War Culture: Social Change and Changing Experience in World War Two Britain* (London: Lawrence and Wishart, 1995), p. 62. Chagrin and Meyer were the first composers employed in the 1940s; Seiber began contributing in 1942, developing into Halas and Batchelor's principal composer. Another Hungarian, György Ranki, worked briefly for the company in 1948.

24. Meyer's cinema output in the GDR, ranging in time between 1950 and 1972, consists of three documentaries and six features, crowned by two elaborate biographical films about Karl Liebknecht.

25. For material on the Free German League's theatrical/musical activities, see Günter Berghaus (ed.), *Theatre and Film in Exile: German Artists in Britain, 1933–1945* (Oxford: Berg, 1989).

26. *Musik im Zeitgeschehen* (Berlin: Verlag Bruno Henschel und Sohn, 1952), p. 161. The assault reads even more ferociously in German: 'Kitsch ist eine heute sehr verbreitete Erscheinung von Pseudokunst, die durch folgende Eigenschaften gekennzeichnet ist. Äußerlich verwendet er schein-volkstümliche, klassizistische oder romantisierende Stilmittel, die den Massen leicht eingehen. Er lebt aber von der Wiederholung von bereits früher einmal Gesagtem, das banalisiert wird; er führt nicht vorwärts, sondern stagniert. Er appelliert an niedrige Instinkte in den Menschen und hat verlogene, unechte Inhalte. Sein Gefühlsgehalt ist nicht wahr, sondern vorgetäuscht. Er ist eine typische Erscheinung der Massenproduktion im Zeitalter des Monopolkapitalismus. Er ist Ausdruck imperialistischer Dekadenz und geistiger Unproduktivität.'

27. Entry for 15 November 1952 in Bertolt Brecht, *Arbeitsjournal 1938 bis 1955* (Frankfurt am Main: Suhrkamp, 1973), p. 991. Bear in mind, too, Eisler's comments in his published conversations with Hans Bunge about friends who 'politicize light music in an idiotic manner'. 'Overpoliticizing the arts,' he says, 'leads to barbarity in aesthetics'. See 'Ask Me More About Brecht', in David Blake (ed.), *Hanns Eisler – A Miscellany* (Luxembourg: Harwood Academic Publishers, 1995), p. 423.

28. Yevgeni Yevtushenko, *A Precocious Autobiography* (Harmondsworth: Penguin Books, 1965), p. 74.

29. *Kinematograph Weekly*, 19 December 1946, p. 33.

30. Maschwitz, *No Chips on My Shoulder*, pp. 125–26.

31. George Mikes, *How to Be an Alien* (London: Allan Wingate, 1946), p. 10.

Chapter 17

I KNOW WHERE I'M GOING!
HEARING GERMANIC MUSIC
IN THE SCOTTISH ISLES

K.J. Donnelly

Shot in the mid-1940s, *I Know Where I'm Going!* continued Michael Powell's interest in the Scottish islands which he had explored in his earlier films *Edge of the World* (1937) and *The Spy in Black* (1939). The film's narrative concerns Joan, who is going to the island of Kiloran to marry her boss who rents it. With progress blocked by bad weather, she instead falls in love with Torquil, the real laird of the island. The film's team included a number of immigrants to Britain: most notably Powell's close collaborator, screenwriter Emeric Pressburger, production designer Alfred Junge, German-born cinematographer Erwin Hillier and composer Allan Gray.

Despite his name, Gray was not Scottish, or even British, although he had some experience of Celtic culture, being interned on the Isle of Man as an 'enemy alien' in 1939/40 for four months. Allan Gray is a strange name for a mittel-European. According to some, his *nom de plume* was inspired by the protagonist in Oscar Wilde's *Picture of Dorian Gray*, although it could also be derived from the protagonist of Carl Theodor Dreyer's *Vampyr – Der Traum des Allan Grey* (*Vampyr: The Dream of Allan Grey*, 1932). In post-First World War Berlin, the Anglicisation of a name might have been a political statement, like the sculptor Helmut Herzfeld reinventing himself as 'John Heartfield'.

Gray was born Josef Zmigrod in 1902 in Tarnow, Galicia, part of the Austro-Hungarian empire that subsequently was incorporated into Poland in 1919. He moved to Berlin and became a student of Arnold Schönberg in 1926, along with such figures as Alban Berg, Anton Webern and Hanns Eisler. At the same time he worked for Max Reinhardt's Deutsches Theater on the Kurfürstendamm. Becoming Reinhardt's musical director in 1928 and even occasionally appearing on stage, Gray met and worked with musicians such as Erich Wolfgang Korngold and Friedrich Hollaender, and wrote cabaret music alongside composers such as Mischa Spoliansky, Hans May (see Geoff Brown in this volume), Hanns Eisler, Rudolf Nelson and Werner Richard Heymann. It seems Zmigrod became 'Allan Gray' to avoid embarrassment, so that maestro Schönberg would not be teaching a composer of 'maintenance music'.[1] Apart from stage and cabaret work, Gray scored films such as *Emil und die Detektive* (1931) and *F.P.1 antwortet nicht* (1932), but never used Schönberg's revolutionary twelve-tone serial technique in scores. This artistic mode was fully divorced from the popular idiom Gray used in his commercial musical ventures. Any personal schizophrenia about his origins and identity was reinforced by a cultural schizophrenia.

This divide between 'Gebrauchsmusik' and 'serious music' solidly differentiated art and commerce, between music made for a living and music emanating from a calling. This is a very Germanic divide. If we think of the ambiguous status of some of Rossini's highly popular arias, or of Satie's or Chopin's parlour piano pieces, none of these have the sense of gravitas characteristic of Germanic music.[2] Jan Swynnoe argues that the divide in classical music between German and French music is essentially a division between concerns with form and structure on the one side and sound and atmosphere on the other.[3]

By the early twentieth century German music had come to dominate serious, respectable 'classical music'. For many decades there has been discussion of what is commonly called 'Germanic music'. The term indicates a theoretical and musicological concept more than it necessarily points to the ethnicity of composers and music. 'Germanic music' denotes a style, a mode of musical operation, tending towards the use of a specific form (often based on 'sonata form') and reaching its apex in the symphony format. Its structure is premised upon dialogue, where themes interact and develop in a logical manner. Germanic music is usually equated with profound seriousness and abstraction. This provides both a tradition and a convention, and is usually traced to a trajectory from Mozart through Beethoven, Wagner, then Brahms and, according to some, its reinvention by Schönberg in the early part of the twentieth century. It should not be forgotten that Wagner has been an absolutely crucial influence on the development of film scores. Avoiding the central notion of artistic status connected to Germanic music, perhaps we could think of some maintenance music as being 'Germanic' in formal terms, most clearly in possessing a sense of clarity, purposefulness and some degree of abstraction.

The 'ethnicity' of music and its connection to specific nationality is now overwhelmingly thought to be culturally accrued rather than innate.[4] However, this is not to deny the national rootedness or implications of certain music. During the Second World War, the BBC set out to remove all music from German and Austrian composers from the airwaves, whether current or not, deeming that the political or ideological resonance of a piece of music was detectable in its sonic materiality:

A ruling maintained that the political or ideological resonance of a piece of music was detectable in the *sounds of the notes* alone … As for the music publishers, who imagined, since they were never told otherwise, that the banning criteria were all to do with copyright, the hidden political filter remained hidden, and they were fobbed off with explanations relating to 'artistic' considerations in the building of music programmes.[5]

The BBC's identification of sonic essences is startling and appears unreasonable, at least to more recent ways of thinking about music's intrinsic value and ideas. However, perhaps on another level the BBC got it right. Music is a potent discourse, and its transmission of ethnic information is often one of its important powers.

The Classical Film Score

The 'classical film score', as Kathryn Kalinak terms it,[6] was established ten years before *I Know Where I'm Going!* as a film music blueprint that increasingly became an international standard. It mixed 'Germanic' dramatic form (a synchronised underscore written for a precise fit with the film's requirements) with 'non-Germanic' (perhaps one could append this as 'French') musical atmosphere (not closely synchronised music that depicts place or mood). This division matches a common metaphor for film music (although one that bizarrely conceives of sound as image). Incidental music in film can either be conceived as being like camerawork, part of the film's narration, which would make it tend towards being stylistically transparent, or it can be conceived as part of the set, an integral part of the drama itself, and thus more likely to be interested in (and indeed, feature) local colour and singular atmosphere.

The process of achieving 'ethnic' film music follows a strong tradition of techniques and a specific film music language repertoire. It is a form of 'shorthand', taking certain musical aspects and using them as an essence of different musical cultures. In film scores both old and new, the 'trick' is to use these forms of shorthand in a manner that foregrounds them as an effect within a musical fabric that is not premised upon such ethnic musical language. Thus their communicational content very commonly outweighs their material and sensual aspects. 'Ethnic' aspects become stylistic decoration, not an essential part of the music.[7]

According to Thomas Fitzgerald, modern ethnicity works through the use and manipulation of symbols.[8] There are some extremely obvious musical examples that appear regularly in film music, among other places, such as the large warpipe version of the bagpipes wielded regularly to indicate Scotland and the use of heavy percussion to denote the African continent. The employment of the simple five-note pentatonic melodic scale tends to suggest bucolic or folk music, while modes with flattened seconds, such as the Phrygian mode and the 'Gypsy' minor scale, are used to provide a clear denotation of the Orient, particularly the Middle East.[9] The use of these clichés is premised upon music as a system of representation, which utilises quite circumscribed codes in order to evoke certain distinctive images and ideas. The rigidity of such music-image coding can be illustrated with recourse to the 'problems' noted by some commentators when James Horner used the Irish bagpipe, the uilleann pipes that are played under the arm and sound far more intimate than the larger warpipes, for the Scottish-set *Braveheart* (1995).

The characteristics of what is thought of as 'Scottish music' are all derived from highland music, neglecting the Scottish lowlands and their traditions, while only aspects that are radically different from the mainstream norm register as distinctive. These tend to include simple pentatonic melodies (following a basic version of the scale and used in most folk music), the 'Scotch snap' (a rapid grace note, highly notable in Strathspey dances), drones (commonly involving a melody often over a single repeated or sustained chord or note), particular timbres, most notably the characteristic bagpipes (or the 'war pipes' as this strident instrument is known to Scots) and to a lesser degree the Clarsach harp, and certain laments and dances. Some of these characteristics are evident in art music's rendering of the Scottish, such as in Hector Berlioz's *Rob Roy Overture* and Max Bruch's *Scottish Fantasia*, both of which also feature the melody from the song *Scots Wha Hae*.[10]

Representing Scotland

I Know Where I'm Going! establishes conventions for representing Scotland, although it appears to be highly conscious of them. Emeric Pressburger stated that the film fulfilled an 'expectation' of Scotland.[11] According to Werner Sollors, modern ethnicity centres on images and objects,[12] therefore imagery and sounds constitute a highly contested area of ethnic production, politics and cultural (and other) repression. Similarly, Colin McArthur points to the representation of Scotland through 'tartan and kailyard' (kilts added to rustic and parsimonious Calvinism).[13] A crucial influence on the international perception of Scotland was 'Ossianism'. In the late eighteenth century, James Macpherson published what were allegedly translations of Scots Gaelic epic poetry, including *Fingal: An Ancient Epic Poem in Six Books* and *Temora: An Ancient Epic Poem in Eight Books*. These were attributed to the poet 'Ossian' and became very popular. Also, in the wake of Ossian, Robert Burns's writings and Sir Walter Scott's epic poems such as *The Lady in the Lake* and novels such as *Waverley* made an important international impact.

This particular brand of Scottish culture became internationally popular, particularly in Germany. Goethe included Ossian's *Songs of Selma* in his book *The Sorrows of Young Werther* (1774), while Johann Gottfried von

Herder looked to Europe's margins to escape the stultifying effect of neo-classical models that had assumed a seemingly universal status. So, while the margins might have been seen, from outside, as having cultural potential, this interest was not extended to the natives of the regions. This is underlined by the irony that at the height of this export of a Romantic vision of the Scottish past, around 1800, the Highland Clearances were taking place. Thus, while cultural exports might have been effective, conditions at home were terrible for those very people being romanticised. Culturally, the reality of Scotland was less important than the symbolism – where it came to represent what the rest of Europe had lost. Working through basic (global, general) terms loses the specificity of the representation of Scotland (and specifically the Hebrides in the case of *I Know Where I'm Going!*), converting the images of Scots into mere ciphers for consumption elsewhere. Colin McArthur notes,

> Clearly an analogous process [to that with Scotland] was at work with regard to the discursive construction of Ireland. *The Maggie* [(1953)] and *The Quiet Man* (1953) are discursively almost identical – an American being humanised and 'feminised' through his encounter with the 'other-worldly' Celtic milieu … Malcolm Chapman in his magisterial study *The Gaelic Vision in Scottish Culture* calls the process 'symbolic appropriation'. The truly terrifying dimension of this, however, is that *homo celticus* will come to live within the discursive categories fashioned by the oppressor to the extent of casting himself in the imposed role in the stories he makes about himself.[14]

The film's symbolic matrix opposes Scottishness and Englishness, but identifies the former with a residual Celtic way and the latter with a more modern, more international, northern European way of life and set of values.[15] This is a figuration of the relationship between the vanquished Celt and the Saxon, between the intuitive tribal and the 'sophisticated' but soul-less societal. This is mediated very directly by the incidental music in *I Know Where I'm Going!* which mixes the two as sonic modes: firstly, the sophisticated Germanic music of drama, moulding the action and integrated with the film; and, secondly, the rural, liminal 'Scots' music that evokes place but is not formally integrated (being more like musical pieces on its own). This division is embodied in the Saxon–English purposefulness ('I know where I'm going!') on the one hand and the Scots stasis (Joan will not reach her wedding on Kiloran) on the other.

Music

Gray's musical style was eclectic rather than distinctive. Tim Bergfelder argues that 'his film scores in Britain were playfully eclectic in style, alternating between haunting romanticism, catchy melodies, and occasional stark modernist touches'.[16] Jan Swynnoe suggests that 'his scores were generally competent and unmemorable. It was not until *Black Narcissus*, the first feature film to be scored by Brian Easdale, that the music in the Archers productions attained the level of other elements of their films.'[17] This is an unfair dismissal. *I Know Where I'm Going!*'s music is impressive, emotionally effective and well integrated. It tends to be illustrative and reactive, doubling images and concepts in dialogue.[18]

The music for the film was conducted by German émigré Walter Goehr. Apart from scoring several film productions, most notably David Lean's *Great Expectations* (1947), Goehr led the Hallé Orchestra in Manchester. Gray remained in 'light music', most famously writing the score for John Huston's *The African Queen* (1951) and mentoring Canadian light music composer Robert Farnon. While most of the score could be attributed to Gray, some sections were written by Goehr. The song 'I Know Where I'm Going!' was arranged by Farnon, while the dance music was by Phil Green and his orchestra.[19]

I Know Where I'm Going! is strongly thematic in musical terms, mixing repeated leitmotifs and incidental music. The film does not have a continuous 'wall-to-wall' score, although it is more akin to Hollywood film music than British, in that it is more 'functional' and tied more closely to image activity and the dynamic requirements of the moment, rather than simply being separately written pieces that are not directly matched to on-screen activity. However, the score includes some notable musical incongruities, such as the blues-style trumpet when Joan takes the taxi, or the plaintive solo harmonica as Ruaridh Mor and Bridie wait for the boat to return from the Corryvreckan whirlpool. The sequence where the boat faces the whirlpool contains no music apart from a small triumphant flourish at the end when the threat vanquishes. According to Tom Gunning, there is a short quote from Jacques Offenbach's *Barcarole* (from *Orpheus in the Underworld* [1881]) when it transpires that Torquil, Joan and Kenny are safe from Corryvreckan.[20] Immediate safety is indicated musically by a short burst of the film's title theme, although subsequently there are two alternated chords reminiscent of the opening of the verse in Offenbach's song but executed at roughly twice the tempo.

The film has seven notable musical themes in its score. The first is the title theme, textbook romantic music associated with the character of Joan. It consists of a main melody with a punctuating supporting countermelody that becomes more active at the end of each main melodic phrase (bearing a similar structure to Max Steiner's principal theme for *Now, Voyager* [1942] or Tchaikovsky's *Romeo and Juliet* overture). The next to appear is the song 'I Know Where I'm Going!', derived from a folk song of Scottish or Scots-Irish origin. In the restaurant, we hear a playful jazz tune, reappearing in different form as incidental music on the train and later when Joan and Torquil talk at neighbouring windows. The train cues the appearance of a kinetic theme that follows dominant conventions for music depicting locomotives, as well as those of Scottishness. Indeed, it sounds very like *Coronation Scot*, a very famous piece of light music depicting a Scottish train, composed by Vivian Ellis in 1948. The similarity between these pieces (both lilting pentatonic string melodies) illustrates the limited range in conventions for aural depiction – in this case of both locomotives and Scottishness.[21]

More specifically location-based music includes a slow *misterioso* theme consisting of two alternated chords and a four-note motif, when Joan arrives at Kiloran in the mist and meets Torquil. Another musical aspect of some mystery constitutes the pentatonic string melody in the 'Scots' style that appears when Moy Castle is on screen and the associated curse is being discussed by the characters. Along similar lines, a theme associated with Kiloran consists of a minor mode run upwards on an oboe, which appears when the location is mentioned. We may never get to see Kiloran, apart from at a great distance, but we constantly hear its musical manifestation!

The film's score consists of small cells of music and melodies that are woven together into a fabric. The succession of musical themes is demonstrated vividly when Joan first meets Torquil at the quayside in the mist. The slow *misterioso* gives way to the theme for Kiloran at the point where she exclaims, 'I intend to spend the night at Kiloran.' The seals then begin their 'singing', another little melody commences (which is related to the jazz melody from the restaurant) and then we return to the *misterioso* accompanied by a faded-in male voiceover reading some of her itinerary as she watches some of its pages float in the water. As the Aberdeen Angus cattle appear and Joan approaches the house, accompaniment involves wordless female choral music derived from the music for the Curse of Moy Castle (slightly reminiscent of some of the more saccharine Disney music). Although the music is near continuous, thematically it seems fragmented into a succession of signifying cells. At times there are some bizarre key shifts. This can be described as a musical 'montage', a diverse succession triggered by action – with its logic sometimes obscured. The music parallels developments in image and dialogue. It is not in a collaborative, organic relationship with these other elements of the film, and any sense of development does not arise from them. The music exhibits a high degree of stasis in that it involves block repetition of themes (such as the *misterioso*), and of small motifs (such as the Kiloran theme), and the use of musical pieces that have their own integrity apart from the film (such as the female voice choir piece that accompanies the cattle in the mist). In much film music, there is a tension between movement and stasis (purposeful scoring and atmospheric 'place' music). Here stasis is paramount, something of a rarity in film scores. In *I Know Where I'm Going!*, this appears to be a reflection of the film's economy of stasis, of blocking progression that is central to the plight of protagonist Joan.

The sequence where Joan first meets Torquil mixes 'place-music' with Germanic dramatic musical styles. The film's establishment of 'liminal space' between two states is not only on screen but also to a degree in the music. The music has a border of sorts between the dramatic, logical (and functional), Germanic music and the magical fantasy (dreamy Scottish aspects – the local colour). Yet the 'place music' is held within the logic of the overall scheme and, perhaps conversely, rendered functional.

The thematic density evident in the music in *I Know Where I'm Going!* derives from 'tight' musical logic – what might be identified as an essentially Germanic aspect in musical terms. This strategy emanates from the logic of musical composition. The result is not Germanic music as serious 'art', but one derived from some aspects close to the heart of Germanic music, namely a sense of the dramatic, the purposeful and the abstract as virtues and ultimate aims of musical production. Ethnic difference is merely subsumed as fleeting detail.

Conclusion

A number of commentators have invoked the mythical Scottish island of Brigadoon in relation to the film. Tony Williams writes that 'the film is no sentimental escapist Brigadoon',[22] while Pam Cook notes that, '[a]s in the case of Brigadoon, the protagonists make a choice to remain in an imaginary past rather than embrace the future, seeking a recovery of lost innocence'.[23] Robert Murphy states: 'The Scottish settings are real enough … but Powell and Pressburger transmute them into a Brigadoon-like Never-never land. The characters … sharing their dim, ruined halls with dogs and eagles, belong as much to Gormenghast as to Scotland.'[24] Yet the film is sensitive in its representation of Scotland, at its conclusion dedicating itself: 'For all true Scotsmen'. There are many non-Scots accents, but attention is given to vocal authenticity, most notably on the bus ride to Tobermory (crediting Malcolm McKellag as Gaelic adviser).[25] The céilidh[26] functions as a set-piece of authenticity for the film (positioning the rest of the film's music in relation to its status), and includes unaccompanied solo singing, although it is in reality a rather polite, professional choir (Sir Hugh Roberton and the Glasgow Orpheus Choir). It also provides the film with its most dramatic moment, the *coup de théâtre* where Torquil proposes to Joan through translating the Gaelic song. In a succession of precise timing, he intones 'You're the maid for me', shoots a meaningful stare at her, she demurs and the pipers burst into a rousing tune.

I Know Where I'm Going!'s music is not related to the specific ethnicity of composer Allan Gray (or Goehr or any other contributor) in any simple sense, but at least partially from convention and from the milieu of Germanic music. Film histories acknowledge the international impact of German Expressionism but have failed to note the influence of Germanic music in the cinema, despite Max Steiner, Franz Waxman and Erich Wolfgang Korngold's key roles in establishing the classical film score in

Hollywood. In *I Know Where I'm Going!* the incidental music alternates Germanic dramatic functionality and the 'Scots' place music. The score not only encompasses both but mediates between the two as musical-philosophical positions. The dramatic music and that associated with the train provide a sense of forward movement. However, with the characters waiting for the boat to Kiloran at the shore, the music tends to be static, dominated by *ostinati*, repeated block themes, and pieces with their own structural integrity, which amounts to music going nowhere.

Notes

1. 'Allan Gray', entry in www.powell-pressburger.org/Reviews/GrayAllan02. His musical collaborator on *I Know Where I'm Going!*, Walter Goehr, had also been a pupil of Schönberg.
2. This was a common divide for composers in Britain, between their film music and their 'serious' concert hall music. Examples include William Walton, Arthur Bliss, Arnold Bax and Alan Rawsthorne, among others.
3. Jan G. Swynnoe, *The Best Years of British Film Music, 1936–1958* (Woodbridge, Suffolk: Boydell Press, 2002), p. 34.
4. Although Richard Middleton states that there is an accrued (and generally accepted) 'meaning' which can be seen as 'interior' to pieces of music. *Studying Popular Music* (Milton Keynes: Open University Press, 1990), p. 10.
5. Robert Mackay, 'Leaving Out the Black Notes: the BBC and "Enemy Music" in the Second World War', *Media History*, vol. 6, no. 1 (2000), p. 79.
6. Kathryn Kalinak, *Settling the Score: Music and the Classical Hollywood Film* (Madison: University of Wisconsin Press, 1992), pp. xv–xvi.
7. See the chapter on ethnic film music in K.J. Donnelly, *The Spectre of Sound: Music in Film and Television* (London: BFI, 2005).
8. Thomas K. Fitzgerald, 'Media, Ethnicity and Identity', in Paddy Scannell, Philip Schlesinger and Colin Sparks (eds.), *Culture and Power: A Media, Culture and Society Reader* (London: Sage, 1992), p. 116.
9. Or historical connections to the East, such as Moorish Spain, European Gypsies or Jews.
10. Mendelssohn's *Hebridean Overture: 'Fingal's Cave'*, op. 26 (1832) was certainly inspired by Ossian's *Fingal*, yet does not utilise stereotypical musical signifiers of Scotland. One of the most popular 'Scots' concert hall pieces was written by a Scottish composer, Hamish MacCunn's *Overture in the Land of the Mountain and the Flood*, op. 3 (1885).
11. 'Certainly *IKWIG* draws on all the available clichés of Scottishness, not least in including a curse *a la* Walter Scott because, as Emeric Pressburger put it, "People will expect it".' Pam Cook, *I Know Where I'm Going!* (London: BFI, 2002), p. 33.
12. See Werner Sollors, *Beyond Ethnicity: Consent and Descent in American Culture* (Oxford: Oxford University Press, 1986).
13. Colin McArthur, 'Scotland and Cinema: the Iniquity of the Fathers', in McArthur (ed.), *Scotch Reels: Scotland in Cinema and Television* (London: BFI, 1982), p. 40.
14. Colin McArthur, 'The Necessity of a Poor Celtic Cinema', in John Hill, Martin McLoone and Paul Hainsworth (eds.), *Border Crossing: Film in Ireland, Britain and Europe* (Belfast: Institute of Irish Studies/BFI, 1994), pp. 118–19.
15. The appearance of the Robinson family's acquired castle inspires an ironic overblown fanfare that is reminiscent of Erich Wolfgang Korngold's music for *The Adventures of Robin Hood* (1938).
16. Tim Bergfelder, 'Allan Gray', in Brian McFarlane (ed.), *Encyclopedia of British Film* (London: BFI/Methuen, 2005), p. 278.

17. Swynnoe, *The Best Years of British Film Music*, p. 179.
18. Powell was interested in 'the composed film', a holistic musical unity. Michael Powell, *A Life in Movies: An Autobiography* (London: Faber and Faber, 2001), p. 181.
19. Alexander Gleason, 'Allan Gray'. www.powell-pressburger.org/Reviews/Gray/Gleason.html
20. See Tom Gunning, 'Going and Not Going, Loving and Not Loving: *I Know Where I'm Going!* and Falling in Love Again', in Ian Christie and Andrew Moor (eds.), *Michael Powell: International Perspectives on an English Filmmaker* (London: BFI, 2005).
21. It is also worth noting the similarity the sequence has to *Night Mail* (1936), which had music by Benjamin Britten.
22. Tony Williams, *Structures of Desire: British Cinema, 1939–1955* (Albany: SUNY Press, 2000), p. 71.
23. Cook, *I Know Where I'm Going!*, p. 72.
24. Robert Murphy, 'Conclusion: A Short History of British Cinema', in Robert Murphy (ed.), *The British Cinema Book* (London: BFI, 1997), p. 259.
25. It is worth noting that two years later, in a Belfast-set British film called *Odd Man Out*, there was a similar ambiguity in its depiction of local colour, as well as in accent and music. For a further discussion of *Odd Man Out*, accent and music, see K.J. Donnelly, *British Film Music and Film Musicals* (London: Palgrave Macmillan, 2007).
26. The céilidh (written céilí in Ireland) is a large informal dance often with boisterous music consisting of jigs and reels. Sometimes recitation and poetry form a part of the proceedings.

Chapter 18

'AN ANIMATED QUEST FOR FREEDOM': MÁTYÁS SEIBER'S SCORE FOR *THE MAGIC CANVAS*

Florian Scheding

Part of the Austro-German musical avant-garde until he was forced into exile, Hungarian-born composer Mátyás Seiber became one of the outstanding figures in British musical life. Despite the significant influences he exerted both as a composer and as a teacher on a younger generation of British composers – Hugh Wood, Peter Racine Fricker, and Don Banks were amongst his pupils – his sometimes puzzlingly eclectic output has thus far received surprisingly little scholarly attention. Most of the few articles published on Seiber highlight his versatility that ranged from progressive modernist avant-garde to incidental music for radio and film and light music such as arrangements for salon orchestra and pop songs. Focusing on his film music alone, Seiber composed the scores for nearly sixty productions, most of them short films (among them propaganda films for the British Ministry of Information), as well as feature films such as the animated adaptation of George Orwell's *Animal Farm* (1954), the war film *A Town like Alice* (1956), and the thriller *Chase a Crooked Shadow* (1957).

Seiber considered himself as part of the avant-garde throughout his life and by and large dissociated himself from the light and incidental music he had to compose out of financial necessity. He was eager to promote avant-garde music in Britain and thus his own 'more "abstract" works',[1] as he once called them. Although in a more stable financial position from the 1940s onwards, particularly after his appointment as a teacher at Morley College, London, in 1942, Seiber never forgot the years of struggle for economic survival, and he continued accepting commissions of light music, and particularly film music, until his death.

The output of numerous émigré composers reveals a shift from serious to lighter music after their flight from Hitler. And while one should avoid constructing too neat analogies between an artist's creative work and their personal circumstances, the fact that many émigrés struggled in their new host countries with significantly different cultural environments undoubtedly exerted an influence.[2] As Theodor Adorno, one of the most prominent exiles of the European intellectual diaspora of the first half of the twentieth century, wrote in the early 1940s: 'Every intellectual in emigration is damaged, without any exception, and he had better recognise this himself, if he does not want to be taught a cruel lesson behind the closely shut doors of his self-esteem.'[3] *Minima Moralia*, the book from which this quote is taken, seeks to highlight the émigrés' viewpoints, experiences, and circumstances against the background of the host society, and to contemplate the native society that expelled them. Subtitled 'Reflexionen aus dem beschädigten Leben' (Reflections of a Damaged Life), *Minima Moralia* addresses the exiles' difficulties in the host country. In being expelled from their native countries, the émigrés were dispossessed of the cultural background that developed their artistic language.[4] In the aftermath of the war, many exiles were ignored in their native countries or accused of having cowardly deserted their country rather than remaining to fight its inner enemies. However uncalled for such an argument is – as leaving Nazi-occupied Europe was for many a matter of life or death – the exiles themselves struggled to justify their leaving. Their thoughts remained with the ones left behind – friends, family, former colleagues and pupils. Although it is true that the phenomenon of exile has been transformed into a potent, even enriching motif of modern culture, 'the achievements of exile', as Edward Said puts it, 'are permanently undermined by the loss of something left behind forever'.[5] The doubt as to whether they could have helped the ones left behind was a cruel one to overcome. In 1937, the exiled psychologist Erich Stern in his extraordinary book *Die Emigration als psychologisches Problem* (Emigration as a Psychological Problem) argued that the larger the quantity of fellow-sufferers, the easier the self-justification of the reasons for escape.[6]

It is against this context of the exile's experience that this chapter wishes to comment on Seiber's film work in Britain, with particular reference to the short *The Magic Canvas* (1947/48). Before addressing this film in more detail, however, it is necessary to sketch Seiber's biography and artistic background. Born on 4 May 1905 into the melting pot of Budapest, Seiber's musical formation mirrors the two-sided outlook of his birthplace. While he belonged to, and was conversant in, the Austro-German musical tradition, his education with Zoltán Kodály, the high representative of a rising Hungarian musical idiom, accounts for his affiliation to Hungary's national school of composition.[7]

Following Béla Bartók, who exerted a strong influence on him, Seiber's early work represents an attempt to combine traditional Western art music with a Hungarian colour. After the proto-fascist regime of Admiral Miklás Horthy seized power in Hungary in 1920, anti-Semitism started to grow rampantly. For Seiber, an assimilated Jew, the hostilities and discrimination became unbearable and in 1925 he left Budapest to settle in Frankfurt am Main, where he accepted a professorship in jazz at the prestigious Hoch Conservatory. This jazz class achieved a tremendous *succès de scandale* and became the first of its kind worldwide. Frankfurt was one of Europe's centres of musical avant-garde at the time, and Seiber enjoyed the stimulating environment of feverish experimentation. He became one of the first composers to employ the so-called dodecaphonic method of composition[8] outside Arnold Schönberg's circle, and moved in the most stimulating artistic and intellectual environments including Max Horkheimer's and Adorno's neo-Marxist Institut für Sozialforschung (Institute for Social Research), whose principal notions he shared.

In 1933, after the Nazis had seized power, Seiber was dismissed in a *Säuberungsverfahren*, an act of ethnic cleansing. The so-called Gesetz zur Wiederherstellung des Berufsbeamtentums (Law for the Restitution of the Professional Civil Service), promulgated on 7 April 1933, that banned all 'non-Aryans' from official positions, was implemented in Hoch's Conservatory over the period when the students where absent for the Easter holiday. Seiber was popular amongst staff and students and the decision to dismiss him and others during the break – including Alfred Auerbach (head of the theatre department), and director Bernhard Sekles – may have been intentional in order to avoid an upheaval amongst students and other staff. After an odyssey that brought Seiber back to Hungary, and briefly to the Soviet Union, he arrived in London in 1935, where he remained until his premature death in 1960.[9]

Besides friends, pupils and colleagues, Seiber left behind his parents and two younger siblings in Hungary. There are no extant private letters between Seiber and his family (and in any case letters between Jewish Hungarians and émigrés in Britain would rarely have reached their addressees during war). One can therefore only imagine the anxieties Seiber endured regarding the well-being of his relatives. Considering the fact that 90 per cent of Hungary's half a million prewar Jewish population was killed during the Second World War in Horthy's Hungary and during the German occupation,[10] it is a miracle that Seiber's family survived the Holocaust. After the war, when contact and visits were again possible, Seiber frequently visited his family and tried to help as best he could. For example, in May 1948 he enquired with the BBC about job opportunities for his brother who apparently sought to emigrate to Britain.[11]

Although Seiber eventually established a reputation for himself as composer, conductor, and one of Britain's best composition teachers, his first years in exile were marked by the struggle for economic survival. For almost a decade, he did not compose any music that could be said to continue the line of his avant-garde compositions of the years in Frankfurt. Instead, he found work as an arranger of light and popular music. To give but two examples, his commissions included an arrangement of Mozart's *Rondo alla turca* from the Piano Sonata, no. 11, K. 331, entitled 'Turkish March' (c.1938), for one accordion, and an arrangement of Gioacchino Rossini's overture to *Il Barbiere di Siviglia* for three accordions with double bass and timpani ad lib (1938). The former professor of one of Europe's outstanding institutions in musical education now authored a multi-volume manual for amateur accordionists. Seiber's ten-part *The Mathis Method of Piano Accordion Playing*, published in London in 1938 by Hohner Concessionaires Ltd under the pseudonym George S. Mathis, is a desperate attempt to draw attention to his abilities as a teacher. Other commissions for incidental and popular music included arrangements and pieces for salon orchestra for Schott, London, such as his own light composition *Evening in the Puszta: Hungarian Fantasy* (c.1936) and an arrangement of Eric Arthur Smith's *Dance of the Midgets* (1939), amongst others.

A considerable part of Seiber's catalogue comprised incidental music for radio, particularly for the BBC, which had become a haven for many émigrés (besides Seiber, Hans Keller and Mosco Carner spring to mind). Although an investigation of the BBC's programming during the first years after the war suggests that Seiber's avant-garde compositions were tacitly ignored, his musicological knowledge and expertise were highly regarded and he was often present as a lecturer on the BBC's European Service, the Home Service, and the Third Programme. In addition to authoring music-related programmes and appearing on air, Seiber composed music for radio plays, performances of which he often also conducted for broadcast. 'The Saga of Grettir the Strong' (broadcast 27 July 1947), 'Johnny Miner' (23 December 1947), 'The Two Wicked Sisters' (19 July 1948), 'The Christmas Child' (19 December 1948), 'The Marvellous Shoemaker's Wife' (2 July 1954) and 'Faust', a series of six programmes with a duration of over six hours altogether (broadcast in November 1949), are some examples of over thirty pieces of incidental music for the BBC.

The compositional approach of all of Seiber's light music contradicted his modernist artistic conviction in the Adornian progressiveness of avant-garde composition. It is clear that by writing and arranging commercial music, he saw himself forced to compromise and make concessions to popular taste. Contrasting sharply with his 'serious' works, all of this incidental music followed the tradition of major-minor tonality that had been challenged after the First World War by composers such as Bartók, Stravinsky and Schönberg, all exiles themselves during and after the Second World War. While Stravinsky's art was to an extent appreciated outside continental Europe, Schönberg and Bartók struggled for recognition. Bartók died in the United States in poverty in 1945, and

Schönberg's compositions, now considered crucial landmarks in the history of Western art music, were often ignored or deemed incomprehensible.

The rejection of formerly accepted, performed and broadcast music had devastating effects on many composers, tantamount to a loss of artistic language, an experience of being silenced. Seiber had to face problems similar to those of Schönberg and Bartók. Written in 1944, his own account of this period is that of a composer who, through economic necessity, is forced to compose what he would not have composed in ideal circumstances:

> Today […] a serious composer often feels that his music is not needed, that his aims in composing run contrary to the wishes of society. So he has the choice either of continuing to express what he wants to express with the danger of isolating himself more and more and ending in a vacuum – or of turning to the composition of music for his living, in which case the writing of serious music often becomes a hobby – a very unhealthy state of affairs.[12]

Despite modest successes Seiber had with his film music – particularly with *Animal Farm* – he loathed the process of composing functional music for film and had great reservations about the film industry. Seiber very rarely voiced his views on the subject, but his bitter complaints about Hollywood's 'cheap propaganda [having] built up a sugary, mysterious picture of the composer most likely showing him sitting picturesquely at the piano'[13] indicates his low opinion of commercial films and the culture industry in general. Not unlike Hanns Eisler and Adorno, he held Hollywood partly responsible for implanting 'glamorous and childish pictures' (like that of the over-romanticised genius effortlessly composing pleasing melodies for the masses) 'in the average mind'.[14] As late as the year of his death, in 1960, he told his brother-in-law, Deszö Keresztury, about his plans to escape to the continent for some creative peace, 'which I need very badly, as I've just had another of those spells of too much filming'.[15]

While the compositional approach in almost all of his film music was geared towards the functional, and marked by expediency, *The Magic Canvas* represented an exception. One of the first animated films produced commercially in Britain, this ten-minute production was directed, written and co-produced (with Joy Batchelor), and co-designed (with Peter Földes) by John Halas. Like Seiber, Halas was a Hungarian-born émigré, and the two collaborated repeatedly, most notably on *Animal Farm*.[16] *The Magic Canvas* differed from other films Seiber worked on in several respects. While in most cases the composition of film music followed the actual filming process, in this case the score was written and recorded first. Indeed, the film follows the music closely enough to speak of a post-synchronisation process. In Seiber's own words, *The Magic Canvas* was 'one of the rare cases when, within the framework of the story, it was possible to create an autonomous musical composition'.[17] Seiber's lighter film music is marked by the late romanticist style with pastiche and leitmotif techniques characteristic of a majority of scores for classic narrative films. In sharp contrast, the music for *The Magic Canvas* was composed in the dodecaphonic style of the Second Viennese school, mostly unknown in Britain at the time. Recorded for the film by the progressive Blech String Quartet with flautist Gareth Morris and Dennis Brain playing the horn part, it would probably have seemed alien or even shockingly experimental to many audiences. Several further differences suggest that the composer distinguished his music for *The Magic Canvas* from his other film scores. Besides the music – the dodecaphonic score for *The Magic Canvas* stands amongst almost sixty tonal film scores – an analysis of the autograph scores reveals clear differences between the handling of incidental and serious musical material.[18]

The significance of this particular score for Seiber becomes evident when one studies surviving documents and other associated materials. In contrast to the avant-garde 'fantasia', as Seiber called his music for *The Magic Canvas*,[19] no sketches, parts, copies or excerpts in the body of his other film music scores exist. For his lighter film scores Seiber often included cues in different colours. If a director did not like a certain melody, Seiber would instruct the musicians to play the red, or green, notes instead. With the 'fantasia', Seiber was much less flexible, and did not alter the score for *The Magic Canvas*. Although he had some of his film scores bound for his private archive, he did not make attempts to have any of these disseminated to a wider public – unlike the 'fantasia', which was published by Milan-based Edizioni Suvini Zerboni in 1956. While the latter score includes the place and time of the composition in the fair copy (the work was written in St Bees and London during August and September 1945), there are no dates in the scores of any other film music.[20]

The 'fantasia' represented one of the first pieces of abstract, serious music Seiber had composed for almost a decade. The fact that the year of the composition coincides with the end of the Second World War and, maybe more importantly, the end of Nazi terror, is in fact more than a coincidence. Seiber hoped that there could be a chance for greater acceptance of modernist avant-garde music and the dodecaphonic style. He was a committed internationalist and passionately believed in the role art could, and should, play for a better future. As he wrote in 1945:

> I hope ... that the danger of isolationism, always inherent in an island community, will be avoided. Such an attitude, which is understandable in war-time, would be a fatal mistake in a post-war world, the greatest hope of which is international collaboration. Music is often said to be an 'international language'; let us hope that when the world is at peace again, music will play its part in helping to promote understanding between nations.[21]

On a personal level, Seiber hoped to regain the international recognition for his music that he had lost with his emigration to London. In Britain, Seiber actively supported the performance of new music, with a particular focus on the modernist music of Bartók and the dodecaphonic style of Schönberg. In 1943, Seiber helped establish the Committee (later, Society) for the Promotion of New Music (spnm), and in 1945 he founded the Dorian Singers, an ensemble dedicated to early (pre-classical) and new (contemporaneous) music. After the war, Seiber, more than other composers living in Britain, tried to establish close links to musical circles on the continent. He frequently visited the newly established, or revived, festivals of avant-garde music, particularly those of the International Society for Contemporary Music (ISCM), whose first Vice-President he became in 1960,[22] and those of Donaueschingen[23] and Darmstadt.[24]

Seen against this context, *The Magic Canvas* represented an attempt to increase the general interest in – and, consequently, understanding of – avant-garde music, attesting to a didactic aim in Seiber's approach. 'It seems to me', he wrote with regards to audiences' interest in the avant-garde style of Bartók and others, 'that people want to know; they want to know more and they want to know better. We must see to it that this healthy curiosity, this interest in musical matters remains with us. [Audiences] should be encouraged to retain and even to deepen that interest.'[25]

The preface to *The Magic Canvas* refers to this idea. Before the opening credits, we read on the screen, 'here is something different from the ordinary cartoon film … Here is something new and exciting. Relax and let your ears and eyes enjoy it'. The musical score, although in one movement, is subdivided into various sections, and the film can be separated accordingly into several segments. Following the credits, in the prologue of the film we see an opening eye. The camera zooms into the pupil, where the whole film takes place. Synchronised with the string quartet's atmospheric and meditative *lento* passage, various shapes appear, move, fuse to create new shapes, until, with the entry of the horn's warm tone (bar 29), a human body emerges. As the musical movement accelerates, the figure moves more and more agitatedly, until it breaks into two. While one of the figures, keeping its human shape and associated musically to the horn, is suddenly enclosed behind bars, the other one, represented musically by the flute, escapes, flying skywards in the shape of a bird (bar 45). The rest of the film follows the flight of the bird.

In the following sequence (*allegro con brio*, bar 49), storm clouds gather and a terrifying storm commences. Two black hands clasp and darken the canvas until everything is covered in black. Accompanied by breathlessly short successive *fugato* motives in the music (*fugato* translates as 'escape'), the bird re-emerges and continues its flight from the storm. Although the human figure is hidden from the screen, its fate is suggested musically. Image and sound thus interweave the flight of the bird with the fate of its imprisoned other. In a ferocious passage (bars 100–109), the horn's *fortissimo* arpeggios imply the imprisoned human's desperate fight for survival, until the cacophonic and persistently monotonous chords of the strings, as if intoning a marching army, further increase their force to overpower the prisoner (*più forte*, bars 106–109). Suddenly, his cries die down (bar 109). Having first strengthened the horn's arpeggios with complementary lines (bars 103-109), the flute now repeats the horn's motif in a downward spiral (*diminuendo* and *ritardando*) and increasingly fragmented motion (bars 110 onwards).

Finally, the bird succeeds in escaping, but is beaten down to the ground, where it lies still and exhausted. The storm abates in the background, the sun rises, flowers blossom, and the bird revives (note the word *ravvivando*, 'reviving', in bar 130 in the score), until, accompanied by a quasi-recitativo *andantino pastorale* section in the music, it begins to recover at the revival of nature. All that remains from the imprisoned human is a short *piano* call in the horn, which, not referred to in the moving image, resounds as if from a distant memory (bars 152–156; note the combination of the *sospirando* ['sighing'] motif with the very Hungarian accent on the strong beat).

The next section of the film stands out somewhat oddly and, with its sudden joyous mood (*giocoso* in the score in bar 161), represents an abrupt shift in musical register. Having escaped the thunderstorm, the bird enjoys a playful ballet with waves and white sails. This sequence quite openly recalls Disney's *Fantasia* (1940) and its use of Stravinsky's ballet *The Rite of Spring*. Music and movements are synchronised in a bold manner and, while the drawings are more concretely figurative than in the rest of the film, the *scherzando* passage is harmonically less complex than the score's other sections. As if mocking British musical life at the time of his arrival in London,[26] Seiber suddenly avoids the dodecaphonic (or any other non-tonal avant-garde) principle and replaces it by an initially blatant tonality (note the *glissando* major chords in the cello and the parallel motifs in the upper strings in bars 160 and following) that is increasingly extended and fragmented, but never abandoned. The bird/flute sings along in uninspired and musically unsubstantial arpeggios. Might this section be seen as a concession to popular taste?

Having regained its strength, the bird subsequently flies back through the dissolving storm clouds, then down, earthwards, in search of its imprisoned other. Finally, it finds the lifeless body of its double. The bars disappear, and, carrying the human body, the bird flies up into the sky and disappears in the distance. The music recapitulates the first slow *lento* section of the score. Compared to the sombre atmosphere of the first *lento*, this section is remarkably transparent and high-pitched. Thus replacing the 'brooding mood as it appeared originally',[27] as Seiber put it, the piece – and therefore the film – is marked by a movement from darkness to light, an almost transcendental transfiguration, until the solo violin, *pianissimo* and in the highest register, fades away into the distance with the two figures. The focus zooms out of the pupil, and, with the closing eye, the film ends.

In addition to the insights an analysis of the music can reveal, *The Magic Canvas* opens up to, and invites, psychological and symbolic analysis. The opening and closing eye that frames the narrative suggests an eyewitness account. Is this the eye of the émigré we are looking into and behind which we discover the tale of their hardship? The flight of the bird which, persecuted by the horrific grip of an unnamed force storming across the lands and darkening all that it encounters, finally succeeds in escaping and, although exhausted, manages to regain strength on the shores of a free country across the sea, may represent the odyssey of many émigrés fleeing fascism. Additionally, the white bird, or the dove, an emblem of peace and a Christian representation of the Holy Spirit and the soul going to heaven, imposes itself upon the viewer. The bird of peace cannot find peace at home.

The human figure, left behind in imprisonment, appears to have an even stronger effect in this context. Yearning to be reunited, and, maybe, driven by guilt for having abandoned its other captive self, the bird returns, only to find the lifeless body. This image can be seen to represent the experience of many exiles in the immediate aftermath of the war, of learning that their closest friends and relatives had been murdered in the prisons and concentration camps of the Nazis. All that remains for the bird/exiles is to bury the dead, collect the pieces of what was dear to them and hope that they may be elevated to a higher level. The soul of the victim finds peace in the afterlife; the remains of a shattered culture are liberated from their oppression and carried forward by those who had escaped, by the exiles. Bertolt Brecht, in exile from 1933 until he remigrated to East Berlin in 1947, summed up the nightmarish feelings of guilt that haunted exiles in his poem 'Ich, der Überlebende' (I, the survivor):

Ich weiß natürlich: einzig durch Glück
Habe ich so viele Freunde überlebt. Aber heute Nacht im Traum
Hörte ich diese Freunde von mir sagen: "Die Stärkeren überleben"
Und ich haßte mich.

(I know of course: only by luck
Have I survived so many friends. But last night, dreaming,
I heard these friends of mine say: 'The stronger ones survive'
And I hated myself).[28]

In summary, if such a reading is a sensible and permissible one, and I believe it is, *The Magic Canvas* stands symbolically for the main aspects of the hardship of exile from Nazi Europe.

Unfortunately, only very few materials survive of the production process to allow for a definitive assessment of how Halas and Seiber themselves envisaged *The Magic Canvas* and its aims and intentions.

Besides the uncommented autograph score and further material amongst Seiber's papers, only a title cell and a storyboard are available.[29] Encompassing six pages with a total of fifty images and one additional page with further sketches, the storyboard comes without any explanatory text (indeed, the only word is the word 'end' on the last image). Furthermore, very few people were involved in the making of the film – Seiber, Halas, Peter Földes and Wally Crook – and all four of them worked too closely together to necessitate correspondence. Apart from meetings at the Halas & Batchelor premises in 10A Soho Square in London's West End, Seiber and Halas, who were good friends, will probably have discussed the film in private.

In their publications, both refrained from discussing the film other than on a technical level, never going beyond a mere summary of the narrative.[30] The preface of the film speaks of 'a ballet in which the dancers symbolise two aspects of man – one part of him soars up bravely like a bird...the other stays imprisoned and waits to be set free'; and a Halas & Batchelor press release refers to *The Magic Canvas* as 'an animated quest for freedom'[31] – a particularly poignant comment in the tense political context of 1948 that saw the beginning of the Cold War and Hungary's isolation from the West behind Stalin's Iron Curtain.[32] Despite Seiber's complaint that 'some of the synchronisation of movements to music was not quite perfect',[33] however, it is apparent that they held the film in high esteem. After numerous propaganda films and sponsored productions, increased financial security after the war made *The Magic Canvas* one of the first experimental and more personal projects at the Halas & Batchelor studio. It was the only film music Seiber decided to publish, and John Halas selected it to be screened alongside three other shorts and *Animal Farm* in a Seiber memorial at the National Film Theatre on 30 April 1961.

Likewise, one can only speculate about the extent to which contemporary viewers might have interpreted *The Magic Canvas*. The few reviews of the film at the time refrain from an analysis of the narrative and include only very brief and limited references to Seiber's contribution. One critic mentions the 'distinctive musical score' and summarises the film as an 'artistically designed production, attractive in colour and animation'.[34] Another reviewer calls *The Magic Canvas* 'a bold attempt at advanced impressionist cinema art' that is suitable 'for better informed patrons only'.[35] Although the film was selected for, and screened at, the 1950 festivals in Cannes and Edinburgh, it did not have a huge impact on British, or international, filmmaking, and is hardly mentioned in secondary literature and academic publications. Unlike quite a few other, more accessible, productions produced by Halas & Batchelor with film music by Seiber,[36] *The Magic Canvas* did not receive any awards and was not distributed widely. The one-off screening as supporting film for Jean Cocteau's *Orphée* (1949) at the 4th Midnight Matinee Film Performance (arranged by the Birmingham Film Society and held at the Futurist

Cinema in Birmingham in early October 1951) is among its very rare public performances. Today, *The Magic Canvas* is awaiting its rediscovery as an unusual piece of émigré filmmaking in Britain – or, for that matter, as an exciting film in its own right.

Notes

1. Mátyás Seiber: 'Folk Music and the Contemporary Composer', *Recorded Folk Music* 2, July–August 1959, p. 9.
2. While the fact that enforced migration affects immensely the biographies and personal lives of individuals (sometimes tragically, sometimes triumphantly so) is undisputed, investigating exile's impact on the artistic output of these very individuals is less straightforward. Thus far, (musicological) exile studies has only very rarely discussed the extent to which the context of exile informs and shapes artistic production as a separate entity from biographic fates, and how tensions between the two, should they arise, can be captured by analysis.
3. 'Jeder Intellektuelle in der Emigration, ohne alle Ausnahme, ist beschädigt und er tut gut daran, es selber zu erkennen, wenn er nicht hinter den dicht geschlossenen Türen seiner Selbstachtung grausam darüber belehrt werden will'. Theodor Adorno, *Minima Moralia: Reflexionen aus dem beschädigten Leben* (Frankfurt: Suhrkamp, 1980), p. 35. My translation.
4. Ibid.
5. Edward Said, 'Reflections on Exile', in Said, *Reflections on Exile and Other Essays* (Cambridge, Mass.: Harvard University Press, 2002), p. 173.
6. Erich Stern, *Die Emigration als psychologisches Problem*, published at his own expense in Bologne-sur-Seine, 1937.
7. Seiber studied composition with Kodály and violoncello with Adolf Schiffer at Budapest's Ferenc Liszt Conservatory.
8. Pioneered mainly by Arnold Schönberg around the late 1910s, dodecaphony, or twelve-tone technique, is based on a series of the twelve notes of the Western musical scale related one to another. The method was linked initially to the so-called Second Viennese School (particularly Alban Berg, Anton Webern, Hanns Eisler, and Schönberg himself). In the 1950s, it became one of the prevalent methods of avant-garde composition. Composers such as Luciano Berio, Pierre Boulez and Luigi Dallapiccola extended it, serialising not only pitch, but also other musical elements, such as duration, dynamics and method of attack.
9. South African universities had invited Seiber as a guest lecturer. During this visit Seiber died in a car crash in the Kruger National Park on 24 September 1960. Zoltán Kodály, György Ligeti, and Seiber pupil Peter Racine Fricker dedicated compositions to Seiber's memory.
10. This information is taken from Paul Tabori, *The Anatomy of Exile* (London: Harrap, 1972), p. 252.
11. The BBC rejected Seiber's request because 'the nationality question might make great difficulty for [Seiber's brother] with regard to employment at the BBC'. See file RCONT1/Matyas SEIBER/ARTISTS/File 1: 1941–1951 with (unpublished) correspondence between Seiber and the BBC, held at the BBC Written Archives Centre in Caversham.
12. Seiber, 'Mozart and Light Music', *The Listener*, 15 June 1944, p. 673.
13. Seiber, 'English Musical Life: A Symposium', *Tempo* [London] 11, 1945, p. 5.
14. Ibid.
15. A letter from Seiber, quoted without documentation in Dezsö Keresztury, 'Mátyás Seiber (An Obituary)', *New Hungarian Quarterly*, vol. 2, no. 2, April–June 1961, p. 171.
16. Seven years Seiber's junior, he was born Janos Halász on 16 April 1912 in Budapest. After experimenting with animation in his native city, he moved to Paris before he

migrated to London in 1936. Here, Halász pursued various projects, which had him return briefly to his native country. Just before the Second World War, he adopted the anglicised spelling of his name, John Halas, and finally settled in Britain. In 1940, he founded the production company Halas & Batchelor, in partnership with the British animator and scriptwriter Joy Batchelor (22 May 1914–14 May 1991) whom he later married. The company was immensely successful almost immediately (particularly with short propaganda films made during the war for the British government), but had a relatively small output of purely artistic films – the most noticeable exception being *The Magic Canvas*. Whether in spite of, or because of, that, it 'became the longest lasting production company in animated film in Western Europe and one of the most prestigious in the world' (Giannalberto Bendazzi, *Cartoons: One Hundred Years of Cinema Animation* (Bloomington and Indianapolis: Indiana University Press, 1994), pp. 153–54.

17. Seiber, 'The Composition and Recording of Music for Animated Films', in John Halas and Roger Manvell (eds.), *The Technique of Film Animation* (London and New York: Focal Press, 1959), p. 249.

18. The British Library holds twenty bound volumes of Seiber's film music, mostly in manuscript form (call marks add. 62841 – add. 62860).

19. A carefully handwritten fair copy, a photocopy, and autograph parts exist in his meticulously organised papers (British Library manuscript add. 62803).

20. Unfortunately for the historian researching Seiber's large body of incidental film music, the surviving documents do not mention the name of the commissioning body, producer or producing company, or director of the film the music was composed for, or the date, place or occasion on which the film received its premiere.

21. Seiber: 'English Musical Life: A Symposium', p. 6.

22. The International Society for Contemporary Music (ISCM) was founded in Salzburg in 1922 as an international network of composers. It was (and still is) devoted to the promotion and presentation of contemporary music. Except for an interruption between 1943 to 1945, the festivals are held annually and hosted by one of the ISCM's national sections.

23. The annual Donaueschinger Musiktage were founded in 1921 as a festival dedicated to premieres of contemporary music. It is the oldest festival of its kind worldwide. Prewar premieres included progressive works by Hindemith, Berg, Schönberg and Webern. Suspended in Nazi Germany, the festival was revived in 1950 and attracted avant-garde composers like Pierre Boulez, Olivier Messiaen, and Hans Werner Henze.

24. Founded in 1946, the first forum for contemporary music in Germany after the Second World War, the so-called *Internationale Ferienkurse für Neue Musik Darmstadt* was frequently visited by internationally renowned figures like Theodor Adorno, René Leibowitz, Heinz-Klaus Metzger and Carl Dahlhaus, and composers including Varèse, Messiaen, Krenek, Cage, Stockhausen, Boulez and Nono, amongst others. Organised by the Internationales Musikinstitut Darmstadt, the festival initially aimed to reintroduce the 'degenerate' music of composers such as Schönberg, Berg, Webern and Bartók, and quickly established itself as one of the world's most prestigious centres for musical avant-garde.

25. Seiber, 'English Musical Life: A Symposium', p. 5.

26. Brahms allegedly called Britain 'das Land ohne Musik' ('the land without music'), a statement that still resounded strongly in the ears of many continental European composers and musicians who considered Britain musically inferior to Austria, Germany and France, for example.

27. Seiber, 'The Composition and Recording of Music for Animated Films', p. 249.

28. Written in May or April 1942, it is the penultimate of fifteen poems included in *Gedichte im Exil* [Poems in Exile]; I have used the version edited by Werner Hecht, Jan Knopf, Werner Mittenzwei and Klaus-Detlef Müller, *Bertolt Brecht: Werke 12* (Berlin and Weimar: Aufbau; Frankfurt: Suhrkamp, 1988), p. 125. My translation.

29. Held at the Animation Research Centre (ARC) at The Surrey Institute of Art & Design, University College, in Farnham, Surrey. I am indebted to the staff of the archive for their friendly and helpful assistance.
30. See particularly Halas and Manvell (eds.), *The Technique of Film Animation*.
31. Held at the ARC without call mark.
32. Seiber and Halas's later collaboration, the feature *Animal Farm* (1954), was promoted as an explicitly anti-communist parable: 'Rumours persist that the film was funded by a CIA covert operation, but Halas insisted that it was humanist and anti-totalitarian rather than anti-communist.' Paul Wells, 'Halas and Batchelor', Reference Guide to British and Irish Film Directors, http://www.screenonline.org.uk/people/id/581849/index.html
33. Seiber, 'The Composition and Recording of Music for Animated Films', p. 249.
34. *The Cinema and Today's Cinema*, 16 October 1950, p. 3.
35. *The Cinema*, 6 June 1951, p. 16.
36. These are the shorts: *Modern Guide to Health* (1st prize at the 1947 Brussels film festival), *As Old as the Hills* (1st prize, Venice, 1950), *We've Come a Long Way* (2nd prize, Venice, 1951), *Down a Long Way* (Diploma of Merit, Venice, 1955), *To Your Health* (Diploma of Merit in Edinburgh, 1956, 1st prize in Cork, 1957, and Golden Reel Award in Chicago, 1958), and *Speed the Plough* (Certificate of Merit, Cork, 1957). *Animal Farm* was awarded a Diploma of Merit at the 1956 Durban festival.

NOTES ON CONTRIBUTORS

Tim Bergfelder is Professor in Film at the University of Southampton. He is the author of *International Adventures. Popular German Cinema and European Co-Productions in the 1960s* (Berghahn, 2005). His co-edited or co-authored volumes include *The German Cinema Book* (BFI, 2002), *The Titanic in Myth and Memory. Representations in Visual and Literary Culture* (I.B. Tauris, 2004) and *Film Architecture and the Transnational Imagination* (Amsterdam University Press, 2007).

Geoff Brown is a music and film critic for *The Times*. Publications include *Directors in British and Irish Cinema* (BFI, 2006; associate editor), *Der Produzent: Michael Balcon und der englische Film* (Volker Spiess, 1981), *Launder and Gilliat* (BFI, 1977). He contributed to *All Our Yesterdays* (BFI, 1986), *The Unknown 1930s* (I.B.Tauris, 1998), and *Tonfilmfrieden/Tonfilmkrieg* (edition text+kritik, 2004). Recent research areas are émigrés and British film music.

Christian Cargnelli has been working on the project 'German-speaking émigrés in British cinema, 1925–1950' at the University of Southampton, funded by the Arts and Humanities Research Council (AHRC). His co-edited volumes include *Aufbruch ins Ungewisse. Österreichische Filmschaffende in der Emigration vor 1945* (Wespennest, 1993), *Schatten. Exil. Europäische Emigranten im Film noir* (PVS, 1997) and *Carl Mayer, Scenar[t]ist* (SYNEMA, 2003). He is the editor of *Gustav Machaty – Ein Filmregisseur zwischen Prag und Hollywood* (SYNEMA, 2005).

K.J. Donnelly is Reader in Film Studies at the University of Southampton. His research is on film and television music, as well as British and Irish cinema. He is the author of *Pop Music in British Cinema* (BFI, 2001), *The Spectre of Sound: Music in Film and Television* (BFI, 2005), and *British Film Music and Film Musicals* (Palgrave, 2007). He is the editor of *Film Music: Critical Approaches* (Edinburgh University Press, 2001).

Laurie N. Ede is a Principal Lecturer in Film at the University of Portsmouth. He has written extensively on issues of film aesthetics, including recent articles on production design for *Screen* and the *Journal of British Cinema and Television*. He is currently completing a history of British film design for publication in 2008.

Gerd Gemünden is the Ted and Helen Geisel Third Century Professor in the Humanities at Dartmouth College. He is the author of *Framed Visions: Popular Culture, Americanization, and the Contemporary German and Austrian Imagination* (University of Michigan Press, 1998) and *A Foreign Affair: Billy Wilder's American Films* (Berghahn, 2008). He is co-editor (with Mary Desjardins) of *Dietrich Icon* (Duke University Press, 2007).

Tobias Hochscherf is a lecturer in film and television studies at Northumbria University. He has published articles on the role of German-speaking émigrés in the British film industry from the late 1920s to the end of the Second World War. His research interests include Second World War propaganda films and contemporary German cinema. He is associate editor of the Controversial Films section of the journal *Film & History*.

Brigitte Mayr is the Scientific Secretary of SYNEMA – Society for Film & Media (Vienna), an interdisciplinary platform acting as intermediary between theory and practice, art and science of audio-visual media. Her co-edited volumes include *Carl Mayer, Scenar[t]ist* (SYNEMA, 2003), *Peter Lorre. Ein Fremder im Paradies* (Zsolnay, 2004), *Film Denken/Thinking Film – Film & Philosophy* (SYNEMA, 2005) and *Wolf Suschitzky Photos* (SYNEMA, 2006).

Lawrence Napper gained his PhD from the University of East Anglia in 2001 where he taught for a number of years. His research interests are in British cinema and popular culture in the early twentieth century. He is the author of *British Cinema and the Middlebrow in the Interwar Years* (University of Exeter Press, 2008). He currently lives and works in London.

Michael Omasta is the film editor of the Viennese weekly *Falter*, and has published prolifically in the area of film history. He is a board member of SYNEMA – Society for Film & Media (Vienna), and a co-editor of several SYNEMA publications, including *Carl Mayer, Scenar[t]ist* (2003), *Claire Denis. Trouble Every Day* (2005), *John Cook – Viennese by Choice, Filmemacher von Beruf* (2006) and *Wolf Suschitzky Photos* (2006).

Kelly Robinson wrote her PhD thesis at the University of Southampton on the influence of German cinematographers on British filmmaking in the 1920s and 1930s. Her research was part of the Arts and Humanities Research Council (AHRC)-funded project 'German-speaking émigrés in British cinema, 1925–1950'. She has lectured in film studies at the University of East London and the University of Southampton.

Amy Sargeant is Reader in Film at the University of Warwick. She has written widely on British silent and sound cinema, and British and European émigrés and exchange, being the co-editor of *British Historical Cinema* (Routledge, 2002) and author of *British Cinema: A Critical History*

(BFI, 2005). Qualified as an architect, she is especially interested in aspects of design in film.

Florian Scheding is a PhD student at Royal Holloway, University of London. His research interests include music in the Weimar republic and by exiled composers. He has published on Mátyás Seiber in the encyclopaedias *Die Musik in Geschichte und Gegenwart* (Metzler & Bärenreiter, 2006) and *Komponisten der Gegenwart* (edition text+kritik, 2006), and on Menuhin and Furtwängler's 1947 Berlin concert in the online journal *Euphonia* (2004).

Sarah Street is Professor of Film at the University of Bristol. Her publications include *British National Cinema* (Routledge, 1997), *British Cinema in Documents* (Routledge, 2000), *European Cinema* (Palgrave, 2000, co-edited with Jill Forbes), *Costume and Cinema* (Wallflower, 2001), *Transatlantic Crossings: British Feature Films in the USA* (Continuum, 2002), *The Titanic in Myth and Memory* (I.B. Tauris, 2004, co-edited with Tim Bergfelder), *Black Narcissus* (I.B. Tauris, 2005), and *Film Architecture and the Transnational Imagination* (with Tim Bergfelder and Sue Harris, Amsterdam University Press, 2007).

Chris Wahl is a researcher at the Institute of Media Studies, Ruhr University Bochum. His main research interests include the impact of language(s) on fiction films; international strategies of filmmaking, distribution and exhibition in the 1930s; film aesthetics: slow motion and double exposure; local cinema history; relations between film and theatre. He is the author of *Das Sprechen des Spielfilms* (WVT, 2005).

Michael Williams is Senior Lecturer in Film Studies at the University of Southampton. He is the author of *Ivor Novello: Screen Idol* (BFI, 2003) and co-editor (with Michael Hammond) of *'Goodbye to All That': British Silent Cinema and the Great War* (University of Exeter Press, 2008). Other publications include chapters on queer readings of the heritage film in *Screen Method: Comparative Readings in Screen Studies* (Wallflower Press, 2006) and landscape and sexuality in *Queer British Cinema* (Routledge, 2006).

Barbara Ziereis is a historian working at the Haus der Geschichte Baden-Württemberg, Stuttgart. Her special interests are history and fiction film. An abridged version of her thesis was published as 'Kriegsgeschichte im Spielfilmformat. Der Erste Weltkrieg im Tonspielfilm der Weimarer Republik', in *Krieg und Militär im Film des 20. Jahrhunderts* (Oldenburg, 2003). She also wrote 'Bausparen im Kino', in *Zuteilungsreif. Bausparergeschichten aus dem Südwesten* (Haus der Geschichte Baden-Württemberg, 2005).

BIBLIOGRAPHY

Adorno, Theodor W. 1978. *Minima Moralia: Reflections from Damaged Life* [Minima Moralia. Reflexionen aus dem beschädigten Leben, 1950], trans. E.F.N. Jephcott. New York: Verso.

Affron, Charles and Mirella Affron. 1995. *Sets in Motion: Art Direction and Film Narrative*. New Brunswick, New Jersey: Rutgers University Press.

Aldgate, Anthony and Jeffrey Richards. 1999. *Best of British: Cinema and Society from 1930 to the Present*. London and New York: I.B. Tauris.

Allen, Jerry C. 1993. *Conrad Veidt: From Caligari to California*. Pacific Grove, Cal.: Boxwood.

Asper, Helmut G. 2002. *'Etwas Besseres als den Tod ...' Filmexil in Hollywood. Porträts, Filme, Dokumente*. Marburg: Schüren.

———. 2005. *Filmexilanten im Universal Studio, 1933–1960*. Berlin: Bertz und Fischer.

Aspinall, Sue and Robert Murphy, eds. 1983. *BFI Dossier, no. 18: Gainsborough Melodrama*. London: BFI.

Babington, Bruce, ed. 2001. *British Stars and Stardom – from Alma Taylor to Sean Connery*. Manchester: Manchester University Press.

Balázs, Béla. 1948. *Filmkultúra. A film müvészetfilozófiaja*. Budapest: Szikra.

Balcon, Michael. 1969. *Michael Balcon Presents ... A Lifetime in Films*. London: Hutchinson.

Banks, Leslie. 1949. *The Elstree Story*. London: Clerke and Cockeran.

Barr, Charles. 1977. *Ealing Studios*. London: Cameron & Taylor.

———, ed. 1986. *All Our Yesterdays. 90 Years of British Cinema*. London: BFI.

———. 1999. *English Hitchcock*. Moffat: Cameron & Hollis.

Baxter, John. 1976. *The Hollywood Exiles*. New York: Taplinger, 1976.

Belach, Helga and Wolfgang Jacobsen, eds. 1990. *Richard Oswald. Regisseur und Produzent*. Munich: edition text+kritik.

Bemmann, Helga. 1989. *In mein' Verein bin ich hineingetreten: Kurt Tucholsky als Chanson- und Liederdichter*. Berlin: Lied der Zeit.

Bendazzi, Giannalberto. 1994. *Cartoons: One Hundred Years of Cinema Animation*. Bloomington and Indianapolis: Indiana University Press.

Benedetta, Mary. 1936. *The Street Markets of London*. London: John Miles.

Bergfelder, Tim. 2005. *International Adventures. German Popular Cinema and European Co-Productions in the 1960s*. Oxford and New York: Berghahn.

———. 2005. 'National, Transnational, or Supranational Cinema? Rethinking European Film Studies', *Media, Culture and Society* 27(3): 315–31.

———, Erica Carter and Deniz Göktürk, eds. 2002. *The German Cinema Book*. London: BFI.

———— and Sarah Street, eds. 2004. *The Titanic in Myth and Memory. Representations in Visual and Literary Culture.* London and New York: I.B. Tauris.

————, Sue Harris and Sarah Street. 2007. *Film Architecture and the Transnational Imagination. European Set Design in the 1930s.* Amsterdam: Amsterdam University Press.

Berghaus, Günter, ed. 1989. *Theatre and Film in Exile. German Artists in Britain, 1933–1945.* Oxford, New York, and Munich: Berg.

Bergner, Elisabeth. 1978. *Bewundert viel und viel gescholten. Unordentliche Erinnerungen.* Munich: C. Bertelsmann.

Bergonzi, Bernard. 1978. *Reading the Thirties: Texts and Contexts.* London: Macmillan.

Berry, Dave. 1996. *Wales and Cinema – The First Hundred Years.* University of Wales Press.

Betjeman, John. 1938. *An Oxford University Chest.* London: John Miles.

Bhabha, Homi K., ed. 1990. *Nation and Narration.* London: Routledge.

Blake, David, ed. 1995. *Hanns Eisler – A Miscellany.* Luxembourg: Harwood Academic Publishers.

Blomfield, Reginald. 1934. *Modernismus.* London: Macmillan.

Bock, Hans-Michael, ed. 1984–. *CineGraph. Lexikon zum deutschsprachigen Film.* Munich: edition text+kritik.

———— and Claudia Lenssen, eds. 1991. *Joe May. Regisseur und Produzent.* Munich: edition text+kritik.

———— and Michael Töteberg, eds. 1992. *Das Ufa-Buch.* Frankfurt am Main: Zweitausendeins.

Borchardt-Hume, Achim, ed. 2006. *Albers and Moholy-Nagy: from Bauhaus to the New World.* London: Tate Publishing.

Brecht, Bertolt. 1973. *Arbeitsjournal 1938 bis 1955.* Frankfurt am Main: Suhrkamp.

————. 1988. *Werke 12.* Ed. Werner Hecht, Jan Knopf, Werner Mittenzwei and Klaus-Detlef Müller. Berlin and Weimar: Aufbau/Frankfurt am Main: Suhrkamp.

Bretschneider, Jürgen, ed. 1992. *Ewald André Dupont. Autor und Regisseur.* Munich: edition text+kritik.

Brown, Geoff. 1981. *Der Produzent – Michael Balcon und der englische Film.* Berlin: Volker Spiess.

————. 1984. *Michael Balcon: The Pursuit of British Cinema.* New York: The Museum of Modern Art.

Bruno, Giuliana. 2002. *Atlas of Emotion: Journeys in Art, Architecture and Film.* New York: Verso.

Bucher, Felix. 1970. *Germany: Screen series.* London: A. Zwemmer.

Burrows, Jon. 2003. *Legitimate Cinema. Theatre Stars in Silent British Films, 1908–1918.* Exeter: Exeter University Press.

Burton, Alan and Laraine Porter, eds. 2000. *Pimple, Pranks and Pratfalls. British Film Comedy Before 1930.* Trowbridge: Flicks Books.

————, Tim O'Sullivan and Paul Wells, eds. 2000. *The Family Way. The Boulting Brothers and Postwar British Film Culture.* Trowbridge: Flicks Books.

Cardiff, Jack. 1996. *Magic Hour: The Life of a Cameraman.* London: Faber and Faber.

Cargnelli, Christian, ed. 2005. *Gustav Machaty. Ein Filmregisseur zwischen Prag und Hollywood.* Vienna: Synema.

———— and Michael Omasta, eds. 1993. *Aufbruch ins Ungewisse. Österreichische Filmschaffende in der Emigration vor 1945.* Vienna: Wespennest.

—— and Michael Omasta, eds. 1997. *Schatten. Exil. Europäische Emigranten im Film noir*. Vienna: PVS.

Carrick, Edward. 1941. *Designing for Films*. London and New York: The Studio Publications.

——. 1948. *Art and Design in the British Film*. London: Dennis Dobson.

Carter, Erica. 2004. *Dietrich's Ghosts. The Sublime and the Beautiful in Third Reich Film*. London: BFI.

Caruth, Cathy, ed. 1995. *Trauma: Explorations in Memory*. Baltimore and London: Johns Hopkins University Press.

Chapman, James. 2005. '"The true business of the British movie"? *A Matter of Life and Death* and British Film Culture', *Screen* 46(1): 33–49.

Christie, Ian. 1985. *Arrows of Desire. The Films of Michael Powell and Emeric Pressburger*. London: Waterstone.

—— and Andrew Moor, eds. 2005. *Michael Powell. International Perspectives on an English Film-Maker*. London: BFI.

Claus, Horst and Anne Jäckel. 2005. '*Der Kongreß tanzt* revisited', *CINEMA & Cie*. 6: 76–95.

——. 2005. 'MLVs in a changing political climate', *CINEMA & Cie*. 7: 48–78.

Coe, Peter and Malcolm Reading. 1981. *Lubetkin and Tecton: Architecture and Social Commitment*. London: The Arts Council of Great Britain.

Cook, Pam. 1996. *Fashioning the Nation. Costume and Identity in British Cinema*. London: BFI.

——, ed. 1997. *Gainsborough Pictures*. London: Cassell.

——. 2002. *I Know Where I'm Going!* London: BFI.

——. 2005. *Screening the Past: Memory and Nostalgia in Cinema*. London: Routledge.

——, ed. 2007. *The Cinema Book*. 3rd edn. London: BFI.

Crowe, Cameron. 1999. *Conversations with Wilder*. New York: Alfred Knopf.

Cull, Nicholas John. 1995. *Selling War: The British Propaganda Campaign Against American 'Neutrality' in World War II*. New York and Oxford: Oxford University Press.

Danischewsky, Monja, ed. 1947. *Michael Balcon's 25 Years in Films*. London: World Film Publications.

——. 1966. *White Russian – Red Face*. London: Victor Gollancz.

Dittrich van Weringh, Kathinka. 1987. *Der niederländische Spielfilm der dreißiger Jahre und die deutsche Filmemigration*. Amsterdam: Rodopi.

Donald, James, Anne Friedberg and Laura Marcus, eds. 1998. *Close Up 1927–1933. Cinema and Modernism*. London: Cassell.

Donnelly, K.J. 2005. *The Spectre of Sound: Music in Film and Television*. London: BFI.

——. 2007. *British Film Music and Film Musicals*. London: Palgrave Macmillan.

Dove, Richard, ed. 2005. '*Totally un-English?': Britain's Internment of 'Enemy Aliens' in Two World Wars*. Amsterdam and New York: Rodopi.

Drazin, Charles. 2002. *Korda: The Definitive Biography*. London: Sidgwick & Jackson.

Droste, Magdalena. 1990. *Bauhaus 1919–1933*. Berlin: Bauhaus-Archiv/Taschen.

Eisner, Lotte H. 1994. *The Haunted Screen. Expressionism in the German Cinema and the Influence of Max Reinhardt* [*L'écran démoniaque*, 1952]. Berkeley, Los Angeles, and Oxford: University of California Press.

Elsaesser, Thomas, ed. 1990. *Early Cinema: Space, Frame, Narrative*. London: BFI.

——. 1996. 'A German Ancestry to Film Noir?', *Iris* 21: 129–44.

———— and Michael Wedel, eds. 1999. *The BFI Companion to German Cinema*. London: BFI.

————. 2000. *Weimar Cinema and After. Germany's Historical Imaginary*. London and New York: Routledge.

Everson, William K. 2003. 'Program Notes for the New School for Social Research', *Film History* 15(3): 279–375.

Exil. Sechs Schauspieler aus Deutschland. 1983. Berlin: Stiftung Deutsche Kinemathek.

Eyman, Scott. 1993. *Ernst Lubitsch: Laughter in Paradise*. New York: Simon and Schuster.

Fergusson, Bernard. 1937. *Eton Portrait*. London: John Miles.

Fischer, Lucy. 2003. *Designing Women: Cinema, Art Deco and the Female Form*. New York: Columbia University Press.

Frankfurter, Bernhard, ed. 1997. *Carl Mayer: Im Spiegelkabinett des Dr. Caligari*. Vienna: Promedia.

Friedrich, Otto. 1977. *City of Nets: A Portrait of Hollywood in the 1940s*. Berkeley: University of California Press.

Gänzl, Kurt. 1986. *The British Musical Theatre*. London: The Macmillan Press.

Gemünden, Gerd. 2006. *Filmemacher mit Akzent: Billy Wilder in Hollywood*. Vienna: Synema.

———— and Anton Kaes, eds. 2003. *New German Critique* 89.

————. 2008. *A Foreign Affair. Billy Wilder's American Films*. Oxford and New York: Berghahn Books.

Gifford, Dennis. 1986. *The British Film Catalogue, 1895–1985: A Reference Guide*. Newton Abbot, Devon and London: David & Charles.

Gillman, Peter and Leni Gillman. 1980. *'Collar the Lot!': How Britain Interned and Expelled Its Wartime Refugees*. London: Quartet.

Glancy, Mark. 1999. *When Hollywood Loved Britain: The Hollywood 'British' Film, 1939–1945*. Manchester: Manchester University Press.

Gledhill, Christine, ed. 1991. *Stardom: Industry of Desire*. London: Routledge.

————. 2003. *Reframing British Cinema 1918–1928. Between Restraint and Passion*. London: BFI.

Gloag, John, ed. 1946. [1934] *Design in Modern Life*. London: Allen and Unwin.

Gottlieb, Sidney, ed. 2002. *Framing Hitchcock: Selected Essays from the 'Hitchcock Annual'*. Detroit: Wayne State University Press.

Gough-Yates, Kevin. 1971. *Michael Powell in Collaboration with Emeric Pressburger*. London: BFI.

————. 1991. 'The European Film Maker in Exile in Britain, 1933–1945'. PhD dissertation. Open University.

————. 1992. 'Jews and Exiles in British Cinema', *Leo Baeck Yearbook* 37: 520–21.

Gunning, Tom. 2000. *The Films of Fritz Lang: Allegories of Vision and Modernity*. London: BFI.

Güttinger, Fritz, ed. 1984. *Kein Tag ohne Kino. Schriftsteller über den Stummfilm*. Frankfurt am Main: Deutsches Filmmuseum.

Haasis, Hellmut G. 1998. *Joseph Süß Oppenheimer, genannt Jud Süß: Finanzier, Freidenker, Justizopfer*. Reinbek: Rowohlt.

Hake, Sabine and John Davidson, eds. 2007. *Take Two: Fifties Cinema in Divided Germany*. Oxford and New York: Berghahn.

Halas, John and Roger Manvell, eds. 1959. *The Technique of Film Animation*. London and New York: Focal Press.

Halle, Randall and Margaret McCarthy, eds. 2003. *Light Motives. Popular German Cinema in Perspective.* Detroit: Wayne State University Press.

Hammond, Michael. 2006. *The Big Show: British Cinema Culture in the Great War (1914–1918).* Exeter: Exeter University Press.

Hansen, Mathias, ed. 1976. *Ernst Hermann Meyer: Das kompositorische und theoretische Werk.* Leipzig: Deutscher Verlag für Musik.

Harper, Sue. 1994. *Picturing the Past. The Rise and Fall of the British Costume Film.* London: BFI.

Helbig, Jörg, ed. 1998. *Intermedialität: Theorie und Praxis eines interdisziplinären Forschungsgebiets.* Berlin: Erich Schmidt.

Higson, Andrew. 1995. *Waving The Flag. Constructing a National Cinema in Britain.* Oxford: Oxford University Press.

———. 2003. *English Heritage, English Cinema. Costume Drama since 1980.* Oxford: Oxford University Press.

———, ed. 1996. *Dissolving Views. Key Writings on British Cinema.* London: Cassell.

———, ed. 2002. *Young and Innocent? Cinema and Britain 1896–1930.* Exeter: Exeter University Press.

——— and Justine Ashby, eds. 2000. *British Cinema, Past and Present.* London and New York: Routledge.

——— and Richard Maltby, eds. 1999. *'Film Europe' and 'Film America': Cinema, Commerce and Cultural Exchange 1920–1939.* Exeter: Exeter University Press.

Hilchenbach, Maria. 1982. *Kino im Exil. Die Emigration deutscher Filmkünstler.* Munich: K.G. Saur.

Hill, John, Martin McLoone and Paul Hainsworth, eds. 1994. *Border Crossing: Film in Ireland, Britain and Europe.* Belfast, Dublin and London: Institute of Irish Studies/BFI/University of Ulster.

Hirschhorn, Clive. 1975. *The Films of James Mason.* London: LSP Books.

Hjort, Mette and Scott Mackenzie, eds. 2000. *Cinema and Nation.* London and New York: Routledge.

Holmes, Colin. 1988. *John Bull's Island. Immigration and British Society 1871–1971.* Basingstoke: Macmillan.

Horak, Jan-Christopher. 1986. *Fluchtpunkt Hollywood. Eine Dokumentation zur Filmemigration nach 1933.* Münster: MakS.

———. 1993. 'Rin-Tin-Tin in Berlin or American Cinema in Weimar', *Film History* 5(1): 49–61.

———. 2005. 'Sauerkraut & Sausages with a Little Goulash: Germans in Hollywood, 1927', *Film History* 17(2/3): 241–60.

Horrocks, Roger. 2001. *Len Lye.* Auckland: Auckland University Press.

Huebner, Michael O. 1986. *Lilli Palmer. Ihre Filme – ihr Leben.* Munich: Heyne.

Hulbert, Jack. 1975. *The Little Woman's Always Right.* London: W.H. Allen.

Huntley, John. 1947. *British Film Music.* London: Skelton Robinson.

Hurd, Geoff, ed. 1984. *National Fictions. World War Two in British Films and Television.* London: BFI.

Jackall, Robert, ed. 1995. *Propaganda.* Basingstoke: Macmillan.

Jacobsen, Wolfgang, Anton Kaes and Hans-Helmut Prinzler, eds. 1993. *Geschichte des deutschen Films.* Stuttgart and Weimar: Metzler.

Jarvie, Ian. 1989. 'John Grierson on Hollywood's Success', *Historical Journal of Film, Radio and Television* 9 (3): 309–326.

Jäger, Anne Maximiliane, ed. 2006. *Einmal Emigrant – immer Emigrant? Der Schriftsteller und Publizist Robert Neumann (1897–1975)*. Munich: edition text+kritik.

Jobling, Paul. 2005. *Man Appeal*. Oxford: Berg.

Jowett, Garth S. and Victoria O'Donnell. 1992. *Propaganda and Persuasion*, 2nd edn. Newbury Park, Cal., London and New Delhi: Sage.

Jürgs, Michael. 2000. *Gern hab' ich die Frau'n geküßt. Die Richard-Tauber-Biographie*. Munich: List.

Kaes, Anton. 1987. 'Literary Intellectuals and the Cinema. Charting a Controversy (1909–1929)', *New German Critique* 40: 7–33.

Kahan, Hans. 1930. *Dramaturgie des Tonfilms*. Berlin: Mattisson.

Kalinak, Kathryn. 1992. *Settling the Score: Music and the Classical Hollywood Film*. Madison: University of Wisconsin Press.

Kaplan, E. Ann, ed. 1998. *Women and Film Noir*, rev. edn. London: BFI.

Kasten, Jürgen and Armin Loacker, eds. 2005. *Richard Oswald: Kino zwischen Spektakel, Aufklärung und Unterhaltung*. Vienna: Filmarchiv Austria.

Keresztury, Dezső. 1961. 'Mátyás Seiber (An Obituary)'. *New Hungarian Quarterly* 2(2): 171.

Kirkham, Pat and David Thoms, eds. 1995. *War Culture: Social Change and Changing Experience in World War Two Britain*. London: Lawrence and Wishart.

Klaus, Ulrich J. 1995. *Deutsche Tonfilme, 6. Jahrgang: 1935*. Berlin: Klaus.

Klöckner-Draga, Uwe. 1999. *'Wirf weg, damit du nicht verlierst …' Lilian Harvey – Biographie eines Filmstars*. Berlin: edition q.

Knilli, Friedrich. 2000. *Ich war Jud Süss: Die Geschichte des Filmstars Ferdinand Marian*. Berlin: Henschel.

Koepnick, Lutz. 2002. *The Dark Mirror. German Cinema Between Hitler and Hollywood*. Berkeley: University of California Press.

Kostelanetz, Richard, ed. 1971. *Moholy-Nagy*. London: Allen Lane.

Kracauer, Siegfried. 1947. *From Caligari to Hitler. A Psychological History of the German Film*. Princeton: Princeton University Press.

Kugelmann, Cilly and Fritz Backhaus, eds. 1996. *Jüdische Figuren in Film und Karikatur*. Sigmaringen: Thorbecke.

Kulik, Karol. 1975. *Alexander Korda, the Man Who Could Work Miracles*. London: Allen & Unwin.

Lafitte, François. 1988. [1940]. *The Internment of Aliens*. London: Libris.

Landy, Marcia. 1991. *British Genres: Cinema and Society, 1930–1960*. Princeton, NJ: Princeton University Press.

Lant, Antonia. 1991. *Blackout. Reinventing Women for Wartime British Cinema*. Princeton: Princeton University Press.

Larkey, Edward, ed. 2000. *A Sound Legacy? Music and Politics in East Germany*. Washington, D.C.: American Institute for Contemporary German Studies.

Leong, Karen. 2006. 'Anna May Wong and the British Film Industry', *Quarterly Review of Film and Video* 23(1): 13–22.

Lewison, Jeremy, ed. 1982. *Circle: Constructive Art in Britain 1934–40*. Cambridge: Kettle's Yard.

Loacker, Armin, ed. 2000. *Unerwünschtes Kino: Der deutschsprachige Emigrantenfilm 1934–1937*. Vienna: Filmarchiv Austria.

Loewy, Ronny, ed. 1987. *Von Babelsberg nach Hollywood: Filmemigranten aus Nazideutschland*. Frankfurt am Main: Deutsches Filmmuseum.

Loiperdinger, Martin. 1999. *Film und Schokolade. Stollwercks Geschäfte mit lebenden Bildern.* Frankfurt am Main and Basle: Stroemfeld/Roter Stern.

London, Louise. 2000. *Whitehall and the Jews, 1933–1948. British Immigration Policy, Jewish Refugees and the Holocaust.* Cambridge: Cambridge University Press.

Low, Rachael. 1979. *Documentary and Educational Films of the 1930s.* London: Allen & Unwin.

———. 1985. *The History of the British Film 1929–1939. Film Making in 1930s Britain.* London: Allen & Unwin.

Loxley, Simon. 2006. *Type.* London: I.B. Tauris.

Luft, Herbert G. 1972. 'Carl Mayer. Film Scriptwriter Extraordinary of Post-World War I Germany', *Films in Review* 23(9): 513–26.

Macdonald, Kevin. 1994. *Emeric Pressburger: The Life and Death of a Screenwriter.* London: Faber and Faber.

Mackay, Robert. 2000. 'Leaving out the Black Notes: the BBC and "Enemy Music" in the Second World War', *Media History* 6(1): 75–80.

Manvell, Roger and John Huntley. 1967. *The Technique of Film Music.* London: Focal Press.

Marris, Paul, ed. 1982. *Paul Rotha.* London: BFI.

Martin, Leslie. 1939. *The Flat Book.* London: The Architectural Press.

Maschwitz, Eric. 1957. *No Chips on My Shoulder.* London: Herbert Jenkins.

McArthur, Colin, ed. 1982. *Scotch Reels: Scotland in Cinema and Television.* London: BFI.

McFarlane, Brian, ed. 2005. *Encyclopedia of British Film.* London: BFI/Methuen.

Meyer, Ernst H. 1946. *English Chamber Music: The History of a Great Art from the Middle Ages to Purcell.* London: Lawrence & Wishart.

———. 1952. *Musik im Zeitgeschehen.* Berlin: Verlag Bruno Henschel und Sohn.

———. 1979. *Kontraste, Konflikte: Erinnerungen, Gespräche, Kommentare.* Berlin: Verlag Neue Musik.

Middleton, Richard. 1990. *Studying Popular Music.* Milton Keynes: Open University Press.

Mikes, George. 1946. *How to be an Alien.* London: Allan Wingate.

Moholy-Nagy, Laszlo. 1947. *The New Vision and Abstract of an Artist.* New York: George Wittenborn.

———. 1947. *Vision in Motion.* Chicago: Paul Theobald and Company.

———. 1967. [1925]. *Painting Photography Film.* London: Lund Humphries.

Moholy-Nagy, Sibyl. 1969. [1950]. *Moholy-Nagy: Experiment in Totality.* Cambridge Mass.: MIT Press.

Monk, Claire and Amy Sargeant, eds. 2002. *British Historical Cinema.* London: Routledge.

Moor, Andrew. 2005. *Powell and Pressburger. A Cinema of Magic Spaces.* London: I.B. Tauris.

Morgan, Guy, ed. 1948. *Red Roses Every Night.* London: Quality Press.

Moss, Robert F. 1987. *The Films of Carol Reed.* Basingstoke: Macmillan.

Mowl, Timothy. 2000. *Stylistic Cold Wars: Betjeman versus Pevsner.* London: John Murray.

Munby, Jonathan. 1999. *Public Enemies, Public Heroes. Screening the Gangster from Little Caesar to Touch of Evil.* Chicago: University of Chicago Press.

Murphy, Robert. 1992. *Realism and Tinsel: Cinema and Society in Britain, 1939–49.* London and New York: Routledge.

————, ed. 1997. *The British Cinema Book*. London: BFI.

Mühl-Benninghaus, Wolfgang. 1999. *Das Ringen um den Tonfilm. Strategien der Elektro- und der Filmindustrie in den 20er und 30er Jahren*. Düsseldorf: Droste.

Naficy, Hamid, ed. 1999. *Home, Exile, Homeland: Film, Media, and the Politics of Place*. New York and London: Routledge.

————. 2001. *An Accented Cinema: Exilic and Diasporic Filmmaking*. Princeton: Princeton University Press.

Neagle, Anna. 1974. *Anna Neagle Says 'There's Always Tomorrow'. An Autobiography*. London: W.H. Allen.

Newman, Teresa. 1976. *Naum Gabo*. London: Tate Gallery Publications.

Niemann, Konrad. 1971. *Ernst Hermann Meyer: Für Sie porträtiert*. Leipzig: Deutscher Verlag für Musik.

Noble, Peter, ed. 1946. *The British Film Yearbook*. London: British Yearbooks.

————. 1946. *British Theatre*. London: British Yearbooks.

Oakley, C.A. 1964. *Where We Came In*. London: Allen & Unwin.

Omasta, Michael, Brigitte Mayr and Christian Cargnelli, eds. 2003. *Carl Mayer, Scenar[t]ist. Ein Script von ihm war schon ein Film/A Script by Carl Mayer Was Already a Film*. Vienna: SYNEMA.

Omasta, Michael, Brigitte Mayr and Elisabeth Streit, eds. 2004. *Peter Lorre: Ein Fremder im Paradies*. Vienna: Zsolnay.

Oxford Dictionary of National Biography. 2004. Oxford: Oxford University Press.

Palmer, Lilli. 1974. *Change Lobsters – and Dance*. London: W.H. Allen.

Panofsky, Erwin. 1995. *Three Essays on Style*. Cambridge, Mass.: MIT Press.

Parker, John, ed. 1952. *Who's Who in the Theatre. A Biographical Record of the Contemporary Stage*, 11th edn. London: Pitman.

Parkinson, David, ed. 1993. *Mornings in the Dark. The Graham Greene Film Reader*. Manchester: Carcanet.

Passuth, Krisztina. 1985. *Moholy-Nagy*. London: Thames and Hudson.

Petrie, Duncan. 1996. *The British Cinematographer*. London: BFI.

————. 2000. *Screening Scotland*. London: BFI.

Petrie, Graham. 2002. *Hollywood Destinies. European Directors in America, 1922–1931*, rev. edn. Detroit: Wayne State University Press.

Pevsner, Nikolaus. 1956. *The Englishness of English Art*. London: The Architectural Press.

————. 1975. [1936]. *Pioneers of Modern Design*. London: Penguin Books.

Phillips, Alastair. 2004. *City of Darkness, City of Light. Émigré Filmmakers in Paris 1929–1939*. Amsterdam: Amsterdam University Press.

———— and Ginette Vincendeau, eds. 2006. *Journeys of Desire. European Actors in Hollywood*. London: BFI.

Powell, Michael. 1986. *A Life in Movies: An Autobiography*. London: Heinemann.

Prawer, S.S. 2005. *Between Two Worlds. The Jewish Presence in German and Austrian Film, 1910–1933*. Oxford and New York: Berghahn.

Pross, Steffen. 2000. *'In London treffen wir uns wieder'. Vier Spaziergänge durch ein vergessenes Kapitel deutscher Kulturgeschichte nach 1933*. Berlin: Eichborn.

Raab Hansen, Jutta. 1996. *NS-verfolgte Musiker in England: Spuren deutscher und österreichischer Flüchtlinge in der britischen Musikkultur*. Hamburg: von Bockel Verlag.

Read, Herbert. 1934. *Art and Industry*. London: Faber and Faber.

Richards, Jeffrey. 1982. 'The British Board of Film Censors and Content Control in the 1930s: Foreign Affairs', *Historical Journal of Film, Radio and Television* 2(1): 39–48.

———. 1997. *Films and British National Identity. From Dickens to Dad's Army.* Manchester: Manchester University Press.

———, ed. 1998. *The Unknown 1930s. An Alternative History of the British Cinema, 1929–1939.* London and New York: I.B. Tauris.

——— and Dorothy Sheridan, eds. 1987. *Mass-Observation at the Movies.* London: Routledge & Kegan Paul.

Rieser-Wohlfarter, Klaus. 1996. *Filmische Passagen in die neue Welt. Entwürfe ethno-amerikanischer Kulturen im Migrationsfilm.* Trier: Wissenschaftlicher Verlag Trier.

Robertson, James C. 1993. *The Hidden Cinema: British Film Censorship in Action, 1913–1975.* London and New York: Routledge.

Rose, Sonya. 2003. *Which People's War? National Identity and Citizenship in Wartime Britain, 1939–1945.* Oxford: Oxford University Press.

Rotermund, Erwin and Lutz Winckler, eds. 2003. *Exilforschung. Ein internationales Jahrbuch, Band 21: Film und Fotografie.* Munich: edition text+kritik.

Rotha, Paul. 1933. *Celluloid: The Film Today.* London: Longmans, Green and Co.

———. 1936. *Documentary Film.* London: Faber and Faber.

———. 1951. *The Film Till Now: A Survey of World Cinema*, rev. edn. London: Vision Press.

———, ed. 1952. *Portrait of a Flying Yorkshireman. Letters from Eric Knight in the United States to Paul Rotha in England.* London: Chapman & Hall.

Sahl, Hans. 1990. *Memoiren eines Moralisten. Das Exil im Exil.* Hamburg: Luchterhand.

Said, Edward. 2000. *Reflections on Exile and Other Essays.* Cambridge, Mass.: Harvard University Press.

Salt, Barry. 1992. *Film Style and Technology: History and Analysis*, 2nd exp. edn. London: Starword.

Sargeant, Amy. 2005. *British Cinema. A Critical History.* London: BFI.

———. 2005. 'Review of *Reframing British Cinema 1918–1928*', *Modernism/Modernity* 12(4): 731–33.

Saunders, William. 1935. 'Songs of the German Revolution', *Music and Letters* 16(1): 50–57.

Scannell, Paddy, Philip Schlesinger and Colin Sparks, eds. 1992. *Culture and Power: A Media, Culture and Society Reader.* London: Sage.

Schaudig, Michael, ed. 1996. *Positionen deutscher Filmgeschichte. 100 Jahre Kinematographie. Strukturen, Diskurse, Kontexte.* Munich: Schaudig & Ledig.

Schöning, Jörg, ed. 1989. *Reinhold Schünzel. Schauspieler und Regisseur.* Munich: edition text+kritik.

———, ed. 1993. *London Calling. Deutsche im britischen Film der dreißiger Jahre.* Munich: edition text+kritik.

———, ed. 1995. *Fantaisies Russes. Russische Filmmacher in Berlin und Paris 1920–1930.* Munich: edition text+kritik.

Sedgwick, John. 2000. *Popular Filmgoing in 1930s Britain. A Choice of Pleasures.* Exeter: University of Exeter Press.

Soister, John T. 2002. *Conrad Veidt on Screen.* Jefferson, NC and London: McFarland.

Sollors, Werner. 1986. *Beyond Ethnicity: Consent and Descent in American Culture.* New York: Oxford University Press.

Soukup, Uwe. 2001. *Ich bin nun mal Deutscher. Sebastian Haffner. Eine Biographie.* Berlin: Aufbau.

Spicer, Andrew, ed. 2007. *European Film Noir.* Manchester: Manchester University Press.

Stent, Ronald. 1980. *A Bespattered Page: The Internment of 'His Majesty's Most Loyal Enemy Aliens'.* London: Andre Deutsch.

Stern, Erich. 1937. *Die Emigration als psychologisches Problem.* Erich Stern: Bologne-sur-Seine.

Stern, Selma. 1929. *Jud Süss: Ein Beitrag zur deutschen und zur jüdischen Geschichte.* Berlin: Akademie Verlag.

Stevenson, Robert. 1934. 'A Year in German Studios', *Proceedings of the British Kinematograph Society* 20.

Street, Sarah. 1997. *British National Cinema.* London and New York: Routledge.

———. 2002. *Transatlantic Crossings. British Feature Films in the USA.* New York: Continuum.

———. 2005. "'Got to Dance my way to Heaven": Jessie Matthews, Art Deco and the British Musical of the 1930s', *Studies in European Cinema* 2(1): 19–30.

———. 2005. *Black Narcissus.* London: I.B. Tauris.

Sturm, Sibylle M. and Arthur Wohlgemuth, eds. 1996. *Hallo? Berlin? Ici Paris! Deutsch-französische Filmbeziehungen 1918–1939.* Munich: edition text+kritik.

Sudendorf, Werner, ed. 1977. *Marlene Dietrich.* Frankfurt am Main, Berlin and Vienna: Carl Hanser.

Surowiec, Catherine A. 1992. *Accent on Design. Four European Art Directors.* London: BFI.

Sweeney, Kevin. 1999. *James Mason: A Bio-Bibliography.* Westport and London: Greenwood Press.

Swynnoe, Jan G. 2002. *The Best Years of British Film Music, 1936–1958.* Woodbridge, Suffolk: Boydell Press.

Tabori, Paul. 1972. *The Anatomy of Exile.* London: Harrap.

Tashiro, Charles. 1998. *Pretty Pictures: Production Design and the History Film.* Austin: University of Texas Press.

Taylor, John. 1994. *A Dream of England.* Manchester: Manchester University Press.

Taylor, John Russell. 1983. *Strangers in Paradise: The Hollywood Émigrés 1933–1950.* London: Faber and Faber.

Taylor, Philip M., ed. 1988. *Britain and the Cinema in the Second World War.* Basingstoke: Macmillan.

Thompson, Kristin. 1993. 'Early Alternatives to the Hollywood Mode of Production: Implications for Europe's Avant-gardes', *Film History* 5(4): 386–404.

———. 1996. 'National or International Films? The European Debate during the 1920s', *Film History* 8(3): 281–96.

Tippett, Michael. 1992. *Those Twentieth Century Blues.* London: Hutchinson.

Traber, Habakuk. 1998. 'Hollywood rief nicht: Der Filmkomponist Hans May in seiner Korrespondenz mit Paul Kohner', *Filmexil* 10: 24–28.

Treuner, Hermann, ed. 1928. *Filmkünstler. Wir über uns selbst.* Berlin: Sibyllen.

Wahl, Chris. 2005. *Das Sprechen des Spielfilms. Über die Auswirkungen von hörbaren Dialogen auf Produktion und Rezeption, Ästhetik und Internationalität der siebten Kunst.* Trier: Wissenschaftlicher Verlag.

Warren, Patricia. 1983. *Elstree: The British Hollywood*. London: Elm Tree Books.

Weno, Joachim. 1957. *Lilli Palmer*. Berlin: Rembrandt.

Willett, John. 1978. *The New Sobriety: Art and Politics in the Weimar Period*. London: Thames and Hudson.

Williams, Melanie. 2006. '"The most explosive object to hit Britain since the V2!": The British films of Hardy Kruger and Anglo-German relations in the 1950s', *Cinema Journal* 46 (1): 85–107.

Williams, Michael. 2003. *Ivor Novello. Screen Idol*. London: BFI.

Williams, Tony. 2000. *Structures of Desire: British Cinema, 1939–1955*. Albany: SUNY Press.

Winn, Godfrey. 1949. *The Bend of the River. A Journey in Ten Stages*. London: Hutchinson.

Wood, Linda. 1986. *British Films 1927–1939*. London: BFI.

Yevtushenko, Yevgeni. 1965. *A Precocious Autobiography*. Harmondsworth: Penguin Books.

Yorke, F.R.S. 1962. [1934]. *The Modern House*. London: The Architectural Press.

Young, Freddie. 1999. *Seventy Light Years: A Life in the Movies*. London: Faber and Faber.

Youngkin, Stephen D. 2005. *The Lost One. A Life of Peter Lorre*. Lexington: University of Kentucky Press.

Zsuffa, Joseph. 1987. *Béla Balázs. The Man and the Artist*. Berkeley: University of California Press.

INDEX